After the Nation

After the Nation

Postnational Satire in the Works of Carlos Fuentes and Thomas Pynchon

✦

Pedro García-Caro

Foreword by Jean Franco

NORTHWESTERN UNIVERSITY PRESS
EVANSTON, ILLINOIS

Northwestern University Press
www.nupress.northwestern.edu

Earlier versions of sections of part 2 of this book appeared as "La nueva izquierda y la agonía del nacionalismo mexicano en *La muerte de Artemio Cruz*" in *Alma América,* vol. 1, edited by Vicente Cervera Salinas and María Dolores Adsuar (Murcia: Universidad de Murcia, 2008): 287–304; and "Damnosa Hereditas: Sorting the National Will in Fuentes' *The Death of Artemio Cruz* and Pynchon's *The Crying of Lot 49*" in *How Far Is America from Here?*, edited by Paul Giles, Theo D'Haen, Djelal Kadir, and Lois Parkinson Zamora (Amsterdam, New York: Rodopi, 2005) 323–45.

An earlier version of chapter 7 in part 3 appeared as " 'America was the only place . . .': American Exceptionalism and the Geographic Politics of Pynchon's *Mason & Dixon*" in *The Multiple Worlds of Mason & Dixon*, edited by Elizabeth Jane Wall Hinds (New York: Camden House, 2005) 101–24.

Printed in the United States of America

10 9 8 7 6 5 4 3 2 1

ISBN 978-0-8101-3215-3

The Library of Congress has cataloged the original, hardcover edition as follows:

Garcia-Caro, Pedro, author.
After the nation : postnational satire in the works of Carlos Fuentes and Thomas Pynchon / Pedro Garcia-Caro ; foreword by Jean Franco.
pages cm
Includes bibliographical references and index.
ISBN 978-0-8101-2995-5 (cloth : alk. paper)
1. Pynchon, Thomas—Criticism and interpretation. 2. Fuentes, Carlos—Criticism and interpretation. 3. Nationalism in literature. I. Title.
PS3566.Y55Z654 2014
813.54—dc23

2014007870

♾ The paper used in this publication meets the minimum requirements of the American National Standard for Information Sciences—Permanence of Paper for Printed Library Materials, ANSI Z39.48-1992.

For Cecilia

For Lulú and Flor

At home everywhere we go

CONTENTS

FOREWORD

Jean Franco

For those without papers, traveling north from the global south, the U.S.-Mexican border is a formidable and increasingly militarized wall. It is not only a dangerous crossing point for thousands of men and women from Mexico and Central America but also a dramatic and sometimes a tragic place that divides families, ethnicities, and tribes and that reminds Mexicans of a history of loss and defeat. It has also figured as a protagonist in a growing archive of border literature that includes Cormac McCarthy's astounding *Blood Meridian* and, on the Mexican side, a border literature in which the fence has become a protagonist. As Pedro García-Caro points out in the preface to *After the Nation,* the U.S.-Mexican border marks the limits of two national territories whose societies, culture, and economics are "increasingly integrated and also mutually distrustful," with Mexico being placed in a "radically subaltern position on the other side of the wall." Not surprisingly, a scarcely suppressed sense of grievance moves writers in the south while underscoring the porosity of the dividing wall despite the fact that it is highly militarized, so that it also signals the "increasing erosion of the modern nation-state." To the north, the heroic version of American conquest and expansion cannot obliterate a history of violence while to the south, the frontier—once a line in the sand—is now increasingly a fortified blockade.

After the Nation focuses on two writers, Carlos Fuentes and Thomas Pynchon, one from Mexico and the other from north of the border, both of whom, using the tools of parody and satire, have held their respective nations in contempt and have steadily dismantled the idea of a hegemonic national culture and the narrative of progress that upheld it. Both writers began publishing in the early sixties during a period dominated by "American nationalist globalism" while, in Mexico, many prominent Mexicans had begun to view the revolution of 1910 as a failure or a betrayal. *After the Nation* explores the dissenting narratives of betrayal of the Revolution to the south and of American imperialism to the north through the writing of Fuentes and Pynchon.

In a short story of that name included in the collection *La frontera de cristal,* Fuentes represented a transparent but impassable barrier that stands in the way of a human contact not governed by power and law, a barrier between two nationalities. The barrier has also stood in the way of a comparatist approach to the Americas as if the border hindered the crossing of ideas so that American literature and Latin American literature occupied two distinct compartments. Perhaps that is why a comparative literature that encompasses both North and South America has had, to the present, relatively few practitioners. *After the Nation* not only fills this critical vacuum, but offers a thoroughgoing meditation on what is involved for the critic faced with such a varied and complex cultural field.

By focusing on two prolific writers, Fuentes and Pynchon, Professor García-Caro is able to encompass a vast area of cultural history that includes the sixties counterculture and the New Left revision of history. Both writers are satirists who, in their early novels, represent the modern city and its underworld of "ghostly, monstrous, magical, or mythical forces" and its picaresque actors and observers. However, *After the Nation* is not simply a work of literary criticism but engages in a wide-ranging cultural history of both Mexico and the United States. Thus, for example, in discussing Fuentes's early novel, *La región más transparente,* the author takes on Mexico's intellectual history from Alfonso Reyes to Octavio Paz and beyond, while the discussion of Pynchon's early novel, *V.,* encompasses what, according to the critic Robert Holton, "seems to be a remarkable history of Western racism from the atrocities of colonialism to the somewhat more covert racism of America at the time of writing." *After the Nation* is also a chronicle of a melancholy counterculture. Although the sixties are often evoked as a time of hope for change, in fact, as I well remember, there was also a substantial amount of dark prophecy, which is amply reflected in the novels under review and especially in those of Pynchon. Indeed, one of the important contributions of *After the Nation* is the ability of the author to reimagine the sixties, the period of both Fuentes's and Pynchon's early writing, in all its complexity between, on the one hand, the American belief in "national greatness, global responsibility, and anticommunism" and on the other the fear of nuclear war, the doomsday scenario of the Cuban missile crisis, and the ongoing war in Vietnam, all of which contributed to the grim carnival that Pynchon, in particular, so deftly narrates.

After the Nation reminds us of how near the brink of a nuclear war we came in the sixties and how an author like Pynchon captures the anxieties of the time. Yet García-Caro also seems to suggest that these two writers have lost their prophetic power for, he argues, the novels "were also immediately immersed in the cultural machine, the educational machine, and they became instantaneously recycled back into the academic milieu, incorporated into syllabi and the canon of American and Mexican national literatures respectively." Is this such a sad fate? Perhaps being "incorporated into the syllabi" is not the worst thing that can happen to an author.

After the Nation is an extraordinarily rich book that encompasses more than literary criticism—the cultural history of divergent nations that cannot or should not be ignorant of each other's culture nor of its dissident voices.

PREFACE

Divided by the U.S.-Mexican border, the city of Nogales has two distinct sides: one in Arizona, the other one in Sonora. A long rusty metal strip made up of corrugated steel panels welded to metal posts crowned with barbed wire segregates the two neighborhoods. On the Mexican side, a procession of houses overlooks the wall along the Avenida Internacional; a few feet separate their front doors from the tall metal structure across the Avenida, adorned with graffiti, white crosses, and other decorations. The barrier goes up and down the many small hills whose geographical configuration clearly defies and predates the drawing of the international dividing line between the two sovereign nations, a title that sounds too large for the bizarre urban partition generated by this unpretentious, even shabby, structure. On the American side, only a handful of houses dot West International Street past the old Federal customs house. A watch road runs parallel to the wall on the northern side; looking westward, both the wall and the dusty road seem to extend for miles into the Arizona desert. Looking at an online interactive map of the two Nogales, one can see the roads that run north-south along the old narrow pass, but they are mostly now divided by the metal structure: human traffic crosses the border in both directions through several tollgates. Bizarrely, one can virtually explore most of southern Nogales online with direct glimpses at street level, but on the northern side there is an unofficial ban on public access to ground images.[1] The Northern nation-state classifies and sequesters information about its side of the borderland, outlawing access to its territory even virtually, while the South is opened up to the satellite's gaze and to the mounted camera that captures street views for virtual tourists on the Internet.

Also out of sight, underground tunnels challenge the superficial division offered by the metal wall: drain channels, passageways, and *narcotúneles* reconnect these two neighborhoods and defy the unyielding control of the U.S. border patrol. So many such tunnels carved by drug smugglers have been exposed in the past few years that a running joke in northern Nogales suggests the town may soon collapse "into a giant sinkhole."[2] The proliferation of these tunnels seems to undermine U.S. federal efforts to close and "secure" the border, but they also challenge the notion of a hermetic territory—a neatly demarcated national space. Over the last two decades, large-scale plans to build and redraw the U.S.-Mexican border on the ground have been ironically paralleled by one of the most ambitious free-trade agreements signed after the fall of the Berlin Wall. So, unlike that now-vanished, almost-forgotten wall, the Nogales barrier does not set apart two rival geopolitical blocs; instead, it signals the 3,141 kilometers of international border between two major trading partners, the United States of America and the United States of Mexico: the longest boundary separating a rich and a developing country. As with other borders, a line was first drawn on a map and then onto the ground; its ideological purpose to substantiate the territorial confines of two nation-states. If the Berlin Wall delineated the divisions of two ideological versions within one alleged national body, the U.S.-Mexican border traces and sanctions the limits of two national territories whose societies, cultures, and economies are increasingly integrated but also mutually distrustful.

These complex and asymmetrical processes of cultural and economic separation, annexation, and integration have been in place well before the 1994 North American Free Trade Agreement (NAFTA).[3] However, the North American integration is unlike any other in its unevenness: these restrictions to human traffic contrast with the free circulation of capital, commodities, and tourists, a paradox which places Mexico in a radically subaltern position on either side of a wall built from the northern side, with American (borrowed) dollars and in some cases by Mexican (undocumented) workers.[4] At one million legal or documented crossings a day,[5] the border sutures two social and political bodies while it organizes and regiments their asymmetries and their interdependent roles in this concealed transnational conglomerate. The line's manifest porosity, like its arbitrary delineation across a town, a valley, or a desert, is a hallmark of the instability of national constructs and their institutional state practices as well as of the increasing erosion of the modern nation-state. The contradictions of integration and separation at work in the two Nogales exemplify well the combined processes of territorialization and deterritorialization so thoroughly described in Wendy Brown's book *Walled States, Waning Sovereignty.*[6] In an avowedly counterintuitive move, Brown argues: "it is the weakening of state sovereignty, and more precisely, the detachment of sovereignty from the nation-state, that is generating much of the frenzy of nation-state wall building today" (W. Brown, 24). Brown goes on to posit these new walls as icons of the nation-state's "erosion" in the contemporary era. The erosion is met with the "theatricalized and spectacularized performance of sovereign power" in the form of the "theological remainder" (26), the hurried construction of global walls in an increasingly globalized postnational setting.

Whether as theological remainders or as postnational kitsch, entrenched nationalist symbols on each side of the border such as the flag or the map continue to codify and demarcate the territorial imaginings of a phantasmal national space. In Ambos Nogales, as elsewhere along the U.S.-Mexico border, nationalist symbols abound with a profusion hardly seen in any other place on the planet, staking out the theological territory of the nation even as the social, economic, and political bodies become gradually more amalgamated. The alleged immanence of the nation in the projected territory, its perceived organic relation, is still perhaps the most successful tenet of nationalist rhetoric. And so, the ubiquitous presence of national markers continues to question the legitimacy of alternative, transversal codes of belonging and the legality of other bodies and narratives except those sanctioned by the totalizing, seemingly unchanged and unchangeable national subtext. The North American continent is far from being "beyond" or "after" the nation despite the signs of tiredness of rhetorical nationalisms, despite the partial collapse of the nation-state as an economic and cultural unit in an ever more interconnected global society, despite the noticeably ever-increasing—if uneven—integration of these two nation-states. It appears as if in the face of a postnational globalization that replicates earlier asymmetrical exchanges and neocolonial relations, nationalism could still be capable of re-creating both a sense of postcolonial resistance and its supplement—imperial narcissism.

If the geographic imaginings of the national map aim to contain and retain the nation within its projected borders, the narratives of national histories have as their central subject the teleological discourse of modernity as an experience of national fulfillment. The literary narratives studied in *After the Nation,* in contrast, aim to unravel and denounce those combined hegemonic processes while they start to contemplate the ensuing postnational constellations. These are literary narratives that playfully point to and debase "holy" borders, international borders as well as the internal lines where narratives of nation are embodied and consecrated.

In order to overcome the ideological limitations imposed by nation-centered narratives of literary production, cultural history, and criticism on each side of the U.S.-Mexico border, *After the Nation* proposes a series of new approaches to novels, essays, and short stories by Carlos Fuentes and Thomas Pynchon within the framework of a postnational, hemispheric American Studies. I propose here a comparativist approach to the contemporary American and Mexican literary canons and their underlying nationalist encodement through the study of a wide range of texts by Pynchon and Fuentes which question and historicize in different ways the processes of national definition and myth-making deployed in the drawing of the literary borders of these two neighboring nations. This approach disavows and resists the desire to re-create the patriotic dissensus within consensus inherent to the institutionalized academic habits of U.S. and Mexican literary criticism, and places my discussions and analyses within the emerging field of Comparative American Studies. My central claim is that for more than fifty years now, the works of Carlos Fuentes and Thomas Pynchon have challenged the nationalist narratives promoted by Mexican and U.S. literary histories by underscoring the controlling and manipulative nature of the cultural and institutional practices implicated in their narrative foundations. Despite working within two very distinct national and linguistic literary cultures, these postnational satires engage with official and mainstream definitions of the nation and in so doing, they parody authorized histories, consensual presents, and manifest futurities and their iconic versions, packaged for mass consumption through cultural institutions and the media.

After the Nation also investigates the ambiguous relations between the self-proclaimed autonomy of the literary field and the textual, critical deployment of national identity and the modern nation-state in the works of Carlos Fuentes and Thomas Pynchon. This book draws attention to a recurring series of tropes and shared textual practices that demonstrate a comparable effort to erode the consensual narratives of nation enforced by mainstream media and other dominant cultural institutions in both Mexico and the United States. The postnational expression of being "after the nation" in the title does not then exclusively refer to a moment or a periodic delineation; it also denotes a spatial kinetic meaning, as the novels studied here go after the nation and in their satirical pursuits they vilify, oppose, besiege, and deterritorialize its foundational myths.

These mostly canonical texts anticipated, intuited, and represented postnational sentiments and practices, even as they became invested with a symbolic political and cultural capital in their respective national literary fields, which paradoxically turned them into national and international canonical commodities. The works of these two authors are customarily recycled into official literary histories even as they perform a full-scale distortion of Mexican and American national discourses. *After the Nation* deals with the complex and critical processes by which these two popular contemporary writers have interpolated national institutions and symbols in Mexico and the United States respectively, while acquiring a singular status in their national literary canons and abroad. I argue that Fuentes and Pynchon examine official national histories, foundational myths, the sense of a national shared presence, and the anticipation of its futurity, through similar narrative strategies such as parody, satire, historiographic metafiction, and playful games with the spatial and temporal limitations of national experience, highlighting the socially constructed nature of national identities and the hegemonic strategies set in place by the collusion of cultural and political discourses.

In contrast to the dominant postmodernist reception of their work, which places a greater emphasis on linguistic and epistemic issues, favoring uncertainty, a vague political cynicism, and the formal erasure of authorial control, I locate these works within their historical contexts, revealing a more specific political and social critique of the hegemonic discourses of belonging.[7] Thus my approach seeks to unveil the epistemic entrapment of thinking within the national framework. I set out to chart the cultural history surrounding these fictional writings to place them in the context of the emergent international New Left during the Cold War. I trace here the beginnings of their postnationalist aesthetics, at once anti-totalitarian and internationalist, as originating from a New-Leftist standpoint and against the Cold War nationalist consensus of the 1950s. However, a lasting legacy of poststructuralism subsists here in the alertness to the socially constructed character of cultural discourses, institutional practices, and the knowledge(s) they produce. I develop the conception of postnational satire by drawing on historiographic notions such as the "invention of tradition" by Hobsbawm, and narratological definitions of satire by Bakhtin, Hutcheon, Rose, Genette, and others. I argue that postnational satire promotes a non-hegemonic view of invented national traditions through the creation of alternative, non-epic temporalities that challenge the threefold temporal structure of prevailing nationalist discourse: foundational pasts, consensual presents, and manifest destinies. Postnational satire also dismantles the imagined geographies of the nation by displaying and toying with the subterranean undercurrents, crevices, margins, and borders of the national map and by underlining and historicizing the ideological production of these mappings.

While I outline the opposition by both Pynchon and Fuentes to these consensual narratives of Mexican and American nationalism, I also examine the ways in which their dissent is paradoxically reinscribed into the plurality of national affects. By elaborating a critique of the social and cultural homogenization promoted by industrial modernity and by engaging in a New-Leftist questioning of the postcolonial status quo of white, oligarchic, and patriarchal definitions of the body politic, these postnational satires reframed the role of canonicity and the moral and patriotic mandates of literary institutions as conceived throughout the nineteenth and most of the twentieth century.[8] The old national canons of foundational romances and settler epics have given way in the contemporary period to a postnational canon that encourages migrant, transnational, polygenetic, and hybrid literary imaginings.[9] Seeking to insert dissent into the national consensus, such institutional nationalist practices have paradoxically incorporated these critiques of official discourses into their respective national literary canons, thus inadvertently allowing for the emergence of a critical postnational epistemic framework.

Calling for a decentering of the nation-state, a wealth of monographs and anthologies have been published over the past two decades that delineate and define the scope of Hemispheric American Studies, their stated goals to "chart new literary and cultural geographies" and to "excavat[e] the intricate and complex politics, histories, and discourses of spatial encounter that occur throughout the hemisphere" which are routinely obfuscated by nation-based studies.[10] This book seeks to contribute to the production of that wider "comparativist and dialogical approach" advocated by scholars such as Donald Pease, Amy Kaplan, José David Saldívar, Caroline Levander, Robert Levine, Anna Brickhouse, Vera Kutzinski, Djelal Kadir, and Alejandro Herrero-Olaizola, among many others.[11] This is a comparativist exercise for which the subject of literary and cultural history is not the national formation, but rather the plurality of creative, critical impulses across languages, literary traditions, cultural fields, and state borders in the Americas and beyond.

Carlos Fuentes's literary production has constantly responded to the changing social and political landscape of postrevolutionary Mexico. There are few themes or literary genres that Fuentes has not incorporated into his all-encompassing oeuvre—from the totalizing novel of dictatorship (*Terra nostra,* 1975); the fragmentary dissolution of the subject and new forms of social control (*La muerte de Artemio Cruz,* 1962; or *Cambio de piel,* 1967); the U.S.-Mexico border (*La frontera de cristal,* 1995); and the survival of Mexican pre-Hispanic myths in the face of modern development (*Días enmascarados,* 1954; *La región más transparente,* 1958); through the present-day narco war (*La voluntad y la fortuna,* 2008) or horror fiction (*Inquieta compañía,* 2004; *Carolina Grau,* 2011). Fuentes stands as a key figure representing the role of public intellectuals in Latin America and their conflicting relation with the state and its (re)production of a national culture in the twentieth and twenty-first centuries. With over twenty major novels and short-story collections and at least seven notable collections of essays (*La nueva novela hispanoamericana, Cervantes o la crítica de la lectura, Tiempo mexicano, Valiente mundo nuevo, El espejo enterrado, En esto creo, La gran novela latinoamericana*), a constant involvement in international political debates through syndicated newspaper articles and interviews, and his participation in lecture circuits in several countries, Fuentes has often been portrayed as a "Superstar writer" (Jean Franco) and as a "Guerrilla Dandy" (Enrique Krauze).[12] Both labels underline his proclivity for the limelight through his self-appointed position as cultural diplomat and socially committed socialite. My study reveals, however, his uneasy relationship with official and populist definitions of Mexicanidad, and challenges the standard depiction of his works as mere transposition into the literary arena of earlier academic and public debates about *lo mexicano.*

In marked contrast, the elusive figure of Thomas Pynchon is characteristic of the retreat of U.S. public intellectuals from the political and social scene in the context of the Cold War and the popular culture promoted by commercial mass media, with its avowed anti-intellectualism.[13] Associated with Cold War paranoia and the countercultural movements of the 1960s and 1970s, with its playful but deep-rooted acts of resistance to mass marketed "square" values, Pynchon's work has remained a sturdy icon of the American New Left.[14] His latest works, *Against the Day* (2006), *Inherent Vice* (2009), and *Bleeding Edge* (2013), demonstrate a seamless continuity in the authorial project I identify in *After the Nation:* a critical assault on both the national historical archive and the dominant practices of socioeconomic control and cultural hegemony at work in (post)industrial U.S. society.[15] Much of Pynchon's academic reception in the United States and abroad coincided with the surge of deconstructionist and poststructuralist approaches to the literary text in the 1980s and 1990s, and has as a result been masked by impenetrable, often obscure exercises in high theory, frequently concealing or overlooking the more historical and political interpretations of his prose.[16]

Despite Pynchon's withdrawal from public life and a critical reception drawn toward formalism, wordplay, and opaque conceptual abstraction, I propose readings of his works side by side with his paratexts—letters, essays, blurbs, and other published contributions—to reconstruct a sense of an authorial project. I advance a theoretical framework rooted in textual commentary and cultural history, as well as archival research within which to understand Pynchon's works as a postnationalist denunciation of American imperialism and its related jingoistic practices.

An introductory section is followed by seven chapters, each dealing with a different novel; these are clustered into the three thematic, chronologically sequenced sections, or parts, and each section is headed by an introductory comparative essay. The introduction, entitled "Bordering Can(n)ons: Postnational Satire in the United States and Mexico," draws on theories of nationalism and nationalist discourse to reconsider the narrative tropes on which national narratives rely to constantly reassert a multi-class consensus. I review the debates over the function of the novel in the forging of a national culture in Mexico and the United States, to situate the political nature of postnational satires.

The first part, entitled "Narrative Undergrounds of the Postnational City," consists of two chapters dealing with two cities, Mexico City and New York respectively, as the sites for the contradictory constitution and institutionalization of national myths. Here I look at the city as the space where political control and social experimentation are shaped under the banner of modernity—but where they are also invariably contested. In each of the two chapters in this section, I analyze narratives that dismantle the teleology of nationalist historical discourses, which implicitly endorse progress as the logical time frame of the narrated nation (Anderson, Balibar). The works analyzed in this section are Fuentes's *La región más transparente* (1958) and Pynchon's *V.* (1963). These novels present an urban landscape, a polis, governed by the reign of national mythical essences driven by the machinery of cultural homogenization.

The three chapters in the second part, "Dissenting from the Nation: The New Left," look at the emergence of a critical anti-nationalism at the height of the Cold War by studying issues of patriarchalism, inheritance, and social conditioning in relation to the construction of a hegemonic culture that seeks to appear as national consensus. Here I read together two novels by Fuentes, *La muerte de Artemio Cruz* (1962) and *Cambio de piel* (1967), and Pynchon's *The Crying of Lot 49* (1966). I look at these works as articulations of critical anti-nationalist discourses within the context of the eruption of the 1960s New Left.

In the third part, "(Post)Colonial Enlightened Origins: Americanism Born," I consider the complex relations between the Enlightenment and the practices of nation building in the Americas fictionalized in two historical novels, Fuentes's *La campaña* (1990) and Pynchon's *Mason & Dixon* (1997).

In both texts, the foundational myths of Creole nationalists who symbolically established themselves in the place of Native Americans vis-à-vis European metropolitan powers re-created paradoxically the colonial violence of settlement and prepared for future expansion through the containment and removal of indigenous cultures across the Western Hemisphere as unviable political elements for the newly founded nations.

In the final section, I discuss some of the latest works by Pynchon and Fuentes (*Against the Day*, 2006; *Inherent Vice*, 2009; *Bleeding Edge* (2013); *La frontera de cristal*, 1995; and *Federico en su balcón*, 2012) and the active relevance of postnationalism as a practical intellectual interpretive framework, which also allows for the critique of neoliberal cosmopolitanism. Despite the seemingly stable borders dividing both nations and both literary traditions, the parallel but distinct trajectories of these narrators feature the common tropes of nationalist rhetoric across the hemisphere and their paradoxical complementarities to the projects of modern globalization and neoliberal capitalist expansion.

As I start out to cross back and forth the virtual but tangible borders that restrict and codify both the nation-state and its literary and cultural histories, I am all of a sudden once again reminded of the paintings on the dividing wall along Los dos Nogales: the myriad graffiti that protest and puncture the inflated importance of the (inter)national edifice challenging its implied stability and its martial severity. Like the paintings on the wall, the fictions studied here erode and tarnish, rehumanize and sarcastically adorn the national boundaries of Mexico and the United States, asking their readers to place themselves *after* the nation—in playful pursuit of its myths and icons, on the other side of its imagined geographies and temporalities.

ACKNOWLEDGMENTS

As I reread the final manuscript for *After the Nation* at the end of 2013, I reminisced about the many voices and people who helped me in the long road that began as a Ph.D. dissertation at King's College, London, at the turn of the century, and culminated as the book you have in your hands or on your screen. There are too many friends, colleagues, and institutions to acknowledge here and I cannot do full justice to each and all of them in such short space, but I hope that the final product will be a fair record and a tribute to their unfailing engagement with this project. All the errors and oversights the reader may find in this book, however, are mine alone.

I remember well many conversations and discussions with Clive Bush in London and at Yale, and here in Eugene more recently, and how they always pushed me to apprehend the historical specificity in which these fictions were conceived. His lifelong commitment to literature, cultural history, and American studies and his generous mentorship offered encouraging models to pursue this project. At King's and in London the help and advice of Shamoon Zamir, Kasia Boddy, Burhan Tufail, and many others provided a great environment in the early stages of my research. An intensive year at Yale University thanks to a doctoral fellowship from the U.S.-Spanish Fulbright Commission and my many research visits afterward provided lots of engaging conversations with Roberto González Echevarría, Rolena Adorno, Cristina Moreiras, Josefina Ludmer, Moira Fradinger, John MacKay, Fernando Rosenberg, Guillermo Irizarry, Anke Birkenmaier, Luis Martín Cabrera, Nadia Altschul, Cecilia Enjuto-Rangel, and many others.

While teaching at Oxford and MIT the final shape of the dissertation and the debates that I have sought to raise in the book were enhanced through discussions with many faculty and students, notably, at Oxford, John Rutherford, Ian Michael, Alberto Mira, Clive Griffin, Robin Fiddian, Dominic Moran, Kirsty Hooper, Manolo Puga, Pepe Bellón-Aguilera; and then, in Massachusetts, with Elizabeth Garrels, Luis Fernández-Cifuentes, Doris Sommer, Teresa Gilman, Roxana Pagés-Rangel. I received very useful feedback and all forms of enlightenment from these very engaged colleagues and friends. The vibrant and resourceful libraries at all these places—London, Yale, Oxford, and Harvard—were key resources that substantially helped me to complete my initial research.

As I took up a job at the University of Oregon, the book started to take a decisive shape around issues of narratology, temporality, and critical postnationalism, which allowed me to revisit and rethink some of my earlier readings, fully revise the entire book, and completely rewrite the introduction and conclusion. I have to thank all my colleagues and friends here for fostering such a collaborative and welcoming space, and in particular Juan Armando Epple, Carlos Aguirre, Gina Herrmann, Michael Stern, Lynn Stephen, Edward Olivos, Barbara Altmann, Leonardo García-Pabón, Evlyn Gould, Bob Haskett, Stephanie Wood, Gabriela Martínez, Paul Peppis, Gordon Sayre, Fabienne Moore, Michael Hames-García, Luis Ruiz, Leah Middlebrook, Sangita Gopal, Amalia Gladhart, Alejandro Vallega, Nathalie Hester, and Karen McPherson for their friendship and support at different junctures over the past few years. The rich intellectual environment of the campus here is the work of generations of committed humanists and I am both humbled and proud to be part of it. Many discussions with students and their readings in several seminars I have taught on Carlos Fuentes at Oregon have helped me understand his works more fully.

As a speaker in two summer seminars at the Universidad del País Vasco, I was able to reformulate ideas about national discourse and the literary field; I thank the other participants and particularly Andrés Zamora and Jon Kortazar. Many others have contributed and helped with their insightful readings, feedback, or generous support at different stages: Steven Boldy, Elizabeth Jane Wall Hinds, Fernando Arrabal, Theo D'Haen, Djelal Kadir, Francisco Collado, Allan Lloyd-Smith, Ilya Kliger, Vicente Cervera Salinas, Jean Franco, Julio Ortega, Julián Rodríguez, and the participants at an MLA roundtable on postnationalism that I organized in 2011. At Northwestern University Press, *After the Nation* acquired its final form under the careful, detailed process of review initiated by Henry Carrigan and with the hospitable, constructive feedback of two anonymous readers. I thank Anne E. Gendler for her copyediting and guidance in the final stages of readying the manuscript for the press. A subvention from the Oregon Humanities Center helped me secure funds for indexing the book, a job that was carried out by Steven Moore, who has carefully offered excellent final corrections to the manuscript. Thank you also to the College of Arts and Sciences, University of Oregon.

Throughout all this time Cecilia Enjuto-Rangel has been the most steadfast reader of this book, a patient partner and colleague who has constantly encouraged me to pursue its publication, even as I moved into other exciting projects over the past few years. It is thanks to her, to her unyielding support and faith, that this book is finally a reality. I could not inscribe the book to anyone else but to Ceci, and to our two amazing daughters, Lucía and Julia, as this book is their older sibling.

After the Nation

Introduction

✦

Bordering Can(n)ons: Postnational Satire in the United States and Mexico

"And yet, as contentious and frustrating and messy as our democracy can sometimes be, I know there isn't a person here who would trade places with any other nation on Earth." (Applause.)

—Barack Obama, "State of the Union," January 25, 2011

The Nation and Its Narrative Tropes

"Democracy" and "nation," the two apparent opposites in the epigraph from Barack Obama's 2011 State of the Union Address, underline the perceived disconnect between political practices—"contentious," "frustrating," "messy"—and the exceptionality of American national sentiment, with its associated across-the-board loyalties. This paradoxical contrast between the emotions of nationalism and democratic political debate points to the elusive matrix of the modern nation-state where dissent, confrontation, and competing agendas can be seamlessly reconciled under the mantle—and perhaps the terror—of a national consensus.[1] As the quote from Obama makes clear, the hollow center of national consensus is not so much a well-defined common ground, but a territorial opposition between the felt exceptionalism of those who belong "here" versus the undesirable "there," the other, more defective nations. At the heart of Obama's quote there is then a double exercise in figurative language: a central antithesis compares messy democracy with national reunion, while litotes aggrandizes the elided central concept, "America," by negating the legitimacy or desire to belong elsewhere.[2] Contrasted with the welcome disagreements of democratic practice, or with the uninviting promises of other national experiences, the image of the nation emerges as antithetical to other national feelings at home and abroad. Appealing to homey but abstract principles of identification and semblance, the discourse of the nation statically refers to a persistently malleable body politic. It derives its strength from its adaptability to changing conditions and its resilience in the face of economic, social, or technological change. A self-righteous narrative of privileged belonging, nationalism short-circuits internal debate while it discredits international or universal narratives of commonality and shared aims. Contoured against the non-national experience of faulty foreignness, which it helps resist and control, and also against the diversity of political and social positions, nationalism capitalizes on identity to secure the boundaries of belonging and the homeland. Outside this geographical conception of the nation lies the world, a space conceived as "the place where international agreements are to be violated, treatises wrecked, other people's land poisoned, and military bases positioned."[3] Though this quotation comes from Terry Eagleton's *After Theory,* published in 2003, with the Bush administration in mind—its Patriot Act, and its one-sided view of international relations—the consensual rhetorical strategies operating within nationalism are also at work in Obama's speech, and their opposition between "America" and the "rest" outlines the border that sets the exceptional experiment of America apart from an outside discarded world, ready for intervention.

Nationalism is the a priori ideological discourse of the nation, its constituting ideology.[4] It is a language with only two indispensable pronouns: the first- and third-person plural, "us" and "them," used to metonymically define and confine all the possible subjects of its national narratives. As a narrative trope, metonymy redirects naming, it points to an element that will signify a whole: "us" in the nationalist playbook stands not just for those who are part of a conversational act, but it refers symbolically to an entire imagined community, even if "they" are absent from "our" conversation.[5] Only through a metonymic act could such a large community of interlocutors be conceived. In his chapter in Bhabha's *Nation and Narration,* Geoffrey Bennington emphasizes the oppositional binary dualities on which the narratives of nation are built. Bennington underlines the centrality of binary games in all national narratives, at heart driven by the fundamental opposition between "us" and "them." He writes, "The idea of the nation is inseparable from its narration: that narration attempts, interminably, to constitute identity against difference, inside against outside, and in the assumed superiority of inside over outside, prepares against invasion and for 'enlightened colonialism.' "[6] As spokespersons for the nation's will, nationalists resort to processes of symbolic utterance to dialectically embody, imagine, and narrate a community against its negated others.

Personified through allegory, the nation's story is typically that of her struggles through history to succeed in fulfilling her manifest destiny: her selfsame unity, her spatial culmination, or both. Circular and linear at once, the typological narratives of nation re-create the figure of a moving spiral: the epic journey forward of the imagined community. This trajectory erases differences between remote pasts and alternate projected futures, but also among the different constituencies and individuals that have populated the alleged homeland over time. Nationalist renderings of history create the fantasy that the nation is a continuum of affects and practices, as if cultural history was the result of essentialized static repetitions rather than a series of conflicts, crises, innovations, and imitations within a shifting community of individuals and groups over time. The nationalist reification of cultural history extensively edits and openly utilizes the archive to create a packaged set of traditions and rituals, displacing and negating the relative autonomy of culture vis-à-vis the national state. This reified iteration aims to forestall cultural representations of diversity and difference; in other words, it seeks to repudiate the heterogeneity, the conflicts and the traumas inherent to cultural production. The desire to provide a neat uninterrupted history of the community in a coherent lineal relation purposefully excludes dissident voices from the genealogy of the nation; it forecloses their presence in the invented tradition, except in the form of an outside or defeated "other," the essential enemy within and without.[7]

"Invented" and "mass produced" are the two adjectives used by Eric Hobsbawm to describe the manufacture of national traditions in the industrial age. These terms evoke images of factory workers producing *charro* hats, stars and stripes nylon flags, and other patriotic paraphernalia, but they also underline the inventive genesis of these signs. Their fabrication is not so much the outcome of a historical falsification, but rather the result of a concerted effort by nationalist elites to metonymically signify the national experience. National bric-a-brac is commercialized en masse to celebrate "Día de la independencia" or 4th of July, birthdays of Mexico and the United States as postcolonial nations—for despite their seeming permanence, nations are themselves born and reborn. Central moments in the outwardly unchanging annual rituals of nationhood are also invented culinary traditions such as Thanksgiving Day, or the tricolor "chile en nogada." Indeed, the colors of the flag can be displayed and also consumed, a form of national communion which cleverly reunites factions, parties, and individuals into a solid flock. The map and its borders, the schoolbook and its histories, the state and its flag, the language and its accents, are all signposts demarcating and signifying the nation itself. If the nation is the text being written, fabricated through discursive and institutional practices, then nationalism is the common language—the ideology—that all fabricators, nation-builders, storytellers, and legislators understand and share: a language whose universal grammar consists of absolute beginnings, perfect preterits, indicative presents, and a manifest futurity.

For over three decades cultural historians have examined and outlined the characterization and substance of nationalism as a key political and cultural discourse of industrial modernity. Positing that national phenomena are historically grounded, culturally constructed texts, and that "the idea of the nation is inseparable from its narration,"[8] theories of nationalism are intimately concerned with its discursive practices, its institutional language as well as its body of literature. The resulting definitions and descriptions of national phenomena point to their textual and socially constructed nature, their cultural overdetermination. Eric Hobsbawm's and Terence Ranger's fundamental suggestion that the hegemonic practices of industrialized societies, with the nation-state at their center, promoted an "invention of traditions" first appeared in 1983, the same year as Benedict Anderson's enormously influential *Imagined Communities,* and Ernest Gellner's *Nations and Nationalism.*[9] The Anglo-American hyper-nationalist conglomerate of the Thatcher-Reagan partnership is the necessary backdrop to locate these three significant studies. Positioned toward the triumphant end of the Cold War, these three books scrutinized the ideological and historical articulations of nationalism modeling similar anti-essentialist propositions to underscore the specific ideological and institutional constructs of nation and nationalism throughout the nineteenth and twentieth centuries, in particular the close relationship between nationalism and the emergence of liberalism, between the industrial bourgeoisie and the modern nation-state.[10] Ernest Gellner defined nationalism as an ideology whose central aim is to equate nation and state: "a political principle, which holds that the political and the national unit should be congruent."[11] For Gellner, the historical concurrence of nationalism and industrial modernity is not at all coincidental, but rather a central condition of possibility for the materialization of the modern nation-state.

In *Imagined Communities,* Benedict Anderson located the origins of modern nationalism in the hemispheric struggles for independence in the Americas from the 1770s to the 1820s, proposing that "nationalism emerged first in the New World, not the Old."[12] For Anderson, the rhetoric of civic nationalism, of enlightened republicanisms, effectively shrouded the ethnic nationalism of American-born Europeans or creoles throughout the hemisphere. However, the civic nationalist foundation of the new republics encapsulated what Anderson calls the "doubleness of the Americas": as they were founded out of colonial social systems, American nations were from the start "internally riven" by racial and ethnic conflicts in ways "unmatched in Europe" (*Imagined Communities,* 202). Anderson's work spins around the central claim that nineteenth-century printed media—namely newspapers and realist novels—"provided the technical means for 're-presenting' the *kind* of imagined community that is the nation" (25). Specifically, Anderson's study focuses on the emergence of print capitalism in the nineteenth century, exemplified by the upsurge in periodical publications and novels, among them the first Mexican novel—*El Periquillo Sarniento* (*The Mangy Parrot*) (1816) by José Joaquín Fernández de Lizardi. Here Anderson deploys his theory of the novel as a "device for the representation of simultaneity in 'homogeneous, empty time' " (25), a key narrative dimension for imagining the futurity of national life. The older, Benjaminean concept of "empty time" is reclaimed by Anderson as a future, teleological dimension of "calendric time" whereupon such fictions were inscribed. Empty time is the temporal locality on which the national narrative moves linearly toward its destiny, its (always) future fulfillment: "the idea of a sociological organism moving calendrically through homogeneous, empty time is a precise analogue of the idea of the nation, which is also conceived as a solid community moving down (or up) in history" (26). The central figuration of national(ist) narratives is thus based on the complex imagining of a transhistorical entity, Anderson's "solid community," one which can be traced back to a mythical moment of origins, but perhaps more importantly, as an enduring community united by its shared existence in time-space, and projected toward the future.

Etienne Balibar characterizes the historical teleology of the nation as constituted upon "a narrative which attributes to these entities [nations] the continuity of a subject."[13] Balibar depicts this narrative trope, "the continuity of [the] subject," as founded on a twofold illusion: an invariant substance and a necessary destiny. The first effect "consists in believing that the generations which succeed one another over centuries on a reasonably stable territory, under a reasonably univocal designation, have handed down to each other an invariant substance" (Balibar and Wallerstein, 86). "Destiny" is the second element of this dual impression as portrayed by Balibar: "[it] consists in believing that the process of development from which we select aspects retrospectively, so as to see ourselves as the culmination of that process, was the only one possible, that is, it represented a destiny" (86). The "invariant substance" highlighted by Balibar is the totemic essentialist cultural construct that projects national identity into the future in the shape of a common destiny. Thus, the "illusion of national identity" is thoroughly linked to the symmetrical narrative figures of "project" and "destiny." In other words, there is what we could call a diachronic syntax of the nation, one that looks at history in search of the narratives of a particular subject, the national body, and which naturalizes its futurity as a matter of course: the future is the natural progression of communal time.

In nationalist narratives, the past almost always prefigures the present as it shoots out into a shared futurity. This concept of destiny, and its implied narrative teleology, is a central ideological tenet in which both national beliefs and the quasi-theological faith in the universal progress of humankind coalesce. This temporal configuration of national narratives appears to be specific and characteristic of Occidental enlightenment modernity, the emergence of present-day nation-states, and it is particularly fraught with contradictions in the interstices of the Occidental projects of Eurocentric acculturation, "emancipatory" colonization, and endless expansion of the Western universalist-though-local episteme.

Mexico: *Mestizo* Nationalism as Erasure

How does, for instance, Mexican or Peruvian Creole nationalist rhetoric—mostly in Spanish—account for the disruptions to a self-fashioned indigenous national subjectivity provoked by the violence of conquest, colonization, and acculturation? What symbolic operations were necessary for American (U.S.) nationalism to imagine itself as native, to both account for the removal and genocide of Native Americans, and still create a viable postcolonial identity vis-à-vis Europe despite its patent white Anglo-Saxon Protestant lineages? Even though nationalism is often cast as a way of locally contending with a metropolitan or imperially imposed modernity, with what Arjun Appadurai has framed as a "modernity at large," I want to make a case for nationalism as one of modernity's most successful, if contradictory, by-products, as Ernest Gellner and many others have persuasively argued.[14] Claudio Lomnitz has succinctly summed up this insightful and anti-essentialist definition of nationalism by presenting it as "a cultural product that is generated in a web of transnational connections."[15] Specifically in the cases of postcolonial societies such as Mexico and the United States, nationalism was from the outset the project of the "national bourgeoisie" whose interests and national definitions were couched within Western global capitalism despite the nativist rhetorical gestures, and despite the apparent ruptures performed through institutional acts of emancipatory self-determination.[16]

Situated by Anderson at the forefront of the modern nationalist revolutions promoted by the onset of postcolonial identity formations, the Americas would seem to offer a particularly apt site to study the inner workings of Occidental nationalisms and the cultural machinery of print capitalism which placed the novel at its core from the beginning. *Periquillo Sarniento,* Mexico's first novel, published in serialized form in 1816, five years before Mexican independence, exemplifies well Anderson's model in its proposition of the nation as an imagined community of consumer-readers by alluding from the outset to the purchasing power of a new national reading (re)public. This ethnically diverse, modern reading public—made up in part of "plebeyos, indios, mulatos, negros, viciosos, tontos y majaderos"[17] ("plebeians, indians, mulattos, blacks, vicious, silly, and foolish men")—to which Lizardi refers in a tongue-in-cheek tone in his prologue, not only makes the literary venture financially possible, it also reflects and constitutes the post-imperial, post-aristocratic society onto which the novel is grafted. And yet, one single novel does not a literary system make, let alone birthing a whole nation-state—Mexican intellectuals would speculate for decades after the publication of *Periquillo* over the existence of a Mexican national literature, and indeed over the character and definition of Mexican identity. "¿Tenemos una literatura nacional?" asked seventy years later, in 1885, Ignacio Manuel Altamirano, one of the leading liberal intellectuals of nineteenth-century Mexico.[18] In characteristic fashion for his times, instead of proposing the more prosaic novel genre—of which he was nevertheless a foremost defender and major practitioner—as a sign of national literary soundness, Altamirano went on to argue in favor of national epic poems as a required genre for the existence of an observable and respectable national literature. A department in which he found Mexican literature still deficient until that very moment: his rhetorical question-and-answer was part of the prologue for such an epic poem by Guillermo Prieto, *El romancero nacional* (1885). Throughout his essay, Altamirano situated Mexican literature in a creative tension with its Spanish formal and linguistic roots, and in an unfavorable comparison with the already well-established literary production of other American republics, namely Argentina, Peru, and the United States. Altamirano's optimism conceived of the intellectual mandate to fill the gaps of an imagined literary canon, where certain genres simply had to exist for there to be a national literature, a corpus which in turn would demonstrate the existence of a national sentiment. This counter-intuitive movement was distinctive of nationalist elites the world over in their pains to fulfill the perceived requisites of national culture: a flag, an army, and logically, epic poetry.

For Enrique Florescano, one of the problems with nineteenth-century Mexican nationalism was its promotion and cultivation of the "myths which supposedly had given birth to the nation," which in turn became "inviolable foundations of the nation, essentialized things, a condition which made them immune to the real social forces that continuously re-created the historical process."[19] The nascent Mexican nationalism, in Florescano's description, "excluded the indigenous population from its purview, and consequently the independent state declared a fight to the finish on them."[20] Subsequently, and in a complementary contrast with these top-down forms of national institutionalizing, the official culture propounded by the Mexican state arising out of the 1910 Revolution forcefully succeeded in promoting the kinds of popular epic narratives (*corridos,* novels of the revolution) and the pictorial icons (murals, films) that the Creolized elites of the nineteenth century could only intuit and long for. Between Mariano Azuela's serialized publication of *Los de abajo* (*The Underdogs*) in the Texan newspaper *El Paso del Norte* in 1915 and Carlos Fuentes's *La muerte de Artemio Cruz* (1962), for five decades a significant share of the Mexican literary output thematized sociopolitical conflicts under the banner of "*the* Revolution," its ramifications and its aftermaths.[21] Despite the fact that much of this "Literatura de la Revolución" offered a central set of premises by which the Revolution was portrayed as chaotic, violent, and leaderless or excessively *caudillista,* it was nevertheless "paradoxically and simultaneously" institutionalized as a central corpus in the emerging postrevolutionary national literary field supplying the prescriptions of "lo mexicano."[22]

Even as the reification of popular, indigenous, and mestizo cultures through museums, public large-scale murals in government buildings, archaeological interventions, and tourist propaganda was taking place, it was nonetheless characterized by a concerted effort to generate a hegemonic, centralized Mexican national identity whose core values were industrialization and social homogenization through educational programs, and whose language of choice was none other than Spanish. The emergence of this contemporary

Mexicanness as a form of national culture was aimed at doing away with the heterogeneity of ethnic, regional, and linguistic affiliations in order to foster the creation of nationalized Mexican citizens. Mexicans had to be made. The bible of the postrevolutionary mestizo state was made up of a corpus of essays defining "lo mexicano" which extolled the virtues of *mestizaje* as the foundation of a "cosmic race" (*La raza cósmica* by José Vasconcelos, 1924); it proposed the acculturation of indigenous people through cultural *mestizaje* as the way to "build the motherland" (*Forjando patria* by Manuel Gamio, 1940) and in order to effectively nationalize—"mexicanizar" was the buzzword—Mexico's large indigenous population, thus doing away with one of "the great national problems" (*Los grandes problemas nacionales* by Andrés Molina Enríquez, 1909): the need to extend a unifying linguistic and national culture to the entire population. Néstor García Canclini detects this fetishization of the "foundational events of the nation" in the National Anthropological Museum in Mexico City.[23] As elsewhere, nationalism is based on a political and cultural discourse that defuses, through a broad consensus represented in the all-inclusive "mexicanidad" of the mural or the museum,[24] the contentious aspects of cultural difference, be it ethnic, generic, or linguistic, either by hegemonically including them or by excluding and erasing their heterogeneity from the nation-state. The central narrative of this mestizo nationalist rhetoric portrayed indigenous identity as a dead past.[25] While it acknowledged its important place in history as a point of origin, it discredited its status as a feasible practice in the present or as a national destination: indigeneity—as a linguistic, cultural practice—was thus narrated as unsuitable for the project of Mexican modernity except as a past narrative.

A prominent theorist of Mexican nationalism, Roger Bartra, proposes anti-essentialist definitions of nation and nationalism to underline their hegemonic consensual impulse, and to formulate with great precision the ideological interaction among these various elements: the ruling class, the state, popular culture, and the discourse of nation. Bartra characterizes nationalism accordingly "as a body of political theory which expresses the hegemonic vocation of the ruling class through a multi-class alliance founded on the supposed originality, itself subjectively reconstructed, of the national peculiarities and their identification with the state."[26] Through a critical rendering of this avowed identification, Roger Bartra defines nationalism somewhere else as a hegemonic discourse, as "the transfiguration of the supposed characteristics of the national identity to the ideological field."[27] Bartra follows Hobsbawm's "invention of tradition" theme to underscore the hegemonic class motivation of nationalist discourses. A nation is not then a phantasmal body politic, unchangeable regardless of the human heterogeneity or the historical conflicts that nationalists purport to signify as a unity, but rather a set of hegemonic cultural narratives to which a "multi-class alliance" constantly refers. Mexicanness as defined and staged by the cultural agencies of the Mexican state throughout the twentieth century sought to incorporate in its visual and narrative scope other ethnic groups, and to narrate other historical origins in the all-encompassing venture of asserting mestizo hegemony. This hegemonic project, and its implicit consensual claims, are at the heart of the satirical deconstructions that I will identify in Carlos Fuentes's novels throughout *After the Nation.*

In moving against and away from the national narratives of Mexicanness, Fuentes encountered and helped (re)found an alternate transnational Latin American literary field. Latin Americanism allowed Fuentes and some of his fellow travelers of the literary "boom" to interpolate the national landscape and to challenge local exceptionalities by alluding to a whole series of postcolonical continuities and similarities: hypernationalist, hypermasculine leaders and dictators, widespread violence, neocolonialism, and intellectual intolerance among other themes are at the heart of novels such as Rosario Castellanos's *Oficio de tinieblas* (1962); Gabriel García Márquez's *Cien años de soledad* (1967) and *El otoño del patriarca* (1975); Augusto Roa Bastos's *Yo el Supremo* (1974); José Donoso's *El lugar sin límites* (1966); and Mario Vargas Llosa's *Conversación en la catedral* (1969) and *La fiesta del chivo* (2000). While many studies have dealt with this Latin American literary "boom" and its aesthetics of hyperbolic, neo-baroque excess that some have come to associate with magical realism (for example, Parkinson Zamora, Faris, Bell-Villada), the extent to which these aesthetics were employed to challenge and deface the projects of the national bourgeoisies and to unravel their ur-narratives of nation has remained largely unexplored. As a comparativist study of Fuentes's postnationalist literary practice, *After the Nation* places his texts in a larger context of the hemispheric New Left to reposition and revisit his satirical project from a different angle.

The Melting U.S. Cauldron

In the editor's introduction to *The Invention of Tradition,* Hobsbawm pointed out how new traditions emerge at times of crisis or during a "rapid transformation of society" (4) when either "the social patterns for which 'old' traditions had been designed" (4) are weakened or destroyed, or when old traditions are no longer "sufficiently adaptable and flexible" (5). The apparently oxymoronic but prevalent idea of the "new tradition" is then born out of the tension between a social body in search of formal authority and a cultural order whose hegemony has been challenged by new material conditions. New traditions are by definition governed by their hegemonic aspiration and their eager adoption by the social group whose status is sanctified or in other words legitimized by the newly incepted tradition; these traditions are in a way their narrative, circular claim to authenticity. Parades, public festivities, culinary habits, sports events, the long list of "modern traditions" studied in Hobsbawm's and Ranger's collection highlights the prevalence, or the "assiduity"—to use Hobsbawm's more specific term—of a cultural practice that for them typifies the contemporary period: the constant (re)-invention of traditions. That time frame coincides with the mounting success of the modern nation-state in establishing and regimenting social and individual identifications and cultural practices throughout the last two centuries. Eschewing essentialist outlooks on social customs, Hobsbawm maps out the interrelation between social change, the nation-state, and the modern need for "new devices to ensure or express social cohesion and identity and to structure social relations" (263).

Discussing the case of U.S. nationalism, Hobsbawm portrays late nineteenth-century invented traditions as largely aimed at "assimilat[ing] a heterogeneous mass . . . of people who were Americans not by birth but by immigration" (Hobsbawm and Ranger, *Invention of Tradition,* 279). Productively, Hobsbawm tackles the ways in which differentiated ethnic groups and their popular cultures became part and parcel of U.S. national culture over time. Such mass-marketed traditions include national holidays that celebrated "the Revolution and its founding fathers (4th of July) and the Protestant Anglo-Saxon tradition (Thanksgiving Day)" (279). "Americans had to be made" he summarizes, inadvertently echoing Gertrude Stein's *The Making of Americans* (1925). To the earlier national traditions, newer, invented or adopted traditions such as Saint Patrick's Day, Columbus Day, and others were gradually added, assimilating the "collective rituals of immigrants" into the narrative of U.S. national traditions. For Hobsbawm, national "assimilation" is not a one-way road—it is not a mere sort of patriotic exam, or a frequently performed oath of allegiance, but a process that underlines the shifting definition of what stands for national experience. In Hobsbawm's rendition, American nationalism appears to be distinctly malleable and successful in its seemingly inexhaustible ability to redefine itself, and to offer a constant two-sided assimilation of subjects who become Americanized, and whose ethnic traditions are rapidly adapted into the packaged set of practices, reified into the nationalist pantheon, thus constantly allowing for new circumstances, and new national subjects. Ronald Bush has discussed the consensual narratives of national identity as informative of the construction of an American literary tradition: "Searching for authentic origins is an old story in American intellectual life, which for two centuries has reacted to the dispersion of distance and industrial transformation and ethnic diversity by seeking to create an overriding national story."[28] In contrast with the accomplishments of American nationalist culture to create such a successful narrative telos, one that both obfuscates its shortcomings and promotes itself as a new hegemonic identity of planetary dimensions, other nationalist discourses are represented as regionally bound, archaic, or flawed.[29] Nonetheless "if ever there was an imagined community, surely it is the United States of America," as John Fousek put it in his historical account of Cold War American nationalism.[30] For Fousek, U.S. national rhetoric is embedded in a millenarian and imperialist conception of its mission in the world, an ideological formation he defines as "American nationalist globalism." American nationalism, particularly after World War II, was set on a global scale, defined in contradistinction with other social and cultural narratives of communitarian belonging, to highlight its universalist, imperial claims: "The belief that the universal nature of American national values justified and even necessitated the global expansion of U.S. power embodies the essence of American nationalist globalism in the postwar era" (7).

One of the main objects of study for Americanists is to inspect how these celebratory, omnipresent discourses of American nationalism, with their attendant silences, their erased flaws, and their implied expansionist agendas, rearrange historical materials in a teleological fashion. If Americanists—to paraphrase Amy Kaplan—aim to offer a critical remapping of America by looking at those "geographies that traverse and challenge [its official] borders," we need to avoid its recuperation as a spatial whole, which, as Kaplan indicates, would present the danger "of reinstating a teleological lineal narrative of historical continuity, of viewing American history, even in its imperial dimensions, as a singular march."[31] As I show in this book, for Thomas Pynchon the universal claims of this American nationalist globalism, and the narrative tropes and temporalities through which they are imagined—untainted origins, social consensus, manifest destinies—offer a wide range of targets in his satirical pursuits. Despite the remarkable breadth and depth of his output, and the persistent anti-nationalist project that I outline here, Pynchon is not alone in the U.S. literary field in broadcasting this satirical rewriting of national histories to critically delineate Americanness. The works of many of his contemporaries can be read within a similar nonrecuperative, non-Americanist framework. Some notable examples are: John Barth's *The Sot-Weed Factor* (1960); Thomas Berger's *Little Big Man* (1964); Robert Coover's *The Origin of the Brunists* (1969); Don DeLillo's *Americana* (1989), *Libra* (1991), and *Underworld* (1997); and Toni Morrison's *A Mercy* (2008). While the larger narrative of the post-Americanist literary field awaits to be written, *After the Nation* offers one contribution to that wider debate of how and where to locate these satirical interventions.

Postnational Satire: Subverting the National

The comparativist proposition at the center of this book is to set side by side the satires of Carlos Fuentes and of Thomas Pynchon in order to replicate and challenge the juxtapositions and the dialogic relations of the two national constructions—Mexico and the United States respectively—within which they operate, and to offer new insights into the manner in which national narrative tropes are refashioned, altered, and critiqued in these two distinct but increasingly connected cultural contexts. A comparativist approach such as this is particularly productive when discussing not only the literary uses of frontiers, flags, and anthems, but also the satirical carnivalization of pop icons, "national" and "foreign" languages, cosmopolitan and autochthonous cultures.

If the progression of the people through history to fulfill their national unity is the basic narrative telos of nationalist rhetoric animating its epics, in this book I look at contemporary novels from Mexico and the United States to propose a complementary allegation: the novel as postnational*ist* satire, as the central narrative site for the discrediting of national epics. In the novels and other texts by Thomas Pynchon and Carlos Fuentes studied here, the attempted demolition of nationalist rhetoric operates by satirically foregrounding its narrative tropes, its temporal structures, and its thematized iconographies. The idea of a hegemonic national culture is assailed through a series of satirical re-narrations and parodic reenactments of official national histories with the intent of rebuilding a conflicting heterogeneity constantly threatened by national conformity and cultural uniformity. As a literary mode, postnational satire shakes the discursive foundations on which the national consensus rests, parodying its rituals, its sacralized essentialist epics, and its longing for geographic and historical exceptionality. Such satirical renderings of national history, of national heroes, national essences and myths, underline the constructed nature of the patriotic compromise—as well as its political underpinnings—while they parade the voices of dissensus, the images of marginalized identities, the failed promises, the unfulfilled revolutions, and the cracks and contradictions of an impossible community. These archival excavations of the mass-produced paraphernalia that daily define national paradigms critically reconstruct both history and the "present" while they successively create a burnt museum of the satirized nation, that is, a museum, or rather a fun-house, where the sacrosanct myths of the national pantheon are torched. As the cozy grand narratives of belonging are collapsed, these texts do not engage in community (re)construction or in foundational audacities, nor do they embrace the globalized—read Americanized—postnational fair; instead, they offer the bitter satirical spectacle of the parodist's cynical grin.

Contrary to the notion that the epic mode, or the foundational romance, is the dominant formulation of the novel as a literary genre, Mikhail Bakhtin proposed both parody and satire as the two historically defining features of the novel. Bakhtin's description of the novel as a heteroglossic, hybrid genre moves away from more conventional depictions of the novel as a monologic, linear epic. As Timothy Brennan puts it: "If the novel for Bakhtin tended to parody other genres, the epic was the genre the novel parodied in its nation-forming role."[32] Characterized by its modernity and its genetic tendency to destabilize the epic genre, the novel as defined by Bakhtin in his essay "Epic and Novel: Toward a Methodology for the Study of the Novel" revolves around a playful criticism of social hierarchies and power structures. As in the Menippean satire, where according to Bakhtin, "nothing is left of the distant epic image of the absolute past," (26) the historical past reenacted in the novels studied here is staged with the intent of cannibalizing and carnivalizing it. While the constitutive feature of the epic is for Bakhtin "the transferral of the world it describes to an absolute past of national beginnings and peak times" (15), in these satirical incursions into national histories "the entire world and everything sacred in it is offered to us without any distancing at all, in a zone of crude contact, where we can grab at everything with our own hands" (26). Bakhtin's image of the novel as a "zone of crude contact" can be appropriated here to define the critical spaces where the present meets the commoditized past seeking to reverse the processes by which it has been sacralized: the teleological epics of the nation are confronted with alternative narratives that satirically reenact the vaunted myths of origins.

Three main narrative features are the basis for the Bakhtinian definition of the novel as an inherently satirical genre—temporal destabilization, dialogism, and authoring. The first of these narrative practices, temporal destabilization, is particularly significant for the subversion of the national sequence of "mythical past-consensual present-manifest destiny" that I have been identifying as the innermost nucleus of nationalist rhetoric. Postnational satire's playful use of the past blurs many interpretative options, it becomes unstable and dynamic, a narrative where neither the nation's mythical beginnings nor the distinctive essentialism of presence in nationalist discourse can be found, let alone be founded. Nor does postnational satire allow for Anderson's projection into that future "homogeneous empty time" necessitated by the narratives of national fulfillment. That is, postnational satire as a narrative mode and as a subgenre within contemporary, postmodern writing actively plots against the deployment of destiny in its representation of temporal progress. For Alvin Kernan satire "never offers that direct, linear progression which is ordinarily taken as plot,"[33] a point also underlined earlier by Bakhtin when commenting on Dostoevsky's work. Morson notes the disappearance of "rhythms" and of inevitability in a plot full of "loopholes," which leads him to conclude that the work is "always directed forward but without teleology."[34] Rather than linearity and progress, postnational satires promote a narrative breakup, what Alvin Kernan referred to as a "satiric disjunctiveness." In the postnational satires studied here, this "disjunctiveness" performs a critical departure from the consensual teleologies of national histories.

The more conventional description of the novel as associated with the epic genre is at the center of Benedict Anderson's work on how both the novel and the newspaper imagine and narrate the national community.[35] The simultaneity offered by print commodities on which Anderson sets his archaeological excavation of national discourses is thus only attached to a particular narrative mode characterized by its linearity and its teleological impetus. As we saw earlier, Anderson borrows from Walter Benjamin the concept of synchronous "empty time" in which national imagined communities are narrated, but according to Homi Bhabha he fails to "locate the alienating time of the arbitrary sign in his naturalized, nationalized space of the imagined community . . . [and h]e fails to read that profound ambivalence that Benjamin places deep within the utterance of the narrative of modernity."[36] Bhabha underscores Benjamin's proposal of the "non-synchronous, incommensurable gap in the midst of storytelling" as a more complex and acute reading of the relation between time and modern fiction, the nation and its narration. Bhabha's critique is thus a valuable reflection on the ways in which the linear narrative of the nation is contested from the interstitial "margins of modernity" as they evince a cultural heterogeneity that cannot be incorporated into the national metanarrative. As Bhabha aptly points out: "From the margins of modernity, at the insurmountable extremes of storytelling, we encounter the question of cultural difference as the perplexity of living, and writing, the nation" (311). Disappointingly, Bhabha fails to distinguish between the literary corpus analyzed in Anderson's *Imagined Communities*—nineteenth-century novels from Mexico and the Philippines, among others—and the text at the heart of Benjamin's essays, Baudelaire's *Le peintre de la vie moderne*. This clear differentiation between Baudelaire's studies of national and urban development in imperial France and those analyzed by Anderson, which originated in late colonial and postcolonial settings, could have allowed Bhabha to explore in a more historically specific and succinct way the relations between modernity and nationalism as they developed in the European center and in its postcolonial peripheries. And yet, Bhabha's evocation of the discontinuities in the temporal narratives of the nation elicited by the non-hegemonic, culturally heterogeneous narratives of the margins, and of cultural heterogeneity, is a fitting though paradoxical model for the postnational satires studied in this book as they disrupt and disavow the temporality and, in particular, the teleology of national histories through a reenactment of its elided others. It is paradoxical, however, because the voicing of a national heterogeneity obliterated from the nation's celebratory epic narration is carried out in both Pynchon and Fuentes from the vantage position of the nation's literary "center" rather than its margins. While the disavowal performed by these postnational satires of the narrative logic of national progression refutes the national claims of exceptionality and the contradictions of modernity's advances, it is that very narrative process that allows these texts to be subsumed into an emerging postnational literary canon.

The title of this introduction deliberately plays with the idea of the national literary canon as both a constellation of texts that construct, define, and regulate national culture and as an educational arsenal that parallels the contours of the national military geography and its state borders. Literary texts and literary scholarship from the nineteenth and twentieth centuries went hand in hand to define these symbolic bordering can(n)ons—their prevailing principle was the design and affirmation of the exceptionality of national character by the ruling postcolonial elites.[37] One of the questions that first spurred this project is precisely the extent and meaning of literary canonicity in the context of satirical articulations of national narratives, and in particular the peculiar relation with cultural hegemony and the literary field exercised by these two authors and their widely studied and commented texts. These are texts that confront the canonical expectations and standards of literary texts enshrined throughout the long foundational period of the Mexican and American literary fields. While they are characterized by an inherent transgressiveness, a constant questioning and a symbolic undoing of the hegemonic projects of the nation-state and its global ramifications, they also have come to represent a specifically New Leftist stance toward the nation-state. Van Gosse proposes to study the New Left through "the original and more inclusive definition as a 'movement of movements' encompassing all of the struggles for fundamental change from the early 1950s roughly to 1975."[38] This "movement of movements" was not however restricted to the United States alone; it was part of a larger international countercultural movement.[39] The New Left was a countercultural internationalism that emerged in the late 1950s from the critique of Cold War institutionalized hypernationalism and which developed a cosmopolitan, postnationalist, postmodern style whose loose center was occupied by the denial of the hegemonic epos of national identification.[40]

Challenging the "rather unified world of the novel" perceived by Benedict Anderson in his description of nineteenth-century literary forms, but also eschewing the proliferation of subgenres that characterized the "vast process of niche-making" in the twentieth century,[41] the novels studied here strive to occupy what Bakhtin called the novel's "zone of crude contact." This is a textual space that also resembles the carnival: an interaction that promotes a destabilization of power discourses and social hierarchies, historical landmarks and institutional boundaries. In their satirical break from Anderson's "calendric, empty time," these texts depart from his definition of the novel as the genre through which national epics are expressed, and of the nation as "the natural if unspoken frame of the novel."[42] The mechanical correspondence between novel and nation proposed by Anderson in his earlier work appears in both Pynchon's and Fuentes's novels to be eschewed, the "frame" torn and exposed as either too small or simply flawed: a political narrative structure whose tricks are halted as they are derided. As in the postcolonial satires of V. S. Naipaul, Chinua Achebe, and Salman Rushdie analyzed by John Clement Ball, there is an emphasis in both Pynchon and Fuentes on the political reworking of the past, provided by satire's playful critique—a "mode of resistance and critique engaging the political."[43]

In Bakhtin's descriptions of parody and satire, the polyphonic form of the novel, and its double voice, typifies the author's participation in configuring alternative, dialogical narrations. Dialogism and authoring, the second and third narrative strategies that define satire as the foundation for the novel as a genre, operate in a concerted manner in the Bakhtinean model. The "authorized" parodic stance follows narrowly Bakhtin's definition of the dialogic or double-voiced texts as "utterances that clearly indicate which of their conflicting voices is to be regarded as authoritative."[44] In these fictions the authorial disappearance is a carefully crafted device, much like Dostoevsky's in Bakhtin's rendering. Chalene Helmuth has summarized the effect of these narrative techniques and the ensuing plurality of readings in relation to Carlos Fuentes's novels: "In essence, there is an authorial loss of control, a carefully orchestrated loss wherein the traditional hallmarks of narration—chronology, authority, and identity—are gradually decimated or utterly transformed. The resulting fictions ardently advocate plurality not only of construction, but of reading, interpretation, and implication."[45] Yet this paradoxical "authorial loss of control" outlined by Helmuth could be best described as an authorized, satirical proliferation of meaning which encourages a critique of the monological and teleological discourses that characterize the narration of national origins and myths. The "plurality" detected by Helmuth in Fuentes's works can also be recognized in Pynchon's texts, where the multiplicity of narrative voices, the narration's dialogic composition, promotes a satirical plurality of viewpoints. In its plural aspect at least, Chalene Helmuth's definition of the—postmodern—novel is close to Bakhtin's demarcation of the genre as a whole. Thus, following Bakhtin, it would be possible to perceive the most accepted feature of "postmodernism," namely its defiance and questioning of metanarratives—and the nation is clearly one such grand narrative—as inherently imprinted in the novel form as a genre, and therefore not only part of novels from a specific cultural period or locale.[46] Early modern satirical novels such as Miguel de Cervantes's *Don Quixote,* Jonathan Swift's *Gulliver's Travels,* or Laurence Sterne's *Tristam Shandy,* in which "parodies produce an open-ended dialogical form,"[47] would demonstrate these fundamental, defining features of the novel form and their continuity in the works of "postmodern" novelists would appear to certify the generic filiations of their satires.[48] The exercise of claiming an authorial textual intervention in the creation of a contact zone (i.e., the novel), and in the active parodying of a previous idea or text through temporal disruption and dialogic play is also key to the concepts of parody and self-parody. The recognition of the author's political objectives is related to the identification of the hypotext—in this case, national romances and epics, nationalist discourses and paraphernalia—without which there would be no understanding of the text's parodic mode. The author remains there, despite being, if not completely, at least partly erased, or *sous-rature.*

If, as Julia Kristeva has posited, all texts are in actuality intertexts, both parody and satire are particular and differentiated modes of intertextual relations.[49] Parody is the central narrative strategy deployed by satire to generate reiterative, but alternative narrations. All forms of parody described by both Genette and Rose rely on the semantic persistence of previous texts or ideas, which become hypotexts (Genette) or what Morson calls "targets," "objects," or "the original utterance."[50] According to one of the most productive theorists of parody, Linda Hutcheon, parody is quite simply a form of "repetition, but with a distance or a difference."[51] Parody's repetitive-but-different utterance constantly refers to the palimpsestic, dialogic nature of satirical textuality and to its critical underpinnings. In its intertextual function, and its authorized (political) critique, parody is mobilized as a narrative strategy by the satirical genre in its all-encompassing proliferation of meaning and open saturation of textual references. As such, it is characterized by its necessary identification of the hypotext of which it is a distorted tune.

Here is an excellent example from Pynchon's *V.* of the specific uses of parody within postnational satire: when the radio broadcasts a song about Davy Crockett, Winsome, one of the navy soldiers aboard the *Scaffold,* is considerably upset. A critical look at the mass production of tradition ensues: "This was '56, height of the coonskin hat craze. Millions of kids everywhere you looked were running around with these bushy Freudian hermaphrodite symbols on their heads" (*V.,* 219). The fake psychoanalytic caricature of the western revival fad locates it in the midst of a mass-marketed output of symbols and traditions sanctified by the manufactured national consensus of consumerist society. However, this is only the first moment of Pynchon's satirical scene; a second more important point emphasizes the rewriting of history on which this mass-produced tradition rests:

> Nonsensical legends were being propagated about Crockett, all in direct contradiction to what Winsome had heard as a boy, across the mountains from Tennessee. This man, a foulmouthed louseridden boozehound, a corrupt legislator and an indifferent pioneer, was being set up for the nation's youth as a towering and cleanlimbed example of Anglo-Saxon superiority. . . . The song invited parody. (*V.,* 219–220)

In the context of the novel's commentary on the history of Western imperialism, Winsome's feelings about Crockett—one of the filibustering leaders in the anti-Mexican pro-Anglo Texas rebellion—as a corrupt and deficient national symbol directly reread the nation's racialized, ethnocentric foundation and the persistence of its frontier myths in the popular culture of the twentieth century. In tune with Winsome, one of Pynchon's many singing characters, Gérard Genette's etymological incursion into parody points to the musical origins of this specific narrative mode: "singing beside: that is, singing off key; or singing in another voice—in counterpoint; or again, singing in another key—deforming, therefore, or transposing a melody."[52] This dialogical relation between parodies, which Genette calls hypertexts, and their antecedent, hypotexts, is common to all available definitions of parody from classical to postmodern ones.[53]

As I will show throughout the book, the parodic use of the archive, of national official histories to undermine their embedded epic claims, takes the shape of what Linda Hutcheon termed "historiographic metafiction," a narrative mode that "problematizes the very possibility of historical knowledge."[54] But by fictionalizing history, Pynchon not only problematizes the access to the archive, he also offers an alternate, critical and more ethically productive type of historical account. Cherrycoke, the interposed narrator in Pynchon's *Mason & Dixon* whose voice replicates and parodies eighteenth-century English, asserts the need to see history, and the history of texts, not as a direct line—as lines are the real protagonist of that novel—but rather as an uncontrollable proliferation: "Not a Chain of single Links, for one broken link could lose us All—rather, a great disorderly Tangle of Lines, long and short, weak and strong, vanishing into the Mnemonick Deep, with only their Destination in common" (Pynchon, *MD,* 349). Cherrycoke's chaotic "Tangle of Lines" is a fictional theory of history that advocates plurality of referent and multiplicity of textual connections in the palimpsestic nature of the present text, or hypertext. That novel's central proposition is an incursion into some of those lines, a reading and a reworking of partial events in the history of the United States before its constitution as an independent nation, which seeks to refashion that history in a critical, satirical mode rather than an epic one.

Comparative American Studies: Disciplining the Trans-National

The archival carnivalization offered in *Mason & Dixon* is part of a larger literary tradition: the postmodern destabilization of official history. Santiago Juan-Navarro devotes his study of contemporary literary "archival reflections" to test his initial assertion "that [postmodern historiographic] fiction is a system of knowledge that surpasses empirical historiography in cognitive power."[55] In *Archival Reflections,* Juan-Navarro traces the ways in which works by Carlos Fuentes, Julio Cortázar, Ishmael Reed, and E. L. Doctorow offer alternate, non-official transcriptions of the archive. Juan-Navarro identifies four functions in this hemispheric "aesthetic sensibility": "utopianism, the search for cultural identity, hybridity, and the attempt to create a political pedagogical culture" (14). The already large body of critical reception related to "historiographic metafiction" (Hutcheon) in the Americas has provided the theoretical groundwork and the methodologies for the study of many contemporary novels where history is "carnivalized" (McHale), "hybridized" and "parodied" (Herrero-Olaizola), and where the hemispheric sense of newness turns history into a "usable past" (Parkinson Zamora).[56] My readings of historiographic fictions by Pynchon and Fuentes, however, try to push the envelope a little further and demonstrate that their markedly different aesthetic projects are inflected with a common satirical defiance of official archives in their ideological function as sacred repositories of national essences. I seek to precisely recognize nationalist records as the hypotexts against which satirical fragmentations, parodies, ironic rewritings, and carnivalized heroes are mobilized.

Despite the symmetric similarities that I have been outlining so far, the postnational texts studied here come, however, from two very different national literary traditions—the United States and Mexico. And although one of my goals throughout this book is to underline their convergence through a diversity of critical and narrative strategies that confront and deride nationalist rhetoric, I will also focus on the different histories of state formation on each side of the border, postcolonial and neocolonial policies, and the emergence of both neoliberal and alternative transnational spaces in the Americas. John Carlos Rowe, one of the leading advocates of a Comparative American Studies, has argued in favor of cultural studies that provide "semiotic site[s] where exchanges may occur from both (or more) sides" despite the assumed inequitable "configurations of power."[57] In addition to the correlations and similarities that I identify at this juncture, a comparativist cultural study of the United States and Mexico as the one envisioned here must make constant reference to what Rowe calls the different "cultural affiliations of the Americas" (Rowe, "Globalism and the New American Studies," 24). Aside from these distinct affiliations, the asymmetrical relations between the two countries is a result of the conflicting interactions occasioned by a long history of vicinity, interventions, migrations, and mutual mistrust. Side by side, these two large diverse cultural spaces are constituted by multiplicity rather than uniformity, and they represent two very different versions of European colonization of the Americas, two dissimilar models of independent nation-building, and two discrete postcolonial histories. A wide diversity of indigenous peoples and traditions, vastly different colonial practices, languages, and experiences, as well as distinctive independent trajectories have generated two very singular sets of national tropes and also two separate literary traditions.

The prevalent use of the two major languages, English and Spanish, in which these texts were first published is an excellent pointer to the ambivalence of national sentiment across this border and in the hemisphere: these two idiosyncratic imperial linguistic cultures have given birth to a multiplicity of national communities, and in each of them the local iteration (Canadian English, Argentinean Spanish, etc.) of the former colonial language has become reified as the national code of belonging, a sort of national accent.[58] Conspicuously, national tradition spoke the former colonial tongue in these postcolonial societies. Paradoxically then, English and Spanish play comparable roles as global, postcolonial, and national languages in the Americas while they also interface asymmetrically and influence each other at many different levels and locales. Simultaneously, Spanish is fast becoming a national language in the United States, while Spanglish, the mixture of Spanish and English, has by now become textualized as a literary language.[59] In Mexico, as in Peru, and elsewhere in the Americas, Spanish has been lexically hybridized with pre-Hispanic languages such as Nahuatl or Quechua over the many centuries of contact.[60] Another paradoxical postcolonial status of Spanish turns it into a lingua franca for indigenous people across Latin America.[61] The implications of a local national language, both postcolonial in its scope but also nationally well-defined, adds to the contentious role of the former languages of empire in both the United States and Mexico. National literary fields in these emerging reading republics were from the outset built around linguistic and aesthetic traditions recycled from the ruins of the colonial culture, and whether in dialogue with or in opposition to the metropolis, literature was in both Mexico and the United States mobilized throughout the nineteenth century for the creation of a set of national traditions. This situation reveals one particularly unsettling contradiction of postcolonial nationalisms throughout the Western Hemisphere: by and large the emancipatory projects and the discourses of nation were not strictly speaking Native American, except perhaps at a rhetorical or symbolic level. To this postcolonial continuity of Western culture, the imperial relation of the United States with the rest of the hemisphere, and very particularly with its closest southern neighbor, Mexico, mediates and defines national renderings of hemispheric relations and their history.

The roots of this avowed "new empire" can be seen as coterminous with the origins of the American republic, itself a result of the development of nationalist feelings among North Americans, as much of the contemporary historiography available to Pynchon and Fuentes in the 1960s was already demonstrating.[62] In the United States, an open statement of hemispheric preeminence followed the early period of continental expansion. From the time of the Monroe Doctrine, formulated by President James Monroe in his seventh annual message to Congress on December 2, 1823, the United States established itself as the guarantor of political stability and freedom in the Western Hemisphere, shortly after the Latin American republics had successfully asserted their independence from their European metropoles.[63] Indeed, the Monroe Doctrine can be seen as both "the personification of national unity" and "a fitting symbol of the new nationalism."[64] If the nation gained its "American identity" with the Monroe Doctrine, as Bradford Perkins claims,[65] then the whole of "America" was also redefined in terms of its earliest constituent republic precisely at the time when the former colonies of Spain were gaining their independence. Shelley Streeby has asserted the continuity between ideas of empire at the end of the nineteenth century and the earlier continental "domestic" expansion, a "continentalism" that was presented as "domestic space" precisely to promote "an exceptionalist understanding of the United States as a nonimperial nation."[66]

The hemispheric imperial presence of the United States gave way to the annexation of half of Mexico by 1848 and to the subsequent military intervention in almost all of the other American republics at some time or another over the next 160 years.[67] "America" writ large became a justification for an expansion, which could without difficulty be read in economic and neocolonial terms. This meant that, from the outset, none of the other "American" nations conceived of their economy, politics, and even cultural discourses without some reference to the U.S. Empire. Territorial expansion, as well as economic, political, and cultural power abroad, are constant issues in the history of the United States and have persistently defined the country's relationship with Mexico.

Cultural historians increasingly regard empire as a key subject that has been "ignored" for too long in the study of American culture. As Amy Kaplan suggests in her seminal introductory essay to *Cultures of United States Imperialism,* "empire" and "nationalism" are both closely related terms, as empire is not just an issue of foreign relations: it is also "about consolidating domestic cultures and negotiating intranational relations."[68] Commenting on the glaring absence of references to empire in the histories of the United States, Kaplan stresses the need to acknowledge the closely knit relations between foreign and local policies: "Imperialism as a political or economic process is inseparable from the social relations and cultural discourses of race, gender, ethnicity, and class at home."[69] As the purview of American Studies becomes redefined through a postnationalist perspective,[70] there is a growing need to address the relation between U.S. imperial relations and the definitions of a national identity which often remains "inflexibly unchallenged" or instantly recuperated by "a renewed version of 'consensus' " (Kaplan, "Left Alone in America," 15). Such consensual narratives construct and support U.S. nationalism, defined by Sacvan Bercovitch not in terms of its territorial or ethnic components, but as the product of a political consensus.[71] One of the narrative myths of this American consensus is provided by the westward expansion of the nation in the nineteenth century, which came to equate the imperial frontier with the discourse of modernity; "from being a dividing line, 'frontier' became a synonym for progress."[72]

However, if the annexation of the northern half of Mexico between 1836 and 1852 severed in two what José Limón has termed "Greater Mexico," its social and civil traditions also changed forever the material culture of the northern Anglo-Saxon nation-state.[73] Many of these historic and economic changes highlight once again the transient nature and the versatility of national symbols and assumed national essences. Despite their circulation as commoditized stereotypes and mass-produced traditions and regardless of their constant metonymic representation through national maps—with their well-defined perimeters—national cultures and their transnational avatars persistently move, change, and alter each other, consigning competing sacrosanct traditional icons and myths of national purity to the trash pile of provincial kitsch. Some aspects of Southwestern American popular (agri)culture—whose vaquero and rodeo traditions holler a far cry from the customs of puritanical Boston Common—would provide good examples of the constant metamorphosis of national and regional emblems over time.[74] However dominant in American media, the recycled remnants of nineteenth century *ranchero* culture reveal the Latino roots of its Southwestern Empire and they can be reinscribed to reiterate the ethnic and political tensions unraveled by that expansion and its associated cultural and economic expropriations.[75] Instead, potent nineteenth-century myths of the westward advancing frontier of civilization and the depiction of the continent as an unsettled virgin land have constituted a major source of cultural production in the United States, a process operating through literal and symbolic expropriation not only of Native Americans but also of the ranch lands and commercial and cultural networks of the previous colonizing cultures of Spain and Mexico.[76]

Side by side, American and Mexican nationalisms are at loggerheads, and not just because both are often defined in counter distinction and in opposition to the other, but also because of the inbuilt historiographic and narrative themes of success and failure that dominate both national cultures. Mulling over the aftermath of the Santa Anna dictatorship and the loss of half of Mexico, John Ochoa observes how "successes threaded with failure run deep in the Mexican national imagination, in the collective memory."[77] The Mexican historical and cultural record is strewn with a collective sense of enlightening failures, and a popular national narrative becomes articulated around the continued sentiment of betrayal and shared disappointment. Coinciding with the establishment of the North American Free Trade Agreement, Carlos Fuentes captured well this perceived contrast between the two neighboring nations and their national discourses, between "us" Mexicans and "them" Gringos:

> Estados Unidos ha tenido éxito en todos los renglones en los que los mexicanos hemos fracasado. Ellos se adaptan a los medios necesarios para lograr la modernidad; nosotros somos incapaces de salir del hoyo arcaico. Ellos son democráticos; nosotros, autoritarios. Ellos son prósperos; nosotros, eternamente pobres. Ellos son eficaces; nosotros inútiles. Vivimos un fracaso nacional lado a lado con el máximo *success story* de la modernidad: el imperio norteamericano democrático, poderoso, rico y libre. ¿Cómo no vamos a ver en la potencia vecina el nuevo centro de identidad que nos proteja y que nos cicatrice, de una vez por todas, la herida nacional? No vemos muy de cerca los defectos de la sociedad norteamericana, las graves figuras morales, económicas y sociales de su actualidad. Porque, comparados con nuestra pulmonía, los problemas de E.U. nos parecen un catarrito cualquiera.[78]
>
> [The United States has been successful at everything that we Mexicans have failed at. Americans adapt to the means necessary to achieve modernity, while we are steadfastly loyal to our archaic cave. They are democratic; we are authoritarian. They are prosperous; we are eternally poor. They are efficient; we are useless. Mexico is a national

> failure living next to the biggest success story of the modern age: the American empire, democratic, prosperous, and free. Nationalism should be buried, this attitude proclaims. We should see in the United States our new center of identity, capable of healing, once and for all, our national wounds. The severe wounds in U.S. society are promptly dismissed, though they more and more resemble our own.][79]

Carlos Fuentes's open-ended questioning of the challenges posed to Mexicanness by the new transnational economic configuration dominated by a triumphant American globalism derives from sociological opinion polls carried out at the time in Mexico. This series of distinctions places Mexico's lived national failure next to the success story of U.S. modernity, and it appears to codify once more the seemingly tangible endurance of Mexico's national character and national history defined here in a dialectical, hemispheric pairing with its northern neighbor as disappointment and failure. *After the Nation* seeks to move beyond these recalcitrant binary mass-cultural recitations of U.S. national "mission accomplished," its Patriot(ic) Act(s), and their corresponding post/neocolonial disenchantments south of the border. Instead, the objective of this study is to emphasize the fictional, literary denunciation of the inventedness of such nationalized essentialisms and the revelation through parody and satire of the more complex fractures and contradictions of uneven development on both sides of the imaginary and real line that segregates the continent.

Temporal Ruptures, Spatial Disjunctures

This book is structured into three parts each dealing with alternate, subversive fictional renderings of the temporal sequence mobilized by national narratives: Future (part 1), Present (part 2), and Past (part 3). Part 1 looks at the ways in which modernity and its projection of a national shared futurity is forestalled in Fuentes's *La región más transparente,* Pynchon's *V.,* and other early writings. Concentrating on alternative representations of time, I show how these texts conjure up mythical, cyclical times, the times of apocalypse, the finitude or tiredness of modernity, to address and challenge the alleged destiny of the modern national community. Importantly, the two novels studied in this first section explore the underground and peripheral spaces of the city as the geographic location where the hegemonic discourses of national progress are hampered.

Part 2 shows the experience of the present as originating in a fratricidal act, or as deriving not from a consensual union but as a result of the inherent violence, and vice, of the formation of the nation-state. Thus, the assumption that the national community is located in a synchronous, contemporary space-time dimension, in other words, that its presence can be ascertained in a present tense and time, or on a uniform national map, is questioned through a multiplicity of references to the fractured and divided social body, the contrasting landscapes it occupies, and also to the made-up and enforced consensual narratives of shared aims and locales of national presence. The novels studied in part 2 are Fuentes's *La muerte de Artemio Cruz* and *Cambio de piel* and Pynchon's *The Crying of Lot 49.*

Part 3 discusses the undoing of foundational narratives and the questioning of originating historical times and spaces at the moment in which the nation-state(s) was heroically conceived or born. History in the two novels studied in that last section, Fuentes's *La campaña* and Pynchon's *Mason & Dixon,* is shown as a complex, unhinged set of texts whose coherence is only achieved through the posterior historiographic intervention of nationalist elites. Similarly, the spatial quests of these two novels offer an unequivocally critical survey of the unified cartographic and emancipatory projects of the Enlightenment by revealing the diverse terrains onto which national mappings sought to carve and produce modern space.

The five texts discussed in parts 1 and 2 were published in the space of ten years, between 1958 and 1968, and their appropriation and transformation are carried out through a steadfast reference to the readers' present. As that "present" moment vanishes, however, the text is no longer read from the same historical viewpoint by our contemporary readers: there is an inevitable loss of political currency in the fading away of the contextual conditions which motivated that literature in the first place. One of the goals of this study is to carry out a reactivation of the crudeness of the contact with which contemporary readers at the time of publication must have accessed these texts. By tracing the lineages of a broadly defined postmodern New Left during the long Cold War (1945–90) and beyond, and by placing these texts within the ideological horizons of that "movement of movements," I review the cultural history of the appearance of a critical transnational postnationalism in the Western Hemisphere.[80] In this book I seek to trace a correspondence between the epistemic questioning identified as the trademark of the postmodern period and postnational satire, which places the modern nation-state at its critical center. Famously, François Lyotard defined the postmodern condition as the collapse of the grand narratives of enlightened universalisms, modernist progress, and scientific certainties.[81] Postmodern cultural productions project a critical beam on the assurances of modernist edifices, eroding nationalist discourse and its essentialist claims of communitarian identification, harassing above all those grand narratives built into the modern(ist) state configuration and its associated regimentations of individuals, groups, and territories.[82] This tendency is what Ihab Hassan defined earlier as postmodernism's "will to unmaking."[83] In these postnationalist texts the fabric of the nation is literally unmade: it is revealed as a set of discourses and linguistic practices, promoted by cultural institutions whose hegemonic agendas seek to advance social consensus within the projected boundaries of the state. By disrupting the conventional temporalities of such rhetorical national communions and by exploring the spaces and crevices of resistance, these postnational satires carnivalize and contest some of the ideological shortcomings of nationalism: its homogeneity, its co-optation of the popular, its commoditized icons, to name just a few. While they point to the failures and violence of nationalist modernities, neither Pynchon nor Fuentes decidedly project alternate postnational utopias, but instead they seek to empower or at the very least entertain and irritate their readers through satirical denunciations, parodies, and humor, through the constant questioning of the nationalist's self-evident "truths."

Part One

✦

Narrative Undergrounds in the Postnational City

"Later I would think of America as one vast City of Night stretching gaudily from Times Square to Hollywood Boulevard—jukebox-winking, rock-n-roll-moaning: America at night fusing its darkcities into the unmistakeable shape of loneliness."[1] These opening words from John Rechy's first novel, *City of Night* (1963), announce a nocturnal geography of urban continuities where the whole of America is sensed as an amalgamated "City of Night." The immense city in darkness represents the protracted peripheral geography of the excluded; the murky zone inhabited by the marginal homosexual whose loneliness encompasses the whole nation. El Paso, Los Angeles, New York, Chicago, are all the "darkcities" evoked by Rechy, boroughs of the "City of Night," extensions of the underground spaces occupied by the "sexual outlaw"—the hustler, the drag queen, or simply the gay man—whose solitude is filled with an unending succession of bodies in an intoxicated landscape of sexual overload. For the Texan-born Rechy—the son of a Scotsman and a Mexican woman, and himself a leading proponent of gay liberties in the United States—the City of Night is the alternative time-space to the well-defined city of the square morals, of the married well-to-do WASP, of the suburb. This "darkcity" is also the City *at* Night, a symbol for the nonproductive social dropout, the new flâneur whose cityscape is the whole of America: the City of Night expands across the landscape constituting itself as the negative of the nation.

As the complex space where national and global discourses fuse, where political control and social experimentation are shaped under the banner of modernity, but where they can also be more effectively contested and defied, the city is the literary figure that brings together in this first section Carlos Fuentes's *La región más transparente* (*Where the Air Is Clear*) (1958)[2] and Thomas Pynchon's *V.* (1963).[3] As in Rechy's *City of Night,* the city is an emblem: a figure of modernity and its reverse, the composite location of the global modern, with its bourgeois cultural hegemonic trends, its enlightened rationalization of space and everyday life, its implied futuristic promises, but also of the many shapes of its entrenched negation. These two novels, published at the start of Pynchon's and Fuentes's careers as writers, reveal significant themes that would reemerge throughout the two authors' later literary productions, in Pynchon's *Bleeding Edge* (2013) or in Fuentes's *Todas las familias felices* (*Happy Families*) (2006): the critique of the synchronized discourses of nationalism and technological progress; the symbiotic relationship between the phallic cityscape as the iconic image of the homeland; the monumental nationalist historiography inscribed onto the urban space. These themes interrogate the hegemonic cultural practices promoted by modernity in its mobilization of urban spaces as sites for social and cultural control.

(Big) Apples and (Prickly) Pears

Satirical narratives, with their insistence on rupturing temporal and spatial continuities, take apart the teleology of nationalist discourse, which implicitly endorses progress as the logical time frame of the narrated nation.[4] Both *La región más transparente* and *V.* satirically represent the urban landscape as a space where the contradictory temporalities of modernity's uneven development meet. In these two texts the polis is governed not so much by a political homogeneous future empty time, but by the conflicts, collaborations, and contradictions between national mythical essences, with their circular sacred temporalities, and modernity's machinery of cultural and social homogenization. In their own individual ways, both novels accentuate and re-create through parody, exaggeration, fragmentation, saturation, and through different forms of temporal and spatial disruption, the points of fracture and suture between local and global codes. The global cities in these two novels represent a modern world whose uniformity and redemptive promises are farcically contested by alternative, ghostly, monstrous, magical, or mythical forces, such as the obscure underground network of Catholic rats infesting the New York sewers in *V.*, befitting the world of machine lovers and imperial maniacs who populate the urban surface. Cold War industrialization in Mexico under the presidencies of Miguel Alemán (1946–52) and Adolfo Ruiz Cortines (1952–58) and its associated aggressive and chaotic urban development are also satirically challenged by the alternative temporalities and the return of the repressed pasts in *La región más transparente*. The main protagonist and accidental narrator, Ixca Cienfuegos, is a satirical figure intent on disavowing both the nationalist intelligentsia's calls for compromise and the narratives of material progress.

Ixca Cienfuegos and Benny Profane, one of the main characters in each novel, unambiguously participate in the conventions of the picaresque, an indisputably urban genre. Ixca Cienfuegos is a picaroon whose life in the margins of society, and yet in its midst, is devoted to burning and devastating other people's lives. In turn, *V.*'s Benny Profane is a self-confessed schlemiel—spelled "schlemihl" in Pynchon's reworking—the clown figure of Jewish iconography translated into the American discourse of the urban loser, the bum.[5] Morris Dickstein comments specifically on the use of the schlemiel by two non-Jewish writers, Thomas Berger and Thomas Pynchon, to remark on the indestructibility of the "chronic loser" as he "inhabits the shadowy margin between the comedy of errors and a comedy of terrors."[6] My politically inflected reading of Benny Profane's figure as comedic adheres to Dickstein's suggestion that 1960s "black humor" is "pitched at the breaking point where moral anguish explodes into a mixture of comedy and terror, where things are so bad you might as well laugh" (Dickstein, 97). In Pynchon's first novel, *V.*, as well as in his early short stories, the apocalyptic backdrop ("Entropy," 1960) and even the post-apocalyptic prospect ("Low-lands," 1960) are accompanied by a comic, satirical presentation of the present leading into a blind alley. In it, the future progress with which national discourse plots its narratives is halted, foreclosed.

As marginal urban characters inhabiting alternative social spaces and times, the lives of these two very singular antiheroes are frustrated from the start: they can only offer a farcical and distanced view of a city, the city—Mexico, New York, Valetta—where they are condemned to "bide" as Cienfuegos puts it in his lyrical opening speech. This seemingly passive attachment to the territory, manifested also in Profane's celebrated "yo-yoing" across the Northeastern seaboard of the United States, and on the New York underground sewage system, emphasizes not just their individual helplessness, their lack of modern individual freedom, but also their marginal, ethical positions from the lives of their cities. In an article on the figure of the schlemiel, Feuer and Schmitz allude to Levinas's musings on photography and temporality that underlie some of his ethical paradigms, to explain the place of the schlemiel as occupying a "monstrous interval" which casts him as an "ethical character."[7] Feuer and Schmitz remark how "the endless repetitions of the schlemiel bring the reader into the meanwhile, the space where he lingers nakedly and, as Levinas says, impotently" (Feuer and Schmitz, 96). I propose to look at the temporal and spatial ruptures, the monstrous intervals and disjunctions underwritten by these two picaresque characters, Ixca Cienfuegos and Benny Profane, as signs of a satirical intervention by which the national time-space of futurity and progress, with its implied teleological narrative of destiny, is ethically disavowed.

Their oppositional belonging to the modern urban landscape is treated in very different ways by Fuentes and Pynchon: the fiery Aztec "spirit of the place" who haunts Mexico City in the case of Cienfuegos, or the schlemiel cowboy who hunts albino alligators in the New York sewers. Their central presence in the novels and their subversive or regressive actions critically underscore the fluid iconic relation between the metropolitan city and the nation. They are not just picaresque figures inassimilable by the process of urban modernization and yet condemned to witness it; they are also presented as national buffoons, walking caricatures of the national symbols that they set out to interrogate. They are ethical characters whose circular, repetitive life arrests the narrative progress implied by national teleologies.

By looking closely at the representation of the city, I seek to disclose a common pattern in these first two novels by which the critique of the nationalist discourses of progress promoted by the "national bourgeoisies" is achieved: a critical concentration on the mythical aspects underlying the organization of the national polis. By marking out the city as the icon where the projects of modernity coalesce and collapse, both texts assail central points of reference to Mexican and American nationalist discourses. The two novels are, however, distinctly characterized by their individual encodement of this critique and their differing emphases on certain aspects of the urban landscape. Fuentes is constantly drawn to the Aztec mythical narratives still inscribed in the city, and embodied in the figures of Ixca Cienfuegos and his mother Teódula Moctezuma. In turn, Pynchon delves into the distressing effects of the technological invasion of the human body and of society, an incursion epitomized by the pervasive presence of the mysterious and ever-changing V. figure. Despite this clear distinction in emphasis, both texts allude to ancient myths and to technology, and even to the myths of technology, as repressive cultural constructs while they question the emancipatory, utopian promises of industrial modernity.

Mexico City and New York City, or as Pynchon frequently puts it in *V.*, "Nueva York," stand for two very different versions of the modern; they are metropolitan centers where progress becomes a showcase, a space to try out the imaginings of a complex and uneven modernity, and where its machinery is also exposed in all its uncouthness. In the case of Mexico City, as Fuentes's novel suggests, the multiple layers of urban history work as constant reminders of the failed projects of modernity, or as John Ochoa has more precisely described it: of Mexico's "failed modernities."[8] The overwhelming presence of a large disenfranchised population is an unambiguous sign of modernity's uneven development: they are human vestiges resulting from such failed and asymmetrical projects. As a developing metropolis, Mexico City encapsulates a wide range of extreme realities whose contrast is abundantly exposed in Fuentes's novel: the cosmopolitan nationalist elite and the rural migrant population fighting for social and physical survival. The consensual nationalist discourse promoted by the national bourgeoisie aims to fasten these extremes and resolve their contradictions into a single and unified narrative space. The narrated nation originates from the centers of power and it operates by reifying the oppositional culture emanating from the derelict periphery. That contact zone is precisely the mythical middle ground, the scarred valley that Fuentes sets out to ignite and unsuture. The pyromaniac character at the center of the narration, Ixca Cienfuegos, is a farcical symbol of those human and mythical vestiges that are constantly, though unsuccessfully, incorporated into the allegedly inclusive discourse of Mexico's postrevolutionary nationalist modernity.

After World War II and coinciding with the final institutionalization of the Mexican revolution in 1946, the ruling Partido de la Revolución Mexicana, created in 1929 as the Partido Nacional Revolucionario (PNR) by President Calles, was symbolically rebaptized as the Partido Revolucionario Institucional (PRI). The new policies of import substitution industrialization and the subsequent social changes effected by the parallel growth of urban population began to suggest an unprecedented alteration of Mexican ways of life. These postwar developments had been preceded by two decades during which Mexico had combined the official creation of national symbols boosted by the Mexican Revolution (1910–17), its nationalization of lands and mineral resources, the expansion of educational programs and the emergence of a welfare state, with a controlled participation of investors from the United States and a number of European countries in Mexican industrial ventures, particularly those related to the newly nationalized oil production. The swift efforts to terminate the postcolonial feudal establishment and its enslaving practices across the country were accompanied by the formulation of a new role in the international sphere.[9] Throughout the 1920s and 1930s, revolutionary Mexico had experienced a period of slow pacification, attempts at economic stability based on a wide agrarian reform, and international recognition under the successive governments of Álvaro Obregón (1921–24), Plutarco Elías Calles (1924–28), the "sexenio del maximato," a period of six years with three consecutive governments characterized by the hegemony of Calles as de facto president "máximo," and Lázaro Cárdenas (1934–40). From these years Mexico's international profile would be shaped by a number of symbolic interventions to support certain "causes" in sister Spanish-speaking countries in the name of revolutionary ideals. Mexico would then face up to increasing American intervention in Nicaragua in 1927[10] and to Franco's advance in the Spanish Civil War in the late 1930s,[11] to mention only the two most notable examples. These policies announced both its future political influence among other Spanish-speaking countries, and its growing national self-assurance based on the values of its very idiosyncratic revolution.

The struggle against the educational and cultural power of the Catholic Church was carried out through a number of programs of general and free education led by the influential intellectual José de Vasconcelos as a minister for education in the first stable revolutionary governments.[12] Vasconcelos optimistically described the Mexican mestizo as an archetype of future mankind, the representative of what he termed the "Cosmic Race." In his model, the mestizo is the protagonist of Mexico's national narrative; his celebration of Mexican hybridity sought to overcome the obsession with ethnic purity of both *indigenistas* and occidentalists. Vasconcelos fostered a comprehensive agenda to end illiteracy, alongside an active participation of the state in the construction of national forms of culture that would find its most representative expression in the public mural paintings of Rivera, Orozco, and Siqueiros.

Apart from the more conspicuous work of the painters and architects, that of filmmakers musicians, writers, and poets also contributed to this "rediscovery" of Mexican identity, narrating those roots that had been apparently neglected by the increasingly Westernizing cultural establishment of Porfirio Díaz's liberal mestizo regime (1867–1910). As Joshua Lund has countered through his study of Ignacio Altamirano's novel *El Zarco,* the Porfiriato would set the foundations of what he calls the "Mestizo State" with its embrace of the discourse of *mestizaje* as the viable resolution to the postcolonial sociocultural contradictions of Mexico: "ultimately, the *mestizo* would come to symbolize the resolution of the central political problem of the time, the negotiation of sovereignty and hegemony, the formation of a state that could not only represent but also somehow reflect its nation."[13] After the Revolution of 1910, the close collaboration between the revolutionary state and artists was aimed at developing a strong national conscience through the visual medium where *mestizaje* manifested the emerging and hegemonic Mexican cultural nationalism.[14] In the late 1940s and the 1950s, however, the fracture between this official revolutionary nationalist discourse and governmental policies was further hastened with the displacement of the social democratic practices of Cardenismo and the swift political turn toward the cosmopolitan bourgeoisie by Alemán's government, the first postrevolutionary administration led not by military veterans but by lawyers and economists.

In the revolution's intensive pictorial identification with the historical indigenous struggle for liberation against Spaniards and criollos, and its resolution into a celebration of *mestizaje,* lies also its recognition of the deep-seated obstacles to carry out a wholesale social transformation beyond the realms of the aesthetic and the discursive. The temporary iconographic incorporation is belied by the final defeat of the more radical revolutionary options, the Zapatistas in the south and the Villistas in the north. The discourse of *mestizaje* was unquestionably predicated on the "de-indianization" of the indigenous population.[15] My reading of Fuentes's novel shows how modernity's other, the Aztec or "native" as past, despite its commoditized and aestheticized status during this period of nationalist cultural formation, permeates the textual fabric of the nation in the form of a ghostly remainder: the Aztec past becomes, in Fuentes's assessment of the postrevolutionary period, an obsessive and inassimilable remnant and a constant threatening reminder of the cultural contradictions promoted by modernity's uneven development.

In *V.,* New York is only one—if the most central—of the many besieged cities visited by the mysterious V. figure.[16] The contrast between the two male characters Benny Profane, the yo-yo bouncer schlemiel, attached to the city and bound to the larger-than-life "street," and the sardonically fragmented Herbert Stencil, defined by his attachment to the equally mercurial V., reflects on the different urban sites visited by both. The "sacred" intellectual search for whatever V. might be is juxtaposed to Benny's clearly profane underground hunts and to his schlemiel's search for an uneventful everydayness.

New York, the besieged city of the Cold War, the next step in V.'s history of ghostly visitations, seizes its future not in the inanimate glittering skyscrapers but in the pests that inhabit its inscrutable belly. Nevertheless, even this bleak prospect is humorously attributed to a fearful Catholic priest whose apocalyptic beliefs at the time of the Depression had prompted him to convert New York rats to Catholicism and imagine the rodents as the future inhabitants of the polis and perhaps the nation: "The city—maybe America, his horizons didn't extend that far—would belong to the rats before the year was out" (*V.*, 118). Uttered at the time of publication of the novel in 1963, coinciding with the Cuban Missile Crisis, such uncertainties were possibly closer to reality than ever before in the history of the city. The conscious play with the significant prospects of annihilation is an instance of black humor provoked by the terror of living under the persistent threat of destruction. A contrast between progress and its dangers, which according to Marshal Berman is at the heart of modernity:

> To be modern is to find ourselves in an environment that promises us adventure, power, joy, growth, transformation of ourselves and the world—and at the same time threatens to destroy everything we have, everything we know, everything we are.[17]

In his celebrated study on the literary representation of urban modernity, Berman alludes to Marx's adage that "all that is solid melts into the air" to illustrate modernity's constant erosion of concrete cultural and material signposts, and specifically New York in the 1950s, one of the sites visited by Pynchon in *V.* Berman's claim, stated from a plural first person which offers a constant definition of the subject—"everything we are"—of a nostalgic solidity, often hijacked by the discourse of modernity in the form of the national consensus. A discourse that can hardly be used to oppose or challenge effectively modernity's constant threats, as a vehicle of simplified nationalized versions of modernity.

"U.S.A. is the slice of a continent," reads the opening statement in Dos Passos's catalog of national definitions. This commanding "national overture" for his trilogy *U.S.A.*—often compared with Carlos Fuentes's opening address in *La región más transparente*[18]—offers a random classification of that which defines the U.S.A. The juxtapositions offered in Dos Passos's catalog openly question the relation between elite and popular definitions of what constitutes the nation, culminating with the American accent, the only common feature, and therefore the only truly consensual definition of an American national identity:

> U.S.A. is a group of holding companies, some aggregations of trade unions, a set of laws bound in calf, a radio network, a chain of moving picture theatres, a column of stockquotations rubbed out and

> written in by a Western Union boy on a blackboard, a public library full of old newspapers and dog-eared history books with protests scrawled on the margins in pencil. U.S.A. is the worlds' greatest river valley fringed with mountains and hills. U.S.A. is a set of bigmouthed officials with too many bank accounts. U.S.A. is a lot of men buried in their uniforms in Arlington Cemetery. U.S.A. is the letters at the end of an address when you are away from home. But mostly U.S.A. is the speech of the people.[19]

This breathtaking medley of geographical, cultural, and economic facets that fasten together the country contains key images that propose a fluid relation between economic and cultural establishments. On the one hand, the capitalist institutions and the state, the stock exchange, the banking system, the army, the postal services, the acknowledged driving forces of American "modernity," and on the other, the cultural institutions cited by Lewis Mumford, the press, the cinema, the library. Even the climactic celebration of the "speech of the people," though clearly laudatory in Dos Passos's piece, cannot but remind us of the customary "extirpation of rival dialects and languages" mentioned by Lewis Mumford in his description of the institutionalization of a national culture.[20] Nevertheless, marginal spaces of discrepancy to consensual discourses, "dog-eared history books with protests scrawled on the margins in pencil," are also given credit as part of the definition of the national culture. Dos Passos's influential multi-vocal literary exercise, its outstanding effort to produce a history of the margins, a penciled marginal history, was echoed through many common formal and thematic traits in the early works of Fuentes, Pynchon, and others during the long Cold War. If the narratives of national histories have as their central subject the teleological discourse of modernity, these literary narratives aim to confront the authority of that hegemonic process. However, this literary marginality paradoxically inscribes itself within the national literary canon without short-circuiting it and without losing its critical claims. These two novels posit modernity as either the repetition of failure, and therefore not "a new beginning" but its parodic negative, pure obsolescence, in Fuentes's version; or as the violent imposition of hegemonic discourses and institutions, under the aegis of the proliferation of the obscure V. figure, leading toward an apocalyptic erasure of the human through the assault on the animate by the inanimate. Thus, both texts reinstate obscured past events, or simply *the past,* in order to break the continuities imposed by the hegemonic reading of a lineal history and its attendant triumphant moral teleology, prompting the reader to rethink the ideological inscriptions of the historical record.

The fluid relation of peripheral cultural margins and modern hegemonic discourses is at the basis of modernity itself, as Raymond Williams and others have shown. The malleable composite of narratives and cultural practices that loosely configures modernity demonstrate Williams's observation that "a lived hegemony is always a process,"[21] rather than the singular totalization used to conceptualize it. Williams's reading of the Gramscian concept of hegemony underscores its complex and active features, while it promotes the use of the adjectival form "hegemonic," rather than "hegemony," as the latter tends to become a more "totalizing abstraction" (Williams, *Marxism and Literature,* 112), which can in turn falsely reduce the very real and more amorphous processes of domination and subordination. Therefore, instead of alluding to "hegemony," I will tag along with Williams's proposal and refer to the existence of both hegemonic practices, continuously reassessed and in constant transformation, and counter-hegemonic discourses. These counter-hegemonic interventions are by definition engaged with hegemonic discourses, and they can even become part of a new hegemonic consensus, for instance through their unobstructed academic canonization, confirming Williams's suggestion that "all or nearly all initiatives and contributions, even when they are manifestly alternative or oppositional forms, are in practice tied to the hegemonic" (Williams, 114). Like the marginal scribbles in the history book at the public library alluded to by Dos Passos, counter-hegemonic satirical narratives share the same page, they share shelves with the canonical, foundational epic narratives of nationalism. In the narrative breakup of the historical teleology in literary representation, the "chief 'faults' " of their satirical plots can be found. This disjunctiveness of their plots, as Alvin Kernan pointed out, is directly related to their satirical mode.[22]

However, despite this intrinsic tie of the oppositional forms to the hegemonic, manifested in the case of Pynchon and Fuentes in their obvious assimilation into the cultural machinery of academic explication and canonization, I put the accent on the strategies deployed by these narratives to perform a counter-hegemonic stance. As alternative narratives of the story of progress and national consensus, they are not immediately neutralized as oppositional forms through their inclusion into a system that institutes and endorses nationalist disciplines and schools—American Studies being the most apparent one[23]—but rather they enter into a critical exchange with that very set of linear hegemonic discourses and nationalist cultural practices. Their stance does not revert to Berman's laconic "everything we are"—or were—nor to Marx's nostalgic solidness melted into the air of modernity; rather, it questions modernity and its imagined pasts, the nation and its utopian projections. National myths do not constitute themselves as those oppositional sites to modernity, but rather as the central icons of the hegemonic culture imposed by the national bourgeoisies in their efforts to build a national consensus. In Pynchon's "geography of the fall away from what is human,"[24] and in Fuentes's "alternative times,"[25] we do not find a celebration of co-opted national myths, nor a longing for the national epic dreams of consensual unity, but rather their reverse images. The radical presence of difference, heterogeneity, and dissent are an attempt to jam the nationalized discourses of rationalization and social control, that is, global modernity in its local iteration.

If modernity is a "narrative category" or a trope, as Fredric Jameson has persuasively argued in his *A Singular Modernity,* proposing that "the trope of 'modernity' is always in one way or another a rewriting, a powerful displacement of previous narrative paradigms,"[26] then the literary projects contained in these two novels satirically revisit that process of displacement by which modernity rewrites previous narrative paradigms. It is not a discourse that nostalgically returns to those "previous narrative paradigms," but a rewriting of modernity—in other words a postmodernity—that can laugh at itself and at its impossible pasts, its failed utopian futurities, if just on the margins of the page. In doing so, these early texts would ratify the validity of the novel as a medium that satisfactorily questions both imperial epics and national histories. Confirming Brian May's proposition that although the novel would appear to be "by its very nature and *telos,* antithetical to the postcolonial, . . . [yet] the same instrument that served those who would establish (wittingly or not) imperial histories of conquest and governance has begun to serve those who would challenge, complement, and even rewrite imperial histories of conquest and governance."[27] These are thus if not "late imperial romances," to use John McClure's denomination, at least "late imperial satires," which sardonically revisit the "sites of stubborn resistance to rationalization."[28]

Homi Bhabha has suggested that cultural difference, and cultural margins in particular, offer a radical challenge to both modernity and the national.[29] Nowhere is this radical difference more clearly expressed than in the urban setting, the cityscape, where "the emigrants, the minorities, the diasporic come to change the history of the nation . . . it is the city which provides the space in which emergent identifications and new social movements of the people are played out. It is there that, in our time, the perplexity of the living is most acutely experienced" (320). This "perplexity of the living" and the undying echoes of a marginalized, eroded past and of alternate critical futures constitute some of the fictional sites visited by Fuentes's demonic narrator as he harasses his fellow citizens throughout *La región más transparente.*

Chapter 1

Modernity Versus Its National Demons: *La región más transparente*

If the "speech of the people" is the common national ground that constitutes Dos Passos's account of the American nation, for Ixca Cienfuegos, Fuentes's menacing narrator at the opening of *La región más transparente,* the nation is identified not with a people but with a mythical geographical site, a space where the ancient origin of the nation is purportedly located. In Cienfuegos's recurrent hunt for the foundational site of the nation in the Valley of Mexico, the ancient lake district of Anáhuac becomes charged with Lewis Mumford's "mystic sense."[1] The mystique of origins in which Ixca's description is embedded can be more accurately described following the contemporaneous anthropological categorization established by Mircea Eliade in his description of the "sacred space," by definition situated at the center of the world: "'Our world' is always situated at the center."[2] According to Eliade, for "religious man," sacred space is not only an interruption of the "homogeneity and relativity of profane space" (22), it also provides a revelation—or hierophany—of "an absolute reality, opposed to the nonreality of the vast surrounding expanse" (21). There are two main features in Eliade's definition: sacred space is a revelation, and a revelation of a differentiated, absolute location. This absolute element is a center that "*founds the world* in the sense that it fixes the limits and establishes the order of the world" (30). It creates the cosmos, or to use Eliade's terminology, it "cosmicizes" a territory (29–31). According to Aztec mythology, Huitzilopochtli, the guiding god of the Mexicas, gave them a sign, a hierophany: they would settle and found their temple—and therefore their city—at the site where they discovered an eagle and a serpent on a nopal tree. In the year 1329 AD the Mexicas, under the guidance of their god Huitzilopochtli, mythically founded Tenochtitlan—literally "the place of the nopal on the stone."[3] The mythical eagle and the serpent on the nopal tree would become later on the national symbols of an independent Mexico, an icon vigorously replicated in revolutionary iconography.[4] The narrative consecration of the Valley of Mexico—and its associated appropriation by the northern newcomers, the Mexicas—follows the exact pattern described by Eliade, for it is the "something that does not belong to this world [and which] has manifested itself apodictically" (28). Even more to the point, it is an animal revelation, which reminds men "they are not free to choose the sacred site that they only seek for it and find it by the help of mysterious signs" (29). Despite the fact that Eliade's analysis does not refer at any point in his *The Sacred and the Profane* to Aztec religious traditions, it can be aptly applied to them: this structuralist system evocatively reconstructs a pattern that seems to be accurately inscribed in most mythological accounts of the foundation of a cosmicized territory, of a religiously ordered space.

In Fuentes's novel, the constant incursion of Tenochtitlan, the foundational "navel" of the nation, the birthplace of the Mexican nation itself, into the homogeneous and undifferentiated place of profane everydayness caustically evokes Eliade's hierophany. This satirical encounter with the national myths is shaped around a multi-vocal, dialogic interpretation of their conflicting relation with the construction of the postcolonial nation. The elusive mythical space of origins is a sign of both historical continuity and of opposition to historical progress, it is a "stone that doesn't change, it is the same forever" (Fuentes, *RT,* 150/102). Ixca's frequent definitions of Mexico's identity in *La región más transparente* present a petrified image of the nation, one that voids the idea of nation as a social referent and commoditizes its founding myths, thus satirically encapsulating the contradictory genetic makeup of Mexican nationalist discourses. In this chapter, I look at the parodic relation between the choral definitions of Mexican identity offered throughout the novel and the earlier responses articulated by intellectuals such as Octavio Paz, Samuel Ramos, and Alfonso Reyes. Though their reified, pseudo-anthropological views of Mexicanness were elaborated through doubtful methodological practices, producing essentializing and overarching theoretical musings, defined by Claudio Lomnitz as "armchair anthropology,"[5] their monumental oeuvres epitomize the textual hypotexts against which the parody of the novel is built. Through this continued parody, through a "double-voiced" presentation of the previous nationalist material, the novel becomes a postnational satire of the dialectical relation between the national bourgeoisie in power and their grafting of the cultural nationalism painfully investigated and carefully elaborated by Mexican intellectuals throughout the four decades that followed the Mexican Revolution of 1910.

Though problematic in their ambitious scope and their sweeping ahistorical generalizations of religious experience across the globe,[6] Eliade's comparativist anthropology and his binary oppositions of sacred and profane spaces and times were also an investigation into the mythical origins of national experience. For Eliade, all religious manifestations are attributed to the perceptions of an abstract "religious man" and are opposed to the daily practices of "profane man." Eliade's conceptions made their way into Paz's *The Labyrinth of Solitude* (1950). In Paz's essay, Eliade's navel of the universe is also the "sacred center from which we were ejected," and the existence of modern or profane man, the lonely Mexican, much as Ixca Cienfuegos, is marked by this "nostalgia of the [sacred] space."[7] Cienfuegos believes that "there, in our origin, Mexico still exists, is what it is, is never what it can be, but what it is" (*RT*, 150/102). Cienfuegos's characterization follows closely Paz's description of modern man, "condemned to search for [that center] in forests and deserts or in the twisting alleys and in the subterranean passages of the labyrinth" (Paz, 254). However, once uttered by the picaresque figure of the limping devil—the Diablo Cojuelo—a classical picaresque figure on which Fuentes acknowledges to have articulated his satire, the dogmatic prescription of Mexican identity "Mexico is what it is" becomes suspicious.[8]

Underneath the Street

Ixca's voice establishes a satirical "contact zone" between the nationalist founding myths and their irrecoverable positioning in relation to contemporary culture, inhabiting a "subterranean city, the city of subterranean labyrinths where the ancient gods reside."[9] This nostalgic search through the subterranean passages of the labyrinth of modernity to unearth the sacred center of the world also summarizes the nationalist longing for a golden past. It is a farcical re-creation of the melancholic loop on which the nationalist myth of the subverted Eden—the untarnished agricultural garden of origins—rests, and which according to Roger Bartra is at heart anti-utopian: its function is to "define the 'authentic' national essence in opposition to any utopia that may attempt to revolutionize (or contaminate) it."[10] Bartra's definition of the anti-utopian melancholia of what he calls "primordial mourning" appears to echo Fuentes's fictional opposition between the recurrence of the mythical origins and the historical time of modernity.[11]

In one of Fuentes's earliest published short stories, "Chac Mool," in his collection *Los días enmascarados* (1954), the subversive, carnivalesque use of Aztec mythologies is directly related to an overhaul of the nationalist dream of an Edenic origin.[12] In "Chac Mool," the disruption of the Aztec past through the arrival of Europeans and the Christian conquest of Mexico is jokingly summarized as "a checkmate to Huitzilopochtli" (13). For Pepe, the sarcastic narrator of the story, the Mexican past can only be read as a continued occurrence of religious violence, consensual only in its constant dissent. Filiberto, his Catholic nationalist friend, interested in antiquarian history, records in his diary Pepe's opinions about the historical continuities between the native Aztec religion and Christianity, suggesting that "in its warm, bloody version, its sacrifice and liturgy, [Christianity] is a natural and innovative extension of the indigenous religion." Pepe, the story's narrator, whose perceptive vision of Mexico's violent history is confirmed by the Chac Mool visitation, is reading Filiberto's diary. His chronicle of how the Chac Mool, a Mayan votive sculpture that Filiberto has recently purchased, becomes alive and slowly occupies his house and his life, culminates in Filiberto's confession: "I am his prisoner." This image of the lonely bureaucrat becoming a prisoner and finally a victim of an ancient messenger deity made flesh purveys a parodic image of the domesticated national myths through their violent incursion into everyday life.

Paz had seen in this return to the mythical national center a desire to stop history in its tracks, bringing about "the kingdom of the perpetual communion, and of a fixed present" (258). Correspondingly, Ixca's answer to Rodrigo Pola's recurrent question "What is this country, where is it going?" is that "What Mexico is, is fixed forever, incapable of evolution" (*RT,* 150/102). Ixca's visions of the origins of the city, the manifestation of a sacred space, assail the unstoppable train of progress while they attempt to regress history to myth. Progress and the chronological, lineal perception of time are thoroughly inscribed into Western historical thinking. As Collingwood noted, "progress is not a mere fact discovered by historical thinking: it is only through historical thinking that it comes about at all."[13] *La región más transparente* sets in motion well-established dialectical oppositions between progress and regress, history and myth, profane and sacred. The arresting dichotomy, either progress with its profane chronological time, or regress into a mythical sacred time, characterizes what Paz called the "dialectics of solitude." The sacredness of the original site where the eagle and the serpent were spotted in fulfillment of Huitzilopochtli's announcement presents throughout the novel a spatial point that could break the lineal time of progress, bringing about a monstrous timeless loop.[14]

There is also an associated apocalyptic terror promoted by Cienfuegos, and which relates to the novel's contrast between the two competing notions of time, the mythical and the historical. "Every culture close to its origins lives in terror: having known a recent catastrophe in the past, it fears that the apocalypse is near," suggests Fuentes in his *Tiempo mexicano.*[15] In that essay, Fuentes also referred to Collingwood's ideas of progress and historiography to discuss the complementary contrast between Western ideas of time and history, permanence and change, imported with the Spanish conquest and the Aztec mythical fears of apocalypse. In *La región más transparente,* in the face of the constant vanishing of the sacred site, of its replacement by profane space, Ixca offers a protracted search that turns both the lost roots and the hunt itself into an exercise in spectral monstrosity. Lurking over the everyday profane lives of Mexico City dwellers, whose existence is marked by a profane solitude, the echoes of the lost sacred space voiced by Cienfuegos are not, however, a call for a religious or mystic experience, but a double-voiced reminder of the destructive results of the modern obsession with authenticity, purity, the myths of origin and its supplement: the myth of endless future progression on which national narratives also rest.

Maarten Van Delden bases his entire reading of the novel on this conflict whereby the reader is left suspended "between a world ruled by profound mythological rhythms, and an alternative, modern world of drift and contingency."[16] Still, the significance of these two disparate realities, the mythical and the modern, is not due to the fact that Fuentes "never fully decides which of these two pictures is finally truer to the reality of Mexico" (19), as Van Delden suggests. In his evocation of *the* reality of Mexico and his apparent yearning for its "truer picture," Van Delden misses Fuentes's ironic tone and his complex satirical dialogism. These two alternative realms, the mythical, demonic background of the cityscape and the contemporary world with its economic and social relations, are contrasted in order to critically investigate their mutual interdependency. *La región más transparente* repetitively contends that life in Mexico City is inescapably governed by the irrational forces of the mythical past: a direct charge against the national bourgeoisie in their adoption of the pre-Columbian iconography through the cultural discourses propounded by the renewed postrevolutionary rhetoric of Mexican nationalism, while failing to enfranchise the victims of Mexico's traumatic colonial history.

In the novel, the central space of the nation—the "navel of the moon" of ancient Aztec mythology—is not described as a place of consensual reunion, but rather as a geopolitical determination where "we fall" (*RT,* 20/4). At least three immediate narrative associations with this predetermined space of the nation, the nation's mythical site, are brought to the fore in Ixca's opening speech. Firstly, the geographical determinism itself: the site of origins is thus the place "donde nos tocó" ("where we bide"), a Heideggerian "Dasein,"—in its literal sense of being here—mere existential contingency. Secondly, the site "la región más transparente del aire"—poorly rendered in English as "where the air is clear," a version which subtracts the superlative quality of the original—has lost any creative and life-giving powers, and it is now a "meseta de joyas fúnebres" ("tableland of jeweled death") (*RT,* 20/4). The wasteland of origins is more akin to a funerary urn than to the exceptionally clear region of the air, a phrase that acquires a radical sense of contextual irony at once. The vanishing of the region's exceptionality is only the most apparent sign of the parodic erasure of its original mythical meaning in the desecrated nationalist pantheon. Finally, this vacated spatial condition—the lost but spectral location of national origins—is narratively concurrent with the *genius loci,* the spirit of Anáhuac—"land by the water" in Nahuatl[17]—who becomes the mute interlocutor of Ixca's address.

Cienfuegos's opening address contains a detailed gradation of reference, a progress through four different personal pronouns,[18] starting with Ixca's first-person singular "My name is Ixca Cienfuegos" (*RT,* 19/3), a third-person singular that points to the spirit "who does not crush grapes but hearts" (*RT,* 19/3), addressed then directly in the second person "you burned your ships that other men could use your decay to build an age" (*RT,* 20/4). As the gradation reaches the first-person plural "Here we live you and I" (*RT,* 20/4), a crescendo movement from the individual speaker to the communal voice has been reached, culminating with the twice-asked question "What are we going to do about it?" (*RT,* 20/4), an echo of the political mobilizing moment, which in itself could be a possible site for the origins of the polis. What appears as a question in the English translation is differently phrased in the Spanish original as a statement of impotence, "qué le vamos a hacer" ("what can we do") (*RT,* 20/4, 21/5), a tone that agrees well with the physical determinism: "aquí nos tocó" ("we were allotted here") (*RT,* 21/5).[19] Despite this sense of being unwillingly thrown into the city, it does not provoke the initiation of political action; instead it underlies and promotes the satirical distance of the passage. Thus, the struggle between this awareness of the geographical conditioning which has initially raised Ixca's pondering mood, and his farcical celebration of that very spatial determinism "fall with me on our moon-scar city" (*RT,* 20/4) is situated in the realm of the rhetorical. At the end of the passage, and perhaps most importantly at the end of the novel, the unanswered rhetorical question, with its use of the first-person plural, completes the slow ironic identification of Ixca with the spirit of Anáhuac. The syntactic juxtaposition of the two nouns in the expression "spirit of Anáhuac" transfers the semantic features of one onto the other, and thus the inescapable and desecrated place of origins becomes a specter, the haunting figure to which Ixca addresses his opening speech. This very process of semantic transference is subsequently extended to Ixca as he gains Anahuac's spectral figuring throughout the novel.

The mythical transparency of the air alluded to in the title and at the end of this opening passage ironically contrasts with the smoke rising from the hundred fires provoked by Cienfuegos. The spirit of Anáhuac's demonic presence in the city is paralleled by Ixca's impish relation with the other characters of the novel. As he increasingly becomes the violent "spirit of Anahuac" who obscurely "hunts himself in a black liquation of tortured stones and jade colored eyes" (*RT,* 19/4), the answer to the preempting political interpellation "qué le vamos a hacer" becomes ever more elusive, and its deferral a sign of the imp's reflexive hunt. Furthermore, Ixca's provisional response "cling to me, brother. If only to see if our fingers touch" (*RT,* 20/4) becomes a sinister laughing gesture in view of the demonic destructive figure who utters it: Ixca's "touching" becomes a symbol of destruction throughout the novel. The extended prose poem, Menton's "national overture," is hence not only a statement of submissive national feelings yielded to the spatial predeterminations, but one that in its narcissistic political passivity becomes actively nihilistic.

Ixca's identification with the spirit of Anáhuac and his quasi-ritual acts of violence against himself and others embody the vengeful violent presence lurking over the inhabitants of Anáhuac/Mexico City that permeates the whole novel. The fires suggested by Ixca Cienfuegos's name—"burning one-hundred fires" in Nahuatl and Spanish—refer literally to the many burning fires and acts of violence across the city, which constantly remind us of the rough and ready status of urban life in Mexico City. Friends and acquaintances suffer his contact: he forces his way into Rodrigo Pola's car and tries to crash it with Pola inside by violently putting his foot on the accelerator; the intellectual Manuel Zamacona is gratuitously killed; the businessman Federico Robles is ruined; Ixca's lover, Norma Larragoiti, is burnt in a house fire; the list is lengthy.

As Fuentes himself asserted in his interview with Claude Dumas in 1972, this satirical panorama of Mexican society is directly related to his reading of Balzac's *Histoire des treize.*[20] In particular, the figure of Ixca is related to the demonic presence of the band of thirteen friends, who rule over Parisian society:

> having a foot in every salon, their hands in every coffer, elbowing their way through every street, a head on every pillow, unscrupulous in their furtherance of every whim. They had no leader for no one of them could claim supremacy; quite simply, priority was given to the liveliest passion or the most urgent need. They were thirteen kings—anonymous, but really kings; more than kings: judges and executioners too, they had equipped themselves with wings in order to soar over society in its heights and depths, and disdained to occupy any place in it because they had unlimited power over it.[21]

Although Ixca is a lonely "anonymous king" in his meandering journey through Mexican city life, an obvious contrast with Balzac's cryptic band of thirteen, his winged presence, "soar[ing] over society," also appears to overrule any other political or social norm outside his own through his "unlimited powers." Like Balzac's *Thirteen,* Fuentes's satirical homodiegetic narrator is "a judge and executioner" who has access to all quarters of society and is able to burn them all in their complacent everydayness.

As a satirical hero, he parodically replicates through his double-voiced performance the romantic hero described by Deleuze and Guattari, "a hero of the earth; he is mythic, rather than being a hero of the people and historical."[22] If Ixca is the earthly mythic hero of the nation, his demonic destructive configuration opposes him to the absence of a community; he increasingly becomes the isolated, mourned idol of national constructions. Fuentes invites his readers to dismantle the encounter between the myths of origins and the construction of the modern city. Mexico's emptied territory resembles those Romantic constructions described in *A Thousand Plateaus* where "the territory is haunted by a solitary voice; the voice of the earth resonates with it and provides it percussion rather than answering it" (Deleuze and Guattari, 340). "Haunting" is definitely a suitable adjective for Ixca's voice, and his ghostly appearance as the spirit of the place is a demonstration of the Deleuzian statement that "what romanticism lacks most is a people," and worse, that "even when there is a people, it is mediatized by the earth, it rises up from the bowels of the earth and is apt to return there: more a subterranean than a terrestrial people" (340). In *La región más transparente* this social undercurrent is evoked through the images of the buried Aztec city, hidden under the layers of the modern city. The buried city is also occasionally noticed by the bourgeois protagonists in their encounters with Deleuze's "subterranean people." These subterranean images reflect on the continued cultural oppression exercised over Mexico's indigenous cultures, cast by Samuel Ramos as "a chorus who silently witnesses the drama of Mexican life" (*Profile of Man and Culture in Mexico,* 63). Ramos did not advocate for a nostalgic return to the mythical origins, but rather for a respectful contemplation of "the unknown subterranean world" as the site in "whose depths history begins and later unfolds in the full light of day" (ibid., 114). The ghostly return of the impoverished indigenous faces at the gates of Federico Robles's house, waiting for his weekly act of charity, is perceived by Manuel Zamacona as "identical in all epochs, all ages. Like a subterranean river, indifferent and dark, flowing far below idea or change" (*RT,* 310/215). The submerged indigenous otherness imagined by Zamacona is an unreal, monstrous apparition, much like Cienfuegos. This ahistorical, cyclical, out-of-time depiction of indigeneity is reminiscent of more contemporary versions of "deep Mexico" such as Bonfil-Batalla's,[23] which according to Claudio Lomnitz "nostalgically reconstructs the deep Mexico, which is a kind of transcendental Indian character that survives, practically unblemished, beneath the asphalt."[24] In Zamacona's rendering the subterranean river of deep Mexico is incorporated into modernity only as a perpetual subaltern, a relational other against which the criollo Mexican national bourgeoisie can define itself as "central," as the subject of national history. At the gates of Federico Robles, the "revolutionary" plutocrat, who advocates for Alemanismo and its developmental practices—the "trickle down" economics of global capitalism's uneven development—justice and redistribution are recast and transformed into a form of conservative, reactionary charity, and as an act of appeasement. In the meantime, his own indigenous origin is "carefully disguised by cashmere and cologne" (*RT,* 131/88) and thus literally deeply buried once again.

The Glittering Nation to Come

Fuentes's satirical illustration of Mexican social and racial contradictions is shaped in a kaleidoscopic series of episodes that alternatively focus on the chaotic urban life of "cocktail-party intellectuals" (*RT,* 306/212), but also cab drivers, filmmakers, prostitutes high and low, revolutionaries rich and poor, poets and writers, and the constant presence of the tireless Ixca Cienfuegos who touches all their lives, visiting and destroying them as a deadly godlike figure. From the nihilistic forces inherent in the obsession with origins and represented by Cienfuegos's radical nationalism, to the modernizer Federico Robles whose ephemeral career as an industrialist is a sign of the very nature of capitalism's evanescent modernity, all the symbolic male characters of the novel stand for completely disparate versions of Mexico that fashionably oppose each other around a coffee table. As they argue and debate over Mexico "what is the meaning of it, the nameless tumult, the twisted mass of blood and rancor which we call Mexico?" (*RT,* 430/298), they also wrestle over their masculine status as the "chingones": the fuckers who have to be in control to impose their prescriptions of national identity.

The novel parodically echoes the remarkable male public interest in defining Mexican national identity throughout the first half of the twentieth century, proposing a wryly distanced look at the different positions held by Mexican intellectuals in the debates over Mexican exceptionality. The intellectual obsession with the mythical origins of the present and the apparently inexhaustible search for a narrative of Mexican particularity constitute the hypotexts of the novel's parodic reconstruction. The reader sieves through different ideological propositions put forward by characters who symbolize distinct stances vis-à-vis the nation's contradictory relation with modernity, only to discover that they are all parodically assailed. The novel of ideas, the postnational satire, is set in motion through the constant interplay of a consistently stereotyped cast of characters who stage in their daily lives the impossible avenues proposed by their failed national projects. In turn, their repeated failures, together with the parodied discourses of future accomplishment, institute the satirical authorial view that Mexico's national condition precisely revolves around the painful lack of a consensual and truly inclusive discourse to consolidate its communal life.

As Jean Franco has suggested, maleness was often the central unspoken debate at stake in contemporary Latin American discussions on the nation: "The problem of national identity was thus presented primarily as a problem of male identity, and it was male authors who debated its defects and psychoanalyzed the nation."[25] Jean Franco sees in the relegation of the female body to an outside position and in this preference for the exploration of maleness, even in its satirical modes, one of the failures of the Latin American literary "boom," to which Fuentes was one of the main contributors.[26] As Franco remarks, "in national allegories women became the territory over which the quest for (male) national identity passed, often at best, as in Juan Rulfo's *Pedro Páramo* (1955), the space of loss and of all that lies outside the male games of rivalry and revenge" (*Plotting Women: Gender and Representation in Mexico,* 131).

The marginal place of women in relation to the heady debates over national identity in *La región más transparente* appears to follow Franco's description. And yet, it is through the dialectics of this subsidiary role of women in the novel, of their ostracized placement in society, that we are also able to perceive male obsessions and male hyperbolic prominence as saturated and satirical. Around Ixca everything burns or is broken to pieces in a crescendo of destruction and death that culminates at the end of the novel with his menacing offer to touch yet another victim—Gladys García's fingers. As she looks down on the Nonoalco Bridge, perhaps in a suicidal mood, the city reveals its polluted morning air. After lighting her cigarette, Gladys "breathed in the city's dawn, the steam of locomotives, somnolence of flesh, wisps of gasoline and alcohol and the voice of Ixca Cienfuegos" (*RT,* 539/375–76). Cienfuegos's voice and the relentless devastation that accompanies it have become by this stage of the novel completely identified with Mexico City's flammable, apocalyptic atmosphere. Gladys, introduced at the beginning of the novel, immediately after Ixca's celebrated lyrical opening speech, as a working-class creature of the night, "moored to smoke and concrete" (*RT,* 26/7), is one of the novel's long list of have-nots. As a prostitute, she inhabits the marginal city of night—"most of day was unknown to her" (*RT,* 24/5)—and with it, the trivial spaces of waste in the industrial city, a landscape often visited by Pynchon's early characters as well. Her morning promenade early in the novel across Bucareli Avenue reveals a world at the margins of a society officially controlled and defined by the Kodachrome postcard pictures of Mexican identity: "The avenue was a cornucopia of refuse: wadded derelict dailies, garbage from Chinese cafés, dead dogs, an old crone poking a boot with a stick, sleeping street children stirring in their nests of magazines and newspapers. Dawn had the palest funeral glow" (*RT,* 23/5). The dim light of the new day does not reveal for Gladys a promising start in the modern city—"progress has to have a [big] buildup" (*RT,* 63/36) argues the businessman Federico Robles—or the images of Mexico run by big North American magazines with "scenic highways, hotels, the fronts of hospitals which may or may not have one bed inside" (*RT,* 63/36), but a despairingly bleak "suffocating city." A "creeping blot" (*RT,* 25/7), full of industrial human detritus. Thus the marginal positionality of the female body is an important sign of the masculine nation's inability to build the foundational romance; the convoluted dreams of masculinity to (re)produce the nation have the opposite effect: a burnt landscape of constant destruction and dereliction.

The presence in this decomposed social cityscape of street children and old men is reminiscent of Buñuel's Mexican film *Los olvidados* (1950). At the end of that film, a dead urchin is further marginalized in death with the symbolic treatment of his corpse as junk thrown away into the landfill. Not surprisingly, the main theme in Alma Guillermoprieto's sketch "Mexico City, 1990" was none other than the dysfunctional metropolitan garbage system and the many fantastic urban stories around the issues of trash disposal, purportedly read as symptomatic of an "obsession" for the inhabitants of the city.[27] Symbolically, a group of four revolutionaries, escaped from Belén, the infamous prison used by the Huertista counter-revolutionaries from 1913, are metonymically identified in Fuentes's novel with waste as they hide in a rubbish train: "Four men, four mouths pressed to cracks between boards on the cart-bed, tombed under refuse, their lungs congesting with rotted vegetables and excrement, all their terror concentrated in the act of breathing" (*RT,* 86/53). The juxtaposition of the failed revolutionaries and the prison's excrements not only identifies them with that specific form of waste, but also underwrites the future marginality of their political projects. The 1913 human refuse of the Maderistas, oppressed by the reaction of the U.S.-backed Huertista recoil, finds its contemporary parallel for the 1950s reader in the daily parade of bodies witnessed by Gladys García in her morning walk four decades later. In the novel, Mexico's uneven development is only presented as an unavoidable upshot of the modernizing project of the institutionalized revolutionary governments by its supporters, such as the parvenu plutocrat Robles. Yet there is no clear alternative political agenda proposed in the text, an absence that reinforces Ixca's recurrent cynical question "qué le vamos a hacer" ("And what are we going to do about it?"). Though the sympathetic gaze of the omniscient narrator stops at precise moments in which the underdog can mumble a word or two before being ditched into the dump, it is only a desperate voicing and a pathetic sighting:

> During that journey from Belén to the dump, Gervasio Pola thought that the dead must feel as he felt, wanting to shriek that in reality they were living, had not died, but were only suffocated by mute pestilence and a transient rigor, the coffin should not be nailed around them, earth should not be clodding down upon it. (*RT,* 86/53)

The spectral voices of the "chingados" of Mexican history are the alternative choral sound in the background that belies the cosmopolitan lifestyle of the coteries of intellectuals, artists, and other wealthy Mexican urbanites devoted to partying away the scant benefits of Mexico's renewed economic ties with the United States after World War II. Mexico City is the composite location of the modern, or to use García Canclini's term to describe it, it is a "hybrid city," with several different urban layers.[28] If Mexico City contains the sacred space where violent Aztec myths ooze into the organization of contemporary profane society, it also parades the historical bloody ghosts of internal chaos and foreign intervention that reverberate as a competing mythology. The image of the city is no longer the well-organized, rational location of the community, built for human habitation and bourgeois business, the place where national future is projected and broadcast as a given, but rather the space where layers upon layers of history and myth, garbage and ruins, run riot.

At stake in the novel is the connivance of the nationalist cultural establishment to portray a Mexican progressive quaintness at the service of northern investors, as in the films of Pola's son. A postcard cultural nationalism whose many icons, from the high culture studies of Mexican character, to the pop culture images of tropical mass tourism, are in effect the foundational texts and images, the hypotexts parodied throughout the novel. In *La región más transparente,* questions about the essential marginality of Mexican hybrid identity are laid open with the specific purpose of critically addressing its contradictory relation with the idea of Western modernity. The constant dialogue of a subdued universalism with a nationalist introspection ridden by varying sentiments of exceptionality and of inferiority is at the core of the debates over Mexico's place in the projects of Western modernity.

Lo mexicano is lo mexicano is . . .

The novel's choral rendering of the nationalist obsession with the self, its playful use of the long menu of narcissistic discourses emanating from the male ivory tower of the Mexican national bourgeoisie, has often been read at face value as either Fuentes's "narrative transposition" of Paz's *The Labyrinth of Solitude,*[29] or even worse, as a straightforward case of plagiarism.[30] Yet this apparent automatism on the part of Fuentes is extremely problematic, as it ignores the novel's critical mode: it reads the parodic utterance as single-voiced, rather than antithetical to a tradition which it is simply accused of parroting. The identity quest in the novel is not so much "the conversion of a pre-existing discourse into novelistic material,"[31] but rather the transformation of that preexisting discourse into satirical material through a concise, double-voiced reference to its terms.

By debating the definitions of Mexican identity, "lo Mexicano," Mexican intellectuals had been addressing for decades the question of Mexico's—and by extension, Latin American—participation in modernity, a discussion which inevitably had to deal with its perceived peripheral relation with Western culture. In particular, a prominent theme of these debates was Mexico's problematic insertion in Western culture as a result of its complex hybrid Hispanicized Native American culture, a question which was met with a plethora of answers, from Vasconcelos's racialist celebration of the mestizo[32] to Ramos's elitist perception of Mexico's immaturity which he offered to treat with a broad psychological and pedagogical agenda. During the 1920s and 1930s, Samuel Ramos methodically revised and updated definitions of Mexico's national identity from different anthropological points of view. In his influential *Perfil del hombre y la cultura en México* (1934), Ramos approached Mexicans' contradictory and unsettling relation with Europe and the United States from a psychoanalytic point of view, asserting that Mexican identity suffered a defeatist inferiority complex, filled with distrust and disorientation. In his discussion of "lo mexicano" Villegas summarizes the views of one of the most influential students of Mexican identity as follows: "Imitation and nationalism are phenomena at the level of that very feeling [the inferiority complex] which together with inertia, laziness, machismo, and courage constitute a crust that covers the real being of the Mexican."[33] Frantz Fanon also noticed the psychological effects of what Mariátegui defined before him as cultural "dependency": the colonized are people "in whose soul an inferiority complex has been created by the death and burial of its local cultural originality."[34]

Ramos's metaphor for the artificial way in which European culture had been adopted in Mexico mainly during the nineteenth century is that of the "hothouse flower" (*Profile of Man and Culture in Mexico,* 108). Mexico's "false Europeanism" had produced a "greenhouse culture" (ibid., 75), a bleak reminder that a century after its formal independence the nation was still "spiritually . . . a colonial country" (ibid., 95). The weakness of the transplanted European culture was in great part due to its inability to "take root" in the Mexican soil, and therefore its advocates, the Europeanists, had to keep it in the unreal "hothouse" environment and separate from the reality of the street. Europeanists, such as the positivists of the Díaz regime, and moderate nationalists, such as the revolutionary group of the Ateneístas, Vasconcelos, and others, had offered mutually excluding views of the difficult relation between the seemingly uprooted European culture of modernity and the inherent otherness of the Mexican reality. José Vasconcelos, Alfonso Reyes, and Antonio Caso, among others, worked during and after the revolution in the Bergsonian project of the Ateneo de la Juventud, which in Samuel Ramos's words sought to "rehabilitate the spiritual values that had been so degraded in Mexico under the influence of positivism."[35] Ramos had applied the psychoanalytical solution of the search for the traumatic past, the self-knowledge as the way forward to unearth that:

> The most recent displays of nationalism make us fear that the Mexican, in the intimacy of his psychological world, has cheated himself, that he has concealed his true nature—of which he is ignorant—by the superimposition of a false image. The essential virtue for the Mexican of today is sincerity. Without it he cannot remove the mask with which he disguises his authentic being from himself. (Ramos, *Profile of Man and Culture in Mexico,* 75)

Ramos looks at the struggle between the "Europeanists" and the "nationalists," and using once more a botanical metaphor, hopes for a future synthesis: "that native element which upon undergoing the influence of European culture grafts onto the tree of the latter a new branch, one that will later become an independent cultural unit" (ibid., 98). This ultimate organic Mexican independence was the collective ambition of cultural historians such as Ramos and later on Leopoldo Zea. Apart from organic metaphors like the branching out of the European tree, analogies with an individual's coming of age, a reflection of Latin America's ongoing maturation, are commonly drawn into their discussions.

The generalized perception within this debate of Mexico's immaturity, its underdevelopment and subaltern relation vis-à-vis Western culture has been often summarized with a culinary image put forward by Alfonso Reyes in 1936: (Latin) América's late "arrival to the banquet of European Civilization."[36] Reyes reclaims here the name of América, "Our América," using

José Martí's famous coinage, to discuss the cultural continuities between the ex-colonies of Spain and Portugal. Unfortunately, the image has often been taken out of the context of Reyes's specific argument, and it has been used to emphasize primarily (Latin) America's peripheral status as regards European cultural traditions. An even more pessimistic version of Reyes's formula is offered in Fuentes's novel by Manuel Zamacona, who declares in his heady writings that Mexicans not only arrive late at the banquets of modernization but "when we are savoring its soups, they turn into crumbs of stale bread nibbled by mice" (*RT,* 79).[37] While Reyes had followed Hegel's view of America's "positive inferiority"[38] in suggesting that in America's peripheral participation in European tradition lay its strength, the restless Zamacona echoes a Mexican anxiety about trailing decayed versions of modernity. If for Reyes the supposedly nude American tradition meant that Americans could create culture anew, and therefore a true modernity, Zamacona points to the seeming impossibility of that original moment to constitute the narrative of Mexican modernity.

Octavio Paz's is one of the four books that Manuel Zamacona carries under his arm: "Look" he says to Ixca, "Guardini, *The Labyrinth of Solitude,* Alfonso Reyes, Nerval" (*RT,* 421–2/292). Walking through Mexico City with his friend Ixca Cienfuegos, Manuel Zamacona, the obsessive national intellectual, carries with him a bibliographical cocktail that synecdochically represents his scholarly preoccupations. Another author under his arm is Romano Guardini, the influential Catholic priest and author of works such as *The Spirit of Liturgy, Sacred Signs,* who is credited with much of the liturgical reformation carried out during the Second Vatican Council in 1963. Guardini's influence on Zamacona's thinking is reflected in his Christian longing—"all could die like God because a God had died for all" (*RT,* 427/296)—for a sacrificial redemption of national contradictions: "What interests me is to find solutions which are suited to Mexico and will permit us for the first time to reconcile human and cultural being with lawful forms. True integration of the scattered members of what this country is" (*RT,* 317–18/220).

Octavio Paz's *The Labyrinth of Solitude,* clearly indebted to Ramos's earlier psychoanalytical *Profile,* maintained an optimistic outlook on Mexico's claims to universalism, an indisputable way out of the nationalist introspection that was widely perceived at the time as part of Mexico's cultural peculiarity. In Paz's words: "[Mexico's] nationalism, if it is not a mental illness or idolatry, must end in a universal search. Our point of departure must be a perception that our alienated situation is shared by the majority of the peoples on the earth."[39] Octavio Paz's essay on the definition of the Mexican or "lo Mexicano" is heavily cannibalized by Fuentes in this and in successive novels, parodying its pompous gravity and seriousness. Similarly, Alfonso Reyes and his essay on Anahuac provides the novel with its title and some of its national thematic aspects.[40] Finally, Zamacona is possibly reading Nerval's post-Napoleonic celebration of a renewed revolutionary nationalism, particularly in such poems as "Le peuple," or "Les doctrinaires"—dedicated to Victor Hugo—and which critiqued the failed Napoleonic imperial adventures and inclusively celebrated a "national hymn for the entire nation."[41]

Like the botanical and organic images proposed by Ramos and others, the gastronomic metaphors support diverse attitudes toward the reception of imported modes of thought. For Fuentes's fashionably secluded thinker the staleness of borrowed ideas, their second-handedness—"nibbled by mice"—is the sign of their lack of validity for the American reality, their insignificant nutritional value. By contrast, Reyes notes the occasional audacity of Americans in their "daring leap[s]," characterized by their frequent anticipation in the modern projects, signaled in the rawness of the food: "the new form has the appearance of a food taken from the fire before it has reached its cooking point" ("Notas sobre la inteligencia americana," 133). Staleness contests rawness, in a search for the American "cooking tempo." Latin American and particularly Mexican cultural philosophers have invested much of their time and efforts in such images, as Fuentes's novel sardonically proposes: "Mucha receta, y cero libros" ("Many recipes, zero books") (*RT,* 421/292).

Reyes's powerful image of the "late arrival" has historically taken over the author's whole argument, namely that the American enquiry is about "knowing if the European rhythm . . . is the only possible tempo" ("Notas sobre la inteligencia americana," 133) and whether European knowledge will someday soon "necessitate us" (ibid., 139). Thus for Reyes the key point is the somewhat hidden potential of "our America" for Europe's cultural renewal, particularly after World War II, rather than the much vaunted American marginality, used by some to pessimistically reinforce the *capitis diminutio* of past thinkers, the Latin American inferiority complex which Reyes sees as an instance of "bad conscience" (ibid., 142).

This existentialist turn of Reyes's phrase denotes however a kernel theme shared by Ramos, Paz, and the Mexican existentialist movement of the late 1940s represented by Zamacona in the novel. If Mexicans are to find and fulfill their identity, they will first have to abandon the labyrinth of solitudes of their inferiority complex, a bad faith induced by the apparently irreconcilable relation of the European and the indigenous cultures. A relation which the Hiperión group of intellectuals headed by Leopoldo Zea and others would set out to reconsider in the late 1940s and 1950s,[42] the immediate intellectual background against which Fuentes's novel was written. Rather than attributing Mexico's radical marginality to its pre-Hispanic cultural and social heritage, Leopoldo Zea described it a year before the publication of Fuentes's novel as inherent in the constitution of the Hispanic cultural sphere in Europe.[43] Zea's theorization of a Spanish peripheral modernity and its subsequent repercussion on the Latin American colonization fictionally reverberates in the musings of the anxious Manuel Zamacona, as he observes Mexico City from his ivory tower.[44]

His physical location above the historical landmarks of the city, the Avenida de la Reforma "modeled . . . after Brussels' Avenue Louise" and over the fugitive unhappy Indians is not used to stress the contrast between the European and the indigenous, but to signal his critical separateness from Mexico's social and historical realities, from his high isolated viewpoint, the physical and spiritual location of Mexico City is sardonically excavated. This location produces a *mise-en-abime* reading of the intellectual's marginal position in the marginal history of Mexico. For Cienfuegos, "eccentricity" more than "contrast" is the defining category of Mexico's reality. As he himself is locked away from Mexico's society, he projects his peripheral viewpoint onto the reality of the nation. "Locked inside cloisters, backs turned on the world, we Mexicans cannot feel that either our works or our soul enter any order comprehensible to others or to ourselves" (*RT,* 73/43–44).

Fuentes has attributed elsewhere his love-hate relationship with Mexico to his position as a frequent outsider, thus the centrality of the privileged position of foreign observers—like Natasha (a "foreign performer" of Kurt Weill's songs) who thinks it is a "horrible city, where we feel sick, where the air's too thin and there's nothing except serpents and eagles" (*RT,* 195/137)—who censure Mexico in critical aloofness to immediately confess an irresistible attachment to it: "beside this repugnant show and false courtesy of people like you, there is also the incredible real courtesy of a child or an old servant." (*RT,* 196/137) This ambivalence can be seen as a trace of the author's detached and ironic stance: the privileged power position of the post-national satirist. Fuentes's conflicting relationship with his Mexican identity stems from his status as insider-outsider for whom Mexico "was a source of violent associations and detachments, against which affection was not stronger than rejection."[45] His apparently conflicting views on Mexican reality come to the fore as the novel critically stages the dialogue between cultural determinations and existential responsibilities. Side by side with the mythical world of the serpent and the eagle that shapes the existence of all characters, there is a continuous, if frustrated, effort to escape this very determinism. The city is the place—the "clearest region" of the original title—where these determinations and responsibilities meet face-to-face.

As the novel closes, its title is brought to the fore once more. "Where the Air Is Clear," or rather, "The Clearest Region of the Air"—with its ironic allusion to the once transparent air of the city, now heavily industrialized—if not an ecological declaration, is at the very least a sign of the political disenchantment with the overwhelming expansion of Mexico City and its traumatic social and cultural consequences. And it is a Weberian disenchantment at that.[46] The title announces the significance in the novel of a tarnished (post) national spatiality; it dryly reverses the coveted exceptionality of Mexico's capital city. The title's contention is satirically negated in the novel through the critical dialogues with the fragments of a ubiquitous nationalist discourse and the public scorching of idealized icons and notions of Mexicanness.

Melting into the air is the air's own mythical transparency, the solid symbol of its ecological promise and of the nation's geographical consecration. As the fumes and exhaustion of the modern urban chaos rise into the air, on the ground everyone is set alight in a hopeless, satirical bonfire of social combustion.

Chapter 2

✦

Innocents Abroad and at Home: The Profane History of American Modernity in *V.*

Cold War? Hell, it was a hot war!

—Secretary of State R. S. McNamara, *The Fog of War*

At the end of the 1950s two similar-sounding titles offered a critical view of the informal American empire in Asia: Graham Greene's *The Quiet American* (1955) and William J. Lederer and Eugene Burdick's *The Ugly American* (1958).[1] Both texts voiced anxieties about aggressive American involvement in the chaotic process of French withdrawal from Southeast Asia at a time when the British and Dutch were apparently promoting a "model" and "pacific" decolonization—very often through comparably complicated and disordered processes as evidenced by the violent partition of Pakistan and India and a long list of other cases. The escalation of decolonial crises at the frontiers between the two blocs of the Cold War provided these authors with prescient visions of an impending clash between communism, perceived at the time by many as a clear route for national liberation of former colonies, and American capitalism, portrayed as grotesquely buttressing the decaying networks of Western imperial interests everywhere.[2] Besides the general censure of unsuccessful imperial efforts by the United States, an emerging overarching theme in these two books emphasizes the defective human empathy and cultural understanding displayed by the seemingly naive Americans abroad in their interactions with these new colonial subjects. The quiet and ugly "innocents abroad"—borrowing Mark Twain's satirical rendering of this long-established American stereotype—are here transformed into the spineless spies of *The Quiet American,* and to the army of civil servants and soldiers fiercely caricatured in *The Ugly American.* However, the underlying theses behind these two texts differed drastically. While Greene's portrayal of Western intervention in Southeast Asia openly condemned it, limited by the colonists' inability to break away from their strict and ethnocentric cultural and economic biases, *The Ugly American* tangentially departed from that starting point to offer a number of counterinsurgency measures to compete with the very successful communist movements. Measures such as befriending and infiltrating the "natives" are devised, anticipated, and celebrated as a well-developed set of strategies to bring "the Asians" under American control. The figure of the maverick CIA agent Edward G. Lansdale, a proponent of an Asian route to conservative nationalism that should allow American interests to be exercised without direct military intervention, is the likely basis for both texts as David Wise and Thomas B. Ross suggested in their early denunciation of CIA counterinsurgent practices abroad.[3]

National Souls for the International Souk

Lederer and Burdick's book portray the complex symbiosis between rhetorical tropes such as the United States as a "leader of the free world" and its patronizing corollary, the depiction of childish "natives" in need of liberation through Americanization. The U.S. diplomatic corps and its counterinsurgent playbook are intent on imposing the (authoritarian) nationalist model as the American way out of the alleged postcolonial communist nightmare in Asia. At the other end of the 1960s and a whole decade into the protracted defeat of the United States in the Vietnam War, *The Pentagon Papers,* published in 1971, divulged Lansdale's reports demonstrating that his advice and main efforts were oriented toward a directed process of "nation-building" as part of a neocolonial policy. Landsdale alluded to the success of this nationalist model in the Philippines around the time of its final independence from the United States in 1947. Landsdale's "nation-building" model was according to Michael McClintock the new way to secure U.S. influence in the post-World War II scene.[4] For McClintock, through this version of top-down nationalism "a colonial or imperial power, in [Landsdale's] analysis, could readily harness the potential for nationalism to its own purpose" (McClintock, 131). The failure of the Philippine model in Vietnam meant that the United States had to directly intervene to defend Diem's nationalist regime, and a number of extremely repressive measures against the "democratic" ideals that it purportedly sought to promote, by imposing a "South Vietnamese 'nation' . . . created from the top down," as Richard Slotkin has pointed out.[5] The logical inference established by Slotkin in his exceptional study is that "the various programs of 'reform' and 'nation-building' tended to become programs of Americanization" (446). Communist internationalism, and the postwar, postcolonial emergence of nationalist solidarities, was thus confronted with a more reactionary, organic version of nation—the Romantic, essentialist idea of a nationally, or geographically rooted people, now bankrolled by American transnational business interests.[6] And with it came other modern but undemocratic byproducts of nationalist thought: ethnic differentiations as a basis for the legal organization of society, and racial, essentialist characterizations of cultures and peoples.

Commenting on the American imperial projection in continental Southeast Asia during the Cold War and on the practice of counterinsurgency of which *The Ugly American* was an important exponent, Slotkin uncovers the updated usages of the U.S. Frontier Myth during the renewed period of imperial expansion after World War II. The Frontier Myth had taught Americans "that progress is only achieved by the advance of White European races/cultures into and against the terrain of 'primitive,' non-White 'natives' " (Slotkin, 446). The iconic transfer of racial stereotypes from Westerns is highlighted as one of the ingredients that made *The Ugly American* so popular: according to Slotkin, Lederer and Burdick conformed "to literary and mythic conventions" (447), and they treated " 'Asians' as Hollywood (for the most part) treated 'Indians'—as if they had a unitary racial character transcending differences of culture and nationality" (447–48).

Even *South Pacific,* the 1958 Broadway adaptation of James A. Michener's *Tales of the South Pacific* (1947), for all its patronizing and stereotyped treatment of both "natives" and French, included a poignant critique of how American racism is a cultural narrative, a mind-set "carefully taught" in the domestic suburbs of the motherland, a pattern that follows the dialogue between the domestic and the foreign domains underlined by Amy Kaplan.[7] Despite their unfavorable review of domestic imperial prejudice, Rodgers and Hammerstein shrewdly avoided the final marriage of the American soldier Cable and the local girl Liat, and stayed with the more comfortable and socially safe European otherness of the French plantation owner Emile, who does finally marry the nurse Nellie. In its hushed avoidance of the distressing effects of "racial miscegenation," at the much more comforting price of providing a national dead hero—"after all, that is what our heroes went there for," seems to be the implicit consensual theme—and in its celebration of the new "Western" alliance in the Far East, this domestic finale is one of the earliest metaphors for the American takeover of the French colonies in Asia, which would culminate disastrously in Indochina during the following decades. If this French-American marriage symbolizes the prominent theme of the new imperial frontier in the East in *South Pacific,* the friendship between Herbert Stencil and Benny Profane, the two searching characters in *V.,* reveals and satirically contests the process by which Americans succeeded into the British imperial legacy after World War II.[8]

In 1957, a year before the opening of *South Pacific,* the twenty-year-old Thomas Pynchon returned to Cornell University. Between 1955 and 1957, two years after the Korean War ended, Pynchon had been enlisted in the United States Navy, possibly as a draftee.[9] From his short stories, published between 1959 and 1961, to *V.,* which came out in 1963, Pynchon's early writings delineate his incisive views about the complex relationship between colonialism and national identity. Pynchon's exploration of this conflict traces a subversion of the American paradigmatic nationalist discourse of liberation and progress promoted during the Cold War period. Instead of subscribing to the discourse of America as a historical exception promoted by the "consensus historiography" in the 1950s,[10] Pynchon's satirical narration chronicles U.S. history as a prolongation of the West's persistent territorial expansion and global colonization.

In his popular *Gates of Eden,* Morris Dickstein suitably inserts Pynchon in the group of writers—Joseph Heller, Norman Mailer, and Thomas Berger—who he calls "the first novelists of the new imperial America."[11] Similarly, some significant assessments of *V.* throughout the 1990s concentrated less on issues of postmodern uncertainty and increasingly on the ways in which, according to Robert Cooley, the novel attempts to "provide a theory (actually a group of interlocking theories) of empire and history."[12] Cooley's parenthetical proposal of the "group of interlocking theories" is an interesting model of how the novel presents a series of competing versions of history and the historiography of empire.[13] However, Cooley suggests that imperialism "hovers in the background" only in the novel's six historical chapters, a strangely reductive reading if we consider the indissoluble continuity of metropolitan "domestic" life and the foreign sphere of imperial domination. A considerable part of the novel focuses on the histories of colonial occupation by European powers in Africa and the Middle East in the first half of the twentieth century. But this recurrent theme of the cultural and political aggression of European imperialism—often through the extermination of entire peoples, as in the case of the Southwest African Hereros by the Germans, in Kurt Mondaugen's story in chapter 9 (*V.,* 229–79)—instantly remits to the foundational narratives of Americanness and its genocidal moving borders. In this sense, *V.,* like *Mason & Dixon* more than thirty years later, proceeds by a play of textual juxtapositions to underline the parallelisms between the violent histories of American and African colonization. The first third of *Mason & Dixon* recalls the trips by the two British surveyors to the Cape of Good Hope and St. Helena, off the African coast. As I propose in chapter 7, this series of episodes is used to create a cultural and historical continuity between these two colonial experiences, and to explicitly question American exceptionalism within the history of Western colonialism.

One of Pynchon's scarce commentaries on his work, a published letter to Thomas F. Hirsch, provides an extraordinary insight into his political rationale and his reading of these interrelated histories of colonial oppression: "I feel personally that the number done on the Herero head by the Germans is the same number done on the American Indian head by our own colonists and what is now being done on the Buddhist head in Vietnam by the Christian minority in Saigon and their advisors."[14] The large frame of imperial history on which the United States is founded finds its continuity in the Vietnam conflict and its parallels in the German genocide of the African Hereros. The United States is not an exception but part of the same worldwide Western history that had led elsewhere in the hemisphere to the toppling of the Inca civilization by a "one-time hog drover from Estremadura [*sic*]" (Pynchon, "Letter to Thomas F. Hirsch," 242). These repetitive acts of exclusion, extermination, and historical erasure thematize Pynchon's satirical, decidedly anti-epic, narrative of U.S. (and Western) history. A narrative he goes on to summarize as the "imposition of a culture valuing analysis and differentiation on a culture that valued unity and integration"[15] (ibid., 243).

Cowboy culture, inhabited and mimicked by the novel's main characters in *V.*, is not then a simple allusion, or a postmodern pastiche, of the ubiquitous televised Westerns of the 1950s—instead, it is a satirical reference to the foundational colonial violence of the United States obsessively revisited and reconstructed by Pynchon over the years. In one of the saloon scenes in *Against the Day,* a group of Japanese visitors armed with anachronistic Kodak cameras—and sharp *katanas*—are searching for the secrets of the American "national soul" out in the West: "the American West—it is a spiritual territory! In which we seek to study the secrets of your—national soul!" This tourist-academic search—a possible cover for their industrial espionage of metallurgic technologies—is countered by the noisy laugh of Merle Rideout slapping his knee: "You fellows, I swear. What 'national soul?' We don't have any 'national soul'! 'F you think any different, why you are just packing out pyrites, brother" (*Against the Day,* 293). This encounter between the anti-nationalist U.S. citizen and the stranger seeking for a static image of national essences in the frontier is one more example of Pynchon's many satirical evacuations of the persistent American Western iconography. The suspicion that nationalism is a cultural contraption to obfuscate material enterprises, hiding from sight competing and struggling class interests while obscuring the history of oppression, coercion, and forcible consensus on which it is built, is once more thematized in *Against the Day* through the retelling of "the settling of the West" as a rapacious industrial venture.

National narratives of exceptionality with their rhetorical emphasis on "project" and "destiny" cannot circumvent the historical and current evidence of its material imperial policies and social practices of displacement and erasure, cultural homogenization, and expansive continental settlement. The parallelisms between different colonial histories highlights the process of "mapping" the colonized territories in order to incorporate them into an Occidental episteme. These mappings evidence the indispensable interconnection of cartographic knowledge/power: not merely a scientific observation, but a process of reorganization, appropriation, and violent incorporation into the global map.

A good instance of these dialectics of global mappings and local spaces in *V.* is provided by the urban ordering imposed on Malta's capital, Valletta, by the colonial administrators as they partition the cityscape into a grid of straight streets. "What a warped idea of cities one got in this occupation!" (*V.*, 468), sums up Sidney Stencil's Victorian outlook, bleakly prefiguring the tracing of the Mason and Dixon Line and the computerized spatial arrangement of the San Narciso valley in *The Crying of Lot 49*.[16] Oppositional to this scientific colonial incorporation of space, the "Confessions" of Fausto Maijstral in chapter 11 (*V.*, 305–46) offer a national-mythical reading of the city, alluding to a disemboweled "spirit of the place" threatened and exorcised by the continuous presence of Western imperial powers constantly reorganizing and mapping the city. However, in Valetta, unlike in Fuentes's Mexico City, there is no vengeful Ixca Cienfuegos, no national "othered" ghostly figure haunting the (neo)colonial actors, only a chronic succession of erasures on the cityscape. For Pynchon, the metaphysical configuration of V. and its many threatening avatars represent Western colonial irrationalism and its incessant drive to map, dispossess, erase.

Like European colonialism, V. is a plague or illness that visits and infects Southwest Africa, Egypt, Malta, to name only a few of the prominent colonized landscapes circulating in the novel. The novel proposes a farcical Conradian quest into the records of colonial darkness whose narrative continuity is made apparent by the relentless hovering presence of the mysterious and elusive V.[17] Robert Holton offers a precise description of the relationship between the contemporary locus of the novel and the history of devastation brought by the V. figure: "Under the cover of historical relativism, rather than making events disappear, he is making present what seems to be a remarkable history of Western racism from the atrocities of colonialism to the somewhat more covert racism of America at the time of writing."[18]

With Holton, I maintain that the critical history of colonialism provided in Pynchon's *V.* is used to emphasize the historical continuity of Western imperialism in the late twentieth-century American informal global empire. During the Cold War, celebratory, mass-produced versions of American (imperial) history were broadcast through the new medium of television, in the form of western serials, and through other popular culture items such as comics, magazines, and radio adverts. In these popularized versions of U.S. history, the uncritical epic of the frontier constituted a foundational epos that narrated the American nation as an imagined community in constant imperial expansion. Kennedy's 1961 version of the New Frontier of space is permeated by the nineteenth-century language of territorial expansion, and it disguises a more tangible counterpart: the frontier to "contain" communism in Cuba and Vietnam. In *V.*, the transformation of America into a worldwide power is reflected (and subverted) in the urban geography as well as in its social landscape, politically reinscribed with the renewed nationalist discourse of American exceptionalism.

Among the effects of the "American nationalist globalism" that emerged after World War II some of the most important were performed in the domestic sphere. John Fousek has persuasively described how the United States became ideologically uniformed by the Cold War nationalist consensus, itself based on three major principles: "national greatness, global responsibility, and anticommunism."[19] This ideology, labeled by Fousek as "American nationalist globalism," is best described as a conflation of well-established American nationalist discourses with the country's new international commitments after World War II: the "traditional nationalist ideologies of American chosenness, mission, and destiny" (Fousek, 7), as a crass justification of military intervention abroad to defend America's economic vested interests: "the emerging notion that the entire world was now the proper sphere of concern for U.S. foreign policy" (7). As Fousek contends, America's anticommunist stance was based on "the belief that the universal nature of American national values justified and even necessitated the global expansion of U.S. power" (7).

Fousek critiques the perverse effect of these policies in implementing a variety of transformations of American society that ultimately "justified major departures from national tradition—such as entangling overseas alliances, a peacetime draft, large standing armies, and protracted land wars in Asia" (7). It is easy to perceive in this last statement a certain degree of nostalgia for the pre-Cold War American "national traditions," understood as inherently liberal and democratic, from which the nation was departing. This idealization of the national "soul" is hardly present in Pynchon's work, however, as one can deduce from reading *Mason & Dixon* or *Against the Day.* Benny Profane in *V.* embodies the overlap between the consumer and the citizen, as he paranoically becomes aware that the space he inhabits is a souk: "He walked; walked he thought sometimes, the aisles of a bright gigantic supermarket, his only function to want" (*V.*, 37). This image of America as a large marketplace prefigures the grotesque "Vineland Mall" of Pynchon's *Vineland* (1990); a mall where the nationalist symbols are parodically transferred and occupied by the hegemonic practices of the consumerist scheme, while the citizen is demoted to just a "free" consumer. The stereotyped "American national identity" centered around the Cold War consensus of American chosenness to lead the "free world" in the pursuit of consumerist happiness, an identity easily commoditized and packaged for universal enforcement, is pessimistically represented in Pynchon's writings as a drive toward new physical, geographical, and social autocracy.

"Corroded Histories" and Impossible Futures

From Pynchon's early writings, history appears as a contorted and conflicting set of narratives of the struggles between different spatial mappings. *V.* inquires about its immediate past, the 1950s, and about the historical record of the twentieth century, disclosing a series of patterns that substantiate its history as a story of cultural and cartographic violence. In *V.*, Pynchon's initial interest in the unhinged cultural interaction between metropolitan powers and those subjected to their colonial rule satirically reenacts the consequences of the colonial experience on the identities of both colonizers and colonized through at least two competing and mutually complementary quests.[20] The first of these searches is that of the schlemiel, the bum Benny Profane, in his apparently aimless voyage around the Eastern Seaboard of the United States. The second quest centers on the middle-aged Briton Herbert Stencil, who in his search slowly and unknowingly unveils a signifier of imperial brutality in the blurry symbol "V."

Soldiers and other colonial agents transform both the colonized territories and the "homeland": many of the characters in *V.*'s cast, and in some of his early short stories collected later in *Slow Learner,* are American soldiers marked by their military experience who are either on the go or between "jobs." These soldiers are in action somewhere around the world, even in the United States, as in his short story "The Small Rain." But they are also in the process of returning home, like Benny Profane in *V.,* to become PFCs, "Poor Forlorn Civilians" (*V.,* 13).

Pynchon's first short story, "The Small Rain," is not directly concerned with the role of Americans abroad, but with the conflicting presence in American society of characters who belong to the growing imperial military machine of the Cold War.[21] A peacetime draft was only one of the direct consequences of the growing militarization of American society imposed by its outstretched growing empire. The story deals with a group of soldiers from radically different backgrounds who help clear out the disaster area affected by a hurricane. In contrast with Norman Mailer's tale of the South Pacific front of World War II in *The Naked and the Dead* (1948), the soldiers of Pynchon's story confront a domestic disaster zone, an incident that emphasizes the omnipresence of the army in the militarized American landscape of the Cold War. In virtually all of Pynchon's early works, including *V.,* the recurrence of this military theme reflects on the ethnic makeup of the American nation. As in Norman Mailer's enormously successful epic of early wartime exploits in the South Pacific, Pynchon's short story portrays the American army as the multiethnic nation "on the go": a vaunted melting pot where males from most social and ethnic backgrounds appear to be in conflict.

Writing about his first story in the introduction to *Slow Learner* (1984) twenty-five years after its publication, Pynchon recognized that it was not so much "the quaintness and puerility of attitude" that he found interesting, but "the class angle" (*SL,* 6). He explains that the peacetime service "can provide an excellent introduction to the structure of society at large" (*SL,* 6). There is, nevertheless, no easy or peaceful relationship between the soldiers in the story: class distinctions are effortlessly discernible in the traditional patterns of characterization, which remain unchanged throughout the text. For instance, everyone keeps their social place and regional accents: unsurprisingly, the social mandarins are officers in the army, and the working class makes up the battalion of "men." One of the former, Lieutenant Pierce, is a Bostonian, a graduate of MIT and officer, who spoke "with a precise, dry Beacon Hill accent" (*SL,* 33). Dugan, a university student from Virginia, represents the other side of the nation's North-South fracture, with his incongruous racist paranoid beliefs:

> The NAACP was a Communist cabal dedicated to 100% intermarriage of the White and Negro races, and that the Virginia gentleman was in reality the Übermensch, come at last, prevented from fulfilling his high destiny only by the malevolent plotting of the New York Jews. (*SL*, 29)

A third significant model of Pynchon's early characterization is the stereotypically intelligent and neurotic New York Jew, Levine, at the center of the story and who, for obvious reasons, did not get on well with the anti-Semite Dugan. "Lardass" Levine experiences the army as a way of not taking responsibility, a job that allows him to avoid "going back." At the beginning of the story, he cryptically announces to his friend Picnic: "you don't go back" (*SL*, 35). The theme of the "return home" or "going back" is picked up again in the closing exchange between the two soldiers: "'Damm, it'll almost be a relief to get back.' 'Back?' Levine said. 'Oh, yeah, I guess so'" (*SL*, 51). As they leave the symbolically named community of "Creole," Levine hesitates to wonder about the point of reference that has been lost in communication. For a brief but seminal moment, there is no common meaning to "back," no shared homeland, for these two soldiers.

In the army, Levine can be the perpetual Wandering Jew of his fantasies, one of the first comic characters in Pynchon's fiction to sarcastically think about national identity:

> He had a momentary, ludicrous vision of himself, Lardass Levine the Wandering Jew, debating on weekday evenings in strange and nameless towns with other Wandering Jews the essential problems of identity—not of the self so much as identity of place and what right you really had to be anyplace. (*SL*, 49)

Although this dreamy image is ironically qualified as "ludicrous" and rapidly contrasted with the everyday reality of the bar and Levine's local girl ("Buttercup[,] waiting for him" [*SL*, 49]), the sketchy "identity of place" confirms Pynchon's complexly satirical interest in identity and specifically national identity from a very early stage of his literary career.

Pynchon suggests in his 1984 introduction to *Slow Learner* that the character's conflict in this early story was "where to put his loyalties" (*SL*, 6). Levine's opposition between these two types of identity, "of the self" and "of place," helps to discriminate the realms of private, or individual, and public, or social, identifications. National and social loyalties become profoundly mixed in "The Small Rain." The soldiers' grisly monotonous work of "picking up stiffs" (*SL*, 48), and Levine's dull sexual encounter with Buttercup are combined as a sign of the army's double invasive role in the community of Creole. Levine both saves and intrudes in the community: he easily leaves without a sense of responsibility or attachment to it. The central point of the story is precisely that role of the army which both rescues and alters a community at once. Levine's "right to be anyplace" is above all an existential question about the social responsibilities, or "loyalties," of the soldier-citizen draftee.

The question of "what right you really have to be anyplace" is particularly significant at a time when American foreign intervention was becoming increasingly prominent, while its renewed globalized national melting-pot story opened its doors to hitherto disenfranchised social or ethnic groups such as American Jews. The story's protagonist owes much to the very successful Jewish-American narratives of the escape from the ghetto into the broader national scene.[22]

The image of the "Wandering Jew" alludes to that contradictory figure, nationally defined through his perpetually diasporic life. It describes a national character in constant dialogue with an identity rooted in a permanently deferred space: the Promised Land whose value had been symbolically transferred earlier onto another imaginary space, America—the New Israel of Puritan iconography.[23] "Lardass Levine" is a first draft, the early stage of the drifter ex-sailor in *V.*, whose apparently pointless life traveling "up and down the east coast like a yo-yo" (*V.*, 10) since he left the Navy shapes this first quest in the novel.

That Pynchon's first character suffering from an identity crisis should be a Wandering Jew contextualizes *V.*'s Benny Profane and his presentation as a "schlemihl," the archetypal loser figure of Yiddish literary folklore, now adapted by a non-Jewish writer to his cast of characters.[24] Ruth Wisse suggests that the impulse of "schlemiel literature in general . . . is to use this comical stance as a stage from which to challenge the political and philosophical status quo" (3). Similarly, Profane can be read as a satirical antihero, an inverted image of the western cowboys of which he is a parodic reminder in the novel. Profane himself defines his identity as a schlemihl as "nothing heroic" (*V.*, 288) in contrast with the western myths of masculine heroes broadcast on television and interpreted by Randolph Scott:

> What was a hero? Randolph Scott, who could handle a six-gun, horse's reins, lariat. Master of the inanimate. But a schlemihl, that was hardly a man: somebody who lies back and takes it from objects, like any passive woman. (*V.*, 288)

The description of the real heroes, the western cowboys, is articulated around the control of the inanimate world, something he could not achieve as a schlemihl: "being a schlemihl, he'd known for years: inanimate objects and he could not live in peace" (*V.*, 37). The ambiguous feminization of the schlemihl Profane is however oddly qualified when he afterward drunkenly lies in bed with Mafia. She had previously inquired whether there was a "latent homosexuality" in his anxieties about heroicity and in his odd opinions about "having names for [sex]" (*V.*, 288) as "confused."

Profane's self-perception as a schlemihl reflects on the construction of his masculinity. This is also related to his earlier involvement in the (imperial) Navy. In the opening chapter of *V.* (December 1955) a bar scene at the Sailor's Grave mocks the military musical films of Gene Kelly and Frank Sinatra such as *Anchors Aweigh* (1945) or *On the Town* (1949). Dewey Gland sings a little song to "celebrate [Profane] becoming a PFC" (*V.*, 13). Sung in waltz time, Gland's song stridently closes with an entreaty to "ship me over for twenty years, I'll never be a Pore [*sic*] Forlorn Civilian" (*V.*, 13). Faced with the apparent tranquil anonymity of civilian life, Profane's former shipmates proceed to a violent bar brawl.

In contrast with Gland's valedictory song and its longing for the masculine military institution, the Maltese Paola Maijstral teaches the group of soldiers a song by the French singer and writer Boris Vian, called "Le déserteur."[25] Through Profane's point of view, the reader translates the young Maltese girl's eyes and how she remembered the paratrooper who had taught her the song. At this point, the succession of perceptions is set in a *mise-en-abime:* Profane looks at Paola and supposes that she is remembering the soldier "on leave from the war in Algeria" (*V.*, 18) and how he must have felt tired of the colonial war waged by his country. Sensed by Profane in Paola's memory, the French soldier's subversive voice is thus heard through a complex play of perceptions and suppositions. Profane surmises that the paratrooper was "probably a man-of-no-politics as brave as anyone ever is in combat: but tired, was all, tired of relocating native villages and devising barbarities in the morning as brutal as'd come from the F.L.N. the night before" (*V.*, 19). Profane's intuition projects onto Paola's memory and onto the French deserter an "apolitical" fatigue at the brutality of colonial warfare, itself a reminder of Profane's involvement with his own imperial Navy in the past. The ironic remark (the suggestion that conscientious objection or desertion could be nonpolitical) mocks the political deactivation of the American 1950s, at a time when anti-imperialism was a communist banner. The French song promises to close the door on the dead years of his career as colonial occupier: "je fermerai la porte / au nez des anées mortes" (*V.*, 18). In his article on *V.*, Robert Holton interprets Vian's lyrics perhaps too generally as the French soldier "closing the door on the historical era of colonialism" (341). A more compelling interpretation could highlight Profane's perception of this political episode as reflecting his own anxieties about his friends's recent colonizing adventures. After the Navy, his renewed sense of "imperial mission" is parodically sought in the unlikely frontier of the New York sewers. This alternative underground space contains not only the caricature of the undying detritus of the capitalist, consumerist city; it also encloses a secret, apocryphal history of the nation.

Profane's reading of "an avant-garde western called the *Existentialist Sheriff*" (*V.*, 284) following the advice of his friend Pig Bodine reiterates his personal iconography. Wearing a cowboy hat, the self-declared "schlemihl" volunteers to go underground with his Puerto Rican friends Geronimo and Angel—themselves colonial subjects from the island-territory at work in the bowels of the metropolis—to get rid of the alligators infesting the New York sewers: a pest provoked by kids who had bought baby alligators as pets and then "flushed them down the toilets" (*V.*, 43). In this dense package of parodic allusions there is an underlying critique of blind American consumerism and its fads—"Macy's was selling them for fifty cents, every child, it seemed, had to have one" (*V.*, 43). The underground city of alligators and rats is offered as the parodic mirror image of the city above, its animalized caricature, by stressing the reptilian moral failures of society. As pets turn into pests, the bowels of the city disclose the dark secrets of its inhabitants on the surface: their waste neither vanishes nor is it recycled back into the system; instead, a new underworld is created as a ghostly reminder of the urban ecological transgressions. Fifty years after the publication of *V.*, the New York cityscape is satirically mirrored in *Bleeding Edge* by its unrecycled skyscrapers of toxic waste and landfills, no longer repressed under the street but merging with polluted water courses and oil-driven barges at the crossroads of several environmental "national bad habits":

> Addiction to oil gradually converging with the other national bad habit, inability to deal with refuse. Maxine has been smelling garbage for a while, and now it intensifies as they approach a lofty mountain range of waste. Neglected little creeks, strangely luminous canyon walls of garbage, smells of methane, death and decay, chemicals unpronounceable as the names of God, the heaps of landfill bigger than Maxine imagines they'd be, reaching close to 200 feet overhead according to Sid, higher than a typical residential building on the Yupper West Side. (*Bleeding Edge,* 166)

This logical culmination of hyperconsummerist unsustainable frenzy exposes the national telos of progress and modernity as running toward apocalyptic self-destruction. In the posthuman underbelly of *V.*'s New York, the sewers are not hermetically closed off from the city, however. The mutant alligators grow and populate the sewers—"now they moved big, blind, albino, all over the sewer system" (*V.*, 43)—menacing with their presence to exert their revenge on the citizens of New York.

In their well-known study of the ideological construction of urban space, Peter Stallybrass and Allon White suggest that the underground space of the sewer "like all the [other] 'low and grotesque' systems" often offers a counter-hegemonic vision that cannot be hermetically separated from the homogenized surface: "[it] could not entirely be closed off from above."[26] In Profane's case, the "above" is also a form of grotesque proliferation of inanimate objects and spaces, in particular the street: "Profane had grown a little leery of streets, especially streets like this. They had in fact all fused into a single abstracted Street, which come the full moon he would have nightmares about" (*V.*, 10). Below the street, he can try to escape from his nightmare of becoming disassembled and fragmented, broken into inanimate parts as he had repeatedly dreamed:

> If he kept going down that street, not only his ass but also his arms, legs, sponge brain and clock of a heart must be left behind to litter the pavement, be scattered among manhole covers. Was it home, the mercury-lit street? Was he returning like the elephant to his graveyard, to lie down and soon become ivory in whose bulk slept, latent, exquisite shapes of chessmen, back-scratchers, hollow open-work Chinese spheres nested one inside the other? This was all there was to dream; all there ever was: the Street. (*V.*, 40)

This larger than life Street threatens to consume Profane's life through its overpowering presence and turn him into a multitude of inanimate objects. Unlike Ixca's mythical visitation in Fuentes's *La región más transparente,* the phantasmal presence of the Street is not a vengeful past impossibly returning to exact its reprisal—though this might be one of the possible readings of V. itself—but rather the inanimate future menacing to clear out the planet. Under the Street, Profane can even start to consider shooting, to use "the shotgun under the street, under the Street, might be all right" (*V.*, 43).An action that could only lead him to commit suicide, the only moral action apparently available: "He could kill himself but maybe it would be all right. He could try" (ibid.). But this first nightmarish presentation of the Street is later on in the novel rephrased in Sidney Stencil's political vision of the twentieth century as part of a binary set that interprets left and right in spatial terms, the "street" and the "hothouse" respectively:

> "If there is any political moral to be found in this world" [Sidney] Stencil once wrote in his journal, "it is that we carry on the business of this century with an intolerable double vision. Right and Left; the hothouse and the street. The Right can only live and work hermetically, in the hothouse of the past, while outside the Left prosecute their affairs in the streets by manipulated mob violence. And cannot live but in the dreamscape of the future." "What of the real present, the men-of-no-politics, the once-respectable Golden Mean? Obsolete; in any case, lost sight of. In a West of such extremes we can expect, at the very least, a highly alienated populace within not many more years." (*V.*, 468)

The historical predictions of this entry date from 1919, and they offer an apocalyptic view of the years still to come. At any rate, Sidney Stencil's journal is the testimony of a colonial civil servant whose nostalgia for the "men-of-no-politics" appears as an impossible ideological posture in the context of imperial occupation of the island of Malta. This renders a similar ironic effect to the one offered by Profane's surmise about the French colonial soldier as a "man-of-no-politics." So Profane's fears of the Street could be read in relation to his noncommittal schlemihl yo-yoing, a reminder of the "ludicrous" rootless Jew Lardass Levine.[27]

Apocalypse Now?

Chasing a resilient alligator, Profane "moved across the frontier" (*V.*, 120) and found out that during the Depression sewer rats had been catechized by a Father Fairing who "in an hour of apocalyptic well-being . . . had decided that the rats were going to take over after New York died" (*V.*, 117). Fairing's apocryphal and apocalyptic vision of the city at a time of severe economic crisis had announced the city's future obliteration. In the midst of the financial crisis that followed the 1929 New York Stock Exchange Crash, Father Fairing "foresaw nothing but a city of starved corpses, covering the sidewalks and the grass of the parks, lying belly up in the fountains, hanging wrynecked from the streetlamps" (*V.*, 118). Assuming that humans were about to be displaced by this hidden world of sewer rats, Father Fairing had decided to convert them to Catholicism. The lurking, catechized underground rats in *V.* represent both a displaced horror, but also a fascinating mirror image of the city above.[28] Stallybrass and White have noted a similar ambivalence of fascination and horror in the way in which the urban underground rat is dialectically defined in opposition to the human city dwellers: "The rat, then, furtively emerged from the city's underground conscience as the demonized Other. But as it transgressed the boundaries that separated the city from the sewer, above from below, it was a source of fascination as well as horror" (143).

In its satirical debasement of religion, Fairing's evangelization is reminiscent of the colonial simile employed by Pynchon in his short story "Under the Rose." The narrator in that early story wittily reconstructs an imperial, racialized history of evangelization: "And so it came about that God wore a wide-awake hat and fought skirmishes with an aboriginal Satan out at the antipodes of firmament, in the name and for the safekeeping of any Victoria" (*SL*, 112). Fairing's impossible spiritual colonization satirically evokes the contradictory and patronizing conquests of Western religion as the father tries to convert the rats while he eats and sodomizes them. Related to this farcical representation of cyclical colonizations of the urban underground Profane's incursion—"Father Fairing talked to rats. Profane talked to alligators" (*V.*, 123)—Fairing's story also underscores the apocryphal origins of such underground urban folklore and the alternative ethical dimensions of the sewer:

> The stories, by the time Profane heard them, were pretty much apocryphal and more fantasy than the record itself warranted. At no point in the twenty or so years the legend had been handed on did it occur to anyone to question the old priest's sanity. It is this way with sewer stories. They just are. Truth or falsity don't apply. (*V.*, 120)

Fairing's journal, with its mixture of desire for a New City "whose foundation we lay here" (*V.*, 120) and its anxiety about the rats' tendency toward "Marxist communism," offers parodic echoes of the clash between America's nationalist myths of the "errand into the wilderness" (itself part of the imperialist, evangelizing Judeo-Christian theological discourse), and "Godless" communism: the un-American ideology par excellence. Fairing's last journal entries are said to be delusive, and thus to have manipulated the record, to avoid the unbearable truth: "the bleak truth that his pale and sinuous parishioners might turn out no better than the animals whose estate they were succeeding to" (*V.*, 119). Through the focalization of Profane's reading of the journals, apocryphal history emerges as both a story that runs parallel to the "official history" above and as a story that in its "bleak truth" offers no hope of utopian renewal, not even through or especially not through the "promise" of Catholic rats repopulating the cityscape. At least the reader can laugh at the coming apocalypse, as Paul Celmer has pointed out.[29]

The parallelism between rats and humans, and between alligators and rats, is further satirized by Profane's central reminiscence of the official history of the nation's founding:

> In Independence Hall in Philly, when the floor was rebuilt, they left part of the original, a foot square, to show the tourists. "Maybe," the guide would tell you, "Benjamin Franklin stood right there, or even George Washington." Profane on an eighth-grade class trip had been suitably impressed. He got that feeling now. Here in this room an old man had killed and boiled a catechumen, had committed sodomy with a rat, had discussed a rodent nunhood faith with V., a future saint—depending which story you listened to. (*V.*, 123)

Whatever "that feeling" might be, it relates to the ghostly inscription of the past in spaces such as the sewers or Independence Hall in Philadelphia, which are here parodically linked. The overwhelming history of the nation's heroes, of its founding fathers, is a hypotext now rivaled by its parallel obscure avatar: a political parody of the nation's epic history. Once these two sacred—and profaned—spaces are contrasted, the story of Fairing's colonization and conversion of rats occupies a new level: it is thus not merely another history of hypocrisy, violence, and colonization, but a hypertextual history that contests, through its secluded satirical parallels, the national foundations of the United States.

The second questing character in *V.* is Herbert Stencil, the son of Sidney Stencil, a deceased British Foreign Officer who died working as a colonial bureaucrat in Malta in 1919 "investigating the June disturbances" (*V.*, 52). As Arnold Cassola and others have noted, these riots, usually known as the "Sette Giugno," recall Malta's "first aspirations toward self-government and eventual independence from Britain."[30] Stencil, "the century's child," who was "raised motherless" (*V.*, 52), comes then from a tradition of tyrannical colonial functionaries and, fittingly, he uses the third person: "like small children at a certain stage and Henry Adams in the *Education,* as well as assorted autocrats since time out of mind, always referred to himself in the third person. This helped Stencil appear as one among a repertoire of identities" (*V.*, 62). His discursive dislocation, this rupture of the ego into a "repertoire of identities," satirizes the psychological and discursive control of the subject exercised by the hegemonic globalizing imperialism of which he is a central part. Stencil's splintered identity reflects that of V., whose mercurial changes "force us to consider what constitutes identity, not to mention 'character' " (61), as Elizabeth Campbell has noted. An international vagrant, Stencil trails his father's diary, and he encounters evidence of the presence of V. in most of the historical episodes that he reviews during his search. The riddle of V.'s identity is for him a personal matter, an investigation into his father's life: "a legacy from his father" (*V.*, 155).

An obscure annotation in one of his father's journals from 1899 sets his entire quest in motion: "there is more behind and inside V. than any of us had suspected. Not who, but what: what is she" (*V.*, 53). Whatever or whoever V. might happen to be, its search is presented as a "grand Gothic pile of inferences" (*V.*, 226), an enormous catalogue of acts of violence—Stencil suspected "V.'s natural habitat to be the state of siege" (*V.*, 62)—and colonial exploitation. Stencil often dreams "perhaps once a week" that it had all been a dream and that "the pursuit of V. was merely a scholarly quest after all, an adventure of the mind, in the tradition of *The Golden Bough* or *The White Goddess*" (*V.*, 61). Ironically, when he is finally awake he realizes that it is not an intellectual, scholarly quest, but rather a libidinal quasi-onanistic one:

> . . . again the tiresome discovery that it hadn't really ever stopped being the same simple-minded, literal pursuit; V. ambiguously a beast of venery, chased like the hart, hind or hare, chased like an obsolete, or bizarre, or forbidden form of sexual delight. And clownish Stencil capering along behind her, bells ajingle, waving a wooden, toy oxgoad. For no one's amusement but his own. (*V.*, 61–62)

Stencil's childish isolated "amusement" takes the shape of an encyclopedic plot that sets off in countless directions, providing catalogs of signifiers and of violent events with possible traces of this evanescent signified:

> Finding her: what then? Only that what love there was to Stencil had become directed entirely inward, toward this acquired sense of animateness. Having found this he could hardly release it, it was too dear. To sustain it he had to hunt V.; but if he should find her, where else would there be to go but back into self-consciousness? He tried not to think, therefore, about any end to the search. Approach and avoid. (*V.*, 55)

Stencil's distanced and sardonic point of view, its double-voicedness, suggests that there is in fact a double search: the reader's search for textual and historical patterns and plots through the Gothic pile offered by the novel, and Stencil's own personal quest for meaning. Theodore Kharpertian detects in this distance the key to the novel's satiric parody on historiography: "The ridicule of Stencil's quest by the narrator, by Stencil himself, and by other characters (Eigenvalue and Maijstral, for example) makes it evident, therefore, that the V. narrative serves as a satiric parody of teleological historiography."[31] The reader of the text can follow an unearthing of the history of the first half of the twentieth century, whose narrative is explicitly exposed not as progress or a gleaming futurity, but as a continuum of usurpations, genocides, and wars without the teleological impulse that nationalist ideologues confer on it. *V.* collapses different and competing forms of historical and scientific knowledge, in a cannibalistic conflict that reaches its maximum saturation in Pynchon's *Gravity's Rainbow* (1973), where history's theme is the narration of technological Western progress as the "Kingdom of Death."[32] V. is for Stencil as unreachable as for Oedipa Mass the series of obscure conspiracies that plague the California landscape in *The Crying of Lot 49*. While playfully ("approach and avoid") looking at the history of genocides on which the empire of "the West" is built, the signifiers of a devastated human landscape satirically emphasize the character's blindness to his or her own political and historical responsibility in the apocalyptic events unfolding on the purported national space.

Part Two

✦

Dissenting from the Nation: The New Left

The three novels analyzed in this section, Fuentes's *La muerte de Artemio Cruz* (1962), Pynchon's *The Crying of Lot 49* (1966), and Fuentes's *Cambio de piel* (1967) refer directly to the immediate context of their audiences at the time of publication in order to historicize and subvert the Cold War nationalist consensus.[1] Their explicit parodies of nationalist discourse are inserted as a central part of what I have been calling postnational satires—a novel form which deploys a postmodern defiance of the grand narrative of the modern nation-state. In this section, I explore the primordial and recurrent idea of the nation as a patriarchal legacy, an inherited totem whose terms are critically examined from a different angle in each of these three novels in order to take to pieces the textual nature of the construct "nation." In *La muerte de Artemio Cruz,*[2] this inheritance is examined by the fractured conscience of the dying man in the process of bequeathing the nation to a yet unknown heir. In *The Crying of Lot 49* and in *Cambio de piel,* the nation as legacy is a composite ideological narrative that has to be comprehended and replicated by successive generations. All three novels underline the dysfunctional and privatized uses of national narratives, and the inability of the narrated official nation to account for social change and cultural diversity. While the present of *La muerte de Artemio Cruz* is located at the end of the 1950s, the other two novels are definitely set in the 1960s—*Lot 49* takes place during the summer of 1964 and *Cambio de piel* during Easter 1965. All three texts reiterate and stage central political debates of the period: the generational gap, the disenfranchisement of women, of racial and ethnic groups, the collapse of the American dream, and of the Mexican promise of modernity. The persistent authorial designs shared with the earlier novels *La región más transparente, V.,* and the short stories studied in the two previous chapters are evident: they parody the dominant discourses of modernity encapsulated in the textual, narrative constitution of the nation. My readings of these three novels emphasize their satirical critiques of American intervention abroad and the repressive policies at home—in both the United States and Mexico masqueraded under the shroud of Cold War nationalist consensus. These three critical narrations of the nation underline and denounce all-encompassing notions of national identity promoted by the Cold Warriors at the service of enforcing political consensus while concealing undeniable cultural and social divides.

La muerte de Artemio Cruz is not just a novel about the ways in which the postrevolutionary ruling class monopolized the national discourses of belonging and Mexicanness; it is also a study about the conflicting heterogeneity of Mexico as a postcolonial society. In contrast with essentialist readings of Mexican identity at the service of the nationalist revolutionary establishment, such as the ones put forward by the Hiperión group, and which Fuentes had already lampooned in *La región* as we saw in chapter 1, the author dialectically underscores in *Artemio Cruz* the foundational contradictions and essential heterogeneities of Mexican society. While the postrevolutionary national discourse of mestizo Mexicanness is revealed as yet another malleable and interested narrative, a reinvention of tradition that incorporates the new ruling elite and guarantees its hegemonic rule, the process of constantly unmaking Mexicanness seemingly turns out to be the only practicable national tradition. The "comunidad jánica," or Janus-faced community as the narrator labels it in *La muerte de Artemio Cruz,* is characterized by instability and reappropriation of national traditions by the ruling elites, a process that both necessitates and questions essentialist definitions of Mexicanness.

Political scientist Tom Nairn also makes use of the two-faced Roman deity of thresholds and gates, Janus, to symbolize the constant dialectical volatility of national identifications in industrialized societies. Nairn aims to represent nationalism itself as the ideological result of uneven development in its ambivalence between political cosmopolitanism and local affiliation, rationality and irrationality, as "both progress and regress are inscribed in its genetic code from the start."[3] This duplicitous, tortured nature of the "nation" and "nationalism"—simultaneously agents of globalized uneven development and local self-satisfaction—is extensively explored throughout chapter 3.

The collapse of the pyramid staged in *Cambio de piel* reinforces the image of the nation as a *damnosa hereditas,* a burdensome inheritance, subjugating characters whose only choices are either suffocating participation in the violent rituals of nationalism or exile.[4] Javier, the writer at the center of the novel, sets in motion a tension with Mexican nationalism reminiscent of the conundrum facing Norman Mailer in the early 1950s. For Mailer, the young *American* writer should be defiant of the grand narrative of Americanness, and in opposition to an earlier generation of writers, Dos Passos, Faulkner, Steinbeck, Farrell, and Hemingway, whose journey had come full circle back into the fold of nationalist propaganda: "from alienation to varying degrees of acceptance, if not outright proselytizing for the American century."[5] In Mailer's take, the young American writer should be "more concerned with 'silence, exile, and cunning,' than a strapping participation in the vigors of American life" (190). Thomas Pynchon's internal exilic practice combines the mode defended by Mailer with an unhindered critique of the American grand narrative of progress and nation, a way of proselytizing "against the American century"—"Against the day"—as I show in my analysis of *The Crying of Lot 49* in chapter 4.[6]

During the mid-1960s, relations between Mexico and the United States were dominated by efforts to cool down the region after one of the "hottest" Latin American episodes in the Cold War: the great nuclear scare of the 1962 Cuban missile crisis. Mexico's "privileged" position in the area as a go-between in the conflict over Cuba's growing Sovietization also meant an increase in American influence over Mexico itself.[7] Headed by Torres Bodet in the 1960s, Mexico's diplomacy staged a variety of distancing acts in an effort to disguise the growing American influence—the country had been increasingly flooded by American aid throughout the decade. A package of massive financial assistance to a number of countries in the hemisphere had already been agreed upon in 1961 under the banner of the "Alliance for Progress," as part of the effort by the Kennedy administration to influence the region both politically and economically.[8] Both the Soviet Union's interest in Cuba and later on in Nicaragua, and the United States' continued implementation of the nineteenth-century Monroe Doctrine through the partisan use of the Organization of American States (OAS) reconfirmed the status of Latin America as a disputed postcolonial territory.[9]

In his critique of this new wave of imperialism, *American Power and The New Mandarins* (1969), Noam Chomsky attacked the paternalistic justifications offered by the American liberal intellectual establishment. He denounced American "imperial efforts" in Vietnam, the Philippines, and Latin America as "directed to organizing (or restructuring) the society so as to ensure the domination of those elements that will enter into partnership with us."[10] Chomsky concluded that the new imperialism was being championed by technocrats and liberals alike, and he warned of the similarities between the American urbanization of the peasantry in Vietnam and the Nazi concentration camp. This neocolonial partnership between the United States and certain local "elements" is mobilized as a recurrent theme in Fuentes's fiction from the outset and is the central satirical allegation against the Mexican national bourgoisie.

The three novels studied in this section respond in different ways to the apparent gap between the internationalized ruling elites who economically own the country and culturally control the national discourses, and an increasingly manipulated, internally colonized population. Thus in all three novels we encounter a critique of American and Mexican national discourses and in particular, a critique of their hijacking by the amorphous corporate state in order to encourage consent. This critique does not promote, however, a return to a mystified unadulterated agrarian nation; it rather emphasizes and denounces the conflation of earlier nationalist discourses with the narratives of technological prowess. Chomsky is not alone here in drawing a parallel between the postwar technocracy and the fascist regimes of the first half of the century. Stemming from Hannah Arendt's 1950s study on totalitarianism as a prevalent ideological danger, this bridge between the political practices of both late capitalism, Stalinism, and Nazism is the ubiquitous image used by many political commentators in the 1960s, particularly those associated with the Frankfurt School and the emerging New Left. The worldwide resurgence of nationalism under the cover of a globalized capital constitutes a generalized expansion of political irrationalism, challenging and even defeating—at least in the bleak analysis advanced by Tom Nairn—the ethical and universalist aspirations of Western philosophy.[11]

Both Fuentes and Pynchon identify and strip bare different new ways of (intra)national colonization through transport, urbanization, and the media, which are intrinsically related to commodities that became widely available in the 1960s: the car, the radio, and the television. These new media which conform to what Fredric Jameson has called the "Consciousness Industry,"[12] are directly linked to a new process of colonization that targets the unconscious, a new site opened up for looting by the corporate state.[13] With the colonization of the (national) unconscious—an expression coined in part by Jameson in the first version of his seminal essay[14]—the old model of colonizer/colonized, center and periphery, partially collapses and is substituted by the image of the power web, by a "whole new decentered global network."[15] The two propositions are clearly immersed in the conventional Marxist view that capitalism is a "world system" (Wallerstein) that necessitates a "culture industry" (McLuhan, Adorno) characterized by its transference of "the profit motive naked onto cultural forms."[16] Jameson suggests that the contemporary representations of "some immense communicational and computer network" are "but a distorted figuration of something even deeper, namely the whole world system of a present-day multinational capitalism" (Jameson, *Postmodernism: or, the Cultural Logic of Late Capitalism,* 37). In *The Crying of Lot 49,* the image of the electronic "printed circuit" is noted by the main character, Oedipa Maas, on the San Narciso landscape. Its appearance is indeed a metaphor for the economic system whose assets the character has to chart as she executes Pierce Inverarity's will. Despite these moments of "illumination," I detect in Oedipa's search a failure to defy the perceptual predisposition imposed by the educational programming to which she has been subjected. Therefore the novel aims at unveiling the mechanisms by which national cultures replicate the message of social conformity and compliance to the capitalist mega-machine of internationalized production through a pervasive, allegedly local, nationalist consensus. Its conclusion, or its apparent lack of it, signifies a pessimistic reaffirmation of the inescapability of such a closed system by any single individual.

This mechanical image of the capitalist system is the most compelling description formulated by New Leftist intellectuals at the time: it was extensively explored by Lewis Mumford in his two-volume *The Myth of the*

Machine (1967–70) and by Herbert Marcuse in his *One-Dimensional Man*. In Mumford's account, the ancient mega-machine is resurrected through the new set of mechanizing disciplines imposed on society by a globalized capitalism. In this powerful indictment of the interpenetration of the military-industrial complex, the mega-machine acquires the outward appearance not so much of the urban grid that he had explored in *The City in History,* but of a *Pentagon of Power,* an image that he suitably compared with the ancient pyramids of Egypt and Mexico.[17] Herbert Marcuse also reviewed in *Eros and Civilization* (1955) and, particularly, in *One-Dimensional Man* (1964) the contribution of the two opposing economic systems of the Cold War to the development of a highly industrialized society and a mechanized man. In his two books, Marcuse concentrates on the effects of mechanization on the individual psyche of people living in late capitalist societies, and in particular in the United States, but he is also concerned with the effects of the bureaucratic technocracy of the heavily industrialized communist bloc. In the United States, this control is conspicuously carried out through the conversion of the citizen into a consumer, as Vance Packard had suggested a few years earlier in *The Hidden Persuaders* (1957). This "one-dimensional man" is a reified human being who experiences the "pure form of servitude: to exist as an instrument, as a thing."[18] As Adorno had also anticipated, the mega-machine attains hegemony through the efficient use of the culture industry which "speculates on the conscious and unconscious state of the millions toward which it is directed, [however] the masses are not primary, but secondary, they are an object of calculation; an appendage of the machinery" (Adorno, *Culture Industry,* 99). The sense that the masses have in fact become an appendage, another cog in the machine, is prevalent in the countercultural movements of the 1960s in which these novels are immersed.

Theodore Roszak conceptualized the term "counterculture" in 1968 around its opposition to technocracy defined as a "social form in which an industrial society reaches the peak of its organizational integration."[19] Again, culture is presented as a set of manipulated discourses by which the values of the technocracy are put forward: "Politics, education, leisure, entertainment, culture as a whole, the unconscious drives, and even . . . protest against the technocracy itself: all these become the subjects of purely technical scrutiny and of purely technical manipulation" (6). In both Adorno and Roszak there is an arresting emphasis on the psychological manipulations effected by cultural discourses, particularly on the unconscious drives and on the non-rational aspects of human behavior that owes some theoretical premises to Wilhelm Reich's *The Mass Psychology of Fascism.*[20] Following Reich, they too identify the control of the sexual drives as a prominent objective in the process of domination of the masses by the mega-machine which creates "a truly totalitarian universe in which society and nature, mind and body are kept in a state of permanent mobilization for the defense of this universe."[21]

Fuentes emphasizes these contradictions by carrying out in *Cambio de piel* a Foucauldian exploration of the neocolonial structures of power and knowledge in Mexico through the image of the asylum as a space reserved for political dissent. The political deployment of clinical psychiatry is also contested by Pynchon, particularly in its role of shaping unconscious desires and ideological practices, through the caricature of the Nazi exile Doctor Hilarius. The appearance of Foucault's poststructuralist questioning of Western scientific discourse in *Les mots et les choses* (*The Order of Things*) in 1966, and his earlier *Histoire de la folie* (*Madness and Civilization*) in 1961, were used by Fuentes to build on his already well-established trajectory as a critic of institutionalized normalcy, mainstream identities, and neocolonial dependencies. Breaking away from the solid muralist depiction of struggling nation-states, with well-defined iconic boundaries—an essential item of the national discourses for the postrevolutionary Mexican establishment—Fuentes underlines in *Cambio de piel* the convoluted mixture of individual, corporate, and ideological interests in the clash over psychological, cultural, and economic hegemony.

Perhaps the most innovative aspect of these neocolonial struggles is their effect on the political landscape of the United States. From the assassination of John F. Kennedy to the reorganization of the New Left around university campuses, most of the political events of the decade are linked in one way or another to American intervention in Cuba, Vietnam, and elsewhere.[22] The arms race between the two superpowers throughout the Cold War had a similar double orientation, for it increasingly became not just a source of deterrent power abroad, but also the driving force of the American economy at home. In his much-quoted farewell address, President Eisenhower warned against the loss of political liberties caused by the expansion of the "military-industrial complex," a statement that can be seen as one of the starting points in the public display of distrust toward the emerging technocracy.[23] As Arthur Marwick has pointed out in his *The Sixties*, Eisenhower's phrase "applied particularly aptly to California, the site for the production of much of America's most advanced military technology; here the interpenetration between business, government, and university had reached the highest level."[24] In Pynchon's *The Crying of Lot 49*, California and in particular the city's grid shape in the fictional township of San Narciso is the compelling symbol of the corporate state and its mechanization of the polis. The "lot 49" is itself a direct allusion to the forty-niners, the gold-mining colonizers who flooded the former Mexican state from 1849, after the 1846–1848 war of annexation, and just a few months after the Guadalupe-Hidalgo Treaty was signed.[25] Thus, the ambiguous "crying" of the title announces both the selling out of the American dream-mirage and the mourning for its ancient, impossible promise.

Although countercultural movements risked being absorbed back into the system, as part of a new national "young folklore," their oppositional value resided according to Roszak in their "visionary imagination," that is, in a specifically different perception of reality. As I will show in my readings of *La muerte de Artemio Cruz, The Crying of Lot 49,* and *Cambio de piel,* all three novels construed their critique of the technocratic discourses of containment and affluence precisely around the characters' inability to develop an alternative perspective on reality to the ones offered by the consensual discourses of the modern nation-state. In particular, the play with the role of gazing at reality, or naming reality, is prevalent in the last two texts. At the center of the discussion in these texts is the dissolution of heterogeneity and subjectivity under these new forms of colonization. If the media's message is one of "adjustment and unreflecting obedience,"[26] it is carried out successfully partly thanks to the breakdown of the concept of the subject, and its inability to conceive the system as a whole.[27] Deleuze and Guattari explore in their *Anti-Oedipus* the relation between the discursive practices of Freudian psychoanalysis and the production of what they call "desiring machines." They set off to investigate whether "schizophrenia is the product of the capitalist machine as manic-depression and paranoia are the product of the despotic machine."[28] Their "schizoanalysis" can be of some assistance in the reading of these three novels as they also explore the disjunctions of subjective identities, the schizophrenia of their constitution under the pressures on their unconscious exerted by the new capitalist machine aided by psychiatric technologies. As García Canclini has noted: "It is not simply a question of some forms of domination being superimposed on others and thereby being strengthened. What gives them their efficacy is the obliqueness that is established in the fabric."[29] That obliqueness lies in the way national discourses mobilize political irrationality and colonize the unconscious, breaking up stable or "rational" subjectivities while fostering an international system of production based on an uneven development that remains politically unimpeded.[30]

The role of psychiatry in absorbing individual anxieties and marking the path to social assent and to "moderation" is fiercely critiqued in *The Crying of Lot 49* and *Cambio de piel.* Once psychiatry becomes conflated with nationalist paraphernalia, Oedipa Maas hallucinates with the image of Uncle Sam threateningly pointing at her. Not only Pierce Inverarity and Dr. Hilarius, but also Oedipa and Mucho Maas in *The Crying of Lot 49,* and Franz and Javier, Isabel and Elizabeth in *Cambio de piel* are subjects in crisis; their identities are continuously redefined depending on the media in which they are expressing themselves. Oedipa Maas becomes Edna Mosh as she speaks on the radio. In addition, the four characters at the center of *Cambio de piel* are constantly in motion, their identities interwoven by their names and, at times, by their interchangeable voices. Their striking coincidence with Foucault's vision at the end of *The Order of Things* (1966) where the logical downfall of enlightened reason announces the erasure of "man," "like a face drawn in the sand at the edge of the sea" (387), is symptomatic of a widespread anxiety about the prospect of human extinction through either mechanization or nuclear armageddon. The three texts analyzed here differ in many aspects, as they address and critique specifically different audiences and national discourses, the American and the Mexican. For Fuentes in *Cambio de piel,* the pre-technological system of domination still in place in Mexican society finds its expression in myths and symbols such as the pyramid, Mumford's ancient mega-machine, where contemporary power is also deposited as the new generation inherits and devours the older one. In Pynchon, the overpowering, prescient image of a computer which functions in ones and zeroes and whose technology charts and configures the lot 49 that is California contrasts with the other computer, the analogical "computer of the lost," the mattress where all the private memories, those of the "excluded middles," are stored and immediately put *sous-rature,* both present and absent, legible but hidden. These human remains are unreadable in the either/or binary system.

Even as they countered prevalent colonizing practices, these novels were also immediately immersed in the cultural machine, the educational machine, and they became instantaneously recycled back into the academic milieu, incorporated into syllabi and the canon of American and Mexican national literatures respectively. However, the realization that their critique can be absorbed back into the national mega-machine does not defuse them automatically as political acts, but it should rather underscore their renewed capabilities as internal oppositional texts, narratives that dialectically promote a break in the national discourse of consensus with every new reading, every time they are activated.

Chapter 3

La muerte de Artemio Cruz and the Agonic Mexican Nation

Fuentes's 1962 novel *La muerte de Artemio Cruz* scrutinizes the political and social outcome of the Mexican Revolution through the image of an agonizing revolutionary who stands as a symbol of both the revolution and the Mexican nation reborn in its aftermath. As in *La región más transparente,* the betrayal of emancipatory ideals characterizes the revolutionary ruling classes. *La región más transparente* proposes a full-blown satirical panorama, a complex representation of Mexican society in full, where all Mexicans seem to be existentially condemned for their individual and communal participation in the betrayal of radical ideals. In *La muerte de Artemio Cruz,* the focus of attention is placed on one character allegorically used to parody the figure of the caudillo, the leader and savior who is subjected to a moral scrutiny.

Listen, Yankee!

I will start my analysis of the novel by alluding to a much neglected point of *La muerte de Artemio Cruz:* its dedication. Despite the novel's apparent anti-Yankee jeremiad, the book is dedicated to the American sociologist C. Wright Mills, "verdadera voz de Norteamérica, amigo y compañero en la lucha de Latinoamérica" (true voice of North America, friend and comrade in the Latin-American struggle). Fuentes's little-commented debt to Mills extends well into the end of the decade, surfacing again in his meditations on the contrast between the United States and Latin America at the close of his influential *La nueva novela hispanoamericana* (1969).[1] Perhaps even more important for the social history of the Latin American literary boom of the novel than Fuentes's well-known essay is Mills's bequest to Carlos Fuentes: his literary agent in New York, Carl Brandt. During his fifteen-month-long agony, Wright Mills wrote a couple of letters to Carlos Fuentes. In the last one, dated January 12, 1961, Mills advised Fuentes that "at just this point all kinds of Mexican writers, as well as writers from other Latin American countries (at least outside Cuba!) can find an audience."[2] With this legacy, he was promising Fuentes his future large audience in the United States, while offering a way of entry for the new Latin American novel of the 1960s into the American literary market, a key step in the literary boom that followed.[3]

Wright Mills was one of the founding fathers of the American New Left, born in and of the struggles of the 1950s: a period usually associated with conformity and political containment in the U.S., and which turned out to be the indispensable foundation of the radical 1960s. His writings from this period belong to a long American tradition of independent radicalism—he was a Quaker—which criticized the American establishment as a "white collar" "power elite." These phrases come from two of his most famous books, which thoroughly challenged prevailing national discourses and their celebration of the health of American democracy as the beacon of Western freedom. Norman Mailer and many of his contemporary writers in the New Left would be influenced by Mills's groundbreaking studies of the social makeup of American society. As Fuentes's case demonstrates, these studies also provided a common backdrop for writers of the period outside the United States.[4]

Mills's interest in Latin America, particularly in Cuba at the time of the 1959 revolution, produced a vigorous criticism of the American neo-imperialist involvement on the island, alerting Americans about their role in the creation of the resentful nationalist movement led by Castro. Carlos Fuentes would meet Mills for the first time in revolutionary Cuba in 1960 while writing *La muerte de Artemio Cruz,* just a few months before the publication of Mills's polemical *Listen, Yankee: The Revolution in Cuba* (1960). The novel is dated "La Habana, Mayo de 1960. México, diciembre de 1961." In *Listen, Yankee* Mills tried to produce a Cuban voice that could explain directly to a wide American audience the anti-imperialist stand of the 1959 revolution at a time when it was still unclear if it would side with the Soviet bloc, a prospect Mills himself did not want to publicize much.[5] This pamphlet leads to the third and last point about Mills and his relevance as the dedicatee of the novel: his implicit dissent from Stalinism, the more dogmatic tenets of "real-existing socialism" and its paralyzed, monolithic Marxist dialectics—a dissent that would go on to become the hallmark of the New Left.[6]

In 1960, the situation in Cuba was becoming increasingly tense, and pressure was growing on the revolutionaries to declare their sympathies for one of the two political blocs of the Cold War. Fuentes's new leftist hope for a permanent revolution defined as "the daily conquest of the exocentric margin of truth, creativity, and of a disorder with which to confront the orthodox order"[7] signaled his opposition by the mid-1960s to the ossified Stalinist orthodoxies under which the Cuban Revolution would fall. The Cuban Revolution had disappointingly for him transitioned from a symbol of New Left aspirations to another victory of bureaucratic and *caudillista* dogmatism.[8] Fuentes's joking remark in closing, "give me five, Feodor Mihailovitch and Lev Davidovitch," shows Fuentes's singular mixture of popular American culture with his support for the long-standing tradition of Mexican Trotskyism, a productive combination that pervades these early works. This public statement of Fuentes's political creed can be easily traced in his contemporary fiction. A significant aspect of Fuentes's fluid work, and self-quotation, his continuous transference between his essays and his fiction is made patent by the resurfacing of a similarly worded allusion to the heterodox revolution in *Cambio de piel*, published only a year later: "Permanent revolution is permanent heterodoxy, not a moment of illumination condemned between two Establishments. Permanent revolution is the daily conquest of the outer limits of truth, creativity, the disorder that must always oppose the orthodox. Shake them up, Feodor Mihailovitch and Lev Davidovitch" (*CP*, 287/289). But the narrator of *Cambio de piel* was even more explicit and cynical about the circular, regressive moment in which he saw the Cuban revolutionaries: "as my Cuban cousins who happen to be at bat now would put it: for virtue leads to peace, peace to idleness, idleness to rebellion, rebellion to destruction, destruction to order, and order to virtue, and here we go again in the hall of many mirrors" (*CP*, 286/288–89). At many other points in Fuentes's fictional works narrator and author collude through an unabashed self-citation as a reminder not so much of pastiche or playful intertextuality, but of the political uses of fiction: these fluid literary intertexts constitute a hybrid literary text that points to the shadow of an author. Fuentes's uninterrupted questioning of political dogmatism and orthodoxy in both essay and fiction permanently visits the margins, and yet it is paradoxically absorbed into the literary canon of a refurbished establishment.

Mills, very much like Fuentes, persistently hoped and labored for an independent revolutionary movement in Cuba that would stay away from the bureaucratic nightmares of Eastern Europe, but also from the imposing pressures of American intervention.[9] The ensuing history is well known, and it is only relevant here in one respect: Cuba's revolution declared for the Soviet bloc in December 1961 and began to promote a hegemonic idea of the nation that did not leave room for Fuentes's or Mills's imaginings of more radical internationalist and democratic models. Fanon had identified around those same years the role of leaders in nationalist revolutions of decolonization, and exacted the problematic identification of the nation and the leader who "before independence, . . . generally embodies the aspirations of the people for independence, political liberty, and national dignity."[10] Fanon's radical democratic manifesto reclaimed the nation for the entire people, maintaining that "no leader, however valuable he may be, can substitute himself for the popular will" (*Wretched of the Earth*, 205). It is at this precise point that the complexly nuanced gestures and the tyrannical character agonizing in *La muerte de Artemio Cruz* become relevant.[11]

Fuentes appears to have written most of the novel in Cuba during the first year of the revolution, and yet his main target was clearly postrevolutionary Mexico, and the combined discourses of (institutionalized) revolution and nationalism. Artemio Cruz, the agonizing revolutionary whose fragmented memories are spread throughout the novel, carries the nation on his shoulders; or rather the reified image of the nation hangs around his neck. One of the many lengthy catalogs of the novel exotically summarizes most things "Mexican" carried by Artemio: "the red deserts, the hills of prickly pear and maguey, the world of day cactus, the lava belt of frozen craters, the walls of golden domes and rock thrones, the limestone and sandstone cities, the tezontlestone cities, the adobe pueblos, the reed-grass hamlets" (*MAC*, 366/232). This stereotyped Mexican landscape reminiscent of the ubiquitous postrevolutionary representations of Mexico, such as Eisenstein's celebratory film *¡Que Viva México!* (1932); Rivera's panoramic murals; and many of the other contemporary aestheticized notions of Mexicanness, are constantly contradicted in the novel by the country's very heterogeneity. Mexico, which "is not one; there are a thousand countries, with a single name" (*MAC*, 365/232), is a fragmentary reality whereupon such reductive, centralizing grand narratives of the nation have time and again been forced. This central national project of the revolution is identified with the agonizing Artemio Cruz by the interpolative narrative voice which says to the character: "you will carry these with you and they are leaden, they are stone heavy for one man: they have never moved and you have them bound to your neck; they weigh you down, they have entered your guts, they are your bacilli, your parasites, your amoebas" (*MAC*, 366/232). The tired, institutionalized nationalist discourse breathes and lives *in* and *through* Artemio Cruz. It colonizes the character much as a microorganism would, constituting perhaps one of the most striking images of assimilation of stereotypical national symbols by a single character in Mexican literature.

Thus, the novel would not only be "the first attempt to literarily integrate the social, ethnic and geographic totality of the nation,"[12] as Mexican writer Rosario Castellanos suggested at the time, but more importantly a successful attempt to satirically summarize the nationalist agenda of the revolutionary class. Artemio stands then for that entire national bourgeoisie and its hegemonic PRI rule, with its homogenizing discourse of *mestizaje* and its idealized naturalized community called Mexico. As such, Artemio is an inverted allegory, a full-blown parody, which articulates Fuentes's denunciation of the political uses of nationalist consensus by the postrevolutionary political elite. As the "motherland" he inherits, "heredarás la tierra" ("you will inherit the land") (*MAC*, 367/233), comes to be identified with Artemio Cruz himself, his agony also becomes that of the nation. Cruz carries with him an odd catalog of national symbols that converge on him to constitute the nation, summarized as "la tierra," he inherits, and which in turn he must now pass on as he dies. All these fragments of the nation are amalgamated in a crucible, within the figure of the agonizing Cruz. I want to build my discussion of the novel around this identification, this symbolic and parodic treatment of the postrevolutionary nationalist regime.[13]

Artemio Cruz stands for that entire class of Mexican revolutionaries who institutionalized the revolution through the constant use of nationalist symbols in order to cement a political consensus and to become the new ruling class, what Fanon termed the "national bourgeoisie." Thus, his heritage is among other things that new social position; his heirs "will accept your legacy: the decency that you acquired for them: they will offer up thanks to barefoot Artemio Cruz because he made them people of position" (*MAC*, 367/233). "They," Artemio's heirs, the next generation, won't be able to take refuge in the revolutionary discourse to carry on with the "sanctioned greed": "they will not be able to speak of their battles and captains, as you can, and shield themselves behind glory to justify rapine in the name of the Revolution, self-aggrandizement in the name of the Revolution" (*MAC*, 367/234). As Artemio wonders "what justification will they find?" (*MAC*, 367/234), it becomes clear that cynicism toward the institutionalized revolutionary discourse is Fuentes's driving motif.

The coverage of the Cuban Revolution in Artemio's newspaper is a telling example of the extent to which he has used the revolution for "rapine" and "self-aggrandizement." His newspaper openly supports the institutionalized Mexican Revolution and its nationalist narratives, inventing and broadcasting renewed national traditions. As the American ambassador in Mexico City is preparing a speech on the contrast between the Cuban and the Mexican revolutions, Artemio is generously asked to collaborate with an editorial "to prepare the climate" (*MAC*, 301/173) in exchange for twenty thousand pesos. Artemio's rewriting of the institutionalized "legal" Mexican Revolution as a form of direct advice to the neocolonial representative completes the picture of a cynical self-conscious regime of historical manipulation: "Tell him to establish a clear contrast between an anarchic, bloody movement that is destructive of private property and human rights alike, and an ordered revolution, peaceful and legal, such as the Mexican Revolution, which was directed by a middle class inspired by Jefferson. The people have short memories" (*MAC*, 302/173). While the memory of the nation is bought and deformed by the U.S. embassy, its heroes are in the process compared and transfigured into the American ones, and the national traditions, the nation's history reinvented as both liberal and orderly. Artemio's newspaper, situated at the center of print capitalism and the national consciousness industry, broadcasts an alternate history which serves the purposes of a double colonization: the internal national colonization by the ruling class, and the external colonization by U.S. interests. The contradictory duplicity of Artemio's social class, which narrates its genealogy through the erasure of its historical roots, parallels also the apparent contradictions of its nationalist ideology: a seemingly local discourse at the service of transnational, neocolonial capital.

As much as he opposed American intervention in Latin America and its renewed imperialist forms, Fuentes's affinities with the American New Left also led him to reject the totalitarian nationalist options that had continuously shaped colonial and postcolonial politics in Latin America. His works provide a critical view of nationalist discourses as outlets of a hegemonic postcolonial nationalism that often becomes paradoxically neocolonial in its practices. In *Listen Yankee* C. Wright Mills had also condemned the double standards of the Mexican Revolution: "a revolution that began with the demand for land and for liberty [that] seems to be ending in a plutocracy sitting within their state and on top of a capitalist economy—and full of revolutionary rhetoric" (172). Fuentes's novel is not just a critique of the disconnect between rhetoric and praxis exercised by the new plutocracy emerging out of the Mexican Revolution—most novels of the revolution seem to offer such a critique, according to Max Aub and many others.[14] Apart from formal considerations, the innovative contribution of Fuentes's novel to the genre of the Mexican novel of the revolution appears to be its critique of the flawed revolutionary rhetoric to which Mills had also alluded: corporate nationalism.

The failure by Porfirio Díaz's technocratic regime (1876–1910) at creating a popular national discourse or a liberal democratic Mexican nation-state had simply hidden under the carpet of bureaucratic positivism the multiple layers of ethnic, gender, and class identifications of an ever more multifaceted Mexico. However, Justo Sierra, the towering late-nineteenth-century intellectual and apologist of the early Porfiriato, had identified the period of the Reforma with the constitution of a new national consensus:

> The Republic was then the nation; with neglected exceptions, everyone attended the triumph, all understood that there was a final and completed event, that conquests had been made that would be eternal in history, that the Reformation, the Republic and the mother country were, from that moment onwards, the same thing, and that there was no more than one national flag, the Constitution of Fifty Seven;[15] with it, everyone became a citizen again, a Mexican, a free man. Both winners and losers, by the incontrovertible force of an idea that contained all the future of Mexico, had to be united in a common yearning: to fulfill the rule of laws and rights, to enthrone Justice.[16]

Written at the turn of the century, this reflection by one of Mexico's most respected political philosophers prefigures Benedict Anderson's account of the founding of nations as imagined communities whose genealogies are built around a reassuring fratricidal consensus.[17] The cementing force behind this idea, the sacred text of the 1857 Constitution, effectively creates the nation whose flag and law unify both "winners and losers," "chingones and chingados" in an apparent consensus. For Fuentes, La Revolución Mexicana alleges to have refounded the nation once again in the first quarter of the century as a new expression of a *mestizaje* whose epicenter is the social climber and plutocrat Artemio Cruz. In the novel, a mixed-race Artemio Cruz represents the opening up of national and social imaginings provided by the 1910 Revolution, but which failed to fully enfranchise or genuinely democratize society.[18] His duplicity is a playful avatar of the stereotypical duplicitous nature of the Mexican, a *malinchismo* that cuts both ways: *Malinche* as the originator of the Mexican mestizo, the new race, and as the indigenous female traitor of the community, both the tyrant and its savior.

The sense that history repeats itself, and that the nation continuously betrays its believers and those who sacrificed themselves for its inception is a recurring theme for the generation born during and after the revolution, to which Fuentes and Paz belonged. In *The Labyrinth of Solitude,* Paz analyzed the major contradictions of revolutionary nationalism:

> In a certain sense, the Revolution has recreated the nation; in another sense, it has extended the nation to races and classes that neither the colony nor the XIX century were able to incorporate. . . . [But] the Revolution has not turned our country into a community, or even into a hope of a community: a world in which men can see themselves in other men, and where the "principle of authority"—that is, force, whatever its origin and justification—cedes its place to responsible freedom.[19]

The painful realization of the frustrated attempt of the revolution at creating a community goes hand in hand with the even more excruciating fact that "nationalist capitalism," as Paz calls it,[20] is based on the old patriarchal structure of caudillos and caciques.[21] At this point Paz's and Fuentes's analysis of the revolution seem to merge with Orwell's cynical look at revolution as a replacement of one oppressive elite by another in *Animal Farm* (1945): Mexican nationalism reenacts a cycle of social and discursive renewal which ultimately fails to empower the community.

The Janus Face of the Nation

At its height, the institutionalized revolution celebrated the image of the pyramid as the appropriate symbol of Mexican society, an image that Fuentes fiercely attacks later on in *Cambio de piel.* Throughout the 1950s, one of the major advocates of this pyramidal organization of the postcolonial polity in Mexico was Leopoldo Zea, who demagogically justified the totalitarian practices of the Partido Revolucionario Institucional (PRI), and its reliance on the figure of the male president as the expression of the nation:

> Where this element of national unification is made more patent within the field of affection is in the figure of the President of the Republic,

> greatest leader [*caudillo*] and greatest friend of the Mexicans. He is not, like among other peoples a symbolic figure who works in the name of the Nation, but the highest expression of the only type of specific action and concrete relation of a society like ours. The President of the Republic is perceived, and in fact he is, like the highest manufacturer and supplier of all the national necessities. . . . All the aspects and political means of the Nation depend on this capacity, which in the last analysis is the capacity of a concrete individual to be the friend, not only of a group or a conglomerate, but of all the Mexicans.[22]

Such fatalistic description of Mexican society, and by extension of Cuban and other Latin American societies, as made up of immature people who have to be guided into modernity by a father figure, a "friend of all," who carries the entire nation on his shoulders, celebrates renewed forms of *caudillismo*. Paz noticed how at the center of the Mexican family is "the father" whose figure "is divided in the duality of the patriarch and the *macho*. The patriarch protects; he is good, generous, powerful, and wise. The macho is the terrible man, the fucker [*chingón*], the father who has left, who has abandoned wife and children. The image of Mexican authority is inspired by these two extremes: Mister President, and the *Caudillo*."[23] At the core of the Janus-faced community is the Janus-faced chieftain, the two roles conflated in Artemio—both the savior and the terrible fucker, the *chingón*. The second-person voice of his conscience reminds him:

> You are who you are because you fuck 'em without letting them fuck you; you are what you are because you didn't fuck around: chain-gang of the fucked, linked before and behind, joined to all who have lost and preceded us, to all who will lose and follow us: heir to being fucked by those who stand above you, inheriting the right to fuck those who crawl below you. (*MAC*, 244/123)

The "word," the Mexican curse word *chingar,* is echoed throughout the novel as the defining feature of all that joins and divides Mexicans; for that reason its impossible erasure becomes the painful obsession of Artemio's dying conscience: "murder the word that stands between us, makes stone of us, rots us with its poison mixed of idolatry and the cross: so that it cannot be either our reply or our destiny" (*MAC*, 124). A word which Paz had defined in *The Labyrinth of Solitude* as the Mexican "password," used as a way of affirming a feeling of national belonging, "mexicanidad,"[24] but also at the heart of a "conception of social life as a combat [which] fatally engenders the division of society between the strong and the weak. The strong—the fuckers [*chingones*] with no scruples, dour and inflexible—surround themselves with ardent and interested fidelities" (Paz, 95).

The *chingada,* a national "destiny," is described by both Fuentes and Paz with the image of a chain that joins all Mexicans in the interplay of power politics: an interplay which is also importantly applicable to gender relations, as the first "chingada," is the Malinche, both the mother of the mestizo, ravished by Cortés at the time of the Spanish conquest, and by the same token, the first traitor to an impossible indigenous sense of national purity: Malinche was a key translator and mediator in the conquest. The general inclusion of all Mexicans inside this pyramidal and patriarchal system becomes contested in the novel through the questioning of the frozen temporal structures, linear or circular, on which it rests. At the center of the authorial preoccupations behind or inside *La muerte de Artemio Cruz* is the subversion of the "unity of destiny," Anderson's "empty time," which characterizes the unity of the national state. Such breaking up of the chronological unity of the nation is accompanied by a critique of the patriarchal location of the national discourse. Both the critique of time and gender structures become central themes which give the text its parodic focus.

The fragmented narration in *La muerte de Artemio Cruz,* as in the case of its high modernist predecessors in the English-speaking world such as William Faulkner's *As I Lay Dying* (1930), or Virginia Woolf's *Mrs. Dalloway* (1925), breaks away from the homogeneous, empty time which nineteenth-century nationalist novels promote according to Anderson and others.[25] This fragmentation of the temporal flow in *La muerte de Artemio Cruz* has been accurately described by Edna Aizenberg as "a means of interrogating the nation."[26] As I argue here, however, it can be seen not just as a means of questioning, but also of interrupting the nation's proclaimed consensus and its flow into the future empty time of hegemonic progress.

La muerte de Artemio Cruz portrays the Mexican nation as a community constantly fractured along the cracks of the conflicting temporal spheres of winners and losers—and where the times of the losers, the "chingados," are continuously denied and erased by the official linear times of the "chingones." These two competing time zones construct the Janus-faced failed community of preterit projects and subjunctive desires, as the character's conscience realizes: "Always the two times in this double-faced Janus community, so far from what it was, so far from what it wanted to be"[27] (*MAC,* 128). Fuentes's proposition is echoed in Paz's 1970 addition to *The Labyrinth of Solitude,* his *Postdata,* but there Paz emphasizes heterogeneity as an inherent feature not just of Mexican society, but of all national and social constructs that results from the divides and contradictions taking place at the individual level:

> If man is double or triple, so are also societies and civilizations. Each people performs a dialogue with an invisible interlocutor who is simultaneously himself and the other, his double. His double? Which is the original one and which the ghost? . . . there is no exterior or

> interior, and alterity is not out there, outside, but over here, inside: alterity is ourselves.[28]

Paz's existentialist dialectics evokes the constellation of individual internal fractures of desires and estrangements as a harbinger of social contradictions and opposing alterities. These splintered individual voices overflow onto the "comunidad jánica," a community whose foundational appeal for unity and homogeneity is haunted by the continuously argumentative Janus faces of its individual members. Similarly, from the beginning of the novel, there is a distance that both reifies and fragments Cruz into broken factions and features. Artemio is that "someone else. Someone in a mirror in front of his sickbed" (*MAC,* 118/12). He is always someone else, one other, "another," both self and other, in a *mise-en-abime* succession of identities which foregrounds his status as the avatar of the Janus-like nation.

One of the many indications of Artemio's two-faced principles is to be found in his intellectual affiliation with American capital, besides and beyond his professional activities as an agent of American colonization in Mexico through business deals such as the newspaper article mentioned above. Artemio's inner dialectics reveals the increasing colonization by Northern luxury and consumerism.[29] His Mexican national identity is gradually lived and understood as geographical slippage, a remainder that stops him from becoming fully metropolitan and fully realized: "For ever since you began to be what you are, to learn to appreciate the feel of fine cloth, the taste of good liquor, the scent of rich lotions, all those things that in recent years have been your only, isolated pleasures; ever since then you have lived with regret for the geographical error that has prevented you from being one of them" (*MAC,* 138/30).

This stereotyped opposition between a preterit "chingado" Mexican "us" and a triumphant Yankee "them" confirms that not only has the new ruling national bourgeoisie allegorized by Artemio successfully liquidated the popular revolution through its co-option by U.S. capital,[30] its nationalist discourse of comparative inferiority has also replicated locally the metropolitan view of the unpreparedness, the faultiness of Mexican society that justifies the imposed uneven development: "You admire their efficiency, their comforts, their hygiene, their power, their strength of will, and you look around you and find intolerable the incompetence, misery, dirt, the weakness and nakedness of this impoverished country that has nothing" (*MAC,* 138/30). Artemio physically suffers the process of cultural appropriation: "You ache because you know that no matter how hard you try, you can never be what they are but become at most only a pale copy, a near approximation" (*MAC,* 183/30). The only relief to the impossibility of bridging that "geographical error" of two fractured national identities, the Americanized ruling Mexican, is the refuge in the supposedly pure nature of Mexicanidad, as a distinctly blurred, "mestizo" moral discourse:

> For after all—confess it—has your vision of things, in your best and worst moments, ever been so simple as theirs? Never. Never have you been able to think in terms of blacks and whites, goods and evils, God and the devil. Confess that always, even when it has seemed otherwise, you have found in black the germ of its opposite; your own cruelty, when you have been cruel, has it not been tinged with a certain tenderness? (*MAC,* 138/30)

Faced with the painful realization that the faraway promising future identity would be a borrowed narration "at most only a pale copy, a near approximation," Artemio's conscience points once again to the benefits of a conscious *malinchismo* as the basis for the *comunidad jánica,* one that can be both cruel and gentle at once, and in that process become aware of its permanent contradictions and fragments. The novel itself is not just a collection of fragments, but a novel *about* fragmentation.[31] This ruling principle of moral fragmentation and identity slippage is manifested through the constantly ruptured temporal narratives, syntactic breakages, and multiple narrative voices, a miscellany of textual disjunctions that stand for the protagonist's, or rather the agonist's ontological wreckage. These narrative strategies deploy the satirical disjunctiveness, the shattering of the temporal and spatial apparatus of consensual nationalist rhetoric.

A Novel About Fragments

The ways in which these cinematic fragmentations take shape have been a significant focus of the novel's critical reception. Sarah Radcliffe and Sallie Westwood have noted how after the revolution "film—and not writing—was the medium through which national identity was articulated and consolidated."[32] At the helm of this identity/cultural industry was, however, U.S. investment and local Mexican collaboration with American interests. Seth Fein has amply studied this collaboration in his study of Mexican cinema during World War II which developed a tense "nationalist rendering of anti-Axis collaboration" (161). By looking at productions of historical cinema such as *¡Mexicanos al grito de guerra!, historia del himno nacional* (1943) and critiques of Good Neighbor relations in *Los tres García* (1946), Fein maintains that the Mexican state fostered a "pseudo-anti-Americanism [devised] to fortify its own rule based on a half-century of elite collaboration with the United States."[33] Through the cultural mega-machine of the cinematic medium, the postrevolutionary Mexican polity invested itself with an outer discourse, nationalism, to disprove its veiled participation and even its increasing co-optation by the imperial influence of the United States. In order to substantiate that renewed national iconography, these films also fostered a sense of continuity of time, the time of the nation, and most importantly in the case of *Los tres García,* as Fein makes clear, a humor based on the rearticulation of Mexican masculinity. The lexical slippage of welcoming the rapprochement of the "americanas," female Americans, rather than that of the Americas provides Fein with a turning point for a whole discussion of the cinematic "remasculinization of Mexican identity" (160). These two elements, linear time, the consensual time of Progress, and patriarchal gender relations are time and again at the core of the constitution of Mexican "revolutionary" nationalism, and they are also the main elements targeted by Fuentes's fragmented postnational satires.

Cruz's history is a story of constant duplicity and treason that runs parallel to the nation's flow. In *Artemio Cruz,* the nation is also constituted as a purely male foundation which cannot be inherited by his only daughter, Teresa, who continuously voices her derision for Cruz at his deathbed: "even what he loved, he destroyed" (*MAC,* 301/186).[34] Their mutual dislike is also an "incestuous intercourse" of sorts that secures the family bond through a chain of mutual *chingadas.* Although Teresa's attack is confirmed by Artemio—"my only love has been material possessions, sensual acquisition" (*MAC,* 239/118)—she is in turn seen by him as a wingless bat waiting for her inheritance by his bedside. As they prey on each other, Teresa for Artemio's will, and Artemio on her unfitness as an heir to his media empire, they confirm the pyramidal system of power whose upper places are only reserved for the male.[35] The pathetic search of both Catalina and Teresa for Artemio's will is an important point missed by most of the commentators of the novel who have studied the role of its female characters. These two female figures interestingly symbolize the passive participation, or even the active connivance, of many women in the patriarchal game of power and capital speculation. They also reproduce Cruz's behavior at the end of the revolution when he had married Catalina Bernal in order to inherit her father's state and aristocratic status.

After surviving the firing squad at a Villista camp and sacrificing his military honor for his life, Cruz is able to use his acquaintance with the idealist Gonzalo Bernal in order to enter the Bernal family. Like the lawyers Gonzalo Bernal alludes to in the cell who "want only a half-revolution, compatible with what interests them, their only interest, getting on in the world, living well, replacing Don Porfirio's élite" (*MAC,* 291/164), so does Artemio Cruz, whose revolutionary ideals are increasingly blurred in order to survive. His shift from revolutionary to social climber separates him from "those who wanted a true revolution, radical and uncompromising," and who "are unfortunately ignorant and bloody men" (*MAC,* 291/164), as the idealist Gonzalo Bernal laments before his death. Gamaliel Bernal, father of Catalina and Gonzalo, and the aristocratic liberal who stands for the old regime, the Porfirismo, finally passes his inheritance onto Cruz by symbolically marrying him to his daughter Catalina once he realizes that his time is up and that Artemio represents the new order:

> Artemio Cruz. So that was the name of the new world that had risen from the ashes of civil war. So that was the name of the newcomers who had appeared to dispossess the old order. Unfortunate land, said the old man to himself as he walked slowly back to the library, unfortunate land where each generation must destroy its masters and replace them with new masters equally ambitious and rapacious. The old man thought of himself as the final product of a peculiarly indigenous culture: that of illustrious despots; as a kind of fathers at times hard, in the end good providers and always the custodian of a tradition of good taste, gentility, and culture. (*MAC*, 155/44)

In this pessimistic judgment on the failure of the Mexican Revolution, we can also hear an authorial judgment on the nation, whose "children" have to be cyclically destroyed with the coming of a new generation. By symbolically sacrificing Gonzalo Bernal and the Indian Tobías at the Villista camp, Cruz becomes identified with the nation once again, in its latest devouring frenzy. His duplicity *is* the form of the novel with its constant shifting voices, but it is also the constituting moment of the nation, its "reassuring fratricide," to use Benedict Anderson's terminology. Anderson has pointed to the fact that the nation, that imagined community, is necessarily built on the common fusion through an "emblema ancestral" of the "asesinos" and the "asesinados."[36] If the nation is built on a foundational fratricide, the revolution too is imagined as both that violent rebirth, the regeneration of the community, but also as the impossible drama of cyclical destruction: "There you have Mexico's drama" (*MAC*, 291/164).[37] The absorption of the idealist Gonzalo by Artemio, in this symbolic anthropophagic process, makes Cruz feel he is "not one man but two, with Gonzalo Bernal's life added to his own, as if Bernal when he died had transferred to him the possibilities of his own interrupted existence. Maybe, he thought to himself, the deaths of others are what lengthen our own life. But he had not come to Puebla to think" (*MAC*, 149/39). He only came to Puebla to inherit the land, we could add. Cruz's communion with Gonzalo, or rather his symbolic devouring of him, resembles his assimilation of successive women—Regina, Catalina, Laura. Catalina, Gonzalo's sister, is perhaps the clearest example of a sacrificial female in the novel, as she becomes part of the *patrimony,* the bridge between the old and the new Mexican nation.[38]

In her influential study on the role of romance narratives as foundational fictions in Latin America, Doris Sommer has noted the failure of the Catalina-Artemio pair to create such community. That failure denounces the earlier romances "mak[ing] us confront the habits of romantic longing we have learned from national romance,"[39] thus defying the reader's expectations of a romantic national foundation—"after all, these romances were part of a general bourgeois project to hegemonize a culture in formation" (29). At the same time, it indicts the nineteenth-century "imagined community" whose mirage is constantly uncovered, for as Sommer maintains:

> It is possible that the pretty lies of national romance are similar strategies to contain the racial, regional, economic, and gender conflicts that threatened the development of new Latin American nations. It would ideally be a cozy, almost airless, culture that bridged public and private spheres in a way that made room for everyone, as long as everyone knew where they fitted. (29)

If romance is the foundational narrative model of the nation, then Artemio's failed love relations proclaim the failure of the nation he aims to institute and are parodically reduced to a patriarchal business deal, a matter of transferring a will, rather than creating a society. Rosario Castellanos's perception of Cruz as the "owner" of the country is proved correct;[40] his estate is the nation itself:

> You will bequeath this country: your newspapers, the hints and the adulation, the conscience drugged by lying articles written by men of no ability; you will bequeath the mortgages, a class stripped of natural human affection, power without greatness, a consecrated stultification, dwarf ambitions. A fool's compromise, rotted rhetoric, institutionalized cowardice, coarse egoism. (*MAC*, 368/234)

As they crawl into a closet looking for the piece of paper where their future material security may be inscribed, Catalina and Teresa become the female faces of Fuentes's invective on the Mexican ruling plutocracy. Their desperate figures remind us of the dethroned bourgeois in the contemporary film by Luis Buñuel, *The Exterminating Angel* (1962), who fight each other as their stiff dinner room is transformed into a hermetically closed jungle.[41]

The combined subversion of patriarchy and lineal time collude to recast the official discourses of the nation in a critical, parodic mode. The highly experimental time frame of the novel allows Linda Glanze to describe it as a literary instance of cinematic montage in the style of Eisenstein, a montage that foregrounds the conflict between "recit"—the action of the novel, Artemio's agony and death takes place on April 10, 1959—and the "diegesis" of the dispersed memories spanning seventy years of the character's life.[42] In the novel, thirty-eight narrative fragments are consistently organized around thirteen sequences or episodes. Twelve of these episodes or groupings all have the same internal arrangement of three fragments clustered together systematically according to the voice in which they are narrated: third, first, and second person. The twelve fragments in the third-person singular narrate twelve distinct days in the life of Artemio Cruz, accessed randomly, all sharing in common his moments of *fortuna,* moments in his life where he has been able to choose between alternative paths. Elsewhere Fuentes has described those twelve days as "[Cruz's] twelve definitive days, days which are really twelve options."[43] History, under the appearance of objectivity through the third-person narration, is then a succession of eventful days in the life of Artemio whose recurring epic plot is Artemio's existential freedom to choose the way to the top. The rest of the days in his life are not worth remembering as they do not constitute Artemio's "history": "You, yesterday, did the usual things, just as any day. You don't know if it's worth remembering" (*MAC,* 118/12). The left-over absent history, the buried history of the everyday is not remembered as it is meaningless for the plot of Artemio's progress through life.

The twelve historical episodes headed by an imposing third person are also usually narrated in the past tense, or through dialogues between Artemio and other characters. The past is staged here before the dying Artemio, and before the reader, in the form of a fragmented and yet objective and classical third-person narration. But these twelve days of Cruz's private history rapidly emerge as significant also for the public "official" history of the Mexican Republic: the revolution, the transition from Obregón to Calles, the Mexican aid to the Spanish Republic in the Civil War, and so on. The cyclic succession of passages in the third person by the other more intimate passages in first and second person underscores the detachment of the former, but it also casts that objective narrative style as an alternative narrative mode among many.

Thirteen episodes from Artemio's agonizing present are juxtaposed with these "objective" narrations of twelve key moments of his past. By way of contrast, in these passages the emphasis is placed on repetition: the obsessive mind of the dying man is fixed with the issue of his inheritance. Here, the real presence of his wife and daughter, his son in law, Gerardo, their daughter Gloria, the priest, Artemio's secretary, Padilla, and the latter's son who will soon marry Gloria, contrasts with the ghostly presence of Lorenzo, Artemio's son who died in 1939 in the Spanish Civil War, and Regina, a former lover who died during the revolution. The first group, the people who will inherit Artemio's estate, seen by Artemio as mediocre and selfish, is opposed to the group of those who loved him without a material interest and died, the people Artemio has bought and the people Artemio has loved and lost. As a recriminatory speech to those around his deathbed, we hear Artemio reflect on how "I have had everything, do you hear me, everything that can be bought and also what cannot be bought" (*MAC,* 222/102). An example of the latter is Regina who "loved me when I had nothing, she followed me, she gave me life down there, below" (*MAC,* 222/102). Regina, whose love encounters with Artemio during the early days of the revolution are narrated in the third "historical" section "1913: December 4" (*MAC,* 167–88/55–72), dies at the hands of the Federals and becomes the emblem of love in Artemio's life by symbolically saving him during the battle. Significantly, Artemio's body is "not his body, but hers, and for her that body must be saved: they did not live isolated and each alone now, they had broken the wall of separatedness; they were two but really one" (*MAC,* 180/65). In turn, Artemio left the battlefield abandoning a wounded comrade, a "nameless soldier" (*MAC,* 317/187), whose life he could have saved (*MAC,* 181–82/66–67), establishing himself as the ruthless survivor who fences off all these ghosts haunting him at the time of his agony: "And they both come toward me, one leading the other, with their empty eye sockets, believing that they are going to convince me, rouse my pity. Ah, no. No, I don't owe either of you my life. I owe it to my pride. I challenged, I dared" (*MAC,* 188/72). The faces of those whose lives were absorbed by Artemio in his career for survival, literally those "chingados" to death by him, attend him in his agony, but even then he is able to claim victory.

Cruz's secretary, Padilla, who could be behind the narrator of the third-person episodes, inherits Cruz's latest resource to survive beyond death: his reputation. He has been meticulously recording all sorts of conversations with Artemio, played back to him throughout the novel. Those recordings are also the object of parody as we are reminded, through the characteristic narrative process of what Bakhtin identifies as double-voicing, of their fragile and unreliable nature: the tape is interrupted, and at times it becomes faulty. They are an index and a symbol of how the writing of history works, a writing which depends on documents that may already contain formal defects or ideological biases. These tapes, oddly omitted in the exchange by the translator, are a record of Cruz's business dealings and once edited they will destroy or perpetuate Cruz's name. Padilla is the bearer of his secrets, an authentic secretary as he "merits my trust. Clearly he deserves a good part of my estate, and its administration in perpetuity. Who unless he? He knows everything. [*Translator's omission:* Padilla, are you still collecting all the tapes of my conversations at the office? Padilla, you know everything.] I must pay you well. You inherit my reputation" (*MAC,* 135/27). And yet, the obsessive reminder of the tapes played back to Artemio as he agonizes is countered by the simultaneous biography offered in the historical sequences where Artemio's fame as the nation's savior is disparaged.

Could the narrator of these "objective" sequences be Padilla? Like Horatio in *Hamlet,* Padilla is the travestied witness on whom the transmission of the narration, and with it the reputation, depends: "Oh God, *Horatio,* what a wounded name, / Things standing thus unknown, shall live behind me! / If thou didst ever hold me in thy heart, / Absent thee from felicity awhile, / And in this harsh world draw thy breath in pain / To tell my story."[44] Shakespeare acknowledged in this circularity the difficulties and responsibilities of the chronicler of the kingdom or nation at the time of composing the official history: at the end of the play, we are faced with the only witness of the tragedy, on whom history relies to tell the story. Similarly, in *La muerte de Artemio Cruz* the agonizing character symbolically confides his reputation to his secretary as the witness and future author of the "testimony," thus announcing the novel's ultimate sarcasm.

The sections narrated in the first person increasingly become syntactically dispersed and fragmentary as Artemio's ego dissolves into death.[45] The presence of his son Lorenzo constantly recurs through the allusion to the trip on horseback to Cocuya through varying versions of the phrase "that morning I waited for him with happiness. We rode our horses across the river" (*MAC,* 117/11). This is an obsessive reminder both of Artemio's possible responsibility in taking Lorenzo to his ancestral lands in Cocuya, as well as of Artemio's striking progress in life. By crossing that river back into his ancestral origins, Artemio takes his son to a false point of departure that will mean certain death, as his guilty conscience reminds him. Steven Boldy has noted how Lorenzo, the idealist fighter, evolves into a counter-image of Artemio, "an inverted and magical reflection of his betrayed idealism."[46] Lorenzo's sacrificial death in the Spanish Civil War is then yet another life symbolically consumed by Artemio. His son's ghostly presence accompanies Artemio's dying conscience, reminding him of the impossible alternatives that could have changed the course of their lives:

> You will choose to leave him in Catalina's hands, you will not take him to Cocuya, you won't push him to responsibility for himself, to that fatal destiny which could have been yours: you won't force him to do what you did not do, rescue your lost life: you will not allow, this time, that you die on a rocky path and she be saved: you will choose to embrace the wounded soldier. (*MAC,* 339/208)

All the paths that Cruz chose *not* to take are presented to him by this haunting threatening voice. The series of passages narrated in the second person are the voice of Artemio's living conscience which observes his life in the manner of a future, therefore both possible and impossible, moral prediction. A conscience that recognizes how the narration, his future biography, will be the result of a necessary choice: "you will not know which events of your life will pass into your biography, or which will be suppressed and hidden; you won't know" (*MAC,* 123/16). Fuentes himself has explained that the role of this voice as "a third element, the subconscious, a kind of Virgil that guides [Cruz] through the twelve circles of his hell, and that is the other face of his mirror, the other face of Artemio Cruz: the You that speaks in the future tense. It is the subconscious that clings to a future that the I—the dying man—will never know."[47] The voice seems to be addressing both the agonizing Artemio and the child who is born at the end of the novel, hence completing the defiance of the homogeneous, lineal empty time, by imposing once again circularity on the story and on history.

Fuentes's gothic novella *Aura* (1962) is narrated in this vocative style also to emphasize the challenge of the linear narratives of official history. The narrative strategy splits the main characters into two: a hundred-year-old widow, Consuelo Llorente, and her "aura" who haunts the decrepit mansion; and Felipe the historian who becomes infatuated with the young images of Consuelo/Aura and is transformed into General Llorente as he seeks to rewrite the general's biography. Toward the end of the story the young historian abandons his watch, the time-measuring machine which has become "a useless object that falsely measures a time accorded to human vanity, those little hands that tediously clock the long hours invented to deceive the true time, the time that runs with an insulting, mortal speed that no watch can measure."[48] This is not just "a need to deny time's annihilating force," as Wendy Faris has argued;[49] it also represents a symbolic defiance of the ideological structures imposed by the narration of time in a linear manner. Peter Brooks has noted coincidentally in relation to Fuentes's novella the way in which it "pulls off the tour-de-force of a narrative that proceeds backward, from death to birth, both parodying traditional forms and showing us something about how we always decoded such forms from the end."[50] That "something" to which Brooks alludes, the enlightening contribution of the broken temporality, symbolized by the historian's rejection of his watch, counters and parodies the reader's expectations of a narrative directed toward a future "empty time." If the frustrated romances of Artemio Cruz had failed to found the fiction of a new community, the rupture of the mechanic, calendric time and its substitution by "true time," a time that defies linearity, also reveals the fracture of the grand narrative of the nation into mere "rotted rhetoric."

At a formal level, the multilayered account in *La muerte de Artemio Cruz,* as in Pynchon's "Entropy" (1960), contributes to the foregrounding and critique of the seemingly objective third-person narration. In the short story, constructed around two alternative narrative spaces, there is the question of who is narrating Callisto's last hours. Callisto, who is dictating his autobiography in the third person in the manner of the Henry Adams of *The Education,*[51] is perhaps also the narrator of the story itself. The coincidence of the character's demise with the end of the narrative suggests that behind the quasi-omniscient narrator's voice may also lie the character's perception of his self-dissolution: "[she] turned to face the man on the bed and wait with him until the moment of equilibrium was reached, when 37 degrees Fahrenheit should prevail both outside and inside, and forever, and the hovering, curious dominant of their separate lives should resolve into a tonic of darkness and the final absence of all motion."[52] Pynchon's apocalypse is brought about by an entropic constant temperature which parallels the disruption of conventional time observed in *Aura.* The startling coincidence between the demise of the character and the end of the narrator/narration encourages a sense of ambiguity about the identity of the third-person narrator in the short story and in *Artemio Cruz*'s "objective" historical sequences.

In the novel, the three narrative voices come to an end with the character's death, who is therefore identified with the narrator: "I carry you inside and with you I die. The three, we . . . will die. You . . . die, have died . . . I will die" (*MAC,* 405/265). But the "man on the bed" who awaits and reaches death, or entropy, and relates his story through the narrator's persona is not a mere narrative device, it is ideologically charged, as Hayden White has noted in relation to *The Education of Henry Adams:* "[its] manifest announcement of the end of the ego in the modern age has to be viewed as a message not only personal and subjective but social and historical as well. Insofar as Adams identifies his own ego with that of his class, the announcement of the dissolution of one is also the announcement of the dissolution of the other."[53] In Artemio Cruz's case the dissolution of the character's ego, even more apparent in the first-person narratives which stage a process of erasure and death *in crescendo,* also announces the dissolution of his class, and the final demise of the Mexican Revolution.

The sequences narrated in the third person use the past tense to signify a closure that becomes further reinforced by Artemio's birth and death at the end. As the novel closes, the last third-person section stages Cruz's birth on April 9, 1889: "Drawn up, doubled upon himself in the middle of those contractions with his head dark with blood hanging by the most tenuous of threads at last open to life . . ." (*MAC,* 403/264). This quasi-circular reiteration of dates—birth and death occur on April 10, 1889 and April 10, 1959,—resignifies the temporality of the nation itself—as the community imagined by Artemio at the time of the revolution and beyond—an ahistorical, fictional narrative that will not survive him. It seems doomed to share his destiny, one that does not flow linearly toward a future, but narcissistically, elliptically toward itself.

Incidentally, Fuentes has subsequently used the metaphor of a birth also to signify the birth of the nation as in the case of the two children born at the beginning of the wars of independence in Latin America at the opening of *La campaña* (1990), and which I discuss in more detail in chapter 6. Perhaps Fuentes's most successful twist to this motif is his *Cristóbal nonato* (1987), where an omniscient fetus, Cristobal Palomar, a carnivalesque avatar of Christopher Columbus, narrates his "coming" to a Mexico divided between oil robber-barons and tourist corporations. These numerous births stress the allegorical nature of certain characters in Fuentes's fiction whose lives run parallel to that of the nation. In *La muerte de Artemio Cruz,* the agonizing character is a negative national allegory, who significantly had "inherited" his allegorical attribute from his grandmother Ludivinia, symbolically born in 1810, the year of Mexican independence, and who is said to carry "a century of memory and, in the lines of her wrinkled face, the marks of winds and suns long disappeared" (*MAC,* 382/245). Ludivinia's face is also the memory of yet another story of cyclical destruction, the novel's "hell of memory" as Boldy has put it,[54] that of the Menchaca's, whose estate—itself a product of violent appropriation (*MAC,* 246)—had been burnt and taken away from them. As she hides in her walled refuge of memories,[55] the ritornello "others have taken from us what we took from others" (*MAC,* 250) stands for the plot of the nation's history, one that is not built around the constitution of a community, but on a repetitious depredation.

The novel's constant reference to mirrors, in particular to broken ones, should be understood as yet another feature at the service of picturing the nation as both agonizing and permanently divided, fragmented. As the agonizing Artemio Cruz looks at himself in the broken mirror of his daughter's purse at the opening of the novel, he also discovers a fragmented reality: "I am this, this am I: old man with his face reflected in pieces by different-sized squares of glass: I am this eye, this eye I am: eye furrowed by roots of accumulated choler, old and forgotten and always present; eye green and swollen between its lids: lids, eyelids, oily eyelids" (*MAC,* 115/9). Furthermore, this story of fragmentation is not contradicted by the preterit tense of the third-person episodes nor the powerful future of the second-person narratives. Artemio's constant fragmentation—like that of the nation—is the focus of attention of these narratives:

> Vendors of lottery tickets, bootblacks, women in rebozos, children with their upper lips smeared with mucus swarmed around him as he moved towards the revolving door and passed into the vestibule and adjusted his necktie in front of the glass and, through it, in the second glass, which looked out on Madero, saw a man identical to himself, wearing the same double-breasted suit, but colorless, tightening the knot of the same tie with the same nicotine fingers, a man surrounded by beggars, who let his hand drop at the same instant he in the vestibule did, and turned and walked down the block, while he, for the moment a little disoriented, looked for the elevator. (*MAC,* 128/20)

The recurring splitting of Artemio's image is directly facilitated by the many mirrors scattered throughout the novel. The two "Artemios" splintered by the mirror apparently choose two different moral or political paths, the "real" one inwards into the private space from where Artemio the individualistic "chingón" can hide away from the victims of the economic system on which his fortunes rest, or the "possible" social choice of solidarity outwards into the street where the army of disenfranchised "chingados," those Mexicans who literally "swarm" around Artemio, struggle to survive.[56] As elsewhere in the novel, the fracture of the central character here is a reminder of the fractured community, of a class-ridden society whose divisions are concealed behind the vanishing consensual narrative of the revolution.

Thus in Cruz's splintered image there is always the threat of the internal enemy as the voice of his conscience tells him:

> You will survive Artemio Cruz, surviving by exposing yourself to the hazards of liberty, taking the risk successfully until no enemies are left: and then you will become your own enemy, that the proud battle may go on: all others conquered, there will remain only yourself to be conquered: you will step from the looking-glass of still water and lead your last attack against the enemy nymph. (*MAC,* 195/78)

The mirror is not the place of reconciliation nor of the narcissistic moment of self-knowledge, in the same way that the mirror of history cannot be the place of understanding, of founding the nation, but rather a site for continuous fight and conflict, a perpetual reminder of the labyrinth of solitudes. As the continuous time of the failed nation is countered by the multiple alternative times of a heterogeneous reality, the mirror constitutes itself as the space to look for difference rather than for identification. Wendy Faris suggests that in these mirror images of the fragmented Cruz "we sense a simultaneous desire and reluctance to know himself" (50), but such desire is finally parodied by its supplementary paradoxical reluctance, a kind of self-aversion which reflects on the author's dismissal of the search for the unified national self that has filled Mexican intellectual history throughout its past. If, like the ideologists of the Mexican nation Artemio "would like to be one,"[57] his failure and that of the nationalist project is the persistence of a plurality of voices, of points of view, that constantly defy and satirize the homogenizing efforts of modernity.

Mexico, "un país incapaz de tranquilidad, enamorado de la convulsión" ("a land incapable of tranquility, enamored of convulsion") (*MAC,* 147/37), is not then the abstract entity in search of the complacent self-identification brought about by the sacred text of the American Constitution—the site of another imagined community, which consecrates the fiction of its plural-unified self—"e pluribus unum"—from its official birth certificate: "We the people of the United States of America." Such mirage, eroded in the semiotic excavation of *The Crying of Lot 49,* is the background noise from the North against which Mexican intellectuals have eagerly searched for the defining moment, an origin, while traditions and communities were submitted to a permanent and continuous overhaul in the name of the nation to come. As we saw in chapter 1, Octavio Paz, perhaps the last in the long line of such intellectuals, timidly announced at the end of his major meditation on Mexico the need for an international or "universal" conscience as the culmination of the long postrevolutionary introspection.[58] In Fuentes's work, however, Mexican nationalism is stripped bare of its many deceiving masks; the essentialist vision of the nation is put into perspective, and even denounced as the colonizing discourse of the dominant class. Artemio's slow and painful death, rather than announcing the challenges of "yet-to-be nations," as Aizenberg has put it, pronounces the contradictions and even the impossibility of such a creation. In his following novel, *Cambio de piel,* Fuentes revisits the dead body of the nation in order not so much to mourn over it, but to try to defuse its resurrection.

Chapter 4

✦

The Crying of Lot 49 and the Nationalist Colonization of the Unconscious

The Crying of Lot 49 complexly elaborates a fictional response to the guilt-ridden conscience of the American middle class and the hopeless search for a way out of its reification. In the novel, the commoditized Californian landscape becomes the obsessive reminder of the social and political cost of undemocratic developmental policies during the long Cold War period. The quest through this "infected" landscape is based on an extended parody, a direct though subverting textual reference to Sophocles's Theban tragedies: Oedipa Maas, a Republican housewife in her early thirties, has to make sense of the will of a former lover and land tycoon, Pierce Inverarity. As in *Oedipus Rex,* the tragic character has to ascertain the causes of the plague devastating her city as she starts to determine her own identity. Her name is an early index that facilitates the decoding of the apparently chaotic network of cultural signs that clutter the text. The classical reference participates in the wholesale carnivalization of cultural codes, from thermodynamics to philately, in a move to de-routinize their positioning in (post)industrial consumerist society. This differs from traditional Americanist interpretations, such as the one prompted by Theodore Kharpertian, who maintains that "Oedipa, like her ancient namesake, does come to recognize that the responsibility for the political plague is hers."[1] I will argue that Pynchon's deviation from the Greek myth does not just rest on his feminization of the classical character, but also on the character's inability to assume a responsibility that may commence a new political epoch. Oedipa's revelations are not so much about her identity as about her incompetence to acknowledge the bankruptcy of the consensual national discourse that has colonized her unconscious since a very early age.

Oedipa's Republic

The first textual appearance of Oedipa Maas invites a preliminary observation on both the material context within which her story was written and some of the textual alterations introduced by the author before publishing the novel's final version. An extract with the novel's two first chapters, published as "The World (This One), the Flesh (Mrs. Oedipa Maas), and the Testament of Pierce Inverarity" in the December 1965 issue of *Esquire Magazine*,[2] is enclosed by such a profusion of commercial advertisements that the text is at times hard to trace. In an ironic parallelism with the extended commodity catalogs produced by Pynchon, the juxtaposed images of all sorts of merchandise—from writing machines to golf carts—resituate the fiction in its precise historical moment by pointing at its definite material context: the bulky Christmas issue of a popular middle-class magazine.[3]

For instance, on page 301 the adverts surrounding the piece by Pynchon take up three quarters of the sheet and their bold language, participating in the sexual discourse of the American advertising industry at the time, merits a brief diversion. Obvious signs point to products "for men": after-shave cream "Aztec," "Rooster" ties, Marum boots "Just for Kicks . . . ," and a curious "Hawaiian Room" at the Hotel Lexington. "There's so much going on at the Hawaiian Room, you almost don't have time to watch the gorgeous native hula girls. (Almost)." The world evoked by the adverts is exotic: not just with the kitsch exoticism intended for the 1965 U.S. readers—Aztec, Hawaiian—but exotic in the sense of being outside, outside Pynchon's text, but forever contiguous to it. That other quarter of the page is not a closed invitation to consume other—female—areas of a folklorized world, but part of a project to satirize the rites of a complacent imperial society. The passage is only a short fragment of the scene in chapter 2 in which Oedipa and Metzger, a former actor become lawyer and also a co-executor of Inverarity's will, flirt in their room at Echo Courts, a Californian motel, and drink tequila without lemons and salt, their combination dismissed as "[a] tourist thing" (*L49,* 33). In the meantime the TV shows *Cashiered,* an adventure film where Metzger starred as a child in the role of Baby Igor, a kid who accompanies his British father in a midget submarine to the imperial confrontation against the Turks: "Suddenly a host of Turkish rifles on shore opened up all together, and the massacre began" (*L49,* 36). A threatening fiction about historical encounters with colonials unwilling to be subdued, surrounded by the tamed pleasures of exoticism.

Later on in her quest, Oedipa flees from John Nefastis, a scientist who offers to have "sexual intercourse" with the TV news in the background: "Maybe there'll be something about China tonight. I like to do it while they talk about Viet Nam, but China is best of all. You think about all those Chinese. Teeming. That profusion of life. It makes it sexier, right?" (*L49,* 108). Nefastis and Metzger could understand well the sex appeal of an Aztec after-shave. In either case, the TV set has become the medium against which their daily fantasies rest and the common channel through which to communicate with Oedipa. No background noise seems to come out of it, but rather a meaningful constant flow of information—to use Raymond Williams's terminology—that projects itself on the characters' unconscious.[4] Rather than contributing to the creation of McLuhan's "global village," it reinscribes hollowed-out social and cultural differences through a new medium, putting forward the dominant discourses that favor cultural and economic colonization abroad and homogenization at home.

Very much like the reader of the 1965 *Esquire,* the two characters in the motel room are surrounded by all this exotic fanfare, from Mexico to the Dardanelles and back to the commercials on their TV set: "a loud commercial for Fangoso Lagoons, a new housing development" (*L49,* 31), "Beaconsfield Cigarettes, whose attractiveness lay in their filter's use of bone charcoal" (*L49,* 34), "a Turkish bath in downtown San Narciso, wherever downtown was, called Hogan's Seraglio" (*L49,* 39). After each commercial, Metzger is able to identify Inverarity's estate. The narrator finally sums it all up: "a commercial would come in, each time Metzger would say, 'Inverarity's,' or 'Big block of shares,' and later settled for nodding and smiling" (*L49,* 41). The exotic element in the magazine adverts is here substituted by a too familiar continuum: behind all the commodities on offer lies the same Inverarity.

In her quest, Oedipa ventures into her everyday world of commodities, parenthetically identified as "This One" in the title to the *Esquire* story. Although it is indeed a familiar world for her, throughout her quest she begins to be exposed to that which until then had seemed irrelevant, and which slowly becomes a central issue: the social and moral bankruptcy of the United States. Exactly how relevant this theme should be for a critical reading of the text is made clear by the swift change in the wording of the magazine version, revealing some interesting departures from the text of *The Crying of Lot 49* published four months later. In the 1966 Lippincott edition, as in all others after that, the narrator announces early in the novel that "as things developed, she [Oedipa] was to have all manner of revelations. Hardly about Pierce Inverarity, or herself; but about what remained yet had somehow, before this, stayed away" (*L49,* 20). This line has been widely cited as a demonstration of the ambiguous treatment of the narrator and as a proof of Pynchon's deferral of meaning. Yet in the *Esquire* version, the same narrator appears to be more punning in the first sentence and finally too explicit: "as things developed, she was to find out a lot. Hardly anything about Pierce Inverarity, or herself; but all manner of revelations about what remained: their Republic" (173). The two sentences have undergone a drastic rephrasing in order to defer the disclosure of the United States as the revealed truth. In the final version, "it" literally stays away from the readers, not because the quest varies its course, but rather because we are spared such an early announcement.

"A Lot-by-Lot Grasp" (*Inherent Vice*)

Multiple layers of meaning arise behind the word "lot," creating a pun in which the serious sense of "way of life," and the simpler synonym "manifold," obviously referring to the saturation of cultural references awaiting the reader, are mixed with the specific allusion to both the novel's title and the "lot" number 49. The entire joke is lost in the rewriting of the paragraph. Oedipa is indeed haunted by a "lot" throughout the novel which seems to materialize in the "lot 49"—a collection of subversive stamps that demonstrate the existence of the Tristero (or Trystero), an underground anti-establishment organization—auctioned at the close of the novel.

Another "lot" alluded to in this first chapter of the novel is the car lot where her husband Mucho worked for two years as a used car salesman, before becoming a disk jockey for the KCUF radio station. Here again the word "lot" does not only stand for the straightforward concept, the physical space where the used vehicles were readied and sold, but it also bears the sense of Mucho's old way of life in which he "had believed too much."[5] Mucho's lot—a multilingual pun in itself, particularly considering it together with his surname, Maas: "Mucho más," "a lot more," when read in Spanish—consists of a traumatic experience of material dereliction. His psychological burden is to have beheld the "salad of despair" of a semi-disenfranchised class:

> seeing people poorer than him come in, Negro, Mexican, cracker, a parade seven days a week, bringing the most godawful of trade-ins: motorized, metal extensions of themselves, of their families and what their whole lives must be like, out there so naked for anybody, a stranger like himself, to look at, frame cockeyed, rusty underneath, fender repainted in a shade just off enough to depress the value, if not Mucho himself, inside smelling hopelessly of children, supermarket booze, two, sometimes three generations of cigarette smokers, or only of dust. (*L49*, 13)

The "parade seven days a week" to which he is no longer exposed at the radio station is made up of inhabitants of what could be called an "endotic" world, a world of difference—racial "Negro, Mexican," and social, "cracker," "poorer than him"—contained inside the same geopolitical boundaries: the American republic, and its cultural epitome, California, the object of all revelations. Instead of the exotic products of both the magazine in which the first version of this chapter is embedded, or those broadcasting Inverarity's multiple assets, Mucho had consumed daily the "endotic" remainders of other citizens' lives who could not have been his neighbors in Kinneret-among-the Pines.

In contrast with the effortless appropriation of a stereotyped periphery through direct consumption of its frozen icons, the inner periphery is not easily processed and its rem(a)inders become a traumatic form of waste. His trauma even compares unfavorably to the one suffered by soldiers in the exotic wars of the American empire: "he should have been in a war, Japs in trees, Krauts in Tiger tanks, gooks with trumpets in the night he might have forgotten sooner than whatever it was about the lot that had stayed so alarmingly with him for going on five years" (*L49,* 15). Compared to the toil of colonial wars, the everyday life of ghetto inhabitants is a more painful reminder of the character's social positioning: the parade of the endotic contains a waste that cannot be cognitively processed and which therefore becomes a source of trauma. This cause of distress at the car lot parallels Oedipa's later encounter with the American disinherited during her quest to execute Inverarity's will, and in both cases it points to the Maas as archetypes of the American "little man."[6] Their surname reveals itself as an embedded hint of their ideological compound: read backwards it becomes "Sam," a reminder of "Uncle Sam," the popular icon for the American nation itself.

In Pynchon's later California novel, *Inherent Vice,* the protagonist's politically aware Aunt Reet reflects on how some L.A. developers "make Godzilla look like a conservationist." Doc's Aunt possesses a "phenomenal lot-by-lot grasp of land use from the desert to the sea" (*IV,* 6), demonstrating a "bordering-on-the-supernatural sense of the land" (*IV,* 7). Unlike Oedipa Maas, she is the repository of "stories that seldom appeared in deeds or contracts, especially matrimonial, the generations of family hatreds big and small, the way the water flowed, or used to" (*IV,* 6). Aunt Reet is a living archive of the "long, sad history of L.A. land use" summed up as a long series of devastations, incursions into the space of ethnic minorities—"Mexican families bounced out of Chavez Ravine to build Dodger Stadium, American Indians swept out of Bunker Hill for the Music Center, Tariq's neighborhood bulldozed aside for Channel View States" (*IV,* 17). Much like Pynchon's other California novels, *Lot 49* and *Vineland, Inherent Vice* offers yet another episode in the continuing proliferation of racialized space under the careful watch of white supremacist policemen and land speculators. The mythical settling of the West of nationalist propaganda is retold as a set of speculative capitalist operations which allot a fractured social body onto a dilapidated landscape.

In his article "A Journey into the Mind of Watts," published three months after *Lot 49* came out, Pynchon highlighted the contrast between the "little man" who inhabits suburbia, "meaning not so much any member of the power structure as just your average white L.A. taxpayer, registered voter, property owner, employed, stable, mortgaged and the rest,"[7] and the blacks who dwell in "Raceriotland" Watts. Reflecting on the riots that took place in the black neighborhood of L.A. in August 1965, when a policeman was acquitted after shooting dead a black driver, Pynchon points out the failure of both the "humanitarian establishment" born of the Great Depression of the 1930s, and Lyndon Johnson's administration fighting the War on Poverty.[8] Incapable of understanding the nature of Watts violence, "possibly because it threatens property and status they cannot help cherishing," the "childish semi-optimistic bureaucrats" are the hopeless intermediaries between two cultures that don't share any value:

> While the white culture is concerned with various forms of systematized folly—the economy of the area in fact depending on it—the black culture is stuck pretty much with basic realities like disease, like failure, violence and death, which the whites have mostly chosen—and can afford—to ignore. The two cultures do not understand each other, though white values are displayed without let-up on black people's TV screen. (35, 78)

This emphasis on the use of the television to broadcast white suburban values reveals Pynchon's concern for the cultural invasion of the well-off into the midst of his extended diatribe against the "unreality" of the L.A. white scene, and is a useful index to understand the characterization of the Maas. His description of the gap between the two "very different cultures" used to explain the "mind of Watts" parallels the image of the "two worlds" suggested to Oedipa by the Mexican anarchist Jesús Arrabal in *Lot 49*. For Arrabal, Pierce Inverarity represented "the oligarchist, the miracle" (*L49,* 119), that is, "another world's intrusion into this one," as terrifying "as a Virgin appearing to an Indian" (*L49,* 120). Our Lady of Guadalupe, Mexico's national icon, is set side by side with the other American national icon, Inverarity (Cruz), the owner of the nation. It is not that people like Jesus Arrabal "have been pushed to social estrangement" as Jerry Varsava claims in his consensual reinscription of the novel.[9] They have only figured as the necessary excluded "other" in America's privatized nationalist (and in that sense, liberal-conservative) project. Varsava's reading presupposes a utopian and consensual moment of total inclusion, a middle ground, contained in the values of the founders of the American Republic, something the novel denies through its excavation of the national archaeology of violence, evidenced in the unfair distribution of the land.

Arrabal, like so many of Pynchon's characters, bears a name immediately significant for its many connotations.[10] Fernando Arrabal, the Spanish surrealist playwright, had successfully staged his *Cementerio de automóviles* from 1959 in Spain, Mexico, and France (as *Cimetière des voitures*).[11] In it, people live in abandoned cars—literally in a scrap yard—their attachment to the machine being even more extreme than that witnessed by Mucho at the lot, and under the constant fear of repressive forces, reminiscent of Franco's police state. The central character in the play is a young trumpeter called Emanu, aged thirty-three, whose defiant act is to play his trumpet in the open air, but also to have been sharing his bread and fish with the others. The Christian iconography is consistently kept in his foreseeable punishment—toward the end of the play, the police measure his arm width as he stands symbolically crucified. But Arrabal's play reworks the ideological tenets of Christian peaceful subversion in order to parody it, as Emanu repeats a phrase that can be read as a mantra for social adjustment: "Because when one is good one feels an inner happiness that derives from the peace of the spirit as it feels to be similar to the ideal image of man."[12] In Pynchon's Jesús Arrabal both the Christian allegory and its recent theatrical author are colluded into the Mexican anarchist who had perceived things about Pierce that Oedipa hadn't "as if he were, in some unsexual way, competition" (*L49,* 120). The image of the trumpeter muted by the repressive order is adopted too by Pynchon and transformed into the Tristero's muted post horn through which the world of the disinherited tries to communicate with Oedipa, but that is obviously the novel's clearest irony.

At this point in the analysis of the novel, the title given to the *Esquire* piece becomes significant again: it openly hints at the "world" in which it is published, in the same way in which Arrabal refers to his. Arrabal's definition of a miracle works also in both directions, thus the anarchist miracle consists of "revolutions [that] break out spontaneous and leaderless" (*L49,* 120), reminiscent of the Watts violence described by Pynchon: "far from a sickness, violence may be an attempt to communicate, or to be who you really are."[13] Violence is not then that threatening social ill perceived by the middle-class social workers, but perhaps the only way out for a muted population.

In their study of racial riots in the United States during the 1960s, Joe R. Feagin and Hahn Harlan maintain a relatively similar position when they suggest that the "spreading riot ideology often viewed rioting not only as a method of protest but also as a tactic that might bring actual structural and political change to the cities."[14] A structural change to the urban space is seen as the key to breaking through the patterns of racial divide and ghettoization.[15] Watts's blacks live in a space where the rule of law is suspended—that is, you can be executed at any time—and where life becomes "nuda vita" or "bare life," in Agamben's definition, a life "which dwells in the no-man's-land between the home and the city."[16] A Watts black is indeed the epitome of the *homo sacer,* a "human victim who may be killed but not sacrificed" (Agamben, 83), whose death can go unpunished. Watts is an emblem of the political space inhabited by the blacks elsewhere in the United States, who Norman Mailer described as "living in the margin between totalitarianism and democracy."[17] Mailer and Pynchon, both white northeasterners, turn to the discourse of the civil liberties movement with its critique of Wasp values leaning toward totalitarianism, in search of a response to the "Square" conformity of the 1950s against which they also seek to react. But their responses differ. While Mailer identifies his intellectual posture, the Hipster, with the Negro's "existentialist synapses" (341), hence claiming the birth of what he calls the White Negro, Pynchon promotes a radical critique of the cultural homogenization taking place in American culture during the Cold War. Yet like Mailer, Pynchon recognizes rioting and revolution as an inevitable form of social exchange between two worlds that, regardless of nationalist consensus building, appear to be culturally incompatible. However, he does not dwell much on this inevitability: Pynchon is more troubled by the colonization of the black neighborhood by a white "unreality" obsessed with averting any future destruction of the status quo, a colonization that would soon be contested by leaders such as Malcom X and social movements like the Black Panther Party in an effort to constitute the black nation in the second half of the 1960s.[18]

For Pynchon in "A Journey. . . ," the issue of violence becomes a source of ironic reflection on the hypocritical positioning of the dominant values: "among so much well-behaved unreality, it is next to impossible to understand how Watts may truly feel about violence." White L.A. is determined to "put the area under a siege of persuasion: to coax the Negro poor into taking on certain white values. Give them a little property, and they will be less tolerant of arson; get them to go in hock for a car or color TV, and they'll be more likely to hold down a steady job."[19] This act of offering a minimal share of the white consumer folly in order to appease an enraged black vitality, part of the process of internal colonization, is carried out through the television, here seen mainly as a political medium, whose counter-image is waste, the other contact zone between the two communities. Pynchon notes how in Watts "it's part of their landscape, both the real and the emotional one: busted glass, busted crockery, nails, tin cans, all kinds of scrap and waste" ("A Journey into the Mind of Watts," 78.) These images of the debris in which the California pariah are immersed, but also of the ways in which their illusory expectations are raised by the TV's dreamy displays, both feature in the novel as muted messages which at times undermine the conscience of the white "little man," and of the "little woman," the Maas, as they become exposed to them.

The Eye of the Beholder

In the years of his marriage to Oedipa, Mucho's unconscious has been cluttered with the image of the waste he had unveiled at the lot: the material remainder of countless disempowered lives. As the car is recycled back into the market, it is cleansed of personal and human wastes that cannot be incorporated either in Mucho's cognitive system or back into the marketplace. They have become immersed in Mucho's unconscious in a formless catalogue:

> When the cars were swept out you had to look at the actual residue of these lives, and there was no way of telling what things had been truly refused (when so little he supposed came by that out of fear most of it had to be taken and kept) and what had simply (perhaps tragically) been lost: clipped coupons promising savings of 5 or 10, trading stamps, pink flyers advertising specials at the markets, butts, tooth-shy combs, help-wanted ads, Yellow Pages torn from the phone book, rags of old underwear or dresses that already were period costumes, for wiping your own breath off the inside of a windshield with so you could see whatever it was, a movie, a woman or car you coveted, a cop who might pull you over just for drill, all the bits and

> pieces coated uniformly, like a salad of despair, in a gray dressing of ash, condensed exhaust, dust, body wastes—it made him sick to look, but he had to look. (*L49,* 13–14)

Once characterized as a "salad of despair" by the narrator, the residue of these lives becomes immediately politicized: it signals the entropic tendency of closed systems such as the U.S. Republic.[20] Beyond the existential sense of exitlessness pervading this imagery, there is a calculated, double-voiced parody of the middle-class observer, whose job forces him to "look," but who remains incapable of understanding the nature of the waste. The choice between the violent reality of the black ghetto and the unreal conformity of the suburb are not then those "meaningless binary choices"[21] confronting Oedipa, in the words of Frank Kermode and other critics. Some of these critics transfer the emphasis from the political contradictions underscored throughout Pynchon's writings, which they come to deem "meaningless," to "the normal hermeneutic activity in disease."[22] It is in this movement out of the habitual, of the "normal" activity of gazing at the everyday, that the conscience of these political contradictions becomes conspicuous but also traumatic and unbearable.

This compulsory viewing of the other world that has tortured Mucho's guilty conscience signifies the breaking down of the physical boundary that had hitherto separated his world and the world of waste, "the reality of Watts" and "the unreality of Los Angeles."[23] California is in the novel a "neon-lit wasteland," as Peter Freese has noted.[24] Michael Harrington observed in his *The Other America: Poverty in the United States* that "the problem, then, is to a great extent one of vision. The nation of the well-off must be able to see through the wall of affluence and recognize the alien citizens on the other side."[25] For Pynchon too the breaking of the visual boundary is a first act that would allow white Americans to cross over to the other side. The need for a change of perspective in order to be able to see and perceive the other side of the country is pointed out in his journey to Watts:

> The panoramic sense of black impoverishment is hard to miss from atop the Harbor Freeway, which so many whites must drive at least twice every working day. Somehow it occurs to very few of them to leave at the Imperial Highway exit for a change, go east instead of west only a few blocks, and take a look at Watts. A quick look. The simplest kind of beginning. But Watts is a country which lies, psychologically, uncounted miles further than most whites seem at present willing to travel. ("A Journey into the Mind of Watts," 78)

Mucho's act of looking has to be read not as a deliberate act, "he had to look," and therefore not as the "beginning" to which Pynchon alludes here, but as a traumatic miracle, an incursion from another world into "this one."

In a parallel move, Oedipa's quest can also be said to have an "immediate and important residual effect: the revelation of the disinherited" as Kharpertian has pointed out.[26] As in the case of Mucho, the key point stressed by the narrator is Oedipa's incapacity to make any sense of such revelation as she drifts into "some paranoia" (*L49,* 182). Oedipa is, like her husband Mucho, unable to process and sort out a meaning behind the human waste that she observes. As she unveils Pierce Inverarity's awesome legacy, she confronts a reality that habitually bypasses her. John Krafft offers an Americanist, nationalist, recuperative viewpoint toward Oedipa's search when he states that "in doing literary history, Oedipa has been compelled to do European and American history, and has been enabled thereby to re-envision and perhaps also actually to reinherit America."[27] However, in order for her to reenvision, to see, Oedipa would have to fully deroutinize her sight, and much of the novel is devoted to this impossible process of breaking through the patterns of vision to which she has been culturally conditioned.

In *Invisible Man,* Ralph Ellison extensively articulates the image of the invisibility of American blacks, which the narrator attributes to the white's inability to see: "That invisibility to which I refer occurs because of a peculiar disposition in the eyes of those with whom I come in contact. A matter of the construction of their *inner* eyes, those eyes with which they look through their physical eyes upon reality."[28] Ellison's much celebrated equation of marginality and invisibility was also re-created by Gloria Anzaldúa in her *The Borderlands/La Frontera* (1987). In her manifesto "La conciencia de la mestiza: Towards a New Consciousness" she claims: "I am visible—see this Indian face—yet I am invisible. I both blind them with my beak nose and am their blind spot. But I exist, we exist. They'd like to think I have melted in the pot. But I haven't, we haven't."[29] The use of invisibility to disparage the inclusive image of the melting pot—the ur-narrative of the racial inclusiveness of the post–Civil War American nation—succeeds in bringing it down and exposing it as just a myth. It is not that in the 1960s "the country discovered, in short, that its citizens were not all white and prosperous,"[30] as David Cowart has claimed in his commentary on Pynchon in the 1960s. Cowart's assertion of course implies the existence of a country, a nation, which is by definition white and prosperous, and which all of a sudden "realizes" it is actually not.[31] The use of invisibility is addressed to counter such an argument by emphasizing the permanent blindness, the racial "blind spot" of the Wasp, but also of those incorporated into the national pot. This is a reminder that race, as language and religion—markedly in the case of Muslims (hence the wave of conversions to Islam among blacks in the 1960s and beyond)—are closely related in the United States to nationhood: citizens who are neither white nor prosperous are not in practice citizens at all, or are at most second-class citizens.

Oedipa's sight is described at the outset of the novel as faulty, "as if watching a movie, just perceptibly out of focus, that the projectionist refused to fix" (*L49,* 20). Indeed, the narrator declines to "fix" the character's perception of "reality" in order to stress her deficient sight. Most of the apparent ambiguities highlighted by certain critics can be explained by paying attention to Oedipa's perceptual problems. Her quest puts into action some of the epistemological themes and devices distinctive of modernist fiction and identified by Brian McHale in his *Postmodernist Fiction:*

> the accessibility and circulation of knowledge, the different restructuring imposed on the "same" knowledge by different minds, and the problem of "unknowability" or the limits of knowledge . . ., the multiplication of and juxtaposition of perspectives, the focalization of all the evidence through a single "center of consciousness". . .[32]

The paintings of another exiled Spanish surrealist, Remedios Varo, serve as a starting point, a sort of iconic manifesto at the start of the novel, which addresses the character's defective eyesight. Her wish to be perpetually saddened by the vision of Remedios Varo's *Bordando el manto terrestre* (*Embroidering Earth's Mantle*)[33] lurks over the whole narration. In a flashback to her trip to Mexico City with Pierce Inverarity, Oedipa remembers her wish to "see the world refracted through those tears" provoked by the vision of the prisoners in the tower, embroidering a tapestry of the world. Oedipa's viewing of the painting saddens her as she realizes that she has not escaped from her own tower:

> Oedipa, perverse, had stood in front of the painting and cried. No one had noticed; she wore dark green bubble shades. For a moment she'd wondered if the seal around her sockets were tight enough to allow the tears simply to go on and fill up the entire lens space and never dry. She could carry the sadness of the moment with her that way forever, see the world refracted through those tears, as if indices as yet unfound varied in important ways from cry to cry. (*L49,* 21)

This first act of crying is directly related to the perspective provided by the watertight glasses filled up with tears: as she cries, she also consciously stages a first reaffirmation of her blurred eyesight. Pynchon's use of the green-colored glasses through which to look at the world is reminiscent of Adorno's reference to the use of "stereotypes" which are increasingly "reified and rigid in the present set-up of the culture industry" and which become "clichés that seem to bring some order into the otherwise ununderstandable."[34] Through these clichés "people may not only lose true insight into reality, but ultimately their very capacity for life experience may be dulled by the constant wearing of blue and pink spectacles" (171). In the case of Oedipa Maas, her glasses as well as her crying are two primary ways of dealing with the inescapability of her tower, her manner of circumventing her own responsibility toward the poisonous inheritance which she has to execute.

It is in this context that the Oedipus story becomes immediately useful as a code against which to read hers. The Greek king inadvertently kills his father, marries his own mother, thus fulfilling an old prophecy. Therefore, it is revealed that he is the actual cause behind the plague devastating his city. When he finds out, the reality is too overbearing and Oedipus physically blinds himself. This act of piercing his own eyes defines Oedipus's moment of awareness as literally blinding, emphasizing the character's permanent inability to see: metaphorically, first, Tiresias warns him "I say you see and still are blind,"[35] and bodily as his face becomes "an eyeless mask" (78). Pynchon's version of the tragic character is devoid of the ancient gruesome mutilation, but it contains a more painful defacement as Oedipa is never delivered of her uncertainties. In a move from tragedy to postnational satire, this Oedipa is incapable of ever reaching "the central truth." Her quest—"if it were supposed to end"—consists of a series of turning points after which there is always the possibility of revelation, but which systematically regress to the point of uncertainty, reinforcing the Oedipal inability to discern:

> She could, at this stage of things, recognize signals like that, as the epileptic is said to—an odor, color, pure piercing grace note sounding his seizure. Afterwards it is only this signal, really dross, this secular announcement, and never what is revealed during the attack, that he remembers. Oedipa wondered whether, at the end of this (if it were supposed to end), she too might not be left with only compiled memories of clues, announcements, intimations, but never the central truth itself, which must somehow each time be too bright for her memory to hold; which must always blaze out, destroying its own message irreversibly, leaving an overexposed blank when the ordinary world came back. (*L49, 95*)

As Oedipa's memory is emptied of the "central truth," the reader becomes ever keener to understand what this means. For most of the "compiled memories of clues" refer to the possibility of connections pointing to the network of assets belonging to Inverarity's will, and lurking behind his estate, the hidden meaning of the Tristero stamp collection, the apparent lot 49, unveiling an encyclopedic history of treason and struggle over the delivery of messages. This whole history can be read as the "signal, really dross," the historical waste, the "secular announcement," "destroying its own message irreversibly," and therefore leaving her once again blind to the truth, always unable to realize her own involvement in the plague. At a certain point in her search, she concludes that "everything she saw, smelled, dreamed, remembered, would somehow come to be woven into The Tristero" (*L49,* 81). Like Oedipus, she is unable to see the real connections, her parentage with the inheritors, and therefore unable to ascertain her moral burden.

The Computer of the Lost

The overbearing muted post horn, the emblem of the Tristero, is a simulacrum, the "information that devours its own content,"[36] some sort of historical detritus, or McLuhan's media fallout, whose escalation brings the loss of communication, confirming *avant la lettre* Baudrillard's third hypothesis about the implosion of meaning in the media: "information is directly destructive of meaning" (79). And what is even more relevant to the truth escaping Oedipa, information "devours communication and the social" (80). It is not then that all Oedipa finds is simulacra, but that she is not able to see beyond the simulacra, partly because its connection with reality appears to have collapsed into "unreality," partly because her own perception is culturally jammed. Pynchon's postnational satire challenges the McLuhanite identification of the medium with the message by presenting the proliferation of the Tristero post horn as an index of the historical nihilism of such a collapse. His is not so much "a parable of the failure of the humanist desire for 'meaningful communication' and for inter-subjective communion through symbols" as Ganter suggests,[37] but rather a caricature of the new era of information. In addition, as a caricature, this paranoia is not Pynchon's alternative political mode. The Tristeros—resonant of the early twentieth century antirevolutionary *Cristeros* of Mexico—are not in my reading "American dreams deferred" as the Americanist, recuperative exercises of Decker and others posit.[38] Rather this double-voiced narration, the parodic strategy described by Bakhtin, is decisive to understanding Pynchon's critique. Jameson's flawed reading of the novel fails to discern this:

> The most ominous doubt inspired by this novella, which wants to contaminate its readers and beyond them to endow the present age itself with an impalpable but omnipresent culture of paranoia, is the conjecture that if the fossil record were complete, we would be likely to find the Thurn-and-Taxis post-horn on hominid artifacts as far back as the Pleistocene.[39]

By collating Pynchon's critique with his own prescription of postmodernism as an epoch whose dominant mode is nostalgic pastiche,[40] Jameson's attack on Oedipa's historical paranoia misses the point by neglecting a reading of the story as a postnational satire (not Jameson's "neutral parody") predicated on the character's failure to see beyond the muted post horn. Her paranoia allows her to intuit, but it ultimately overrides the reading of the national landscape of social dereliction: although she can see the signs pointing to the disinherited, she is unable to read this reality in terms of its opposition to the discourse of American inclusiveness. As she travels from San Narciso, the apparent center of Inverarity's empire, down to San Francisco hoping for "the whole thing to go away and disintegrate quietly" (*L49*,

109), Oedipa drifts into the night "at random," not knowing that she is going to be exposed to the "infected city" (*L49,* 117), and that once again she will be blind to the central message of her direct connection with the plague.

Instead of looking, she "played the voyeur and listener" (*L49,* 123), she can only see the simulacrum: "after each alienation, each species of withdrawal, as cufflink, decal, aimless doodling, there was always the post horn" (*L49,* 123). As she hopes for the "central truth" to stay and not blaze out, to have the epileptic seizure, the illumination, and also to remember beyond that moment: "The repetition of symbols was to be enough, without trauma as well perhaps to attenuate it or even jar it altogether loose from her memory. *She was meant to remember.* . . . She tested it, shivering: I am meant to remember. Each clue that comes is *supposed* to have its own clarity, its fine chances for permanence" (Pynchon's emphasis. *L49,* 118). It is at that point that her own conscience places Oedipa in a closed circuit of political impotence: "But then she wondered if the gemlike 'clues' were only some kind of compensation. To make up for her having lost the direct, epileptic Word, the cry that might abolish the night" (*L49,* 118). She may then remember the real, although only through the muted post horn and at the cost of accepting the loss of that "epileptic Word." That is, accepting the silence of the simulacrum. If the abolition of the night, of the underworld of the disinherited, is an impossibility, then there is no escape from the plague.

This arresting conclusion contradicts both hopeful recuperative or Americanist critics, and those projecting openly "postmodern," inconclusive renderings of the character. The views of the former, best represented in Lois Tyson's essay on Pynchon's "Politics of Despair," describes Oedipa's journey as a move "from existential blindness and bad faith to existential awareness and engagement."[41] And notably, the latter, the purely "postmodern" critics, also insist on Oedipa's recovered sight, even going as far as to claim that "[Oedipa's] long dark night, the central event of the novel, represents a radical enlargement of her vision. Significantly, it is the episode in the book that is most conspicuously free of parody."[42] But the prevalent narrative mode of the novel is that of parody as a function of postnational satire: the parody of the classical Oedipus, through its demotion from king to commoner, and the parody of the discourse of political renaissance for America, in the ineffectual recuperation of Oedipa Maas's vision, her ultimate blindness. Her inability to comprehend her own involvement as the impersonation of a system that promotes disinheritance, and to find a way out of it, is strictly critiqued through the use of parody. It is hard to see in Oedipa's political cul-de-sac the contradictory despair which may hopefully inspire a political engagement as envisaged in Tyson's essay:

> If *Lot 49* is a novel about the possibility of constituting an existential subjectivity in this nation today, then it must also be a novel about the politics of despair, about the ways one can continue to

> take meaningful action in a situation that is apparently hopeless and exitless. Despair is evident in the novel's overlapping social, philosophical, and psychological themes.[43]

Indeed, if Oedipa's journey into the night is to be considered as the "central event" of the novel, it is for two different reasons, both evidencing Oedipa's inability to engage politically. First, in her night journey through San Francisco, Oedipa witnesses "a calculated withdrawal" on the part of certain citizens "from the life of the Republic, from its machinery" (*L49,* 124). These are the citizens who may be communicating through the WASTE system, and who have withdrawn into a "separate, silent, unsuspected world" (*L49,* 125). The narrator in Ellison's *Invisible Man* also withdraws into the "unsuspected" underground where he can escape the stifling life of the American national nightmare. But to Oedipa, the underworld system becomes a threat, and she needs to look for her shrink Dr. Hilarius at the end of her journey to ask him "why the chance of it being real should menace her so" (*L49,* 132).

The culminating scene of Oedipa's night journey takes us to the second reason for considering this trip as the "central event" of the novel. As Oedipa reaches the limits of the California cityscape, at the San Francisco Embarcadero, she encounters a dying old sailor who asks her to post a letter for his wife through the WASTE. There, she envisions the core of this alternative underworld in the "secret salts held all those years by the insatiable stuffing of a mattress that could keep vestiges of every nightmare sweat, helpless overflowing bladder, viciously, tearfully consummated wet dream, like the memory bank to a computer of the lost" (*L49,* 126). The sailor's fluids stored in this unscripted "machine," and their clear belonging outside the system of references and properties of Inverarity's estate, their lack of virtual meaning in the lot, positions them as a form of excremental waste that can become oppositional to that very system. Unlike the bones of soldiers, which are recycled back into the consumers' lungs through the Beaconsfield cigarettes, these human remains constitute an alternate "memory bank." Very much like the lost items found inside those cars that Mucho had to recycle back into the commodity system, and whose vision of utter waste had traumatized and jammed Mucho's comfort, the "computer of the lost" stands as Pynchon's arresting image of "the separate, silent, and unsuspected world" where the opposition to the machinery of the Republic is recorded. It is here that Oedipa's inability to turn the curse of the plague is more patent. At the sailor's tearful cry, she can only whisper "I can't help" (*L49,* 126). As she stares at the mattress in awe, she thinks about the erasure of these private histories, "the stored, coded years of uselessness, early death, self-harrowing, the sure decay of hope, the set of all men who had slept on it, whatever their lives had been, would truly cease to be, forever, when the mattress burned" (*L49,* 128). Resigned to her inability to code those "worlds no other man had seen" and to the fact that "nothing she knew would preserve them, or him" (*L49,* 129), she flees to finish her circular trip at John Nefastis's apartment house, "back where she had started" (*L49,* 131).

Ironically, these spaces of the American underworld do not remain silent, but voiced in the form of Pynchon's fiction, and at center stage, the middle-class housewife who is unable to know how to preserve these records, and even what they suggest about her Republic, her nation. The novel thus becomes both the archive of an American underworld of dereliction, and an indictment of the cultural bias that renders Oedipa impotent, victim of her own national identity, a victim of her colonized unconscious. It is not that as Deborah Madsen has claimed "by reading in the debris of her culture the signs of an alternative explanation, an alternative pretext, she is able to see the strategies of cultural repression that have determined her subjectivity and defined her isolation,"[44] but rather the opposite. Her brief viewing of the waste renders her once again blinded: her eyes pierced by the reality, incapable of sorting a way out of her entrapment.

Oedipa is submerged in the social and psychological conditioning of her own nationalist education; her search, as do those of Slothrop or Stencil, in *Gravity's Rainbow* and *V.* respectively, unveils the establishment's conditioning of the citizen through a variety of psychological means. In Oedipa's case her academic literary education and her psychological therapy appear to be the unequivocal reasons for her blindness.

As Oedipa visits Berkeley, in the afternoon before her night journey, she appears to cherish the ways in which she was "mothered" by the National Security State of the 1950s. She visits the campus to try and contact a Professor Bortz, editor of a hardback edition of the play *The Courier's Tragedy,* a text that may contain a key to understanding the Tristero conspiracy. In Bortz's copy there should be a discrepancy with her own edition—precisely the line referring to the Tristero is missing—but to her surprise she finds out that Bortz has moved to San Narciso College. Oedipa has already made certain connections between Inverarity, W.A.S.T.E. (or more simply, WASTE), the underground system of postal communications unveiled by Oedipa; Thurn-and-Taxis, the historical European postal system originating in the Middle Ages (sorry Fred Jameson, not the Pleistocene) and in actual continued service until the nineteenth century; the Tristero, a supposedly subversive alternative system to Thurn-and-Taxis; and the possible representation of these in the fictional Jacobean play *The Courier's Tragedy.* By now San Narciso, center of Inverarity's speculative activities, has become the nodal point that connects all the patterns of the possible conspiracies.

Oedipa walks out of the campus in the afternoon: she feels like a stranger whose "somnolent" educational past contrasts with the modern and radical Berkeley campus over which the repressive machine of government does not seem to exert a firm control. By comparison with her own "Siwash" old university—Pynchon's Cornell?—she finds Berkeley "more akin to those Far Eastern or Latin American universities you read about, those autonomous culture media where the most beloved of folklores may be brought into doubt, cataclysmic of dissents voiced, suicidal of commitments chosen—the sort that bring governments down" (*L49,* 103).[45] The emphasis here on the voicing of dissent, and the autonomy of the cultural media, in this instance the university, is one more instance of Pynchon's unease with the hegemonic role of cultural national institutions in the United States. Far from exercising a critical activity, these institutions are at the heart of the technocratic state reinforcing the amalgamation of the "beloved folklores" of the nation, its self-perception as the land of promise, with the consensual discourse of progress and faith in technology.

Oedipa belongs therefore in an alternate world, separate from the Berkeley campus: "She moved through it carrying her fat book, attracted, unsure, a stranger, wanting to feel relevant but knowing how much of a search among alternate universes it would take" (*L49,* 103). As she looks around for "Secretaries James and Foster, and Senator Joseph, those dear daft numina who'd mothered over Oedipa's so temperate youth" (*L49,* 104), Oedipa just sums that they must simply be "in another world." Senator Joseph—McCarthy—and secretaries John Foster Dulles—secretary of state under Eisenhower, and architect of the CIA—and James Forrestal—secretary of defense at the time—are a sardonic reference to the civil context in which Oedipa has been reared, where anticommunist paranoia and political repression prevailed.[46] Those absent members of the establishment alluded to in the passage are behind Oedipa's educational programming, enabling her to execute Inverarity's will without perceiving the breakdowns in the nationalist discourses of opportunity and democracy. The ironic narrator notes that she is capable of investigating and connecting the patterns arising from Pierce Inverarity's legacy, because "among them they had managed to turn the young Oedipa into a rare creature indeed, unfit perhaps for marches and sit ins, but just a whiz at pursuing strange words in Jacobean texts" (*L49,* 104).

In Pynchon's fiercest critique of the character's inadequacy to question the machinery under which she has been trained, Ganter has correctly identified an attack also on the New Critics and their Derridean offspring,[47] in their break away from extra-textual and socio-historical reality: "Oedipa's attempt to reveal the soul of America's disease with 'books' only reproduces the very plague she seeks—the heart of the Trystero conspiracy is that text has become more important than people" (Ganter, "Rioting, Textuality and *The Crying of Lot 49,*" 69).[48] The possibility that "the symbol has taken over the human" (ibid., 77) is indeed at the center of Pynchon's critique of the ways in which the nationalist cultural industry replaces oppositional, critical codes with those that encourage cultural hegemony and consent. Similarly, Nefastis's hopeless machine aims at connecting "the world of thermodynamics to the world of information flow" (*L49,* 106) through the metaphor of entropy. The latter is in turn Pynchon's warning about the fate of the closed system of technocracy, a political system based on the fusion of the realms of information and technology, psychological conditioning, and the market.

The two parallel stories in Pynchon's earlier short story, "Entropy," literally evolve into two different "stories" of the same building: Callisto's ordered, closed world and Meatball's chaotic party downstairs. In Callisto's third-person narration, the second law of thermodynamics is applied to society: once you stop the circulation of individual ideas, the system is condemned to repeat itself and break down. Accordingly, American society, equaled here to its market structure, is presented as a closed system heading for an entropic end: "in American consumerism [Callisto] discovered a similar tendency from the least to the most probable, from differentiation to sameness, from ordered individuality to a kind of chaos" (*SL*, 88). This apocalyptic, entropic vision of a culture heading for disaster through its short-circuited flow of information, and its enforced sameness, also permeates Pynchon's later works and can be used as a referent of his political positioning in the face of consumerist uniformity. As all ideas become part of a consumer's intellectual menu, they cease to mean: "ideas, like heat-energy, would no longer be transferred, since each point in it would ultimately have the same quantity of energy" (*SL*, 88). Once the oppositional is incorporated into the system, the dialectical flow is stopped by the relative acceptance of all ideas into the closed system, leading to a "heat-death for his culture" (*SL*, 88). This is perhaps Pynchon's most prescient, and damning judgment of the recuperative readings of his postnationalist satires.

Correspondingly, the palpable atmosphere of subversion perceived by Oedipa in Berkeley and the appearance of entire groups of organized citizens that might be either plotting against the federal government or at least establishing alternative means of exchanging information both promote a gloomy look at the insurgent means left for the citizen to express a private opinion in an increasingly controlled and closed system. Both the atmosphere at Berkeley and the Yoyodine postal system are characterized by a certain degree of superficiality. Fallopian's description of the alternative postal service does not suggest any political content to the correspondence exchanged through it, as it merely transmits superficial messages such as: "Dear Mike, it said, how are you? Just thought I'd drop you a note. How's your book coming? Guess that's all for now. See you at The Scope" (*L49*, 53). However shallow the communication among the San Narciso users of the system may be, it provides them with a private voice, which surprisingly enough they have to use compulsorily once a week. In Fallopian's book linking "the Civil War to the postal reform system" (*L49*, 53), we may find yet another possible proof of the establishment's intent on imposing a hegemonic framework. Fallopian perceives the history of the suppression of private delivery systems in the United States—and the creation of a national system, we might add—as "a parable of power, its feeding, growth and systematic abuse" (*L49*, 54). Similarly, the wishful look at the American 1960s of the Berkeley campus is soon confronted with the social reality of their incorporation into the system through consumerism, and the suggestion that the institutional surveillance over the young is more sophisticated, less patent in the 1960s, than in Oedipa's years. The students' background belies their political activities: "But it was English she was hearing as she crossed Bancroft Way among the blonde children and the muttering Hondas and Suzukis; American English" (*L49,* 104). Once qualified by this restriction, the dissident atmosphere becomes ambiguous, suggesting that the Berkeley protest amid the unreality of "muttering Hondas and Suzukis" is once again too far from the reality of Watts, and too easily absorbed back into the system.[49]

Years after the publication of *Lot 49,* in his blurb for Kirkpatrick Sale's *SDS,* a detailed history of the New Leftist "Students for a Democratic Society" group, Pynchon would sound less critical of the 1960s youth movement—"the American Prerevolution"—as he praised the book: "a source of clarity, energy and sanity for anyone trying to survive the Nixonian reaction."[50] His committed, New Leftist political views had found in *The Crying of Lot 49* an accord with the ones promulgated by the founder of the SDS, Mario Savio. In one of his speeches at Berkeley, Savio appeared to coincide with the oppositional views to the machinery intimated in Pynchon's marginal underworld:

> There comes a time when the operation of the machine becomes so odious, makes you so sick at heart that you can't take part; you can't even tacitly take part, and you've got to put your bodies upon the levers, upon all the apparatus and you've got to make it stop. And you've got to indicate to the people who run it, to the people who own it, that unless you're heard, the machine will be prevented from working at all.[51]

Reminiscent of Thoreau's *Civil Disobedience,* and also openly committed to a politics of gaining visibility and a voice, Savio's statement promoted a view from outside the national machine in which the Republican housewife Oedipa could not share. With her educational conditioning, she would miss certain "realities" surrounding Berkeley not mentioned in the novel, such as the fact that napalm was being produced at a plant nearby, and war dogs were being trained in Tilden Regional Park in the hills above Berkeley.[52] Though she does not seem to know it, the California she cruises is deeply involved in the neo-colonial war in Vietnam, as the students in the VDC—Vietnam Day Committee—of the Berkeley sit-in that she witnesses are only too aware.

The Colonization of the Unconscious

Oedipa's failed search is the product of a psychological conditioning that goes beyond her university education, and whose definition involves an analysis of the internal colonization to which I have been referring in this chapter. Three interrelated aspects need to be underscored here: the role of psychology in dulling the critical contours of the American middle class, the role imposed on women by what Betty Friedan called the "feminine mystique," and finally the ideological dimensions associated with the new suburban lifestyle. The manipulations effected on her by her shrink, Dr Hilarius, who is working on a project called "die Brücke," or "the bridge inward," among suburban housewives, assert the coarse interweaving of the three aspects in Oedipa's female suburban psyche.

Betty Friedan examined in her 1963 best-seller *The Feminine Mystique* the psychological cycle of domination exercised over women through the creation of a repressed femininity, maintaining that "the feminine mystique masks the emptiness of the housewife role, encouraging girls to evade their own growth by vicarious living, by non-commitment."[53] This lack of responsibility, transformed in Oedipa in her final preference for schizophrenia over political engagement, cannot be evaded through a "knight of deliverance" or a "shrink," as Friedan observes: "there never will be enough Prince Charmings, or enough therapists to break that pattern now. It is society's job, and finally that of each woman alone" (264). Faced with solitude and an imposed sense of femininity, Oedipa is at the other side of the psychological storm proposed by Freudian psychiatrists Maryana Farnham and Ferdinand Lundberg in their 1942 *Modern Woman: The Lost Sex,* where they recommended "massive use of psychotherapy, government propaganda and awards for good motherhood, cash payments to mothers, and the restoration of such traditional home tasks as cooking, preserving, and decorating."[54] With "feminism" as their visible enemy,[55] Friedan accuses Farnham and Lundberg of having restored the "feminine mystique" during the postwar years, a feminine identity "grafted on to old prejudices and comfortable conventions" (37). The feminine mystique's only message of commitment is with women's "fulfillment of their own femininity" (38), a proposal advanced through the obscure discourse of psychiatry, "inaccessible to all but a few initiates, and therefore irrefutable" (38). Friedan even goes as far as to compare American suburbia and its effects on the female psyche with the Nazi concentration camp (Dr Hilarius in the novel): "there is an uncanny, uncomfortable insight into why a woman can so easily lose her sense of self as a housewife in certain psychological observations made of the behavior of prisoners in Nazi concentration camps" (265). Friedan's observation could be applied to Oedipa's Kinneret-among-the-Pines, a concentration camp of sorts representing another site of internal colonization.[56]

During a three in the morning phone call from Dr. Hilarius, Oedipa suffers a hallucination consisting of "the well-known portrait of Uncle [Sam: Maas read backwards] that appears in front of all our post offices . . . his finger pointing between her eyes" (*L49,* 17). The "we want you" slogan of the federal, national state merges with the hypnotic call from the former Nazi psychiatrist to convince Oedipa to participate in the experiment that he is running at the community hospital "on effects of LSD-25, mescaline, psilocybin, and related drugs on a large sample of suburban wives" (*L49*, 17). The bridge is also the bridge inward, a trip whose purpose is never quite clear, but as in the experiments with the Jews practiced by Hilarius in Buchenwald, what is being tested is probably the drug rather than the individual. With the combined collaboration of psychological science and sociological transformations, the age of conformity, the world of capital investment and material growth, can sacrifice the unified "subject" in exchange for the confused but self-assured consumer. Such practices had been half denounced by Vance Packard in his *The Hidden Persuaders,* where he elaborated on the research carried out by certain agencies on psychological techniques for selling, including research on shopping patterns during the housewife's menstrual cycle.[57]

Although Oedipa apparently rejects Hilarius's advice to take some pills—"would be dammed if she'd take the capsules he'd given her. Literally dammed" (*L49,* 17)—the image of Uncle Sam becomes immediately juxtaposed to Inverarity's forceful request to execute his will. The juxtaposition of these two incursions into Oedipa's previously uneventful existence allows for a conceivable amalgamation of both, particularly as Hilarius sounds on the phone "like Pierce doing a Gestapo officer" (*L49,* 16). Dr. Hilarius is after all a German refugee from World War II,[58] a former Nazi scientist whose work at Buchenwald consisted precisely in altering his patients' perception by working on "experimentally-induced insanity" (*L49, 95*), and who may have become paranoid after the Eichmann trial (1959). During the postwar period, he had been working for the U.S. government in an experiment that seemed to differ little from his earlier work at the camp. In his "A Journey. . ." Pynchon had warned about the role of "an enormous priest caste of shrinks who counsel moderation and compromise as the answer to all forms of hassle,"[59] and who are therefore behind the construction of the L.A. "unreality." Oedipa's paranoia may then be the result not of political consciousness, as so many critics have suggested, but of a fault in the psychological conditioning carried out on her. Hilarius had succeeded in modifying the perception of the Jews at the camp; he may also have manipulated Oedipa's. The Jews would only perceive Buchenwald as a "soccer field" where "fat children would learn flower-arranging and solfeggio in the strangling rooms. At Auschwitz the ovens would be converted over to petit fours and wedding cakes, and the V-2 missiles to public houses for the elves" (*L49*, 95). Oedipa may have not been completely conditioned to perceive her own concentration camp in such a positive light, and this might partly account for her anxiety and her doubts.

A part of the past, the history of psychiatric experimentation with prisoners carried out by German scientists in the concentration camps, has survived into present-day America, much like Von Braun's experimentation with rocketry. That combination of psychology and rocketry would be explored seven years later in *Gravity's Rainbow* through Slothrop's conditioning to Immoplex. And both scientific experimentations are successfully transferred over to the United States by the corporate state whose only (in)visible head in California is Pierce Inverarity. During the autumn of 1965 and the winter of 1966, that is, at the time the novel was going to print, California was going through a public debate on LSD and the U.S. Senate Subcommittee met to outlaw the drug.[60] Pynchon links this contemporary issue to Nazi psychological experimentation in the same way in which in his "A Journey. . ." he had denounced conditioning through chemical products as a central feature of Californian lifestyles: "But alcohol is a natural part of the Watts style; as natural as LSD is around Hollywood. The white kid digs hallucination simply because he is conditioned to believe so much in escape, escape as an integral part of life, because the white L.A. scene makes accessible to him so many different forms of it" (80). In opposition to Roszak's open celebration of Huxley, Leary, and the other public proponents of hallucinogens, Pynchon rejects their effects by incisively linking them to those other forms of escape that dissociate the different racial worlds coexisting in California. But he goes even further as he disguises the cool Lisergic establishment (i.e., Timothy Leary) under the mask of the Nazi shrink Hilarius (read Hi-Leary-us), accusing both of contributing to a massive colonization of the unconscious in the midst of the Cold War.[61] Hilarius's spatial image for the unconscious reveals that he had already established a metaphor by which desires and drives could be tamed:

> And part of me must have really wanted to believe—like a child hearing, in perfect safety, a tale of horror—that the unconscious would be like any other room, once the light was left in. That the dark shapes would resolve only into toy horses and Biedermeyer furniture. That therapy could tame it after all, bring it into society with no fear of its someday reverting. (*L49,* 93)

Pynchon's assault on the psychoanalytical establishment, like Deleuze and Guattari's in *Anti-Oedipus,* is directed at the ways in which its scientific metaphors of the human mind favored adaptation, conformity, and the erasure of the subject. In *The Crying of Lot 49* "egos lose their sharp edges" (*L49,* 94) with the use of LSD, and the distinction between the "I" and the "others" "begins to vanish" (*L49,* 94). However effectively Oedipa protected herself at the very beginning of the narration against the pernicious effects of the pills administered by Dr. Hilarius, she may have been hypnotized by Hilarius's technique of making faces: "Hilarius only made a face at her, one he'd made before. He was full of these delightful lapses from orthodoxy" (*L49,* 11). Through his unorthodox face games, Dr. Hilarius carries out part of a psychological treatment that involves more than just a relapse into childhood: "He claimed to have once cured a case of hysterical blindness with his number 37, the 'Fu-Manchu' . . . as Oedipa's Uncle Sam hallucination faded, it was this Fu-Manchu face that came dissolving it in to replace it and stay with her for what was left of the hours before dawn" (*L49,* 18). Oedipa's "hysterical blindness" derives from a psychology oriented to bringing light into the "room" of the unconscious by extirpating the guilty conscience—and with it any sort of critical consciousness at all—from its patients, whatever the means.

Mucho is finally "cured" with LSD of his painful and traumatic vision/awareness of waste at the lot as Hilarius has "broadened his program to include husbands" (*L49,* 143). His conscious memory of the "bad dream" (*L49,* 144) of seeing the N.A.D.A. (National Automobile Dealer's Association, but also "nothing" in Spanish) sign every day at the lot, its "cracking metal sign that said nada, nada, against the blue sky" (*L49,* 144), is the only remainder of the waste that had so disturbed him. The vision of the daily nothingness is skirted by remembering only its symbolic representation in the "sign," as Oedipa had escaped consciousness and commitment by remembering only the muted post horn. After the treatment, he is said to be "losing his identity . . . less himself and more generic" (*L49,* 140), but like those other "multi-faced" male characters in the novel, his problem is that he is too many people at once: "he enters a staff meeting and the room is suddenly full of people, you know? He's a walking assembly of a man" (*L49,* 140).

Oedipa's potential search for self, underlined by many critics as the key to reading the novel, contrasts with the male mercurial characters who are defined in terms of their change, their unstable selfhood, as Inverarity (non-truth), or Hilarius (laughable). But their ability to "make faces" or "make voices" is not a merely performative ability; it is also a metaphor for their adaptability, their ever-changing capacity for manipulating different people. Pierce and Hilarius come to represent the ambiguity of the ever-switching media, the reactionary side of the carnival, and the dislocation of identities by which the subject is hardly definable.

A year earlier, just at the time when she had unknowingly been named executrix of the will, Oedipa had received a call from Pierce during which he had impersonated various voices starting Slavic, Negro, Pachuco, Gestapo, and finally Lamont Cranston, "the one he had used all the way down to Mazatlán" (*L49,* 11). This versatility of the fragmented subject is one of the preferred objects of parody in the novel, as it is a constituent part of the escape fantasy of white America. As Pynchon's subtle commentary on contemporary Californian society becomes more obvious, Metzger, the co-executor and legal representative of Pierce Inverarity, in his role as an actor become lawyer, also becomes reminiscent of the Republican candidate in 1966 to the governorship of California: the middle-aged actor Ronald Reagan. Oedipa, who had thought Metzger might be the "Knight of deliverance" coming to rescue her from her tower is finally unable to communicate with him, partly due to his acute narcissism: in Echo Courts he prefers to look at his own image as a child on the TV, over making love to Oedipa, and he then elopes with a fifteen-year-old friend with the "Paranoids" band.

As they all abandon Oedipa—"they are stripping away, one by one, my men" (*L49*, 153)—their presence hovers over her like the obscure figure of the lot 49. Oedipa's imaginary pregnancy at the end of the novel returns her to the iconography and techniques implanted on her unconscious by Hilarius as she "dreamed of disembodied voices from whose malignance there was no appeal, the soft dusk of mirrors out of which something was about to walk, and empty rooms that waited for her. Your gynecologist has no test for what she was pregnant with" (*L49*, 175). She is perhaps pregnant with the paranoia induced by all the male intellectual secretions to which she has been exposed throughout the novel. Her paranoia—"they'll call it paranoia. They" (*L49*, 170)—induces her into thinking that everything she has blindly observed is any of four options: either there is a real alternative system, or she is hallucinating it; or it is a plot against her, or she is fantasizing such a plot. She does not like any of these four options and so she turns to schizoid paranoia, "hop[ing] she was mentally ill" (*L49*, 171). Certain critical approaches to Oedipa's final wish worryingly celebrate her "denial of "either/or" constructions as syntactically or experientially meaningful."[62] Kolodny and Peters's approach falls short because of its celebratory identification of Oedipa's self-perception with that of the critical reader: "we've come, like Oedipa, to embrace the reality of ambiguity, uncertainty, and barely-perceived intuition" (79). As Oedipa renounces her fragmentary and momentary sight and chooses mental illness and ostracism, she goes away like the old Greek king into exile from the polis, not so much into the realm of ambiguity, but into a maddening noncommittal suicide, an action difficult to recognize by most recuperative readers.

Chapter 5

✦

Epidermic Metamorphosis? Shedding the Nation in *Cambio de piel*

From 1962, the year of publication of *La muerte de Artemio Cruz,* to 1967, Fuentes worked on his most experimental project, *Cambio de piel* (*A Change of Skin*), a text that would build on the earlier themes but with a much less clear set of answers. If the "monster" Artemio had personified so many of the ills of Mexican society, and his death had announced a potential future break, in *Cambio de piel* the challenges faced by Mexico, reducible once again to perpetual cycles of violence and destruction, are taken out of the national framework and explored within a global framework as part of a universal history of infamy. The exceptionality of Mexico's essentialized relationship with death is here revealed not as a local aberration, or as part and parcel of the national character, but as an echo of the larger history of a violent species bent on genocide and sacrificial murder.[1] The unveiling of the consensual narrative of the nation through the parody of its epic fictions exposes not only that universal atavistic violence but also the contradictions of a global modernity: the narcissistic loops of hegemonic Mexicanness and its underlying narrative of communal progress are targeted and denounced as part of a worldwide process of technocratic homogenization, a new utterance of the old violence. Fuentes's narrative investment in referential saturation and historical panoramas culminates with *Terra nostra* (1975), completing a perceptible shift from (post)national to pan-Hispanic satire.[2] A similar move from the local to the global is also apparent in Pynchon's works in the 1970s as the large Californian deception visited in *The Crying of Lot 49* sprawls to a wider panorama in *Gravity's Rainbow:* the great national lie of consumerist happiness and technological prowess is revealed as an avatar of the universal nightmare of progress.

In Which Fuentes Explicates Himself

Fuentes concentrates in *Cambio de piel* on the apparent contradiction between modernity, a global hegemonic discourse, and nationalism, the local discourse that avowedly resists the modern while stealthily promoting it. But

Fuentes also elaborates here a bolder nihilistic manifesto more readily defiant of the Western idea of progress and its ideological by-products: modernity and the nation. The resulting political cynicism and the central ambiguities are so pervasive throughout the text that David Gallagher dubbed him a Nazi apologist when reviewing the novel for the *New York Times Book Review* in February 1968, while only a few months earlier the Franco regime had prohibited its publication in Spain for its "pro-Semitic and anti-German" allusions.[3] To both paradoxical charges, Fuentes responded with comparable anger though seemingly contradictory references to the "risks of freedom": "put to the test, words always signify the risk of freedom"[4] are his closing words in his response to the Spanish censors. In his rather more elaborate letter to the editor of the *New York Times* he makes obvious his authorial aim:

> I have specifically spelt out in my book a very simple idea: that the impulses of freedom have been, can be, and will be used as justification for extreme oppression . . . Revolutionary thinkers (Sade and Nietzsche included) are not sponsors of evil; they are sponsors of freedom who must courageously recognize that freedom can lead to evil, yet that the risk is worth taking.[5]

Of all the authorial glosses to the novel, this is perhaps Fuentes's most frank statement about the ambitious aim of the book: to chart that grey boundary between freedom and evil, between human progress and its moral confines. He goes even further to clarify both the objects of his parody and therefore his ideological standpoint: "*Cambio de piel* is deliberately designed as a phantasmagoria of the Right—its whole conception of history, love, psychology—seen in a parodic vein from the standpoint of what I believe in. That 'creed' could be called, not 'Nazism' as your reviewer states, but critical revolutionism."[6] After this New Leftist acknowledgment, the real voice of a barefaced totalitarianism in whose parody the novel rejoices, the clerical fascist censor in Spain and his indictment of the text, become key paratexts to understand the political positioning of the novel in its Spanish-speaking historical context.

And yet, despite Fuentes's straightforward definition it is not difficult to understand the upset review in the *New York Times*. After all, Fuentes's noticeable need to explicate the novel in order to authorize a position in the otherwise frenzied fictional play with the moral limits of terror and violence, freedom and evil, civilization and barbarism, is an authorial effort to forestall the most extreme readings of the text. In a way, Fuentes tries to defuse in his essays the more radical aspects of his fiction through an authorial redefinition of the text. His nihilistic performance is then restricted or elevated to a rather optimistic and hazy "critical revolutionism," a transcending internationalist practice that Fuentes makes even more explicit elsewhere: "the nihilistic realization of individual desires will create its antithesis in the full cooperation between humans."[7] The politically hazardous lack of faith in universal truths offered by Nietzsche's nihilism could dialectically give way to a renewed utopia. But this "critical" utopianism, particularly its utopian component, the author's avowed "creed," is obscured by the novel's constant play—in the final analysis, the novel can be better described as a satirical critique than as the utopian manifesto dramatized by the author in his multiple glosses and commentaries. This generic discrepancy may perhaps account for Fuentes's need for constant reminders of his authorial purpose, his vain attempt to control, influence, and demarcate his ideological positioning in the face of the radical ambiguities provoked by his aesthetic and narrative play.

There are at least three other contemporary texts where Fuentes explicates his novel at length: a talk given in Mexico City in the summer of 1965 which then became an article for the collection *Los narradores ante el público,* and two important interviews in 1966 with American academics. The first is a reported conversation with Luis Harss and Barbara Dohmann,[8] and the second an interview with the Uruguayan literary critic Emir Rodríguez Monegal.[9] Looked at chronologically they sketch the evolution of Fuentes's thoughts about the text during the months before its final publication. At a series of conferences of Mexican writers organized by the Instituto de Bellas Artes de México between 1965 and 1966, Fuentes—who spoke on August 26, 1965—was already glossing a novel entitled *El Sueño* (*The Dream*) published nineteen months later under the revised title *Cambio de piel* (*A Change of Skin*). At the conference, Fuentes identified an extensive list of influences and intertexts cannibalized in the book, but most importantly, he confirmed there three of his most significant obsessions at the time: the existential "conflict between an individual and the world";[10] the role of pervasive national myths in art and politics; and finally, the formulation of a theory of the novel beyond the "false dichotomy between pure art or *littérature engagée.*"[11] These three unambiguous themes with notable variations and ramifications become somehow interconnected in the disjointed narrative of *Cambio de piel,* tracing a highly complex texture characterized by the satire and saturation of cultural referents. As I show here, all these three obsessions—existence, national myths, and engaged artistic production—are woven into the chameleon-like narrator, Freddy Lambert, who becomes a performer of these central debates and themes through his one-sided dialogue with the other characters.

The Nation as Madhouse

A humorous combination of Freddy, Friedrich Nietzsche, and Lambert, Balzac's Louis Lambert, the narrator's name is already a playful dialogue between well-established cultural symbols of nihilism and madness. Madness here derives from a blinding view of the world: Balzac's character, described as a real "seer,"[12] cannot endure his holistic view of humankind. He too is an individual at odds with the world, as he has seen and understood its realities in a different light. None of the critics who have reviewed Fuentes's novel have paid much attention to this intertext and its significance in the novel, and yet there are a number of positively self-conscious references that help to understand Freddy Lambert's voice.

The story of Balzac's Louis Lambert represents the failure of an educational system, and of an entire society, to accommodate the mind and ideas of a gifted philosopher and scientist. Although his figure is presented from the sympathetic viewpoint of the narrator, his monumental intellectual trajectory is the cause of his isolation and has ultimately led him to be regarded as a madman. His anguish at the whole history of humanity and his disquieting suggestion that culture can be seen as a large series of failed projects, that "[civilization's] constant disturbance has brought it no progress,"[13] has an undeniable critical bearing on *Cambio de piel* and its ambitious discussion of modernity and progress.

Similarly, in both texts the narrator's voice insidiously suggests that the two Lamberts may in reality not be mad but "right" about the world. Balzac's Lambert fears that his illuminated outsideness might turn him into a Christ figure: "I feel within me a life so luminous that it might quicken worlds . . . We must needs embrace the whole world, and clasp it to our bosoms before we can remake it; but those who have thus clasped it, and thus refashioned it, did they not begin as a wheel in the machine? As for me, those wheels would crush me."[14] Influenced by Emanuel Swedenborg's ecumenical ideals, Lambert is tempted by his millennial visions to see himself as a future savior of the world who could lead it into a new spiritual and scientific era. Instead, he becomes increasingly secluded and introverted until he is clinically declared mad.

At the end of *Cambio de piel,* we also find out that Freddy Lambert is an inmate at an asylum in Cholula, and that like the original Lambert, he is the victim of a society that expels and confines those geniuses whose universal truths cannot be heard. As an inmate at the Cholula madhouse, Freddy Lambert's voice is the sardonic reminder that unreason naturally provides an insight into the inherent organization of institutionalized reason, for in unreason all that reason stands for and all that it denies becomes negated but fulfilled at once. This complementary, dialectical view of madness would also figure prominently in Foucault's *Madness and Civilization* (1961), which appeared in the original French five years before *Cambio de piel.* Foucault had defined madness in terms of its ancillary relation with established reason:

> Joining vision and blindness, image and judgment, hallucination and language, sleep and waking, day and night, madness is ultimately nothing, for it unites in them all that is negative. But the paradox of this nothing is to manifest itself, to explode in signs, in words, in gestures. . . . For madness if it is nothing, can manifest itself only by departing from itself, by assuming an appearance in the order of reason and thus becoming the contrary of itself.[15]

Triggered by the vision of Cholula's asylum, from where the narrator may have escaped, Javier indirectly reminds us of Foucault's study of Charenton, the Paris madhouse, where "'not only madmen were locked up. They also kept libertines and spendthrifts there. The lunatics in Charenton were put on show,' Javier said quietly. 'They were paraded before the good citizens of Paris as a spectacle, and the good citizens went home again with quiet consciences. They would congratulate themselves that they weren't like the patients'" (*CP,* 308/309). This description of madness as a form of social scapegoatism may thus be applied to the narrator at the peril of repeating the same epistemological structures which arguably culminated in the concentration camp. This moral resonates as the four characters themselves may be establishing the same power-relation with the inhabitants of Cholula's madhouse, and in a *mise-en-abimic* move, it stands out as a warning to the reader not to do the same with the narrator.

He warns Elizabeth:

> What didn't occur to you, Dragoness, was that the asylum attendants were like priests. Priests have always watched over madmen, giving them versions of life and the world that they can comprehend, changing their hatred into love, finding peace for them, providing them with the exaltation and the calm that a lunatic needs to go on following his thread. The priest, the writer, the artist, the politician, everyone who supplies the world with images of itself, artificial, false images, interpretations, incantatorial psalms, all of them know that they are manipulating their lunatics. But the madmen, for example my friend Tristam Shandy, don't even hear the rhetoric. They laugh at their mentors and at the same time gradually transform them into the lunatics of lunatics. (*CP,* 308/309–10)

Fuentes insists on the inadequacy of the characters to understand the world from a critical viewpoint because by holding to linear notions of time and conventional mappings they may have taken refuge in a farcical and repressive view of reality. If Balzac's Louis Lambert had written as an adolescent *A Treatise on the Will,* confiscated by his Jesuit teachers, the novel we read, *Cambio de piel,* is also supposedly the confiscated, suppressed work of a madman who speaks uncomfortable heresies.

As we discover at the end of the novel, Freddy Lambert is a madman whose freedom is curtailed so that his expansive mind may be equally contained, but in that process, the creative act of the novel comes into being. He is genealogically related to his contemporary, Cortázar's Oliveira in *Rayuela* (*Hopscotch*) (1963).[16] Once again this intertext is openly suggested by Fuentes himself who had meditatively linked to the two "fathers" of Freddy Lambert in his 1966 review of Cortázar's novel: "Oliveira belongs to the line of the imbecile genius who, from Louis Lambert to Pierrot le Fou, creates the indispensable order of the dispensable. In the madhouse and the hospital, final port of that Nietzsche that we could all become, is the center of the Hopscotch, heaven and hell are reunited and freedom can be exercised from the perpetual cry of need, of dissatisfaction."[17] That "indispensable order of the dispensable" is also the project of Freddy Lambert as he recovers and inspects the vestiges of a dystopian reality where the only apparent freedom is to be found in the secluded space of a madhouse. Sickness was also the condition with which the agonizing voice from underground starts its confession in Dostoevsky's *Notes from Underground:* "I am a sick man. . . I am a spiteful man. I am a most unpleasant man. I think my liver is diseased."[18] Like Dostoevsky's character, Lambert's existential sickness accounts for his visionary stance in front of a decayed civilization. Importantly, Fuentes immerses himself here in the epistemological debate about the relation between the structures of power and knowledge that define the Occident. Finally, another relevant feature seems to have been modeled on Balzac's text: the use of the second person. *Louis Lambert* is partly narrated through the character's epistolary relation with his fiancée to whom he confides his existential anxieties and who, like the narrator, gives support to his genius until the end. Although obviously deformed by the very different scope and organization of *Cambio de piel,* this aspect is nevertheless important as the second person gains here a different use to the one seen in *Aura* or *La muerte de Artemio Cruz.* Klaus Meyer-Minnemann has already pointed out how Lambert's voice is narratologically different to the one found in those earlier texts.[19] The central difference lies in the fact that the second-person narration in those other texts was used as an internal monologue, whereas in *Cambio de piel* it becomes the dialogue between a homodiegetic narrator and some of the characters. This narrative mode affords Fuentes a series of games with the process of writing itself, and with the boundaries of the writer-author-narrator in the novel, an issue further problematized by his constant public reinterpretation of the text.

The dialogic format of the novel, intermixed with flashbacks, dialogues, and internal monologues, offers various stories as a conversation with the two female characters, Elizabeth and Isabel, addressing them as Dragona and Novillera, respectively, in order to continuously deface their individualities and erode their fictional freedom. The prevalence of this narrating apostrophic style combines and pushes back the omniscient and the subjective at the same time; the narrator's violent incursions in the intimacy of the other characters in their dialogues, their thoughts, and in their lives—as an omniscient narrator—is coupled with a constant reminder of his own convictions and desires as a nihilist. The narrator is that "individual in conflict with the world" to which Fuentes refers in his articles and interviews, and as such, it provides a suitable vehicle for a performance of Fuentes's farcical version of existentialism. In particular, two key contemporary interviews provide us with extensive commentary by the author on the existential nihilism of the narrator.

In Which Fuentes Appears as a Beatnik

In his interview with L. Harss and B. Dohmann in *Into the Mainstream*—a milestone in the dissemination of the writers of the Latin American literary boom in the United States of the mid-1960s—just two months before the novel was published, Fuentes advertised his new novel once again as "the story of the conflict between an individual and the world,"[20] introducing Freddy Lambert as "an aging Nihilist, a middle-aged beatnik, a rebel without a cause, who is pushing forty."[21] This explanatory note reveals the author's reply to the narrator's rhetorical question to Elizabeth in the novel: "Am I only another rebel without a cause who has begun to grow old, a middle-ageing beatnik, an angry young man still angry enough but no longer so young?" (*CP,* 73/67). Autobiographical questions aside—Fuentes was thirty-nine at the time of publishing the novel—the author's useful commentary reconfirms his intellectual positioning within the New Left, stressing also his coincidence with Norman Mailer in "many existential, even nihilistic, attitudes" (309). Such attitudes are seen as the basis of his own New Leftist literary and political motivation: "If I have anything in common with Mailer, it's the conviction that a new anarchic [*sic*] left is forming within the neo-capitalist countries, and that this current offers us new literary modes and characters" (309). Among those new literary characters inspiring Fuentes's *The Dream/A Change of Skin* would be the central character in Mailer's 1965 *An American Dream,* the suicidal Steven Rojack, whose facetious abandonment of a comfortable elitist existence by murdering his unbearable rich wife turns him into an archetype of the desperate middle-aged white male in crisis, an echo also of Updike's 1960 success, *Rabbit Run.*

If the "existentialist synapses" of the black hipster described by Mailer were a response to the overwhelming feeling of foreignness in the midst of a racist society, so too Fuentes's decidedly un-Mexican beatnik responds as an outsider to manifold realities: he is outside the nation, outside society, but also outside the world of the other characters. For the two couples at the center of the story, he is an apparition, a resurrection of the dead god mourned and celebrated by Nietzsche. As Fuentes put it in his interview with Emir Rodríguez Monegal,[22] he is indeed the "deus ex machina" of the novel, who stages, transforms and performs the lives of the two couples as he participates in their moral judgment. This outsideness opposes the narrator not only existentially to the world, but also to the foreign nation "Mexico," and to his stories and their characters.[23] In other words, his spatial placement defines him ideologically as *the* outsider, but also as the source of renewal, of heterodoxy and heresy. The dialogue continuously reminds us of its own prominence as a burlesque intellectual "happening" over the fractured plot, foregrounding a "radicalism of fiction" aimed at finding that "new heresy" sought by the author, capable of "renew[ing] that aspiration to liberty, which is perhaps the closest we can come to liberty itself."[24] In other words, the novel as happening is not only a formal feature, a "resource of parody" as Basto has suggested, but also an actual performance through dialogue of the existential theme of overcoming nihilism.[25]

As the self-appointed hammer of the Mexican nationalist establishment, Fuentes also positioned himself at a vantage point: New York, Paris, where the novel was written and signed, but also Tonantzintla, conferring on himself the status of the insider-outsider, a position reflected in the use of the homodiegetic narrator who "observes" and talks to the other characters, while moving in and out of the story. A closer look at the complexly parodic detachment of the existential narrator reveals its centrality as one of the key narrative strategies used by Fuentes to deal at once with his three obsessive themes noted earlier—namely, existentialism, nationalism, and narrative play. The narrator's outsideness goes beyond an intellectual play with the limits of nihilistic freedom—the individual opposed to the world: it also effects a potent critique of the cycles of violence on which the history of the Mexican nation is supposedly founded, while humorously performing a cannibalization of literary forms and theories.

If as Fuentes posits "in Mexico there is an existentialism *avant la lettre,* and very obvious: Mexico is a country of the immediate moment,"[26] then his interposed narrator can be regarded as an individual on a search for the literary form with which to capture that immediacy so as to exorcize it and artistically liberate it from nationalist essentialisms. That form is the "happening."[27] The carnivalesque occurrence of history, the liquidation of the belied exceptionalism of the nation derives in a festive postnational satire attended by the equally defaced characters. In the epigraph to part 2, "In Body and Soul," we encounter a suggestion of definition for the novel as a whole: "Therefore the Narrator quotes Tristan Tzara: 'Tout ce qu'on regarde est faux,' in order to save himself from the Museum, from Perfection, and to participate in a personal Happening, a novel written for immediate consumption: recreation" (*CP,* 23/15). The text is perhaps an instance of the happening defined by Susan Sontag just a year earlier as "an art of radical juxtaposition" and "a cross between art exhibit and theatrical performance."[28] The text is set to be performed in each reading, also as an "impossible feast," one that defies the static occurrence of a linear story, the national "Museum," in favor of a playfully performative (hi)story. A happening whose audience is the reader, but also the characters who are in and out at once, and who suffer, like the reader, the unforgiving performance of the act. As one of the many influences acknowledged by Fuentes, Sontag's description of New York happenings in the early 1960s and their use, or treatment, of the audience can be useful: "Perhaps the most striking feature of the happening is its treatment (this is the only word for it) of the audience. The performers may sprinkle water on the audience, or fling pennies or sneeze-producing detergent powder at it. Someone may be making near deafening noises on an oil drum, or waving an acetylene torch in the direction of the spectators."[29] Spared the oil and the powder, the characters—and the readers—are however ceaselessly interpolated and intellectually teased, references and allusions are showered on them in this surrealist spectacle where history and popular and highbrow culture camply amalgamate: from the Beatles to *Hamlet,* from the Mariachis to Paz.[30] Lambert reminds Elizabeth of the existential use of such farcical games: "And so it goes, sweet Elizabeth. Once you begin to monologue over the skull of Yorick you discover that the Dane's doubt is the only way to affirm the elemental truth that we are, yet we are not; we were, yet we were not; we shall be, yet we shall not be. Now you see me, now you don't: boo" (*CP,* 57/51). The narrator's mockery of all the characters, as the practitioners of the parodied values and ways of life, places them center stage: their well-defined, square concepts of history, of love, of psychology, makes up that "phantasmagoria of the Right" which Fuentes sought to lampoon in the novel.

Nationalism as Sartrean Bad Faith

The four main characters, their opinions and experiences, establish a playful game of complementary and opposing identities throughout the novel. Rather than merely being "signifiers whose signified is 'modernity'" itself, as Jean Franco put it,[31] they could also be read as different moral and aesthetic attitudes toward it. Elizabeth is an American middle-aged woman, later found to be a Mexican Jew; Isabel is a young Mexican who has lived in the States; Javier, Elizabeth's husband, met her in New York and is writing a novel, *Pandora's Box,* about the "secret of love"; and Franz is an exiled German, a former Nazi architect who participated in the construction of the concentration camp of Terezin.[32] In the same way in which Javier is writing a novel inside the novel, there is a parody inside the parody as the judgment carried out on the two couples is staged inside the pyramid at Cholula, a ceremony immediately disqualified "because its sense lies in the parody of the parody."[33] The "Impossible Feast," the happening, has in the meantime actualized the liquidation of the national myths, in particular its central mystery: the exceptionality of Mexican history and the impossibility of national consensus.

If the self-obsession of Mexican intellectual nationalism is perceived as a form of nihilistic existentialism that promotes a sense of predestination, a Sartrean "bad faith," an oppressive sense of historical inevitability, then the role of the New Leftist intellectual is to find a way out. In order to preempt the fixation of the Mexican intellectual nationalists in carving out the exceptionality of Mexican history, Fuentes draws a contrast between the Jewish Holocaust of World War II and the acts of violence committed in Mexico throughout its history, which bring home the international reality of the twentieth century and reunite it with local essentialized traditions of violence and death. Mexico comes out of its singularity to participate in a universal history, as Paz's *The Labyrinth of Solitude* intimated in closing: "we are, for the first time in our history, contemporaries of all humankind" (235). But the historical narrative in the novel portrays universal history as an incessant series of cycles of violence. Fuentes's depiction of this contemporariness emphasizes the ritualistic aspect of Mexican history, a history characterized, like the history of the rest of humanity, by power struggles, oppression, and death. Conflict is seen as an atavistic human feature, rather than either class warfare or national fratricide, and the incursions into European history provide the Mexican traditions of death with a suitable background for the discussion of the relationship between the local geography of violence, represented by the pyramid at Cholula, and the universal suffering epitomized by the Jewish Holocaust. Unsurprisingly then, the Spanish conquest is not the first layer of violence in the Mexican landscape: the Tlaxcaltecas already suffered injustice under Aztec rule, and their collaboration with Cortés in the massacre of Aztec nobles at Cholula is then just another episode of ritualistic, cyclical vengeful death. As they kill three thousand Aztecs "they free those the Cholulans had destined for sacrifice" (*CP,* 16/9). This incessant rewriting of the foundations of the nation as inherently remitting to another originary moment of aggression is common to the other novels by Fuentes analyzed here. In *Cambio de piel,* however, this questioning of the exceptionality of Mexican violence aims to denationalize violence as an inherently human bond—the real plot of universal history is not progress, but the constant repetition of bloodshed and murder. The recurrence of violence and evil is indeed "one of the few certainties the reader has on closing *Cambio de piel,*" as Steven Boldy has noted.[34]

Whereas in *La muerte de Artemio Cruz* the fragmented narrative of the novel formally stages the breaking away from linear history, in *Cambio de piel* the sense of absolute contemporariness, the satire and saturation of an overwhelming "pure perpetual present" formalizes such rupture. In his interview with Emir Rodríguez Monegal, Fuentes makes clear that history has to be understood in this novel as either static or repetitive: "There is a paralyzed history. A history which is turned into a Statue of History, remitting to itself, returned to itself. There is no historical progress, this is what the novel is somehow saying: there is no eschatology, there is only pure perpetual present. A series of ceremonies."[35] Accordingly, history in the novel is presented as a consecutive occurrence of dismal practices instead of the victorious rendering of official national histories, replacing the consensual idea of progress as the thematic argument of history by that of regress.

The echoes of Benjamin's "Theses on the Philosophy of History" are evident: the shape of Fuentes's "Statue of History" is based on Benjamin's apocalyptic image of the angel of history compared, in turn, to Klee's painting *Angelus Novus.* Historical progress for Benjamin's Angel departs from "commonsense" history: "Where we perceive a chain of events, he sees one single catastrophe which keeps piling wreckage upon wreckage and hurls it in front of his feet." [36] This view of history as a catastrophe by which progress is characterized as a "storm" propelling the Angel "into the future to which his back is turned, while the pile of debris before him grows skyward" is arguably close to the nihilistic inspiration and the satirical excesses of *Cambio de piel.* Benjamin's much-quoted tantalizing image of progress, as both an imposed violent movement and as a pile of debris, has also been used by Tom Nairn. For Nairn the dead which the Angel would like to "awaken"—literally, the historical debris—are resuscitated: "through nationalism the dead are awakened, this is the point—seriously awakened for the first time." The asylum where the narrator is held prisoner is the "land where live the dead who resuscitate themselves, this palace of Our Lord Lazarus. . . . He who has given his name to our dwelling place and also to the pyramid and also to the church atop the pyramid" (*CP,* 441/461). The "Land of Lazarus," to which the narrator refers at the close of the novel, is really the imaginary territory of the Nation, the Mexican nation, where its sacrificial victims in the name of historical progress are cyclically incorporated into the machine to fuel its projection into the empty space of the future. As Nairn puts it: "All cultures have been obsessed by the dead and placed them in another world. Nationalism rehouses them in this world. Through its agency the past ceases being 'immemorial': it gets memorialized into time present, and so acquires a future. For the first time it is meaningfully projected on to the screen of futurity" (*Faces of Nationalism,* 4). But Nairn's ambivalent celebration of nationalism forgets its customary alliance with modernity, the "neon-lit pyramid," at the basis of the "screen of futurity." In Mexico, the smoke screen of an ever postponed modernity is blown away by the realization that the machine is not going anywhere, and that "most Mexicans are left without any other possibility than the paradise of the present instant,"[37] that there is only incessant sacrifice and no reward, that there is "a series of ceremonies," but no escape from the loop of never-realized material or moral progress.

A Paralyzed History

Cambio de piel was finished at a time when Fuentes was frontally attacking the agonic soul search of Mexican intellectuals as a trap, or a mirage: "On returning to Mexico, where I finished the novel, I asked myself if any other country, except Russia and Spain, had been as worried about the sense of its nationhood as ours."[38] In his evaluation, the distinct root of Mexican national obsessions is to be found in its mythical sensibility. Mexican myths offer a "succession of consecrated, foreseeable, and repetitive forces" (*Los narradores ante el público,* 138) based on legends that do not allow for narrative suspense, but which merely recite three well-known mythical epics: the unfulfilled promise of the return (Quetzalcoatl), of its mythical destruction through treason (Montezuma-Malinche-Cortés), and of the silent vengeance of the victims over time. As the "denouement is known beforehand" (ibid., 139) there is no real narrative expectation—just bad faith—which would account for an earlier poverty of the narrative genres in Mexico due to the assumed obligation of the postrevolutionary artist: "the patriotic vigilance of local traditions and the national identity" (ibid., 140). Fuentes observed in his polemical talk that even though the new generation of Mexican writers was tired of "the alienating mythology" of the nation, it ran the risk of believing that after abandoning "the landscape of the maguey and the Indian," it was immediately redeemed by entering a "bourgeois universality." The dilemma facing the cosmopolitan, New Leftist, upper-middle-class writers, epitomized by Fuentes himself, was then "to be bourgeois, to live as a bourgeois, and yet to reject the lies that support us."[39] Those lies are without question, and following Fuentes's line of argument, the universalizing mirages of uneven development generated by globalized capitalism, the inequitable economic system hidden by the postrevolutionary Mexican ruling class under the camp national theme park of Mexico, with the Aztec pyramid at its mythical center. This Mexican national bourgeoisie visibly followed the patterns of co-optation and global cooperation described in Frantz Fanon's description of the nationalist postcolonial ruling class that "will be quite content with the role of the Western bourgeoisie's business agent, and it will play its part without any complexes, and in a most dignified manner."[40] Fuentes was even more poignant in his interview with Monegal, when he openly denounced the dangers posed to Mexican society, and by extension to the rest of Latin America, by the enforced and pervasive nationalist consensus: "Chauvinistic isolation favors our true enemies, all our enemies, internal and external. It favors local oligarchies who disguise themselves with the charisma of the flags, the motherland, and the dead heroes, because the heroes who are still alive are forbidden in Latin America; and it favors the reactionary circles in the U.S. who want to maintain the subjugation, the backwardness, and the isolation of Latin America."[41] The marriage between figures representing these mutual "enemies" is vital to the portrayal of the two couples in the novel: Isabel, a Mexican married to a former Nazi architect, and the American Jewess Elizabeth married to the Mexican writer and diplomat Javier.

Fuentes's most brilliant metaphor to represent the hybridization of national symbols with multinational capitalism is "Pepsicoatl" a fusion of the Pepsi-Cola drink and the Aztec god Quetzalcoatl, and defined as "the new goddess, the neon-lit pyramid."[42] With the parodic image of a pyramid commoditized through kitsch, the ludicrous blindfold of the national obsession with progress becomes also fully meaningful in political and economic terms. The nation and its symbols are revealed as commodities to subdue and colonize a politically anesthetized society where even artists are seduced by the nationalist establishment, as Fuentes had also pointed out in his speech.[43] The whole history of Mexico is told as the history of the obsession with a never fulfilled self-definition, a mythical fusion of an obsessive and unrequited narcissism and a Sisyphus-like constant return, which consumes the chances of exercising an authentic self-determination.

In his collection of political and cultural essays *Tiempo mexicano,* Fuentes articulates an attack on the temporal structure of the West as a unified ideological construct superposed and imposed upon the mythical times of the Aztecs, not so much in order to recuperate a lost cultural code, but rather to excavate the site of contemporary Mexican culture: "From Quetzalcoatl to Pepsicoatl: the time of the Western calendar, the time of progress, lineal time, is placed on top of the indigenous mythical time."[44] As he contrasts the temporality of ancient religious practices and myths with the theme of Western history, lineal progress, and Americanization, Fuentes critically looks at the interaction between these two contradictory narratives and the manner in which this contact has contributed to Mexican cultural narcissism and its concomitant inferiority complex. In so doing, the triumphal banner of Mexican nationalism, *mestizaje,* the fruitful exchange of European and Indian cultures, is discarded as a simplifying official discourse, while its two major discursive components—progress and mixed origins—are correspondingly critiqued as empty signifiers. The icon of the "neon-lit pyramid" contains a double critique as it dismantles the two components of the nationalist dream of uniting an idolatrized frozen past with the promise of material progress. Like other national or religious icons, it replaces language and society and puts in its place a semiotic machine whose signified is purely ideological. As an avatar of the modern Mexican nation, Pepsicoatl aims at occupying the site of society: its ideological content is precisely that very replacement.

The novel complexly responds to the narration of Mexico's exceptional history by dismantling the symbols on which it rests. The erosion of the Mexican pyramid, its symbolic collapse at the end of the novel, simultaneously uncovers power structures common to other nations: the church and the asylum. Balzac had also impugned the role of socializing institutions through the Jesuit school in which Lambert's vitality and creativity languished. What is at stake in the novel is not so much a search for that which makes Mexicans different, that which characterizes their identity, but rather a parade of proofs of their "universality," of the many ways in which Mexico participates in the history of humanity, a history whose argument is not Hegelian progress but instead, through a Voltairean twist, violence. In *Cambio de piel,* violence is seen as one of the constituting and recurring features of human existence exemplified by the pre-Hispanic rituals, the Spanish conquest of Mexico, the Nazi camp of Terezin designed by Franz, the judgment by the Monks and the open suggestion that they, the new generation who judge the old one, are also carrying a victim in the back of their Lincoln. By integrating a series of other historical moments into the most recent nationalist holocaust, histories of racial cruelty begin to emerge as a recurrent pattern. In the opening part of the novel, "An Impossible Feast," the juxtaposition of at least three different narratives exposes the fragility of the temporal axis, challenging it with the repetitive image of the entrance into Cholula of three consecutive waves: the first Europeans, the group of four friends at the center of the novel, and the group of six young beatniks called the Monks. In the background, the permanent, out of time, series of religious ceremonies of the Indians whose beliefs are identified with a form of syncretism. The re-creation of the massacre at Cholula by the Spanish and the Tlaxcaltecas stands out as a marker of Mexico's vicious history of tyranny and submission, which may be repeating itself as the chapter finishes with the suggestion by the narrator that he "could hear only the whimpering and sobbing, soft, fused, that I knew came from the trunk of their [the Monks'] car" (*CP*, 21/14). But in the novel, as in a happening, "There is no attempt to cater to the audience's desire to see everything. In fact, this is often deliberately frustrated, by performing some of the events in semi-darkness or by having events go on in different rooms simultaneously."[45]

In *Cambio de piel,* this juxtaposition of episodes from different times and places is maintained throughout the book in order to create what Fuentes has called a "paralyzed history."[46] Textual juxtaposition performs a similar break in the established chronology in José Emilio Pacheco's *Morirás lejos* (1968), where four layers of historical time intermingle, issuing a frozen picture of racial devastation. The opening episode situated in present-day Salonika—the Greek town populated by Sefarad Jews banished from Spain in the fifteenth century, annihilated by the Germans during World War II—is the first of a series of five alternating historical moments reoccurring throughout the novel. The last two sections of that novel are "some other possible dénouements" of a history whose continuity even in alternate times is all intersected by the images of persecutions suffered by the Jews.[47]

Cambio de piel thus marks the turning point in the 1960s at which Mexican obsessions with the national self had entered into a crisis that prefigured a postmodern defiance of grand narratives, and was more specifically linked with the "critical revolutionary" internationalism that emerged in some voices of the (Trotskyite) New Left. Their followers would soon flood Tlatelolco and other public spaces to meet the armed repression of the national postrevolutionary state. How to found such an internationalism avoiding the universalizing claims of enlightened reason and its liberal cosmopolitan avatars is the challenge encountered in the narratives of both Pynchon and Fuentes in the 1990s as they both reviewed the eighteenth-century utopian ideals of Republicanism that had inspired the postcolonial national foundations throughout the Americas at the time of independence.

Part Three

(Post)Colonial Enlightened Origins: Americanism Born

In the two historical novels studied in this part, Fuentes's *La campaña* (1990) and Pynchon's *Mason & Dixon* (1997), the formation of independent nation-states throughout the Americas is portrayed as a continuation of the hegemonic practices of competing European cultures in the Western Hemisphere.[1] Thus the foundational national past is reimagined not as a mythical origin but as another iteration in the long series of acts of conquest, pillage, and interethnic violence that constitute the alternate narrative of hemispheric history. The act of mapping, of tracing a geometric line into the American Western "wilderness" in Pynchon's *Mason & Dixon*, resembles the military campaigns in Fuentes's *La campaña,* as enlightened projects of liberation and the expansion of emancipatory knowledge which contribute to reaffirming and strengthening European/Western control over territories and peoples. In both cases, traveling through an "inhabited" wilderness, and mapping out the space of the nation-to-come reveal and reinstate heterogeneous cultural and social realities that the nascent postcolonial national bourgeoisies sought to homogenize after their political independence from European metropolitan powers. In this sense, both texts emphasize and trace the Western, Creole roots of settler nationalisms throughout the Western hemisphere and connect them with the epistemic revolutions of the Enlightenment: standardization and homogenization of knowledge(s), ethnocentric universalisms, and encyclopedic panoramas.

In *Mason & Dixon* the uncontrollability of the scientific process of mapping new territories is epitomized by the material demarcation of the boundary between Maryland and Pennsylvania: the line gains a life of its own separate from the two surveyors who trace it; they become increasingly aware of the human, cultural, and social consequences of incorporating into the world map previously uncharted territories. The line develops into a "great invisible Thing," a monster analogous to Scholem's Golem, a story to which Pynchon parodically alludes in the novel: another monster of human, Faustian, scientific ambitions. The line is not merely a north/south boundary between two neighboring provinces, but a way westward, a route into the western Indian territories, "a tree-slaughtering Animal" which kills "ev'rything due west of it"—its real "intentions" beyond that, unknown to all.[2] The newly charted territories become "known" and accessible to future colonizers, while the landmarks, codes, and cultures of other societies are erased and confined to a pre-historical past. The line will also provide the official separating incision between North and South during the Civil War one hundred years after it was marked out. As an index to the two mythical efforts articulating nationalist images of Americanness throughout the nineteenth century—the conquest of the West and the North–South divide—the line references not only (post)colonial ambitions, but also national foundations. Unsurprisingly, the story begins at the very moment and place of birth of the United States as a nation-state: Philadelphia, 1786—the year the U.S. Constitution was finally approved. While the story of Mason and Dixon predates this national foundation, Pynchon denounces the historical continuities between the colonial projects, the "enlightened" projects of modernity, and the subsequent expansion of the thirteen colonies onto the continent and beyond.

Both *Mason & Dixon* and *La campaña* address through different textual strategies the postcolonial conflicts arising from the process of enforced incorporation of peoples and places in the Western Hemisphere by the projects of the Enlightenment. In Pynchon's novel, mapping, what Lefebvre called "the production of space," that is, the production of a "readily decipherable" cartography, is accompanied by a parallel process of deterritorialization.[3] As Europeans culminate the invasion and occupation of Native American territories their abstract concepts and their textualization of space invades the realm of an already populated area. The two central characters finally view their scientific intervention onto space and their mappings as another, more abstract form of colonial violence.

In *La campaña,* the ten-year-long campaign for independence in Spanish America also becomes an allegory of the moral limitations of universalist, Occidental forms of knowledge. The campaign itself stands for the process of questioning the dogmas of the French philosophes, and of the European Enlightenment that had been transferred onto the American colonies, and which had precipitated in different ways the revolutionary movements. At the close of the novel, the main character, Baltasar Bustos, replaces his beliefs in a permanent and ideal progress with the activity of endless critical enquiry as the Enlightenment is revealed to be a new dogma. Bustos's realization that the past cannot be erased by the enlightened projects and their faith in endless progress, that the real world cannot be effectively transformed by the written word, places the novel in Fuentes's familiar fictional remodeling of the diverse times coexisting in Spanish America. By promoting the incorporation of the "otros tiempos, los tiempos de los otros," ("the other times, the times of the others")[4] Fuentes is suggesting a decidedly plural politics of culture that contests the lineal and monologic proposals of the Enlightenment. The trip north, the central quest of Fuentes's *La campaña,* traces an imaginary line connecting all the uprisings of Spanish America against its metropolis, a move which reveals the regional differences that will at once separate and unite the newly born nations; and it also shows how the "enlightenment" leaves the racial and cultural boundaries of the colony largely unchanged and unchallenged beyond the moment of independence. The Latin American emancipation from the old Spanish masters is carried out by the local national settler elite, the criollos, and their new hierarchical order is at pains to differentiate its projects from those of the metropolitan colonizers. Baltasar Bustos, the protagonist of *La campaña,* finally comes to visualize the postcolonial authoritarian flaw of the Enlightenment agenda of liberation: the imposition of ideas of modernity and progress, of "future times" on other temporalities.

As they erase alternative mappings and narrative times, the central characters in both novels realize that the Euclidean/Cartesian dimensions of time and space are not universal. Rather than a "civilizing" movement, imposing these Western standards on others is a form of ethnocentric violence.[5] There is a sense at the end of both novels that the characters have become, at a minimum, more aware of the dangers of the hallucinating grand narratives they had so faithfully embraced at the outset. However, the two texts go beyond the mere moral questioning of the right to impose ideas of progress on other cultures. They both assail the concept of progress itself and its allied ideological claims of cultural and social homogenization. Through what Elizabeth Jane Wall Hinds has identified in *Mason & Dixon* as a "counter-Enlightenment movement," ideas of liberation and progress sanctioned by the Enlightenment are critically evaluated and with them the associated projects of Western modernity.[6] This assault is not carried out in order to advance an alternative discourse of liberation, but to denounce and resist the erasure of other languages, worldviews, and cultural formations. It is at the point of voicing the subaltern subject that the two texts are halted. Both novels stay away from voicing the subaltern in order perhaps not to reappropriate and void them. Their silence is geared toward their non-recuperation in the Western language in which both novels are written: these "others" are not included in the dialogues, since they would need to be translated or speak the colonizers' language, becoming a sort of Caliban figure. Thus, both novels re-create the possibility of private resistance to prevalent ideologies, withdrawing from both the apparent complexities, and the simplicities, of a dialectics of colonizer and colonized.

Enlightenments, Inc.

Adorno and Horkheimer's *Dialectic of Enlightenment* describe the supposedly emancipatory philosophy of enlightenment as a destructive process of cultural homogenization: a "line both of destruction and of civilization."[7] This image of the Enlightenment as a destructive civilizing line, the censure of this seemingly unstoppable unifying logic of Western modernity, concurs with the indictment expressed by Fuentes and Pynchon in their novels. Their fictional denunciation of the destructive projects of European civilization in America concentrates on the process of erasure of those other forms of knowledge that Adorno and Horkheimer see as the victims of Enlightenment's demythologizing action.

If "Enlightenment" can be defined as a series of efforts to establish rational and standardized ways of studying and managing nature and society, Adorno and Horkheimer add two main provisos to this definition. The first one relates to the idea that Enlightenment is not only an epistemic revolution, but also a form of domination: its search for knowledge is not an end in itself—"What men want to learn from nature is how to use it in order wholly to dominate it and other men" (4). A second proviso refers to the social hierarchies and the "access to knowledge" promoted by the Enlightenment. For the Frankfurt scholars Enlightenment becomes "wholesale deception of the masses" (42) as its mechanics seem to "liberate" while pursuing domination. Their conclusion that "today machinery disables men even as it nurtures them" (37) is close to Pynchon's paranoia of a post-human techonopolitical order that may or may not know where it is going.

In "Is It O.K. to Be a Luddite?" Pynchon had already used the debate between the "two cultures," the mythical or literary on the one hand, and the logical or scientific on the other, as a pretext for his investigation into the contemporary availability of Luddism.[8] In his essay on the nature and validity of Luddism, not only did Pynchon acknowledge the dated nature of the debate on the "two cultures," but he also addressed the inevitable question of the political and economic implications of technological development. Pynchon situates the passage from religious theology and faith through to the technological theology of Enlightenment in the eighteenth century:

> In ways more and less literal, folks in the 18th century believed that once upon a time all kinds of things had been possible which were no longer so. Giants, dragons, spells. The laws of nature had not been so strictly formulated back then. What had once been true working magic had, by the Age of Reason, degenerated into mere machinery. Blake's dark Satanic mills represented an old magic that, like Satan, had fallen from grace. As religion was being more and more secularized into Deism and nonbelief, the abiding human hunger for evidence of God and afterlife, for salvation—bodily resurrection, if possible—remained. The Methodist movement and the American Great Awakening were only two sectors on a broad front of resistance to the Age of Reason, a front which included Radicalism and Freemasonry as well as Luddites and the Gothic novel. Each in its way expressed the same profound unwillingness to give up elements of faith, however "irrational," to an emerging technopolitical order that might or might not know what it was doing.[9]

In *Mason & Dixon,* the coexistence of "rational" and "pre-rational" beliefs contributes to the characters' hesitation about the ethical dimensions of Occidental reason. The possible validity of "other reasons" to account for the world puts into perspective the ideological discourse of Western reason. Pynchon's preoccupation with the extensive political uses of technology is the clear theme of *V., Gravity's Rainbow, Against the Day,* and *Bleeding Edge,* where experiments with chemistry, conductist psychology, rocketry, electricity, magnetism, mapping, or the internet, commoditize, mechanize and discipline the human body, while they reshape and redefine social and cultural spaces in terms of scientific rationality and capitalist productivity. Pynchon openly connects the social consequences of technologies, old and new, with predatory economic practices. And yet, while Pynchon appears to cherish the old "elements of faith," he is not promoting a return to religious beliefs or to mythical explanations of reality. Adorno and Horkheimer had already warned about the ineffective "opposition" to Enlightenment from earlier forms of knowledge: "Whatever myths the resistance may appeal to, by virtue of the very fact that they become arguments in the process of opposition, they acknowledge the principle of dissolvent rationality for which they reproach the Enlightenment. Enlightenment is totalitarian" (6).

In questioning Enlightenment's universalist claims, the universality of Reason and Knowledge are directly under attack. In his "Qu'est ce que les Lumières?" ("What is the Enlightenment?") Michel Foucault questions Kant's use of the concept of "mankind" (*Menschheit*) as a form of wondering about the location of Enlightenment:

> Do we need to understand that the entire human species is inserted in the process of the *Aufklärung*? And in that case, we should have to imagine that *Aufklärung* is an historical change that touches upon the political and social existence of all the men on the face of the earth. Or do we need to understand that the change is in fact related to that which constitutes the humanity of a human being? And the question then would be what is that transformation. Even there, Kant's reply is not exempt of a certain ambiguity.[10]

The ambiguity to which Foucault refers seems to disguise the belief that the Enlightenment is addressed not to Humanity in general, but to that which constitutes the "humanity of the human being." Kant does not seem to concede that all humans can be enlightened: some of his other writings point out strong racial and cultural biases of which Foucault was surely aware when looking for discursive inconsistencies in Kant's article. They are not all "Enlightened humans" as the ones described by Kant, but victims of Enlightenment's homogenizing projects. *Aufklärung*/Enlightenment is universal; all human societies are already involved in it. But as Adorno and Horkheimer point out, it has become the most efficient dominant force: it is the epistemic agenda of Western colonialism.

In both his article on Luddism and in *Mason & Dixon,* Pynchon explores the possibility of an opposition to Enlightenment's domination in the form of realization and the development of ethical awareness. In this sense, his political agenda may belong to another version of Enlightenment, an Enlightenment inside Enlightenment: we need to know, to liberate ourselves, to get out of the immaturity of the Enlightenment itself. This is built on the template of Enlightenment's popular claim, delineated by Kant in his famous essay "Was ist Aufklärung?" ("What Is Enlightenment?"). Published in the *Berlinische Monatschrift* in 1784 as a response to that same question, Kant uses the metaphor of childhood to explain the process of Enlightenment as one that should "take man out of his immaturity."[11] Kant brings up to date the old motto "*Sapere aude*" as the paramount expression of the enlightened man's challenge.[12] The same motto may be applied to Pynchon's paranoia: "dare to know." Pynchon's characters are motivated to know by paranoia, instead of experimental reason, and their ultimate findings all direct them toward the conviction that they are being manipulated, that they are victims of a conspiracy, which is coincidentally that of the technopolitical order that "might or might not know what it was doing." These insiders who do realize, and grow out of the immaturity of not knowing, become aware of the disenfranchisement of the non-modern, the "Preterite" of *Gravity's Rainbow* and the "Subjunctive" in *Mason & Dixon.* Their knowledge is knowledge of the past, nostalgia for what was destroyed and erased. The Enlightenment is a homogenizing project as the unification of times and measurements proves in *Mason & Dixon.* Pynchon finds in those other lost subjunctive times a form of fictional resistance to the relentless advance of *the* line.

In Fuentes's novel, American-born Europeans, the criollos, liberate themselves from their European masters, and their promises to "liberate" the Others, the Indians, the black slaves, of their (preterite) cultural forms of oppression are also a promise of future homogenization. In some of his nonfictional writings, Fuentes positions himself against the linearity of time imposed by the Enlightenment on Spanish America. In "El Secreto de Diderot" Fuentes nostalgically celebrates the possibility of recuperating, at the end of the twentieth century, "the times of the others," and his genealogy of Spanish American modernity points to the historical moment of his *La campaña* as the age when those other times were abandoned:

> We were born into modernity with the lineal time of the Enlightenment. We forgot the instantaneous, circular, and magical times of our origins in favor of a progressive, irreversible time, destined to a future infinitely perfectible: the time of a secular Christianity, a time without final judgment, but like Christian time, a time shooting towards the future.[13]

Progress, that time "shooting" towards the future, is indeed "shot" on the non-Europeans too. This appears to be part of a nostalgic recuperation of the lost opportunity for an identity made up of a heterogeneous polity, rather than of the homogeneous "sameness" of Enlightened equality. In the failure to acknowledge the subaltern other beyond a passive recipient of their own liberating laws, or their own economic use (and abuse), the enlightened criollos homogeneously perpetuate Western domination over difference.

Many of the critics who have approached *La campaña* have failed to see this nostalgic effort behind Fuentes's re-creation of the process of independence and its emphasis on imported ideas of cultural homogenization. However, Fuentes's ideas are made even clearer in his historical analysis of the period elsewhere:

> Where did barbarity come from? From the city or the country? The ideology of progress avoided all the obstacles. Indians could be sacrificed. And the conquest, was obviously far from over. It was now our turn: we the independent Latin Americans. We were the new conquistadores, behaving exactly as the true descendants of Pizarro and Cortés. Only the uniforms had changed.[14]

In the United States, and in the rest of the Americas, the discourses of freedom, equality, and material happiness originating in the Enlightenment were modeled onto and against preexisting cultures. Cultural differences were erased, languages muted, and alternative histories disappeared in the name of progress and the new national consensus.

Independent Identities

As we saw in the "Introduction," Benedict Anderson traced in *Imagined Communities* the late eighteenth-century dawn of the age of nationalism, a postcolonial ideological framework emerging in the Americas between the 1770s and the 1820s. This new political ideologeme, nationalism, constituted itself as a form of political irrationalism, a modern obscurantism, coinciding with the dusk of religious modes of belonging; in a way, Anderson sums, the Enlightenment "brought with it its own modern darkness."[15] This criticism of the enlightened "liberation" is directed specifically both toward the universality of its claims and toward ethnocentric definitions of the subjects of such liberation. The "man," whose rights are asserted by Paine or by the Declaration of Rights, remains a gendered male, white, and propertied European. In the American Constitution, for instance, property owners, men with an education, who style themselves as freethinking men become the agents of those "universal rights." The sacred, mystical idea of the nation develops from the emptying out of the previous space occupied by the religious justification of royal power and the birthing of the new space, the bourgeois order of the nation-state. This social transformation creates its new hierarchies of power, excluding other groups or classes, incorporating them as outsiders within, originating new identities and a nation: a community imagined and defined by a selected group of political and intellectual leaders. Madam de Staël's proposal of a "république des propriéteurs" comes true after the American and French Revolutions, the two milestones at the outset of that history of liberation. In Anderson's account these projects are not geared to establishing a "truly egalitarian" society, but a new ruling class, the national bourgeoisies, and a political formation which embodies and perpetuates the mystical enlightened despotism of the period: the nation-state.[16]

The historical period to which *Mason & Dixon* and *La campaña* allude spans from 1761, the date of the first encounter between the two British scientists, until 1821, when Baltasar Bustos returns to Buenos Aires after his successful fight for the independence of the Spanish continental possessions in America. During these sixty years, the whole of the Western hemisphere, with the exception of Cuba and Puerto Rico, gained its independence from its European masters. The variety of motivations behind all the many American revolutionary movements reveals a complex process of searching for new national identities in the context of increasing pressure from the European metropoles to reform and regiment colonial societies. Indeed, for many historians, the main economic and political reasons behind the fight for independence are to be found in the enlightened programs of reform initiated during the second half of the eighteenth century by both Spain and Britain, by which colonial subjects, a vast group of which were politically disenfranchised creoles, or descendants of European settlers, were exposed to demanding governmental measures—increased taxation, firmer regulation of trade, among others—which enhanced their insufficient participation in the structures of colonial governement.[17] This period of "enlightened despotism" established the elements for new colonial approaches to their own economic capabilities, and what was initially a response to "taxation without representation" grew into full-blown projects of independence and national construction. As a result of the growing availability of economic and political treatises in the hemisphere, Smith's *Wealth of Nations,* the widespread discussion of these issues in journals such as *El Mercurio de México* or Franklin's *Poor Richard,* middle-class colonial subjects throughout the Americas became engaged in economics. They realized that they could have a direct profit from independent commerce once they shook away the overwhelming structures of control exercised by their European masters. The reforms derived from despotic Enlightenment policies had a pernicious effect on the European interests in America: they fostered revolts by informing colonial subjects of their worth and their capabilities.[18]

In the United States, this transition to "maturity" was the result of the encounter of Enlightened ideas with the Puritan tradition of the "Errand in the Wilderness." Sacvan Bercovitch perceives in the self-assured idea of (North) American "exceptionality" a stronger role in the formation of a separate American identity than in the writings of any of the French encyclopedists.[19] In the thirteen colonies the struggle for independence can be seen as directed toward the establishment of a middle-class republican order similar to the one asked for by Madame de Staël, guaranteeing a property order already emergent in the pre-revolutionary period, but which would soon of its own become self-sufficient, as its political and national symbols became increasingly represented a society devoted to profit (over people) and technological progress (over nature).[20]

The marriage of religion and politics that made the American Revolution so distinct, from the early fear of Episcopacy as a conspiracy against their religious liberties, to the rejection of taxation without representation, underlines the role of the Anglo-American nonconformist tradition in the history of the American colonies in its mixture with Enlightenment ideas.[21] There seems to be a wide consensus among contemporary historians about the role of religion in the formation of the early American identity:

> The subjects of the Great Awakening and the American Revolution, which on one level have tended to displace a fuller consideration of the Enlightenment in America, are in fact the major paradigms within which we must understand most Americans' participation in the international Enlightenment. The instrumentality of much of the American thought is perhaps a commonplace, but in the eighteenth century it certainly seems true that most powerful intellectual currents in America swirled around questions about the soul confronted by nature and nature's God and about man in political society, about salvation and government.[22]

The United States would be founded on the crossroads of the millenarian beliefs and the liberating discourses of Enlightenment. Pynchon's critique of American exceptionalism and of its suitable adaptation into the ideology of the Enlightenment is a central focus of my reading of *Mason & Dixon.*

Spanish American and Anglo-American Enlightenment differ in many aspects, but particularly in the presence in both Spain and Spanish America of deep-seated Catholic intellectual traditions that had survived the Protestant Reformation. The extent to which an imported modernity could be "adapted" and/or "adopted" by the complex colonial societies under Spanish rule had been a debate since long before the first outbreak of the Buenos Aires revolts which open *La campaña.* And it is, to this day, a fundamental issue in Spanish American societies.

One of the main deficiencies of Fuentes's expository prose as well as his fictional recounting of the period is related to his effort to portray the Enlightenment as a force diametrically opposed to the pre-revolutionary order. This contrast may be useful for the purposes of parody, but it contradicts the historical evidence of the deep involvement of Spain and its colonies in the scientific projects of the time.[23] America's "growth into maturity" forged a set of new American identities based on the layers of preexisting European traditions and some indigenous features. At this point, however, Fuentes prefers to maximize the historical positions and depict the revolutionary elements as too disruptive of a problematically idealized colonial order.

The Spanish government had started a wide-ranging program of reform in the colonies and at home under Bourbon rule, particularly under Carlos III (1759–88). Spanish-speaking America had been exposed to enlightened ideas by different means throughout the eighteenth century. Newton, Bacon, and Locke, to whom the French *Encyclopédie* was dedicated, had been introduced in the universities of Mexico, Havana, and Lima long before Napoleon's invasion of the Iberian Peninsula.[24] The works of the Spaniards Feijóo and Campomanes also contributed to the wide-ranging spread of critical ideas in science and philosophy.[25] Thus, a sizable readership among the colonial intelligentsia had been exposed for many decades to the literature on which the philosophes themselves constructed their views.[26] Although the French insistence on self-rule and on the image of the noble savage is often highlighted as the most decisive contribution to the movement for independence, the oxymoronic "Despotic Enlightenment" introduced through Spain, or the even more contradictory idea of "Christian Enlightenment,"[27] appears to have prepared colonial Latin Americans for thinking of themselves as independent societies. In Fuentes's novel, these contemporary historiographic debates about the intellectual sources of Spanish American independence are reinstated, but Fuentes's version ultimately prevails.

In 1990, while finishing *La campaña,* Fuentes was already involved on a project for the BBC to commemorate the fifth centenary of the arrival of Europeans in America. In the book that resulted from this television program, *El espejo enterrado,* Fuentes reviewed the history of the relations between Spanish America and its former metropolis. As such, it is a valuable source of information about Fuentes's opinions and sources as regards his fictional reconstruction of several important episodes in the history of transatlantic cultural relations. In *El espejo enterrado* (*The Buried Mirror*), Fuentes's voice is identifiably his, we assume: the narrator is not a fictional device introducing a polyphony of viewpoints as in *La campaña.* Fuentes's sarcasm when reviewing the intellectual excesses committed by the enlightened American bourgeoisie is patent:

> The mixture was intoxicating and muddled the heads of local parish priests, of provincial lawyers, and of the first national writers in the old capitals of the colonies. They all learned French in a rush, in order to savor all those great writers as if they were old wines from Bourgogne.[28]

That "mixture" to which Fuentes refers is the combination between the new philosophies of the Enlightenment and the old intellectual traditions of scholasticism under review throughout the eighteenth century in the Spanish American colonies. The central characters in *La campaña* will coincidentally be youngsters drunk with enlightened ideas like those identified by Fuentes in his "serious" historical essay. They will also be "inebriated" by the readings of the French philosophers *à la mode.* Fuentes does "imagine" that young seminarist reading Voltaire in the colonial world in his 1990 novel in the inflexible reformer Xavier Dorrego. His friend Baltasar Bustos, a young would-be lawyer, is indeed exalted by "Rousseau's rhetoric and by his moral exigencies." Fuentes's fictionalized history coincides nearly word for word with his own serious "narration." In both texts subversive readings are smuggled into Spanish America with ecclesiastic collaboration; the only difference is in the voice that presents the image in each case:

> The forbidden books entered Latin America in original ways. Because churches and monasteries were exempt from customs inspections, many enlightened European churchmen filled boxes and even sometimes sacred objects such as chalices with forbidden pamphlets and manuscripts.[29]

In *La campaña,* this historical information is provided in the first-person plural, and the narrator and his friends are the beneficiaries of the smuggling activity: "But this also works to the advantage of those of us who love ideas and books: since crates containing chalices and ecclesiastical garments are not opened at customs, friendly priests use them to send us forbidden books by Voltaire, Rousseau, and Diderot" (*LC,* 9/4–5).[30] In these repeated images we can detect Fuentes's own insistent version of the Spanish American Enlightenment as a "Christian Enlightenment" that could have developed its own local version of modernity, based on its own multicultural identity, but which finally went wrong, precisely because it ignored its heterogeneity. If in *Terra nostra* he had obsessively studied the erasure of preexisting traditions under the devastating rule of El Escorial, in *La campaña,* it is the Enlightenment itself that comes under attack for its incapacity to accommodate local traditions of knowledge. The connection between novel and historical essay, *La campaña* and *El espejo enterrado,* demonstrates the nature of Fuentes's historical narratives as two types of exploration of his views on the material. A process that he considers as one of organic relation—the essay as a branch of the novel—is at work in *La campaña.*[31]

Whether the American Enlightenments remain "peripheral" or not in the works of historians on the period such as Peter Gay or Cassirer,[32] the participation of the Anglo-American and of the Spanish-American creoles in its projects and in its ideology remains a patent reality. The observation of the transit of Venus from Ecuador, California, or Massachusetts in 1769 is only one more evidence of the active participation of pre-independent America in the project of calculating the distance between Earth and the Sun.[33] Mary Louise Pratt has pointed out the simultaneous occurrence of these global scientific endeavors: the observation of the transit of Venus from different points of the planet, the Linnaean project of biological classification, which entertained numerous correspondents throughout the Western Hemisphere, and the experiments to improve the calculation of longitude at sea. They resulted in the creation of what she terms a European "planetary consciousness."[34]

My readings of *Mason & Dixon* and *La campaña* show how their rewriting of the histories of the Enlightenment in America identify the inception of diverse American national identities as the result of the postcolonial agency of local national bourgeoisies of European descent. They follow closely Walter Mignolo's assessment of the intellectual absorption of the late eighteenth-century European Enlightenment in peripheral areas "projected from hegemonic local histories and embraced by subaltern ones as a model to be imitated."[35] The local histories suggested by Pynchon and Fuentes in these two novels center around characters who embody their beliefs in the Enlightenment; they *are* precisely because they are "men" as defined by the enlightened agenda: white, educated, Christian, middle-class males. In both novels, the central story spins around these male characters' capacity to survey and map out the extent to which their enlightened projects participate in a wholesale act of Western barbarity: they come to see themselves as agents of European homogenizing practices. Although there are many similarities between the two texts, there is also a vast distance between their critiques and their conclusions. While Fuentes still hopes for a history made up of a multiplicity of identities, and the discourses of transculturation and mestizaje are still preponderant in his agenda, Pynchon's indictment of the past is also a condemnation of a totalizing present. In retelling these stories of the emergence of their American nations, Thomas Pynchon and Carlos Fuentes satirically reinscribe the American Enlightenments and their revolutions as a straightforward change of colonial agents in the Western course of empire. And in doing so, they deconstruct the mythical origins of modern nations throughout the hemisphere by uprooting their foundational constitutions: their sacred histories and their vaunted mappings.

Chapter 6

✦

Enlightened Nationalists: The Conquest Rides Again in *La campaña*

When fighting for Venezuelan independence, Fernando Fonta, one of the protagonists in Arturo Uslar Pietri's *Las lanzas coloradas* (1931), remembers his early enthusiasm for the republican dream: "Fernando remembered his days in the university. His readings of Rousseau. The Republic. Because, when all was said and done, he was there to fight for the Republic. For everything that had once aroused his enthusiasm."[1] The revelation of Fernando's stream of consciousness at a critical moment of the narration emphasizes "his readings of Rousseau" as one of the turning points in the character's political education. He represents a whole generation of Spanish American criollos who set off to sever their societies from the political dependency of Spain, a decadent and chaotic monarchy "beheaded" in the spring of 1808 by the Napoleonic invasion. His readings of the French philosopher, widely acknowledged as having played a fundamental role in the formation of a new intellectual identity among Spanish Americans at the time, figure among the originating texts, the pre-texts of the revolutions for independence.[2] In Fernando's last thoughts, Rousseau's texts coexist with a classical reading, Plato's *Republic,* and with the "claustros," a reference to the Catholic religious orders, such as the Jesuits, in charge of much of the secondary and higher education in the Spanish colonies, and which had become increasingly opposed to the royal projects of secularizing enlightened despotism throughout the American colonies.[3] These three references to the character's heterogeneous intellectual upbringing situate his emergent republicanism as a result of competing European notions of the role of "citizens" in society, power relations, and the political horizons of reform and revolution.

At the close of *Las lanzas coloradas,* Fernando becomes an anonymous hero of the republic by dying in the name of those ideals that had enthused him earlier. His—and the text's—tragic ending confirms the whole narration as an epic account of the revolution for independence, leaving that heterogeneous and even conflicting intellectual background of the struggle for independence unquestioned.[4] Worse, the confirmation, fictional and historical, of the French philosophes as a major influence on Spanish Americans at the time could also be considered as a new form of dependency, one that reveals the Europeanness of the new identities emerging from the wars of independence, their participation in a postcolonial, but western episteme.

Founding Utopias

In contrast with Pietri's tragic though celebratory view, Carlos Fuentes's rewriting of the revolutionary period introduces a "distancing gaze" and a satirical tone which emphasizes the Europeanness of these "new" identities, thus parodying and questioning the earlier epic versions of those foundational narratives. In *La campaña,* the influence of the French philosophers on the movement for independence is imaginatively used to satirize the political naïveté of the criollos, and their enthusiastic wholesale importation of the utopian ideals of the French Enlightenment. At the center of Fuentes's parody is the dubious, possibly pernicious effect of unquestioningly applying French political ideas to Spanish America. Hence, the emerging national identities are not presented as a fresh start: nor do they embody local, pre-colonial cultures, or even the hybrid social groups born under Spanish rule over the previous three hundred years, but rather a struggle between different European/Western ways of approaching modernization. All the characters and debates in the novel circulate around this central fulcrum.

At stake here is the double conflict of the criollos: their determination to abandon their economic and administrative dependency on Spain, and the irreconcilable contradictions of their male (peripheral) European identity in the midst of African, Native American, mestizo, and female subjectivities. *La campaña* stages these two conflicts in Baltasar Bustos's military campaign against the European masters, a campaign in which Bustos symbolically eliminates representatives of all these other social groups. Fuentes seeks once again to articulate a complex analysis of two of the author's most persistent preoccupations throughout his career: the contridictions of challenges of material modernity and the constitution of Mexican national identity,[5] this time expanding his scope to the whole of Spanish America. The disparity between writing (and reading) and reality is symbolized in the gulf between notions of native communal life idealized by the long-standing Americanist intellectual tradition, and their underwriting of utopian colonial projects. This is of course the "ethnographic" base for Rousseau's noble savage,[6] and the political praxis of the emergent postcolonial nation-states throughout the Western Hemisphere: writing foundational constitutions while waging (neo)colonial wars.

The publication of "El secreto de Diderot" in 1986 opened a six-year period in which Fuentes frequently revisited the eighteenth century. In that article, Fuentes claimed that Diderot's treatment of time establishes him as a "novelista actual"[7] ("contemporary novelist" [translations mine]) who "demuestra que el arte no progresa" ("shows that there is no progress in art")

(104). Diderot promotes a concept of art as the site where different times can be accessed and recovered. Echoing Bakhtinian dialogism, Fuentes defines the novel as a genre that performs a "diálogo de géneros, de lenguajes, de tiempos históricos, de civilizaciones, de posibilidades inéditas" ("a dialogue of genres, languages, historical times, civilizations and unheard-of possibilities") (115), a dialogue that had already been mastered by the editor of the *Encyclopédie*. Diderot's secret—a playful enactment of a dialogic present in which past and future times are "contained"—constitutes an alternative to the future paradise on which the enlightened idea of progress is construed. The times of the non-European, and the forgotten "tiempos instantáneos, circulares y míticos de nuestros orígenes" ("instantaneous, circular, mythical times of our origins") (105) become an alternative thus to the Voltaireian idea of the past as a "cueva de la barbarie" ("cave of barbarism") (105).

In his series of lectures at the universities of Harvard and Cambridge, published under the title *Valiente mundo nuevo* in 1990[8]—also the year of publication of *La campaña*—Fuentes criticized the effect that Voltaire's ethnocentric disregard for history and for other non-European cultures may have had on the Spanish American revolutionaries, and in their conflicting relation with their mixed cultural heritage. He sardonically closes his reflection with a lament—it might have been preferable for Spanish Americans to have read Vico rather than Voltaire:

> Deprived of history and humanity—everything that is different is illusory, as Voltaire would say—the peoples of the Western Hemisphere—savages, children, or idiots—teamed up in the enthusiasm of independence, faith in progress and a denial of the past, of that which denied us. This time we wanted to arrive on time to the table of civilization: get over what we considered Indian, mestizo, Spanish, colonial and counter-reformist underdevelopments. We denied what we had done—a developing polycultural and multiracial world—to affirm what we could never be—modern Europeans—without accepting what we were already—indoafroiberoamerican. The political and cultural price was very high. We would have fared better reading Vico instead of Voltaire. (*VMN*, 34–35)

In Fuentes's rendition, Voltaire's disregard for "all that is different" positively inspired the Europeanizing drive behind the criollos' revolts. Two of Fuentes's claims here are instrumental to my reading of *La campaña*. Firstly, he denounces the French influence on Spanish America, principally Voltairean ethnocentrism, as a version of modernity that was in open contradiction with the "real" identity of Spanish America: the idea of enlightened progress erases the emerging, heterogeneous, plural self. Secondly, and related to this idea of a plural self, Fuentes advances a view of colonial society in which some sort of *avant la lettre* cultural modernity—that "developing multicultural and multiracial world" to which he makes parenthetical reference—was already present in Spanish America before foreign, homogeneous, and more coercive versions of modernity were imported—that is, those of Voltaire. Had they read Vico instead, Fuentes suggests, Spanish American colonists would have understood the impossibility of fully erasing history, and would have fought for their own already constituted multiple and complex identities.

Both points, external influences as *the* problem, and the multiracial identity of Spanish America as a given in the eighteenth century, raise a number of problems. For even if we accept that the interaction of the various racial groups that peopled colonial Spanish America was relatively fluid, the uncontested fact remains that colonial society was highly hierarchical.[9] The fact that for Fuentes, Spanish Americans already had a sense of a multiracial "indoafroiberoamericano" identity is particularly problematic.

There are a number of paintings from this period where the various categories of racial mixing are portrayed in an encyclopedic effort to account for the variety of physiognomic characters to be encountered in the colonies. In one of these paintings by Ygnacio María Barreda y Ordoñes, dated 1777 and hanging at the Real Academia Española, sixteen social and racial groups can be distinguished.[10] Even in that painting, social groups are displayed in a hierarchical order: couples from different racial backgrounds are arranged from top to bottom depending on the level of "European blood" that they are supposed to "have" in their veins. Putting into perspective these multifarious classifications, Magnus Mörner recognizes a class division of four or five main groups depending on their racial and civil status: European-born Spaniards, American-born Europeans or criollos, Indians, and blacks, either enslaved or freed.[11]

At any rate, Fuentes's insinuation of a multicultural Spanish America is politically tuned with his critique of the homogenizing cultural adventure which was the Enlightenment—still at work, according to Adorno and Horkheimer—and by extension modernity. His emphasis on the complex aspects of colonial society portrays the coming of the Enlightenment as the erasure of the too idyllic multi-layered society portrayed in the *castas* paintings. A different, less optimistic, or perhaps less nostalgic, view of the colony, which also indicts the race relations of postrevolutionary Spanish America, is provided by historian Tulio Halperín Donghi in his suggestion that "although identification with the Indian inheritors of the pre-Hispanic past became a commonplace of Revolutionary rhetoric, the old attitudes based on a feeling of caste and superiority survived."[12] For anyone familiar with the Native American disguises of the Anglo participants at the Boston Tea Party, the rapid failure of this revolutionary rhetoric may not be too surprising. Yet, the parallelisms between the Anglo and the Hispanic American revolutionaries seem to be limited to this precise moment: their initial search for national symbols.[13] Indeed, the process of loosening racial boundaries would vary immensely from Argentina to Mexico, from New Orleans to New Haven.

But even more alarming than Fuentes's celebration of a presentist colonial multiculturalism is his account of the wars of independence as motivated by an imported faith in progress which denied this glorified past. Fuentes articulates this argument in three different texts from the early 1990s using a stock set of images to describe Spanish American cannibalization of European culture. In *Valiente mundo nuevo* he uses a collective—and somewhat paradoxical—"we" to assert that "this time *we* wanted to arrive on time to the table of civilization" (my emphasis, *VMN,* 35), a civilization that he identifies with the Voltairean utopia of eternal progress. Fuentes's portrayal of Spanish American elites rushing in to participate in the banquet of "progress" is again used in the passage from *El espejo enterrado.* In it, the imagery of intellectual aliment becomes one of excess with the use of the word "embriagado" (inebriated) to describe the effects of French philosophers (he refers here to Rousseau) on Spanish American colonial subjects. And again, in *La campaña* the ironic narrator insists on the image of excess and intoxication by portraying Baltasar Bustos as suffering from an "indigestión elocuente de filosofías" ("eloquent indigestion of philosophies") (*LC,* 26/20).[14]

Fuentes voices his position in the wide debate over the intellectual influences behind the Spanish American uprisings, and the process of identity formation and nation building that ensued. The emphasis on the revolutionary French influence is stressed to the point of satire in order to stage the intellectual conflict that Fuentes perceives as a recurrent pattern behind Spanish American problems: the importation of external, foreign ideologies onto a local reality for which they are ill-prepared. As elsewhere in his work, the author's exploration of the aggressive cultural practices of Western imperialism denounces both its diachronic and synchronic alterations of Spanish American society. On the one hand, the erasure of history is associated with the projects of "modernity"; on the other, identity traits become erased and homogenized under the process of westernization. To these overwhelming external forces, Fuentes offers once again the heritage of *mestizaje* as a feasible alternative.[15]

In order to put forward this critical-political agenda, Fuentes's narratives reduce and exaggerate historical data, a double process that displaces these narratives from exhaustive and analytical positivistic historiography. This process of re-narrating history in favor of a particular set of circumstances becomes instrumental for the author's indictment of extreme and exclusive cultural attitudes. Therefore, his surmise that the Voltairean disregard for history as mere "dark ages" led to the Spanish American rejection of their own past is the basis for his assault on the revolutionary movements.[16] Undoubtedly, the representation of the French philosophes as a contaminating influence is a useful generalization for the purposes of parodying the Spanish American blind importation of foreign sociopolitical models. To favor one of the many grounds for the movement of independence is indeed ideologically effective in order to recount the process of constitution of the new national identities as a product of external influences rather than a result of original internal forces.[17] Even though other factors are offered to the reader, the wars of independence are finally portrayed not so much as a turning point after which Americans gained a new voice, but rather as another step in the incorporation of Spanish American societies into Western modernity without solving the social and cultural contradictions that that very "modernizing" effort had originated. Two aspects of this "re-conquest" are brought to the forefront: the erasure of history, and the unrecoverable interstice between the model society projected by the revolutionaries and their real societies.

In *La campaña,* the three friends at the center of the narration, Dorrego, Bustos, and Varela, are characterized as followers of Voltaire, Rousseau, and Diderot respectively. Their allegorical presentation stages the ideological battle of a priori truths versus dialogical and provisional statements. Fuentes's depiction of the various "faces of the eighteenth century" is clear. Bustos's two revolutionary friends, Manuel Varela, a printer and publisher of forbidden incendiary books who narrates the novel, occasionally inserting letters and documents from other characters, and Xavier Dorrego, a wealthy criollo whose economic interests are at stake in the revolutionary process, represent two alternative philosophical positions,[18] also in conflict with Bustos's passion for the writings of Rousseau:

> Dorrego follows Voltaire; he believes in reason but thinks it should be exercised only by an enlightened minority capable of leading the masses to happiness. Bustos follows Rousseau: he believes in a passion that would lead us to recover natural truth and bind the laws of nature and the revolution together like a sheaf of wheat. They are two faces of the eighteenth century. There is one more: mine, the printer Manuel Varela. I follow Diderot's smiling mask, the conviction that everything changes constantly and offers us at each moment of existence a repertory from which to choose. (*LC,* 25/18)

These three ideological readings of the eighteenth century summarize the main conflicts staged in the novel. The dogmatic utopian agendas of both Voltaire and Rousseau, progress and nature as unchallenged values, are reviewed throughout the text vis-à-vis Diderot's distanced gaze. Dorrego, a zealous follower of Voltaire, believes in a progress directed by "an enlightened minority," but his participation in the campaigns for independence is minimal. He represents the vested interests of the urban criollos who are trying to redistribute power positions placing themselves at the top of the new ladder. Varela, Diderot's proxy in the novel, puts into practice that playfulness underlined by Fuentes in his defense of Diderot. The distance of the satirist who cynically recounts the story of the ideological excesses of these youths behind that "smiling mask" of a printer of subversive writings is also an ideological proposal.

The names of the three main characters in the novel have not so far attracted the attention of the critics who have discussed *La campaña*. Therefore, it has passed unnoticed that Fuentes has alluded here to three historical personages of the revolutionary period around the River Plate region: Juan Bautista Bustos, Manuel Dorrego, and Juan Cruz Varela. Their biographies as revolutionaries are widely accessible, even though they were, as in the novel, second-rank figures. Bustos, an officer born in Córdoba, participated in the defense of Buenos Aires against the English in the early years of the nineteenth century; he also took part in the May revolution and, like the character in Fuentes's novel, fought in the Upper Peru campaigns with Belgrano.[19] His controversial reputation as local strong man in Córdoba during the civil wars of the 1820s can be regarded as an instance of the rebel who contributed to the desolation of the republic through their defense of their petty vested interests, and their intolerant attitudes. Manuel Dorrego also fought in Upper Peru and participated actively in the politics of the 1820s. As a Federalist, he was governor of the province of Buenos Aires, but died in the civil war against the Unitarians.[20] In *La campaña* Dorrego has the lowest profile of the three characters, and yet his differences with Bustos announce the future civil wars of the ensuing decade.

The features of the narrator are inspired in Juan Cruz Varela, a patriotic journalist and poet who was also actively involved in politics as a liberal during the 1820s. He directed a number of journals, some of them oppositional to the established governments before dying in exile in Montevideo.[21] In his poem "Sobre la invención y libertad de la imprenta," Varela praised the printing machine as the basis for the Enlightenment,[22] and in *La campaña* his only political activity is editing—the novel—and printing subversive writings.

In the novel, the narrator's distance reinforces the textual double-voicedness: the narrative is sprinkled with such reminders as "I, Varela," which continuously identify him as the intradiegetic narrator whose scathing presentation of the rest of characters in the novel, particularly Baltasar, confirms the overrunning parodic tone. But Manuel Varela not only selects and controls the information in the novel in a whimsical way, he also inserts his ideological judgments into the narration. From the beginning, both his identification with Diderot and his status as the editor of the novel underscore the prevalence of his political opinions over the other characters.

Claudia Macías de Yoon has pointed out a number of inconsistencies in Varela's voice as a narrator to justify her reading of the novel as an expression of Fuentes's exclusive "discurso único."[23] While it is feasible to argue that Fuentes has traced a critique of the "discursos únicos" ("monologic discourses") of the French Enlightenment, Rousseau's good nature, and Voltaire's utopian progress, to attribute these discourses to the author appears to be a clear misreading of the novel. If the times and voices of Indians, blacks, and mestizos are suppressed it is not so much because Fuentes is excluding them from the novel, but rather as a result of their victimization at the hands of the Enlightened revolution.[24]

Fuentes's narratives also challenge conventional accounts of the historical period which are nevertheless incorporated into both *El espejo enterrado* and *La campaña*. The former seems to include them for the sake of generic consistency; after all, it is a conventional pop-history book; the novel offers these competing explanations of the Spanish American independence—economic, social, commercial, cultural—in order to foreground the violence and contradictions unleashed by the Enlightenment in the Spanish colonies.

The Three Campaigns

Baltasar Bustos's "indigestion" of French philosophy, very much like Don Quixote's saturation of chivalric romance, also results in a successful parody of those texts that had induced it in the first place. The narrator, included in a collective first-person plural, makes explicit the parallelism between the character and Cervantes's intoxicated hidalgo:

> Everyone knew that Baltasar Bustos had read all the books of the Enlightenment; we called him the Quixote of Reason, but we didn't know what to fear most: his eloquent confusion of philosophies or his foolhardy, quixotic decision to test the validity of his readings in reality. (*LC*, 26/19–20)

Through his readings of the Enlightenment, Bustos is presented as a foolish quixotic character whose participation in the struggle for independence becomes doubtful from the outset. But his successful characterization as the "Quixote of the Enlightenment" also derives from his other passion: to his folly as a reader, which throws him into the unfeasible—Rousseauian—adventure of *reinstating* a good and just society, his blind love for a woman, in whose name he will embark in a seemingly personal crusade, is added. The composite name of his impossible beloved, Ofelia Salamanca, signals his Hamlet-like debating act throughout the novel.[25] None of his two loves will come true. For he is not only in love with Ofelia: "I love a woman. I'll never win her unless I do what I must do. I am going to join up with Castelli in Upper Peru, sister dear" (*LC*, 69/61), but also with his books, "What the hell am I—fat, blind, and enamored of my books—doing in these savage and lonely places?" (*LC*, 76/66). Correspondingly, the parody of the military campaign comes from two sources: on the one hand from Bustos's attempt to test on reality his readings of Rousseau, on the other, from his desire to realize his infatuation with Ofelia Salamanca.

As the epic account of the wars for independence loses its heroic gloss, it is challenged by all the alternative "journeys." These three competing accounts of Bustos's journey—his military actions, his search for Ofelia, and his intellectual quest—become alternative campaigns occurring in the novel contemporaneously and interacting with each other through parody. The "obvious" campaign for independence, experienced by the character from 1810 to 1821 as he travels from Buenos Aires to Santiago de Chile, the Andean heights, Maracaibo, and Veracruz, participating in all the wars for independence in Spanish America, becomes parodied by the concurrence of at least two other campaigns: the protagonist's campaign to find his Dulcinea, Ofelia Salamanca; and finally, the character's campaign in search of his own intellectual identity which parodies his earlier political passion.[26] The quest becomes, as in *Don Quixote,* a journey of discovery in which the character's earlier idealizations of love and societal relations are transformed and problematized.[27]

Baltasar Bustos's search for Ofelia Salamanca parodies both his military campaign and his intellectual quest: Bustos may have gone to war not so much in order to help liberate the colonies, but in order to find a woman. He may not after all be looking for answers to his increasing philosophical dilemmas either, but for Ofelia's apparently unparalleled body. Some critics go as far as to describe Bustos's search for Ofelia as "the *real* campaign"[28] or one of the protagonist's "two campaigns."[29] Fuentes uses the structure of *Candide*—itself built on the template of *Don Quixote*—to put forward a similar critique of an intellectualism that does not acknowledge its physical contingencies.[30] In that novel, Voltaire stages a dystopian quest through which Candide realizes the impossibility of finding Leibniz's "meilleur des mondes possibles" ("best of all possible worlds"). Despite its likely "latent Americanism," *Candide* is a classic model for a critique of unrealistic utopianism and of religion, in which parody is the main form of emplotment.[31] *La campaña* resembles Voltaire's novel in the questing character's infatuation with an impossible or forbidden female whose search parodies the other intellectual or political searches. In Fuentes's novel, this parody is complemented with the narrator's final gesture of disclosing his own relationship with Ofelia Salamanca: it is a narrative tool that furthers the satirical effect of the novel. As the reader realizes that the whole story of Bustos's unrequited love has been told by Ofelia's lover—Varela, who is in fact the father of her missing child—the novel's constant challenge of fixed truths is brought to a new stage.

The third campaign, Bustos's quest for intellectual identity, outlines a search by which the character gradually questions the received ideas of the Enlightenment. Fuentes encloses in this other campaign most of the ideological debates, complexly addressing the question of the relationship between Spanish America and the projects of modernity. Bustos's search for ideological identity is strictly a test of the liberating principles of the Enlightenment revolution and their suitability for the Spanish American context. His inflexible ideas about justice and equality at the beginning of the novel become blurred after the character's intellectual journey away from the texts and into reality—a journey which in turn parodies the pass from the Enlightenment belief in progress to the Romantic belief in an organic renewal of society, while it reviews the theory of the noble savage subjacent to both intellectual moments.

The opening scene of *La campaña* sets the farcical tone in which the hero's campaigns for independence are recounted. Baltasar Bustos decides to impart justice by exchanging a black baby, the son of a prostitute who has been publicly thrashed, with the newly born son of the Marquis of Cabra, temporary president of the Audiencia of Buenos Aires, and his wife, no other than Ofelia Salamanca.[32] This initial deed turns into a fiasco as Bustos mistakenly sets the palace on fire and the offense is never discovered. It is also the first of a series of parodic scenes in the novel. Revolutionary justice has symbolically culminated with the burning of an innocent black boy, while the kidnapping of the little Marquis will conclude at the end of the ten-year-long campaign, when Bustos himself adopts the young boy. Xavier Dorrego's dogmatic voice states "Long live justice" (*LC,* 35/28), celebrating the mishap as a success of the revolution. However, ridden by the guilt of the black child's death, Bustos soon realizes that he "had only substituted one injustice by another" (*LC,* 51/43). The revolution seemingly sacrifices the colonial social order, but the new establishment is annoyingly conservative in its outlook on racial and social boundaries: the white boy, representing the newly born nation, taken from his aristocratic parents, is adopted at the end by the republican heroes. Read as parody, the recovery of the white child cannot be regarded as Fuentes's "symbol of hope for America" as Macías de Yoon has suggested in her article.[33] Rather, it constitutes itself as Fuentes's most pessimistic judgment about the whole historical period: its accursed continuity.

A similar Orwellian conclusion is examined by Alejo Carpentier in *The Kingdom of This World* (1947), as the Haitian revolutionaries inaugurate a horrific postcolonial monarchy in a move that emphasizes history as repetition; as González Echevarría has remarked, time in that novel becomes "a daemonic circle in which history, moved by natural forces, [is] entrapped."[34] In *La campaña,* the repetition of the historical cycle is not so much a natural determination as a cultural one: the result of the revolutionaries' obsession with the unreal, utopian doctrines of the French Enlightenment. As the novel closes, the narrator opts to continue publishing Voltaire and Rousseau, rather than warn his readers against the foreseeable collapse of Bolívar's Spanish American federation (*LC,* 252). Both Varela and Dorrego prefer to remain in their inherited trades and continue their lives as *bon vivants* in Buenos Aires. In the contrast between their uncommitted attitude and the persistence of Bustos's determined campaign, a critique of his exacerbated foundational zeal emerges. If the accidental burning of the black boy is the first in a series of racial and sexual transgressions by Bustos's vigorous and farcical campaign, the indolent and idealistic attitudes of his two friends are equally problematic. While the narrator announces at the end that "the campaign was finally over" (*LC*, 260/246), his readers are ironically forced to remember the series of civil wars that tore apart the Spanish American colonies after independence. This projected and unwarranted violent future is the culmination of the growing tension between the disillusioned elitist revolutionaries who are still hoping for a peaceful future in their tranquil European outpost, and the traveled Bustos who knows he is "not going to live that time in peace. Not me, nor Argentina, nor all the Americas" (*LC*, 257/243). His painful realization is the result of multiple quests in which he has become aware of the ever-widening gap between the enlightened declarations and written laws of the lettered city and the real societies whose freedom they claim to administer.

From the moment when he commits his first revolutionary outrage at the Marquis de Cabra's palace until his return to Buenos Aires, he is involved in all the three main areas of conflict in the Spanish colonies: San Martín's Peruvian and Chilean campaigns; Bolívar's far reaching wars to found Greater Colombia in what is today Venezuela, Colombia, and Ecuador; and Hidalgo's failed movement to bring independence to Mexico. But this ahistorical and hyperbolic participation in all three campaigns is parodied by the two other concurrent, alternative journeys in which he is involved, and indeed by the sheer magnitude of his deed. His epic journey for "liberation" could be narrated instead as a fight against all the many subalterns he seeks to contain and suppress: this is perhaps Fuentes's ultimate parody on the national foundations of independent Latin American republics, their postcolonial continuities with the Columbian Conquest.

In his first sally, he returns to his father's farm in La Pampa, and he realizes there the irreconcilable breach between his idealistic dreams and nature. Looking at the mountains, he wishes that they might turn into the stage where "history could be made so that nature and society might once again be united" (*LC*, 51/43). Nature brings back his readings of Rousseau and his romantic passion for an organic society, but his encounter with the gauchos working at the farm signals the flaw of his idealization. His romantic hope for a noble savage is confronted with the sweat and labor of the gauchos who he perceived "as a Mongolian horde" (*LC*, 44/36). The double dismissal of the frontiersmen as unruly savages illustrates the gap between his anthropological faith and his perceptions: "[the gauchos] spoiled his idyllic vision of nature" (*LC*, 44/36).

A "perfect reader of distant ideals" (*LC*, 19/13), his importation of foreign political utopias had started with his effort to "seduce" his fellow revolutionaries: "bubbling with optimism, seduced and now seducing us with the vision of a political idyll, the social contract renewed on the banks of Buenos Aires's muddy, swampy river" (*LC*, 10/4). To the conspicuous impossibility of accomplishing a "political idyll" on the banks of a "swampy river," the satirist adds the depiction of Bustos as an impossible hero whose physical appearance, chubby and short-sighted, identifies him as ideologically blinded and physically unfit to carry out any such deed. The ideological inconsistencies of the character are highlighted by the sarcastic narrator who makes explicit the contradictory role of Rousseau's social thought as understood by Bustos:

> Then his reading of Jean-Jacques would come to his rescue (the same way the romances of chivalry served as models for Don Quixote, said his friends, Dorrego and I, Varela, laughing), to tell him that feeling uneasy in society, or seeing society as an excretion, an excess, was not a sin but a virtue. (*LC,* 51/43)

The cunning narrator reminds us once again, this time parenthetically, of his comic resemblance with Don Quixote. The joke of a lonely revolutionary going away to impose utopia on a society with which he is disengaged at heart is obvious. Rousseau's romantic enlightenment becomes openly problematic once its reconciliation of society and nature are effected despotically, and from an a priori judgment of their vices and virtues. This chasm between the romantic theorization of indigenous otherness or natural life, and the character's experiences, is one of the major discoveries in Bustos's learning trip: it is a form of self-discovery.[35] From the premise that the political ideas of the French philosophes could be put into practice in the Spanish colonies, the character sets off to fight the European masters, but in so doing, he becomes aware that he himself, as a criollo, is actually one of them.[36] At the end of his campaigns, Bustos is convinced of the striking differences between "real" society and the elite's imagined communities.[37]

His own experiences as a destroyer of ethnic diversity evidence his inability to create—or help create—a language by which the new community will incorporate all the individuals already living in the "liberated" territories. When he announces to the Indians in Upper Peru their freedom from servitude and that "the Indian is declared equal to any other Argentine or American national" (*LC,* 83/74) he realizes the hypocrisy of the action: he is speaking from atop his horse—"the horse is authority, . . . the horse defeated them" (*LC,* 82/72), as father Muñecas reminds him—and in Spanish—"how many of these Indians even speak Spanish?" (*LC,* 84/74) he asks the rebel cleric. Thus, liberation, freedom as an abstract concept, belongs only to the distant written law of the new constitution(s), not to the everyday reality of the leftover colonial institutions, the plantation, or the *mita,* which exert forced labor in the fields and mines respectively. As the basic social and economic realities remain unchanged for the majority of the population, the discrepancy between the written and the real world grows wider. The criollo self-awareness turns him into the postcolonial administrator of inequality, feeling "proud of [his] superiority, and at the same time in love with the inferiority of others" (*LC,* 92/82), as Bustos confesses in a letter to his friends.

That sense of superior social status derives from the criollos' access to writing and the written word, their status at the center of the lettered city as the *letrados* who write and imagine the national community. They can create the new nations because they can write their constitutions, the declarations of independence and, with them, their version of the Americanist utopia. When Bustos visits the Mexican rebels he perceives their excitement for the radical written rule "as if winning the war depended on paper and as if only that which was written could be real in our new nations and as if what was real were a mere mirage, to be disdained to the degree to which it did not adhere to the written ideal" (*LC,* 215/202). After all, "no combatían. Escribían leyes" ("They didn't fight. They wrote laws") (*LC,* 228/215). It is their papers, the ten cartloads of laws that account for their military power, as Bustos notices "to make up for the paucity of their artillery, there was an overabundance of archives" (*LC,* 214/201). At this point, the parody of the rebels' failed endeavors to write utopia reaches its narrative culmination. Through a double-voiced reenactment of their utopian campaign, Fuentes pinpoints and underlines the discrepancy between the legal and the real nations in Latin America, between the written laws and constitutions, and the unreachable—and unwritable—*real* society outside the texts.[38]

Much like the second part of Cervantes's book, toward the end of *La campaña* the hero needs to live up to his own story, fictionalized in popular songs, thus acting "to carry out his legendary destiny, which had already been mapped out in popular song" (*LC,* 194/182). Bustos's acknowledgment of his own status as a character of epic folklore is used to challenge further the relation between reality and the text. Fuentes pointed out in his *Cervantes o la crítica de la lectura* the character's awareness of his fictionality as one of the "modern" features of Cervantes's novel: "He ceases being the reader of chivalric novels and starts to act his own adventures" (75). But if the real is always a predetermined—or already written—reality, then the power lies in the ability to write the master texts. "History" would be only "the naïve belief that, first, things happen and then they are written" (*LC,* 194/182), because the text precedes the real—as in the Judeo-Christian creed. And yet, as the novel also suggests, texts are only tentative approaches to a reality that continually defies permanent narratives and stable definitions through the constant chaos of human agency, historical changes, and irrational desires.

The narrator, who hammers this ideological inconsistency on his readers throughout the novel, defends a different kind of critical distance, one by which texts and realities are continuously reread and rewritten according to ever-changing conditions. Nevertheless, even the playful narrator is condemned at the end of the novel when his inconsistent political attitudes are also brought to the fore. As he confesses his preference for leisure and playfulness amidst the growing chaos of the new republic, his activities as printer also become more distanced from the real pressing issues of his society, he becomes exposed as an instigator who essentially prioritizes his own safety. At the end, he himself prefers to edit translations of French utopias rather than Bolívar's diatribes and worried prose. As he refuses to publish a biography of Bolívar by an Aureliano García—a lighthearted allusion to García Márquez's take on the period in *The General in His Labyrinth* (1989) as well as to the Aurelianos, a line of characters in *One Hundred Years of Solitude* (1967)—Varela also starts to remove himself from political participation in his new republic. It is as if the utopias of the Enlightenment could only exist in the vast library of revolutionary philosophy, as if the material world of politics and social affairs was only the imperfect remainder of the need for further shelves and volumes to imagine its alternatives and to plot its overhaul.

In *Tiempo mexicano* Fuentes had already suggested the temptation to interpret Mexican history as a "fight between sacred texts and profane realities."[39] Fuentes alluded to this fracture between the two nations, the real and the legal, when describing the hesitant figure of José de San Martín in *El espejo enterrado:*

> Between the absence of the monarchy and the weakness of civil society, between the façade of the legal nation and the substance of the real nation, a breach opened that would only be filled by what San Martín feared most: the fortunate soldier, the strong man, the tyrant.[40] (276)

In Domingo F. Sarmiento's political program *Facundo: Civilización y barbarie* (1845), the would-be president of Argentina had pointed to the uncontrollable forces of the countryside, in particular to the cattle-raising gauchos, as the anarchic element in the constitution of a modern nation in Argentina. Fuentes's novel partially responds to Sarmiento's proposal of a direct importation of European and North American models—*Facundo* draws frequent examples from the United States—and to his dismissal of the non-European as barbarian and unruly. Fuentes appears to suggest that the civilizing program of nineteenth-century positivism which inspired Sarmiento was an unambiguous continuation of the earlier Enlightened rejection of the past.[41] In Sarmiento's inability to reconcile those "two nations"—which according to Fuentes account for many of Spanish America's ills—Fuentes recognized one more historical failure to comprehend the plural identity of Spanish America.[42]

El Dorado

In the Peruvian highlands, Bustos experiences the indigenous world directly, but his ultimate ambiguity, his inability to come to terms with it, leaves little hope for a foundational postcolonial reconciliation between settlers and natives, between European and Indigenous societies. His first sexual experience results from the sacrifice of an Indian girl, offered to him as a gift: the *acla cuna* or "chosen one" (*LC,* 79) who has to die as she is no longer a virgin who can serve the gods well. Equally, the first man that he kills is an Indian who had to die "because he was Indian, weak, poor, different" (*LC,* 115/107). As in other moments throughout his campaign, the liberation of the colonies is reminiscent of the episodes of pillage and rape of the conquistadors. In Bustos's encounter with the Indian world Fuentes appears to be criticizing his own view of the colonies as enjoying that developing "indoafroiberoamericano" identity which he had eagerly proposed in his *Valiente mundo nuevo.* With this contemporary reworking of the (im)possibility of cultural *mestizaje,* Fuentes is perhaps suggesting that past and present multicultural identities are not fixed and need a continual revision. In the novel, the Spanish criollos, as their Anglo-Saxon counterparts would do, vigorously claim for themselves the Western concept of Americanness, to then impose it on the whole of society in the shape of national "consensus."

The reactionary warning of the Spanish Marqués de Cabra, Ofelia's husband, had already foreshadowed this seemingly inescapable future. When Bustos encounters him in Lima, Cabra insists that

> the mere act of casting out the Spaniards will not make the creoles less unjust, cruel, or greedy. And dictatorship after dictatorship will be necessary to bridge the gap between the country as constituted by law and the country as reality. You will be left to the mercy of the elements, my dear patriots. You will wrench off the roof of tradition. But you do not know how to survive in the new, open air. (*LC,* 139/129)

Cabra's voice is part of the polyphony through which the complex historical situation is staged in the novel. It obviously represents the European determination to see the colonies as a perpetually engaged territory, and as an ever-immature society, never ready to gain its own political autonomy.

Bustos's contradictory response underlines once again the inconsistency of his solution: "'We shall make our own modernity, and it will be unlike that of the English or the French, your lordship,' said young Baltasar, imagining a French roof over the head of his sister" (*LC,* 139/129). His hope for their own version of modernity—perhaps also Fuentes's longing—is rapidly belied by his mental imagining of a French ceiling protecting his sister. And yet, at times the Spanish colonial heritage is offered throughout the novel as an alternative version of modernity which already contains concepts such as popular sovereignty and representative democracy, and where the moral values of Christian and pre-Columbian societies could be merged.[43] Father Ríos, Bustos's Jesuit tutor, longs for a balanced combination of the past and the present in a complex though dialogic encounter: "Would the South American patriots ever understand that without the past they would never be what they desired: paradigms of modernity?" (*LC*, 144/134).

For the liberator of Mexico, the mestizo father Quintana—father Hidalgo, the precursor of independence, in disguise—a solution to the conflicting relationship between Spanish America and modernity could also be found in the "harmonious" amalgamation of the different cultures of the continent:

> What I'm asking you is that we not sacrifice anything, son, not the magic of the Indians, not the theology of the Christians, not the reason of our European contemporaries. It would be better if we gathered up everything we are in order to go on being and to be, finally, something better. Don't let yourself be divided and dazzled by a single idea. (*LC*, 243/230)

Carlos J. Alonso insightfuly perceives in Quintana's words "an argument to counter the exclusive hegemony of Enlightened Reason" (264) and therefore as part of a postmodern revision which in Latin America is "one that has led to the reconceptualization of Spanish American cultural discourse as intrinsically beholden to hegemonic values and concerns" (266). According to him, the novel could be described as "a profound meditation on the contradiction and difficult relationship between Spanish America and modernity" (254). Alonso argues that the novel's intention is to exorcize the "phantom of the lost object of modernity" (260) and that it "is emblematic of the successful passing from melancholy to mourning and beyond, that is, to the final awareness that loss must somehow be turned into totalizing memory if life is to abide and prevail" (262).

Ironically, the image that appears to agglutinate the different components of a possible Spanish American version of modernity is none other than El Dorado. One of the series of epiphanic moments to which Bustos is exposed in his journey, his descent to this underworld reaffirms the separation of man and nature,[44] but it also suggests the reconciliation of past and present. At his father's deathbed he reflects again on his vision, wondering whether tradition and utopia can be harmonized. The "eyes of light" of El Dorado

> contemplated the origin of time and celebrated the birth of mankind. They did not remember their past; they were there always, without losing, because of it, either their immediate present or their most remote beginnings . . . How was it possible to stand next to them without losing our humanity but augmenting it thanks to everything we've been? Can we be at the same time all we have been and all we want to be? (*LC*, 122/112)[45]

Quintana's words also echo this longing for harmony, but the suggestion that Spanish American identity could be all-inclusive, or at best a multicultural El Dorado, is clearly charged with an idyllic tone reminiscent of the earlier Americanists, the conquistadores who sought a city of gold in the "new world." Multiculturalism does not only pose the racial and social problems encountered by Bustos, but it also subverts the concepts of cultural and linguistic purity. If the concept of *mestizaje* and transculturation might promote plurality and the erasure of old boundaries, it also reproduces the problems of hierarchization and acculturation without solving them. What would need to be continually revised and reassessed is the toll that each of the participating cultures has to pay for its successful integration into a multicultural postmodernity.

Like the narrator who is described at a certain point as "an impenitent printer confident he could change the world by throwing words at it" (*LC*, 216/203), Fuentes seems to be replicating the pattern of hoping in writing for what remains unsolved in society. Bustos's conclusion at the end of his ten-year troubles that "hay que ser un problema, siempre hay que *ser* un problema" ("There has to be a problem. There always has to be a problem") (*LC*, 256/242) foregrounds a questioning activity that establishes itself as oppositional to the scientific and political certainties in which he believed at the outset of his campaign. In a similar way, Fuentes's postmodern solution is "in progress," unfinished. Unlike any of the modernist, nationalist, "final" solutions to difference, the minimalism of postnational postmodernity emphasizes the confluence of times, histories, and languages, opposing their plurality to the prevalence of a single one over the others. Exactly how workable this minimalism may be or how much of it may be used to disguise a homogenizing globalization that has found a new, more effective way to broadcast itself is at the core of the ethical questions posed by Fuentes's inquiring characters.

Chapter 7

✦

Surveying American Exceptionalism in *Mason & Dixon*

> But should [the poet] venture upon the dark story of their wrongs and wretchedness; should he tell how they were invaded, corrupted, despoiled, driven from their native abodes and the sepulchers of their fathers, hunted like wild beasts about the earth, and sent down with violence and butchery to the grave, posterity will either turn with horror and incredulity from the tale, or blush with indignation at the inhumanity of their forefathers.
>
> —Washington Irving

> Westward the course of Empire takes its way;
> The four first acts already past
> A fifth shall close the drama with the day;
> Time's noblest offspring is the last.
>
> —Bishop George Berkeley

Irving outlined the troubled, ambivalent attitudes toward the genocide committed against Native Americans by whites: incredulity—confirmed by a silence, which not always sounds condemnatory—or indignation—spoken through many acts of contrition—are only two, perhaps the most prevalent ones, of the many possible outlooks on the American Holocaust. Assuming the relentless impact of the westward expansion of the country, Irving's prediction anticipates the destruction not only of the East Coast Indians, but of all the Native American peoples and their ways of life across the territory claimed by U.S. expansionism in successive years: "They will vanish like a vapor from the face of the earth; their very history will be lost in forgetfulness."[1] With a mixture of liberal nostalgia and historical fatalism, Washington Irving endorsed the prevailing myth of the "vanishing Indian," a theme that would pervade American culture into the twentieth century. The reverse trope of this historical fatalism—its photographic negative—is, of course, the grand narrative of Manifest Destiny: the American nation as a triumphant exception in a history of constant decline and depravation. American exceptionalism, a set of totemic narratives on which the politics of continental expansion—and its associated ethnic cleansing—was built from the time of U.S. independence, is a complex and evolving group of myths about selfhood which range from Protestant millennialism to secular (pseudo)scientific theories about ethnic superiority. Although both epigraphs are united by their dark sense of prophecy, Bishop Berkeley's well-known lines stem from and contribute to a discourse of the English and the English-Americans as the "chosen people," celebrating the "Elect" in opposition to the "Preterite" ones.[2] Berkeley's verses expound the mixture of nationalism and millenarianism subjacent to Anglicanism, ridden by myths such as the "glorious undertaking" or the "errand" and the "chosen people," the idea of England as the New Israel, being transferred here onto the construction of America as an accomplishment of the *translatio imperii.* Sacvan Bercovitch has shown how the beliefs of the New England dissenters were permeated by this millennialism and how it was progressively built into the idea of America through what he terms an "ideological consensus."[3] According to Bercovitch, an American national ideological consensus became ritualized and intimately linked with the process of westward expansion: "As New Israel progressed across the continent, the Westward Movement came to provide a sort of serial enactment of the ritual of consensus."[4] The rhetoric of a westward course of empire behind the nineteenth-century coining of "Manifest Destiny" is but another phase in the evolution of the millenarian discourse that can be easily identified at the root of racial and religious justifications of U.S. imperialism in the North American continent and elsewhere. It is one of the most powerful pieces in the ideological backbone of a "mainstream" definition of Americanness—Bercovitch's "consensual term"—as "time's noblest offspring," it also provides American exceptionalism with a vigorous geographical agenda. America the "consensual term" is thus the unchallenged space for a nationalist "ideological consensus," as Sacvan Bercovitch proposes.[5]

These two epigraphs are good referents of the controversial attitudes in early American history toward the future of Native Americans, particularly in relation to their integration or exclusion into the nascent Anglo-Saxon nation. In its double axis, its Western projection, and its North-South divide, the Mason and Dixon Line embodies two main fault lines on which the historical narratives of the American nation have dwelled since before the time of its independence from Britain: two geographical axes and two subjugated groups, Native Americans and African slaves. These two geographical axes and their position in the formation of an independent American identity are prominently thematized in Pynchon's *Mason & Dixon.*[6] Destructive racial and cultural relations with Native Americans on one hand, and the fracture posed by two conflicting capitalist systems—Northern free-holding farming and industry versus Southern slave-holding plantation—on the other, contest the combined discourses of scientific progress and of enlightened freedom inscribed into the national consensus. *Mason & Dixon* offers a critical interpretation of American colonial history and the ensuing national foundation of the United States, short-circuiting its recuperation into the grand narratives of the American nation as a historical exception.

Pynchon sets out to debase the nationalist histories of American exceptionalism by pointing at the epistemic biases of the discourses of progress and science at the time of the Enlightenment, the intellectual context in which part of the British American colonies became an independent nation. I will explore here the ways in which Pynchon parodically uses historical materials and characters in order to reinscribe into the birth of the nation the cultural erasures and the epistemic violence involved in the narration of American exceptionalism. Pynchon's political intervention in a critical rewriting of history is aimed at showing the lack of national exceptionality in the American history of conquest and cultural homogenization.

The narrator in Pynchon's *Mason & Dixon* is the Revd. Cherrycoke; his voice replicates and parodies eighteenth-century English, and asserts the need to see history, and the history of texts, not as a direct line—as lines are the real protagonist of that novel—but rather as an uncontrollable proliferation: "Not a Chain of single Links, for one broken link could lose us All—rather, a great disorderly Tangle of Lines, long and short, weak and strong, vanishing into the Mnemonick Deep, with only their Destination in common" (*MD*, 349). Cherrycoke's chaotic "Tangle of Lines" is a fictional theory of history that advocates plurality of referent and multiplicity of textual connections in the palimpsestic nature of the present text, or hypertext. Thus, the project of the novel is an incursion into some of those lines, a reading and a reworking of partial events in the history of the United States before its constitution as an independent nation, which seeks to refashion that history in a critical rather than an epic mode. Through a dense use of historical material, and through the use of parody, the novel confirms Pynchon's commitment to a reassessment of American history through satirical fiction. Pynchon critically underlines the inconsistencies between discourses and practices at the time of the formation of the United States as a nation and in so doing, he satirically reinscribes its foundational narratives.

In *Mason & Dixon,* the material demarcation of the boundary between Maryland and Pennsylvania epitomizes the uncontrollability of the scientific process of mapping new territories: the Line gains a separate life from the two surveyors who trace it, and who become increasingly concerned about the human, cultural, and social effect of incorporating into the world map previously uncharted territories. The Line becomes a "great invisible Thing,"[7] a monster of human ambition, not merely a boundary between neighboring provinces, but a way into the western Indian territories, "a tree-slaughtering

Animal" which kills "ev'rything due west of it." Its real "intentions" beyond that are unknown to all. The newly charted territories become "known" and accessible to future colonizers, while the landmarks of previous societies are erased. At the same time, it is noted that the line will serve also as the official separating incision between North and South during the Civil War one hundred years after it was marked out. As an index to the two mythical efforts articulating the nationalist images of Americanness throughout the nineteenth century, the conquest of the West and the Civil War, the line stands at the center of American nationhood. The story itself begins at the very moment and place of birth of the United States: Philadelphia, 1786, the year in which the U.S. Constitution was approved.

"I Make an Effort to Keep to the Margins Close as I May" (*MD,* 69)

Faced with the horrors of slavery in the African colony of Cape Town, Jeremiah Dixon, the Quaker surveyor from Durham, reaffirms, through Pynchon's words, his marginality and his distrust of the practices of the East Indian Company. As elsewhere in the novel, ideas about the characters' marginal relation to the projects of the British Royal Society, the East India Company, or the proprietors of Maryland and Pennsylvania convey a sense of their vacillating participation in those projects. Their status as insiders/outsiders is a position much in tune with the perspective adopted by other characters in the rest of Pynchon's fiction, characters that parallel Pynchon's paradoxical marginality in the national canon of American literature. A suspicion about the location of Pynchon's marginal voice has been expressed often among critics of his work. The coincidence in time between the development of poststructuralist critical practices in the American academy with the early reactions to Pynchon's work, added to the lack of a physical authorial presence, has too often led to the surmise that the point about his novels is precisely the process of avoidance of an authorial voice. Pynchon was, and is to this date, elusive not only in "real" life—no photographs, no interviews—but also in a fiction opened up to many possible readings through the multiplicity of voices.

This celebratory approach may be politically at the service of silencing one of the main qualities of the text, namely Pynchon's critique of the elimination of cultural differences by the homogenizing nationalist projects of enlightened modernity. In particular, the description of the novel as plotless may be aimed at suppressing its politics. This process of political demotion in relation to *Mason & Dixon* is well illustrated in William Logan's article "Pynchon in the Poetic."[8] The title gives away Logan's whole thesis: *Mason & Dixon* is "a poetic act" (424). What for some might be a point of agreement, the novel's excellence in metaphoric language, the dazzling sense of humor, the success of both pastiche and anachronism, turns under Logan's logic—or rather his lack of it—into a classification of the novel as a failure, which is a point that surely will provoke a strong disagreement among other readers. Logan does not equate the language and the formal features of the novel to poetry as a form of praise of Pynchon's mastery, but rather as an excuse to indict its prose as hollow:

> Pynchon may have conceived *Mason & Dixon* as a supreme fiction, a poetic act freed of the slavery of plot and character; but conventions are cruel to those who betray them. As his stand-up comedy becomes merely a seven-hundred-page improvisation, the jokes grow hollow. Here Pynchon's poetics have seduced him: it hardly matters if most poems mean what they say. Poetry is the saying, but fiction (the drama, the action, the consequence, the regret) is the having said. (437)

The conclusion reached by Logan is consistent with his heavily formalist analysis of the novel. He accuses the characters' apparent "purposeful dither" of finally becoming "just dither" (433), failing to notice that the line would *not* be finally completed, not because the "actions of the characters remain empty" (433), but precisely because of their final realization of the moral and cultural implications of the Line they are tracing. Logan's constant use of adjectives such as "empty," or "hollow" to refer to the novel, and his affirmation that the novel's quasi-narcissistic texture is a product of the author's self-complacent attitude, are just two of the strategies deployed by this particular critic to try and defuse Pynchon's satirical reconstruction of the nation's fraught origins and its archaeological fractures.

From a different angle, Pynchon's apparent marginality has been reviewed as part of the features that guarantee Pynchon's entry into the canon of American literature. Michael Bérubé's *Marginal Forces/Cultural Centers* connects Pynchon's seeming marginality with the process of canonization of the author himself, underlining the status of Pynchon's voice as a "consensus criticism of the consensus."[9] This dissenting attitude from inside would be in tune with Bercovitch's characterization of some mainstream American literature as enacting an internal disagreement which finally "serve[s] to sustain the culture."[10] It is in this sense that Pynchon's conflicting voice comes from the center itself and not from the margins. Pynchon might therefore be seen as "one more white man from the Northeast, writing big books about the Puritan origins of the American self,"[11] as Bérubé casts him at a certain point, and his concern for the margins, as in *Mason & Dixon,* might identify him with that future poet previewed by Irving who would finally "blush with indignation at the inhumanity of their forefathers."[12] And yet, the assumption that Pynchon is working inside the framework of the mainstream in terms of his access to the canonizing resorts of a white man from the Northeast with his background should not work to defuse his effort to dissent with the nationalist grand narrative of American exceptionalism. And what if the assumption that Pynchon writes big books about the Puritan origins of the country is a misreading of recuperative, Americanist critics as I have been claiming throughout this book?

Commenting on the film *The Patriot* (2000), Donald E. Pease sums up what he calls the double, Janus-face of American exceptionalism which was "discernible in the national and international reactions to the nation's founding." Yet in Pease's rather conventional description of American exceptionalism this Janus-face is not composed of a negative and a positive face, but rather of two equally potent alternatives to European decadence, the rhetorical-democratic and the factual-imperial: "The advocates of Americans' exceptionalism who set Europe's feudal past against America's democratic future typically invoked the moral exemplarity of the nation's civic nationalism to justify their description of American democracy as the *telos* for the progressive movement of world history. But it was the state's demonstrable military and economic power that inspired international observers to recognize the United States as a political model that constituted an alternative to Europe's."[13] None of these two accustomed celebratory renderings of the United States as an "alternative" to European economic or political models envisions, however, the lineages and continuities underlined by Pynchon in his belying of America's exception to the Western history of expansive destructiveness.

In *Mason & Dixon,* Pynchon does not seek to reconstruct the Puritan origins of the republic to come; instead he explores and critiques the destruction of human difference in the apparently harmless scientific enterprises of observing the transit of Venus or tracing a line through the wilderness. Both historical and fictional characters do become aware of the implications of western expansion and of the brutality and barbarity of its agents. As in *Gravity's Rainbow* and *The Crying of Lot 49,* the questing plot gives shape to the authorial preoccupation with the margins of society, through a trip that takes the characters into a reality which challenges their complacent, trite lives. The direction westward of the Mason and Dixon Line becomes the locus for a critique of the western movement of the Anglo-Saxon Empire, and an indictment of the colonial racial relations that remained largely unchanged after the American Revolution.

Reading as I do Pynchon's text as a denunciation of imperial practices in the formation of the United States as a nation-state integrates the novel into a postcolonial, postnational critique, foregrounding the relation between the production of space and power, and the rewriting of history as the central themes in the novel. Such a politicizing reading of *Mason & Dixon* suggests a view of the text as a contact zone: the humorous and ambiguous aspects of the novel, its various registers, the accurately historical, the concisely anachronistic, Pynchon's mastery as regards the confluence of eighteenth-century styles of English and its parodic resonances at the close of the twentieth century and beyond all come together as part of the textual, political practice of postnational satire. In it, those stylistic features can be read not only as the signifiers of the political, but also as part of the signified, that is, part of the project of ideologically recuperating and reenacting the past from the present time, to which all historiography is committed.[14] A similar preoccupation with the epistemological problems of the interaction between history and fiction is expressed in the novel, through the reutilization of historical material in a parodic mode. As Douglas Keesey pointed out in his survey of the first reviews on *Mason & Dixon,* the novel's carnivalization of history should be approached "with this assumption that comedy is *not* incompatible with history, but a key route to other pasts and futures—an alternative history."[15] Parody is not therefore a mere formal feature, Logan's "hollow jokes," but rather a political movement away from the "want of objectivity" studied by Hayden White, and which usually manifests itself as a "failure to narrativize reality adequately."[16] As the ethnocentric seriousness of enlightened science is questioned by private morals and practices, so are the ethnocentric discourses of objectivity and reason by jokes, laughter, human diversity, and ecological resistance.

In his *Postmodern Cartographies* Brian Jarvis regards space and its politicization as constituting a constant element in the works of contemporary artists, such as David Lynch or Toni Morrison. Published only a year after *Mason & Dixon* came out, Jarvis's book does not discuss Pynchon's most explicitly cartographical novel, yet its perceptive analysis of his earlier fiction proves to be useful as a framework for reading *Mason & Dixon.* In his analysis Jarvis perceives

> an acute geographical awareness in Pynchon's work from the outset, one which manifests itself not in "adestinality" or directionlessness, but in a continual movement *underground,* towards the critical contours of the postmodern landscape. Pynchon's fictions gravitate towards the contraries and contradictions of uneven development, towards the spaces occupied by the underclass and the disinherited and towards the omnipresence of forms of waste, which, potentially, may become oppositional objects once situated as anti-commodities.[17]

In *Mason & Dixon,* Pynchon's "geographical awareness" is brought to the foreground. It demonstrates once more the author's commitment to that "continual movement underground" which Jarvis has identified in Pynchon's other fiction. In this case, the explicitly cartographical endeavor is also an encounter between Europeans and the preexisting cultures whose geographical signposts they help erase. However much their distrust of the political motives behind their two expeditions may be emphasized, they are after all imperial bureaucrats at the service of the British Crown.[18] The contrast between the characters' religious beliefs and their scientific activities is a central aspect of the novel's parodic tone. Although it might be possible to claim that their metaphysical and moral beliefs are challenged by "Reason," their faith in progress is ultimately shattered by their own actions and observations.

As a parody of the grand narratives of scientific achievements of the age of Enlightenment, the novel makes use of double-voice in order to express a disagreement with the established or official discourses about the history of social and racial relations in early American history, critiquing the construction of power groups and the history of the appropriation of knowledge. By doing so, it subverts both the triumphal narrative of the scientific achievement of tracing the line between Maryland and Pennsylvania, and the narrative of progress and democracy underlining the accounts of the American revolutionary period.

"A Tale About America" (*MD,* 7)

To most readers, *Mason & Dixon* will give the impression of an exceedingly complex text. Yet the rewards of a consistent and detailed reading are very promising. Its complexity and the density of the historical material make it almost impossible to refer to the novel's structure without feeling that something is being left out. The novel is divided into seventy-eight chapters separated by three sections which correspond to the three main scientific activities carried out by Charles Mason (1728–1783)[19] and Jeremiah Dixon (1733–1779).[20] These are, in the first and third parts, the observations of the transits of Venus in 1761 and 1769 respectively, and in the second part the tracing of the boundary between the provinces of Maryland and Pennsylvania, and the calculation of a degree of latitude in the Delaware peninsula.[21] The first section, "Latitudes and Departures" (chapters 1–25, pp. 3–253), deals with among other things the expedition to the Cape of Good Hope to observe the transit of Venus, the first occasion on which Mason and Dixon worked together. Although initially appointed to go to Bencoolen in the island of Sumatra, the war between the English and French, and the fact that Bencoolen itself was taken by the French meant first a delay, and finally a change of plans in their destination. In January 1761 they traveled to the Cape of Good Hope and stayed there until October 1761 when they joined Reverend Nevil Maskelyne at Saint Helena. At the end of the first part, Mason and Dixon return to England and sign the contract with the proprietors of Maryland and Pennsylvania that will engage them in tracing the boundary between those two provinces from 1763 to 1768. The second part (chapters 26–73, pp. 255–713), "America," has as the recurring theme Mason and Dixon's five-year-long stay in the British North American colonies. During these five years the personages become close friends, and while carrying out their jobs they also get involved in observing and commenting on pre-Revolutionary American society. In the third part (chapters 74–78, pp. 715–73), "Last Transit," back in England Mason and Dixon observe separately the transit of

Venus from different points. After Dixon's death a decrepit Mason returns to Philadelphia to die with his family.

Mason & Dixon starts in media res: it is Christmas time 1786, and Reverend Wicks Cherrycoke arrived in Philadelphia in October to attend Charles Mason's funeral, although he was "too late for the Burial, as it prov'd."[22] At his sister's, the reverend has been telling stories in exchange for accommodation given that "for as long as he can keep the children amus'd, he may remain." The opening scene of the novel focuses on an exchange between the reverend and part of his audience, the Twins, Pitt and Pliny, who through these months have already heard "the Escape from Hottentot Land, the Accursèd Ruby of Mogok, the Ship-wrecks in Indies East and West—an Herodotic Web of Adventures and Curiosities selected, the Revd. implies, for their moral usefulness, whilst avoiding others not as suitable in the Hearing of the Youth" (*MD,* 7). They now ask for a "Tale about America," "with Indians in it, and Frenchmen" or "French Women" as Pitt mutters. The exchange from which the narration stems, with its implied nostalgic reference to the oral traditions of storytelling and the human interaction in the transmission of information characteristic of the past, offers an indication of the dialogic nature of the narration to follow. Opinions are exchanged between the storyteller and his audience that account for much of the book's metafictional discussions: among other things, they comment on the act of remembering (*MD,* 350, 695). This setting is in turn related by another narrator—the nameless editor of the novel—who will also organize and present quotations from sources such as Reverend Cherrycoke's *Spiritual Journal,* his sermons, and his treatise on *Christ and History.* Such a juxtaposition of materials, the ones used by the heterodiegetic omniscient narrator and those related by the storyteller, provides the novel with the appearance of a collage, out of which the plot and the chronological continuity of the narration emerge.

It is in relation to Cherrycoke's voice that Foucault's questions of "who is speaking?" and "what difference does it make who is speaking?" need to be posed. Cherrycoke, described as Mason's Boswell (*MD,* 718, 744), is *the* witness. He becomes the key character through whom the reader, and his intradiegetic audience, have access to Mason and Dixon. Both his nostalgic mood and his moral expounding conjure up the history of the two British surveyors as an excuse for his "Tale about America." The story-teller is placed at a privileged viewpoint—1786, ten years after the revolution, and twenty after the surveyors' departure from America—from which he can resurvey the past through the many Lines that connect us back with history, "Not a Chain of single Links, for one broken link could lose us All—rather, a great disorderly Tangle of Lines, long and short, weak and strong, vanishing into the Mnemonick Deep, with only their Destination in common" (*MD,* 349). The common destination of time is seen throughout the novel as the principal feature of the Enlightenment's new order. Dixon reacts against superstitious warnings before departing for Cape of Good Hope, stating that " 'tis the Age of Reason," and that Mason and he are "Men of Science To huz must all days run alike, the same number of identical Seconds, each proceeding in but one Direction, irreclaimable" (*MD,* 27). This belief in a relentless progress of time is partially contested by Cherrycoke's activity of remembering, but also by those "other times" and "spaces" that constitute themselves as oppositional to "rational time" and "measurable space": the "eleven missing days" of the old English calendar, and Dixon's exploration of the Terra Concava (*MD,* 740).

Cherrycoke is a self-styled "untrustworthy Remembrancer" (*MD,* 8) selecting and narrating facts in a consciously "moral" way. His access to some information about the lives of the two British scientists immediately poses questions about the accuracy of the stories, the origin of the materials presented,[23] but also about their moral purpose. The narrator has a contradictory political position from the outset as an exiled member of the Anglican Church who represents, in an American context, dissent and "official" views at once. Cherrycoke's ejection from England characterizes him as an outcast, a "madman." The *Seahorse,* a commercial ship aboard which he travels with Mason and Dixon on their first assignment abroad, is described as an "Engine of Destruction" also used to seclude political dissent. His political activity is identified with madness in a way that recalls the exclusion of social "unreason" in eighteenth-century France denounced by Foucault in his *Madness and Civilization.*[24] Cherrycoke's political sin, "the Crime they styl'd anonymity," can be read as analogous to Pynchon's artistic standing and his own anonymity, his withdrawal from the public while engaged in a denunciation of technocracy as a conspiratorial entente in which military and economic powers collude. Cherrycoke's "insanity" is reflected in his anonymous activities:

> That is, I left messages posted publicly, but did not sign them. I knew some night-running lads in the district who let me use their Printing-Press—somehow, what I got into printing up, were Accounts of certain Crimes I had observ'd, committed by the Stronger against the Weaker—enclosures, evictions, Assize verdicts, Activities of the Military—giving the names of as many of the Perpetrators as I was sure of. (*MD,* 9)

All the "Crimes" cataloged here refer to the process of redistribution of communal properties carried out at the time of the Industrial Revolution in England, and of which Dixon was an agent as local surveyor in Durham.[25] It is Cherrycoke's denunciation of those crimes of the "Stronger against the Weaker" that account for his marginal position, for his initial sympathy with margins and excluded people.

For him, America appears to offer an "exceptional" opportunity to banish the corruption of the Old World, expressed in that continuous oppression of the "Weaker." Cherrycoke explains his wish when he remembers how in 1765: "I was back in America once more, finding, despite all, that I could not stay away from it, this object of hope that Miracles might yet occur, that God might yet return to Human affairs, that all the wistful Fictions necessary to the childhood of a species might yet come true, . . . a third Testament" (*MD*, 353). America, as the "object of Hope," belongs to the discourse of the nonconformist traditions established in the American colonies since the seventeenth century, and which had been hoping for the arrival of "Miracles." Cherrycoke's "Third Testament" is another version of the coming of the New Israel, or Berkeley's "Fifth Act" of westward progress of which "Time's Noblest Offspring" is the protagonist.[26]

Yet the predestination of the American people, and of America's sacred territory, is threatened to become part of everyday "Despair" by the mapping carried out by the enlightened scientists:

> Does Britannia when she sleeps, dream? Is America her dream?—in which all that cannot pass in the metropolitan Wakefulness is allow'd Expression away in the restless Slumber of these Provinces, and on West-ward, wherever "tis not yet mapp'd, nor written down, nor ever, by the majority of Mankind, seen—serving as a very Rubbish-Tip for subjunctive Hopes, for all that *may yet be true*—Earthly Paradise, Fountain of Youth, Realms of Prester John, Christ's Kingdom, ever behind the sunset, safe till the next Territory to the West be seen and recorded, measur'd and tied in, back into the Net-Work of Points already known, that slowly triangulates its Way into the Continent, changing all from subjunctive to declarative, reducing Possibilities to Simplicities that serve the ends of Governments—winning away from the realm of the Sacred, its Borderlands one by one, and assuming them unto the bare mortal World that is our home and our Despair. (*MD*, 345)

Cherrycoke's paradise to come in America is incorporated into the "bare mortal World" at once "home" and "Despair." As the "next Territory to the West" is seen and recorded, and Adorno's "line of destruction and civilization" advances, the "Possibilities" of diversity are encroached, becoming profane "Simplicities that serve the ends of Governments," homogenized into the "declarative" tense/time of the Westward Empire. Jarvis has pointed out a similar aggression of the colonial forces on the "spaces of myth" in *V.:* "Pynchon's geography of the fall away from what is human hinges upon the expansion of profane places—for as colonial dependencies and supermarkets are built up, so too are all spaces of myth and magic razed to the ground."[27]

The loss of myth and magic which Pynchon had already denounced several decades earlier in "Is It O.K. to Be a Luddite?" is developed even further here, and given a new dimension with the use for the first time in Pynchon's fiction of "real" personages, whose "real" records are reinterpreted through the narrative act. In the novel, their slow-growing awareness of the loss of the "subjunctive" is accompanied by an increasing hesitation about the righteousness behind the scientific projects in which they are involved.[28] Mason and Dixon's nonfictional *Journal,* written in Mason's first person, also reveals the "restlessness" (*MD,* 705) that they confess at the end of their trip.[29] But in the novel their early suspicion about why "they have been hired again" (*MD,* 250) turns into Dixon's conviction that they "shouldn't be running this Line" (*MD,* 478), and Mason also finally wonders why he is "doing this" (*MD,* 642). Their growing paranoia is one of the many ways in which the transition from personages into characters takes place in the novel. Unlike other apparently unresolved quests by Pynchon, *Mason & Dixon* finds here a conclusive opinion: the characters finally perceive the line as "a conduit for Evil" (*MD,* 701).

The point at which author and narrator "coincide" is precisely in their shared choice of the historical personages, Mason and Dixon, to talk about "Britannia's Dream," to tell through them a "Tale about America." Moreover, the Reverend's pondering on the future of the "realm of the Sacred" is one of the most explicit examples in the novel of the fictionalization of history in order to politicize it. It is conveniently inserted as a parenthetical digression in the Lancaster episode in which Mason and Dixon visit the site of a massacre committed the previous year against the Conestoga Indians. Pynchon does not need to invent some of the main "episodes" leading to their awareness of racial hatred toward the non-European. They are all taken from historical sources, although given the relevance of milestones in the narration: they are re-narrated and placed at moments of "Enlightenment." In the novel, Mason's visit to Lancaster is conveniently followed by an extract from Cherrycoke's *Christ and History* where he defines history as neither mere "chronologies," which concern Lawyers, nor "Remembrance," which belongs to the people. As we were told at the beginning of the novel by that "other narrator," Cherrycoke's histories are "an Herodotic Web of Adventures and Curiosities selected, the Revd. implies, for their moral usefulness" (*MD,* 7).

Of the many points in which Mason the character, and Mason the personage coincide, one of the most remarkably "moral" is in the Lancaster episode. Mason's visit to the scene of the massacre of Conestoga Indians at the hand of the infamous Paxton Boys is recorded in the *Journal,* as one of Mason's trips in the winter of '65:

> Left Brandywine and proceeded to Lancaster (distance about 35 miles) a Town in Pennsylvania, distant from Philadelphia 75 Miles, bearing nearly due West. *What brought me here was my curiosity to see the place where was perpetrated last Winter the Horrid and inhuman murder of 26 Indians, Men, Women and Children, leaving none alive*

> *to tell.* These poor unhappy creatures had always lived under the protection of the Pennsylvania Government and had Lands alloted [*sic*] for them a few Miles from Lancaster by the late celebrated William Penn, Esquire, Proprietor. They had received notice of the intention of some of the back inhabitants and fled to the Gaol (jail) to save themselves. The keeper made the door fast, but it was broken open; and two men went in and executed the bloody scene; while about 50 of their party sat on Horse Back without; armed with Guns, etc. Strange it was that the Town though as large as most Market Towns in England, never offered to oppose them, though its [*sic*] more than probable they on request might have been assisted by a Company of his Majesties Troops who were then in the Town . . . no honor [*sic*] to them! What was laid to the Indians charge was that they held a private correspondence with the Enemy Indians; but this could never be proved against the men and the women and children (some in their Mothers wombs that never saw light) could not be guilty.[30]

Cherrycoke turns the journal entry into a full episode in which both Mason and Dixon go into the jail separately. Dixon puts on Mason's clothes, leaving behind for the first time his "real" red army jacket,[31] both as an external sign of their first ideological identification in the novel, and as a way of bringing Dixon into a fundamental epiphanic moment of the story. Although there is no documented evidence of whether Dixon accompanied Mason or not on this journey,[32] fiction and fact are mixed with Cherrycoke's assurance: "Dixon told me, that Mason had meant to go alone, but that at the last moment, mindful of the dangers attending Solitude in a Town notorious for Atrocity, he offer'd to add Muscular Emphasis, tho' Mason seem'd unsure of whether he wanted him there or not" (*MD,* 341). Mason's "real" horrified account is inserted in Cherrycoke's—and Pynchon's—ideological recuperation of history in order to show the way in which the "subjunctive Hopes" may have become "murderous Hopes," and that as the line progresses, the "indicative" or "declarative" world of the Age of Reason will also advance, absorbing the subjunctive world of the Indians.

Despite his confessed faith in American exceptionality, in the "subjunctive Hopes" that "may yet be true," Mason and Dixon's comparison between Good Hope and America is constant, even talking about America as just "another slave-Colony" (*MD,* 248). He is also able to recount Mason's realization of the apparent "connection" between the acts of racial violence in both continents:

> Mason did note as peculiar, that the first mortal acts of Savagery in America after their Arrival should have been committed by the Whites against Indians. Dixon mutter'd, "Why, "tis the d---'d Butter-Bags all over again."

> They saw white Brutality enough, at the Cape of Good Hope. They can no better understand now, than then. Something is eluding them. Whites in both places are become the very Savages of their own worst Dreams, far out of Measure to any Provocation. (*MD*, 306–7)

If "something is eluding them," it is because they have not yet come to the conclusion that the violent episodes they witness are part of the same project of domination for which they are working. Butter-Bags fill the air every time an act of colonial violence occurs as a metaphysical indication of the outrage, and yet they have not been able to ascertain that "connection." Pynchon's use of Mason and Dixon's African experiences, as a preamble for a "Tale about America" becomes clearer: as in *Gravity's Rainbow,* the African element is used in the text as the index of the "original sin" of slavery and domination. In *Mason & Dixon* the comparison between the two colonies reenacts American utopia just as it was being depleted, turning the "tale about America" into a tale about *the lack of exceptionality of* America.

"Our Thoughts Are Ours, Their Ends None of Our Own"

Mason and Dixon have been made into fictional characters on a few occasions.[33] Ironically, these characterizations are not always inserted in what we could consider "fictional" works. For instance, the words that I am using as a title for this section are "spoken" by Mason and Dixon in Genevieve Blatt's preface to the Commonwealth of Pennsylvania's publication to commemorate the bicentenary of their line. Twenty-five years before Pynchon's novel, Blatt also cast the two surveyors as having been both inside their job and at the same time distanced from their actions. The prefacer takes a fully literary approach when she associates their apparent ambiguous relation with their line: "it is as though Mason and Dixon were two characters in Shakespeare's tragedy *Hamlet*" (iv). Motivated by their aloofness, an obscure functionary sees in the two surveyors a dissenting attitude toward "their ends."

An obscure writer who published an early fictional account of Mason and Dixon's American stay, Susan Lefever,[34] also makes Mason write a letter to Dixon in which he asks: "How did we ever do what we did in that exotic world across the sea?"[35] Mason continues, with a by now familiar paranoid style, to confess his close friendship with Dixon:

> And now though I still suffer depression from what we went through and from the ultimate apathy of our superiors I was so sure would honor us, I feel God gave me a greater gift than all the material honors or promotions that should have been awarded us. He gave me you, Jery. He gave me your friendship, your love, your concern. And never, ever do I wish to lose it. (326)

In Pynchon's infinitely subtler and more complex text, the ideas here condensed in a paragraph are slowly developed. The personages/characters are yet again bestowed with what amounts to distrust for their superiors' "ends," a suspicion which is intractable in any of their published letters or their *Journal,*[36] and which Pynchon elaborates into a full-blown questioning of Western values.

A different case is the first recorded instance to my knowledge in which the two surveyors were fictionalized, on this occasion by a Maryland historian, John H. B. Latrobe, in his speech *The History of the Mason and Dixon Line.*[37] In his 1854 address to the Historical Society of Pennsylvania, Latrobe analyzed the long history of tensions and anxieties on both sides of the Mason and Dixon Line just six years before the outbreak of the American Civil War. Latrobe could look back at the moment when the thirteen colonies had declared independence from the British king seventy-eight years earlier and summarize what appeared to him to be a short history of national and intellectual success, the foundation of a republic "whose rapid development, in all that constituted the true greatness of a people, would be the wonder of the world" (Latrobe, 49). Independent American history so far was marked by two geographical events, inscribed on the map of the Mason and Dixon Line east-west and north-south.

The first of these events could be observed in the Line's westward projection, the advance of the country reflected in the replacement of the woodlands inhabitants, the Indians, by the "monster and the miracle of modern ingenuity" (Latrobe, 37), the train.[38] An achievement which for Latrobe was in marked contrast with the power that the "roving Indians of the wilderness" had had ninety years earlier in cutting thirty-six miles short the assignment of tracing a line between the provinces of Maryland and Pennsylvania.

The other successful event had still to happen and it would reconcile the axis North-South that the Mason and Dixon Line had clearly marked: slaveholding versus anti-slavery states. In the short history of independent America, slavery was the major controversy "whose solution, and its consequences, involved the gravest considerations, and had been supposed to threaten the integrity of the Republic" (Latrobe, 7). Latrobe's racialist "final" solutions to slavery are relegated to the "south" of the text, divided by the separating line of the footnote where his execrable proposals, such as bringing into the country waged white slaves and shipping back to Africa the black population are put forward; they remain there as the proof of his white supremacist ideology.[39] Coincidentally, in Pynchon's novel these solutions are parodied when Dixon summarizes the "Elements common" to all their journeys:

> Slaves. Ev'ry day at the Cape, we lived with Slavery in our faces—more of it at St. Helena—and now here we are again, in another Colony, this time having drawn a Line between their Slave-Keepers, and their Wage-Payers, as if doom'd to re-encounter thro' the World

> this public Secret, this shameful Core . . . Pretending it to be ever somewhere else, with the Turks, the Russians, the Companies, down there, down where it smells like warm Brine and Gunpowder fumes, they're murdering and dispossessing thousands untallied, the innocent of the World, passing daily into the Hands of Slave-owners and Torturers, but oh, never in Holland, nor in England, that Garden of Fools . . . ? Christ, Mason. (*MD,* 692–93)

In Dixon's earlier trip to Virginia "though Slaves passed before his sight, he saw none" (*MD,* 398), but at the moment of summing up their journeys, all the encounters with slavery become connected as the "public Secret," "this shameful Core": the prostitutes in St Helena, who were that "slavery within Slavery" (*MD,* 150), and the American slaves, the chatteled and the chained, are part of the same techno-political system based on different forms of slavery. Even northern waged workers can be considered slaves—at least in this point, Latrobe seems to coincide with Pynchon. In their explicit realizations, Pynchon's Mason and Dixon appear to have traveled a long way from other characterizations of the two personages.

Latrobe, worried about the coming civil war, argues in apocalyptic tones that if the "blessed people" are finally divided, it may mean the demise of the American dream of "a united and homogeneous people." After enumerating the many scientific and political advances which Mason and Dixon would have missed since their deaths, including the foundation of the republic,[40] he hypothesizes about their reaction to the news by guessing that they would be astonished "could they have been told, that the results of this revolution having been power, and might, and majesty, and boundless prosperity, of which every individual in the land was a participant" (Latrobe, 51). In contrast to Pynchon's, Latrobe's Mason and Dixon are presented as weak, subservient Britons. After all, the surveyors who traced the boundary between Pennsylvania and Maryland until stopped at the "war-path" by the "sylvan monarchs" represent those past times and values banished with the new order to come only with the American Revolution. Latrobe even affirms that "they, probably, were not imaginative men, and it is not likely that they indulged in many reflections as to the future of the world of mountain and forest and boundless plains, on which they thus turned their backs" (ibid., 48). Quoting Berkeley's famous line about the course of Empire, Latrobe congratulates himself and his audience that now "an observatory . . . crown[s] the summit of a hill, looking down on a great city [Cincinnati] near three hundred miles westward of the war-path" (ibid., 49).[41] Their final reluctance to finish the line into Indian territory was charged to them by Latrobe as a sign of their ignorance of the new Republican values.

In contrast, Pynchon's Mason and Dixon are cast once again as men whose understanding is subject to moral judgment, rather than to the imperatives of the Line: "Having acknowledg'd at the Warpath the Justice of the Indian's

Desires, after the two deaths, Mason and Dixon understand as well that the Line is exactly what Capt. Zhang and a number of others have been styling it all along—a conduit for Evil" (*MD,* 701). Mason and Dixon's acknowledgment of the "Justice of the Indian's Desires" in Pynchon's novel credits them with an ability to listen to the Other, and to those other reasons, which are absent from Latrobe's speech. Both Mason and Dixon share their increasingly awed views about the colonial horrors of South African and American slaughter of natives and transported slaves. Their reflection on what they have observed during their journeys leads them to the conclusion that white Europeans are the real savages "out of their own worst Dreams."

Finally, Latrobe puts in the surveyors' mouths "words of prophecy" uttered "for the sake of the unity of [his] discourse" (Latrob, 52), that is, in order to complete his presentation of the surveyors as weak British "servants" (ibid., 50), he makes them worry now about the future preservation of the Republic:

> These uses, to which you put the lightning; this erection of cities on river shores, in Indian lands; this tale of battle, and blood-shed and victory; this dethroning of monarchs and uplifting of their subjects, are astounding results that we cannot appreciate, for we see no elements to produce them, and they shock all the prejudices of our education. To time we leave their development. But, that a blessed people beyond all others, in their realization, if realized they *are* to be, and occupying the proudest place among the nations, because of their wondrous unity, under a government that extent of dominion enfeebles not—should willingly permit their Union to be dissolved, we cannot believe; because, here, we are dealing, not with the future of science or politics, but with the principles of humanity common to all ages; and, depend upon it, whatever the few may wish, the many will be true; and this, our line of survey, will, after all, owe its notoriety to ephemeral oratory, in which it figures as a mere phrase of cant, or to addresses, which will bring to light the few brief records we have left of our transactions. (Latrobe, 51–52)

It is at this point that Pynchon's and Latrobe's Mason and Dixon appear as completely diverse personages through their different perceptions of the Line. Latrobe's reconstruction of their voice remains politicized for the sake of his project to save the union, as the "blessed people" need to "be realized." Pynchon's polyphony is equally politicized, but engaged in demonstrating Pynchon's obsession with the predestination of the West to spread its "Kingdom of Death" (Pynchon, *Gravity's Rainbow,* 722) throughout the world. His surveyors encounter numerous opinions favoring that view, such as Captain Zhang's: "Nothing will produce Bad History more directly nor brutally, than drawing a Line, in particular a Right Line, the very Shape of Contempt, through the midst of a People—to create thus a Distinction betwixt 'em—'tis the first stroke.— All else will follow as if predestin'd, unto War and Devastation" (*MD,* 615).

Pynchon's final opposition between the two worlds comes to a halt with the surveyors' stop at the Indian Warpath, the "Membrane that divides their Subjunctive World from our number'd and dreamless Indicative" (*MD,* 677). In their discussion, Dixon uses one of Pynchon's syntactic clichés to describe the Line and to speak for the Indians' fear of "this great invisible Thing that comes crawling Straight on over their Lands" (*MD,* 678). Apart from echoing *Gravity's Rainbow*'s opening image of "a screaming [that] comes across the sky" (*GR,* 1), the sentence insists on Dixon's earlier conviction that the real "Proprietors" are the Indians (*MD,* 468). For Dixon the line is therefore an invasion, "its Life's Blood," similar to the V-2 rockets in *Gravity's Rainbow.* A "living creature, 'tis all of us" (*MD,* 678), says Mason to a disconcerted Dixon whose hesitation is the ultimate paranoid abashment in the novel: "And what of its intentions, beyond killing ev'rything due west of it? do you know? I don't either" (*MD,* 678).

Cherrycoke's reconstruction of history is not so much directed toward claiming truth as toward finding a space for resistance against the dreamless homogenizing drive of the West. His praise of fictional history could stand as a manifesto of the postmodern historical novel:

> Who claims Truth, Truth abandons. History is hir'd, or coerc'd, only in Interests that must ever prove base. She is too innocent, to be left within the reach of anyone in Power—who need but touch her, and all her Credit is in the instant vanish'd, as if it had never been. She needs rather to be tended lovingly and honorably by fabulists and counterfeiters, Ballad-Mongers and Cranks of ev'ry Radius, Masters of Disguise to provide her the Costume, Toilette, and Bearing, and Speech nimble enough to keep her beyond the Desires, or even the Curiosity, of Government. (*MD,* 350)

Cherrycoke's faith in America could be read as being parodied through the oppositional elements advanced in Mason and Dixon's discoveries. And yet, Mason and Dixon's story seems to have also transformed the narrator as he has told the story. He explains how his approach to history belongs to the "common Duty of Remembering" of which "our Sentiments" are a part. By "Sentiments," Cherrycoke parenthetically explains, he is referring to "how we dream'd of, and were mistaken in, each other," and those "count for at least as much as our poor cold Chronologies" (*MD,* 695–96). His "sentimental history" is as much a reconstruction of utopian dreams as a realization of their erring. His America is a thing of the past, it exists in the past subjunctive of the utopia that might have been, but wasn't.

The surveyors discontinue the Line, and Dixon thrashes a slave conductor who was being violent toward the slaves.[42] As their actions become oppositional to the world they have helped advance, and they reassert their "thoughts," they also conclude that America *could* have been different, exceptional: "No matter where in it we go, shall we find all the World Tyrants and Slaves? America was the only place we should *not* have found them" (*MD*, 693). This statement reinforces the subjunctive impossibility of imagining the United States, America, as a moral reservoir at its foundation as a modern nation-state: the imagined national landscape is shown to be harmed by economic and social exploitation from the outset—it is but another site degraded by human ambition and corruption.

Conclusion

✦

Beyond the Nation

The texts studied in this book offer an alternative satirical rejoinder to the "national romances" identified by Doris Sommer in her book *Foundational Fictions*. As Sommer points out, the novels of the Latin American boom "rewrite, or un-write, foundational fiction as the failure of romance, the misguided political erotics that could never really bind national fathers to mothers."[1] In contrast, she chooses to look at nineteenth- and early twentieth-century novels as national romances, narratives where the foundation of nations is symbolized by successful couplings. In Sommer's study, Carlos Fuentes's *La muerte de Artemio Cruz* is singled out as the most programmatic text in this movement to "unwrite" the Latin American foundational romance. Tangentially, the angle through which I have looked at these anti-foundational fictions, these foundering fictions, is not so much romance or its absence, but rather the lack of an epic narrative logic, the active unwriting of a national telos and the befogging of the national contours through satire and parody.

Foundering Fictions

These novels resemble those of the "second postcolonial stage" demarcated by Kwame Anthony Appiah which "far from being a celebration of the nation . . . reject not only the Western *imperium* but also the nationalist project of the postcolonial national bourgeoisie."[2] The foundering fictions of the postmodern New Left eschewed the constitution of alternate states, avoiding the utopian narratives of national romances and epics, and concentrated their creative impulse in unsettling the mechanical relation of the literary field with the national state. As we have seen, these dissenting narratives simultaneously assail the temporal and the spatial conformation of the national construct to unstitch its seemingly stable histories and mappings. Disruptive temporalities in which the past is no longer the repository of ancient essences, the present does not allow for communal encounters, and the future is not a collective destination are a central articulation of these postnational satires. The disruption of the national telos activates alternate images of historical time—fragmentary, circular, spiral, entangled, frozen, parallel—which disavow the necessary linearity of national mythographies. These narrative fractures are also articulated spatially as a defiance of the sacred, "scientific" configuration of national geographies by highlighting the spatial divisions, the porosity of borders, the juxtapositions of irreconcilable heterogeneities, and the ways in which the nation-state is brutally constituted as a hegemonic territory.

Fuentes the Cosmopolitan

In Carlos Fuentes's novels and essays, the indictment of U.S. and Spanish colonial and neo-colonial practices in Mexico is accompanied by an unequivocal postnational satire on the Mexican nationalist bourgeoisie at the service of those transnational and global interests. As I have been maintaining throughout this book, one of Carlos Fuentes's durable contributions is doubtless his ability to capture during a remarkably long productive period of close to sixty years (1954–2012) the contradictions between this postcolonial globalized comprador elite—the Mexican (trans)national bourgeoisie—and its rhetorical and institutional deployment of nationalist consensual bonds. His fictional, critical disruption of the celebratory discourses of Mexican modernity initiated in the context of the Cold War remained unbroken into the post–Cold War era, with NAFTA and the U.S./Mexico border zone as a new center of economic and social practices that exacerbated the earlier paradoxes and contradictions. Fuentes's inroads into the border zone with *La frontera de cristal* (1995) overthrows the glowing mirages of malls and throwaway goods that characterize the new world order of American global expansion with its boundless consumerist ethics and it unabashed neo-colonial interventions. As a collection of short stories, *La frontera* condenses the aggravated sense of social disparity both within Mexico and in the new North American "community" of the free trade zone. Thus, it stages post–Cold War globalism and its triumphant neoliberal internationalism as a dystopian displacement of the postnational network of solidarities envisioned by the 1960s' New Left warriors. Faced with the impossible choices of the glittering transnational depredations of the mall or the nostalgia for a stifling nationalist museum, characters throughout this collection negotiate and rework their individual identities in search of spaces to create communities of affect that coincide neither with the national mapping, nor with televised conformity, nor with the latest consumerist fads.

Two short stories from the collection stand out for their evocation of the hopeless longing for a national space, as local differentiations are disturbingly erased in the celebratory global geographies of the neoliberal mall. In "El despojo" two Mexicans head back south, fleeing from the consumerist nightmare of the North in which they too had become mere commodities.

The title of the story refers to the literal stripping off that they undergo as they run through the desert seeking their origins as a site of salvation. Their renewed identification is a form of rebirth into the nation, itself not found in the flag or the territory, but rather in the more immaterial culinary scents emanating from kitchens on the Mexican side of the border. The scent of bone marrow tortillas stands for an irreducible marker of local sensory identification that can be neither easily translated nor commoditized into the TexMex franchises of the North. As a remainder of the national/local affiliation, this intractable excessive South provides a specific site of resistance to the post-national globalization promoted by the new northern hegemony, and one that also bypasses the old trap of national sameness and consensual orthodoxy.

The title story, "La frontera de cristal," satirically portrays the new transnational corporate mogul, Leonardo Barroso—a character that surfaces throughout the collection as a representative of the new economic elite—as both a sellout and a paternal figure. He pragmatically flies workers to clean windows in New York's skyscrapers as a way to establish alternate new migratory patterns that would resemble a daily commute between the two neighboring metropoles. At the same time, he becomes aware of the vast distances, and the unpreparedness of his workers for the colder northern climate. As Barroso watches the cleaners descend from the plane, he feels an empathic national solidarity for his compatriots who have arrived ill prepared into the chilly morning—he offers them some blankets. This act does not constitute in itself the re-creation of a national community in the transnational space of the airport, but instead an ironic confirmation of two central suspicions furthered throughout the story: first, the possibility that the national construct has been erased in the new transnational space and it is not even visible from the air, as Lisandro, one of the temporary workers, speculates on his way to New York;[3] secondly, that the new community replacing it is not the old inter-class "revolutionary" consensus of national industrialism—Barroso's paternalistic act after all reiterates his hierarchical power position and distance—but rather the impossible romance between the north and the south: NAFTA. The "ironic community" formed by the trans-border romance between Lisandro, as he cleans outside the window, and Audrey, who fancies him from behind the glass, relocates the border away from the state-sanctioned demarcations on the map, emphasizing instead a private negotiation of identity which resolves in a misunderstanding: Audrey draws her name on the glass while Lisandro traces the word "Mexican." National identity is posited here as both an unusable remainder of the old inter-class alliance which had constituted Mexico's uneven modernity as well as a constraint for international solidarity and romance.

The cultural and political consensus promoted by Mexican nationalism is shown in Fuentes's work as incapable of questioning the economic and social dimensions of a hegemonic modernity that has placed Mexico in its periphery, perpetuating its postcolonial exploitation and its sense of insufficiency. In the

A-Z guide to his personal creed, *En esto creo* (2002), Fuentes displays once more his balancing act between his nuanced beliefs in modernity, understood as universal progress, and in a more ethical, democratically controlled cosmopolitan globalization. He writes: "The mission of the new left is to control globalization and to democratically regulate the conflicts that derive from it."[4] This proposal is predicated on the revamping of the New Left as a sort of institutional network of regulations and guarantees to watch over the "free" market, with its neoliberal laissez-faire, and its draconian imperial underbelly. He appears to follow Jürgen Habermas in believing in a postnational constellation of institutional formations as a counteractive to transnational globalization, whose controls and balances could still be guaranteed by the rule of international law and what Habermas called "cosmopolitan solidarity"[5]: "Governed, globalization is an opportunity for everyone. Without a government, it ends up in anarchy and unfairness for everyone" (Fuentes, *En esto creo,* 144). Postnational cosmopolitanism understood in this way is not then a mere cultural or social by-product of neoliberalism, or global capitalism as some critics have intimated,[6] but it derives from an earlier ideological form of internationalism.

In her *Nations Without Nationalism* Julia Kristeva conceptualized the prospect of a postnational cosmopolitanism as a political horizon to move beyond the nation, "beyond the *origins* that have assigned to us biological identity papers and a linguistic, religious, social, political, historical place."[7] Kristeva proposes that "the freedom of contemporary individuals" could be "gauged according to their ability to *choose* their membership, while the democratic capability of a nation and social group is revealed by the right it affords individuals to exercise that choice" (16). It is clear that these individual freedoms and these transnational/postnational state formations are still cast as "in the making," future political horizons, but the important point here is that these postnational filiations are not historically conceived as the mere outcome of a hegemonic globalized market, or as a superficial "ideological compatriot of globalism," as Paul James claims.[8] Instead, as I have proposed throughout this book, there is a postnationalist articulation of cosmopolitanism, which is effectively the logical culmination of Cold War leftist internationalism, that is, of global networks of solidarity, the discourse of universal human rights, and the emancipatory projects of the international New Left.

Fuentes's confessed postnational cosmopolitanism unsurprisingly leaves out the term "nation" from his list of forty-one items of faith. In his entry for "Mexico," however, he underlines the point that the centuries-long waking obsession with Mexican national identity—the "ontological obsession with Mexicanness" which according to a fairly standard line of reception has constituted Fuentes's own "golden cage"[9]—should be superseded by a respect for heterogeneity and a tribute to the network of private feelings and appreciations, the small ethical narratives of what he calls the "realm of small things": "the humbleness of a craftsman and the pride of a female cook. The melancholy of a singer and the cry of a rebel. The discretion of lovers. The beauty, without exception of all the children of Mexico. The innate courtesy of true Mexicans" (Fuentes, *En esto creo,* 183). Identity and its ethical encodement can no longer be controlled by the nation-state, it no longer functions as a hegemonic top-down discourse, but rather like the "tortillas de tuétano" in "El despojo," as a sensory, ethical remainder, as a constellation of affects, private choices, and acts of resistance.

Human, all too human: only two weeks before dying, Fuentes announced from the Buenos Aires Book Fair in May 2012 the forthcoming publication of his new, now posthumous novel, *Federico en su balcón* (2012), a—possibly unrevised—fictional narrative on the creation of a postrevolutionary society with Friedrich Nietzsche as a prominent character.[10] "Don Niche"—as the philosopher is addressed in the novel—asks his interlocutor: "Where is your family? Is it in your blood or in your interests?" Nietzsche, Federico, will rebut throughout the novel the assertion that "regardless of our interests, the first priority is the family. Where we were born. Sometimes where we grew up" (63). The Spanish "donde nacimos" of the original is of course much more resonant of the Latin *nation, nación.* The genetic and social origins of the individual are interfaced with other types of affiliations and values throughout a rather careless narrative where the foundation of a new republic is being imagined.[11]

As we saw in chapter 5, another avatar of Nietzsche had already featured in the tortuous experiment, the narrative "happening" of *Cambio de piel.* Its central character, Freddy Lambert, is a madman and a visionary, a nihilistic beatnik—an avatar of Nietzchean nihilism seen here through Michel Foucault, the birth of the asylum, and against the backdrop of the foreseeable breakdown of PRI hegemony in Tlatelolco a year later. While the novel was censored that year in a Francoist Spain still nostalgic of the Axis days, for being "pro-Semitic and anti-German," David Gallagher branded Fuentes a Nazi apologist when reviewing *A Change of Skin* for the *New York Times Book Review* in February 1968. Only a year later, in March 1969, Fuentes was barred from entering the United States at San Juan, Puerto Rico, and was publicly declared an "undesirable alien" under the McCarren-Walter Act for his alleged communist affiliations and his support for the Cuban Revolution.[12] Two years later, the Cuban cultural apparatchik supreme, Roberto Fernández Retamar, would inquisitorially burn Carlos Fuentes in effigy as "the most conspicuous representative" of the "so-called Mexican literary mafia," after he criticized the Cuban Revolution earlier that year. Fuentes and other writers of the Latin American literary boom, Mario Vargas Llosa and Julio Cortázar among them, had overtly dared to condemn Cuba after the poet Heberto Padilla was first incarcerated and then publicly humiliated and forced to recant his critical comments, in what is still perhaps one of the most embarrassing autos-da-fé of that government. Clearly none of the bureaucratic readers involved in all these processes were able to pin down Fuentes: they did not seem to comprehend his support for what he called in his response to the *New York Times* editor a New Leftist "critical revolutionism." A critical act capable of questioning the undoing of revolutionary hopes by the stifling bureaucratic nightmares of the Soviet bloc, nightmarish even in its seemingly festive tropical adaptation, Fuentes's gesture was also able to denounce simultaneously the marketeering model and capitalist imperial practices of the U.S. military-industrial complex, and the so-called Western "democratic" bloc. In other words, he sought and practiced during the hottest years of the Cold War a critical questioning that would challenge the straitjackets of the two blocks, the two political asylums of the long Postwar. All these critics missed Fuentes's pioneering, ethical balancing act in the context of the Cold War, and what would become Fuentes's unique literary trademark: his radical, humanist self-determination. His elite critique of the elite, be it the Politburo, the PRI, the New England Brahmins, or the emerging NAFTA bourgeoisie, made Fuentes confront head-on institutional hegemonies and their proclivity for intellectual co-optation.

Pynchon's *Internationale*

Pynchon's fictions, insistently closer to an environmental anarchist version of a dystopian world, or perhaps to what Schaub has recently qualified as "wistful libertarianism,"[13] trace a denunciatory postmodern politics suspicious of global progress or its associated all-encompassing consensual narratives, be they science, nation, or capitalist modernity. For Pynchon in *Mason & Dixon*, Europeans behaved as "the very Savages of their own worst Dreams" (*MD*, 307). As we saw in chapter 7, at the end of *Mason & Dixon* the characters listen to the Indian's "reasoning" and they do realize that the line they are tracing into the wilderness is a "conduit of Evil" marking an ethical moment: Mason and Dixon's withdrawal from the line. This realization on the part of the two British colonial agents contours Pynchon's (postnational) ethics molded on their idealized individual act of respect for cultural heterogeneity and ethnic diversity, an ethical awareness discarded from the national narrative and its praxis soon after the revolution. Pynchon explores the pre-national colonial demarcations of space to forestall the narrative process of archival mythmaking and to refute the foundational basis of Americanist nationalism: the exceptionalism of its sociopolitical experiment. Challenging a fairly dominant interpretation of Pynchon's works, which as a form of liberal Americanism can be confidently classified as "Rortian," this book has posited that Pynchon's ideological filiations are closer to a radical New Leftist postnationalism—with ramifications into environmentalist anarchism—than to the consensus-building rhetorical exercises of Americanism. A recent example of the reluctance of this liberal Americanist strand of Pynchon's reception to recognize the postnational, post-Americanist discourse articulated by Pynchon can be found in David Cowart's reading of *Inherent Vice* against the supposedly utopian horizon of *Gravity's Rainbow.* Cowart brandishes here his intimate "knowledge" of Pynchon's deep-seated "nationalist" agenda and of the author's intentions: "Pynchon does not want simply to debunk American exceptionalism: he wants the nation to live up to its rhetoric, to *realize* the special destiny that Tyrone Slothrop's ancestor William would have heard invoked aboard the *Arbella.*"[14] This is just one more example of Pynchon's forcible recuperation for the nationalist literary field—for some English (only) department to comfortably continue broadcasting the messages of national consensus and the American dream-to-come. These types of ideological dogmas, however, do not allow for the deep ethical and aesthetic questions posed by Pynchon's work. True, colonists the world over dreamed of building utopian societies as they traveled to the Americas; many people—including many literary critics—still do, but is this really what Pynchon's work has to offer? Through a comparativist approach to Pynchon's work within the frame of Hemispheric American Studies, this book has sought to participate in what Linda Hutcheon has called the "congenitally contrarian" nature of Comparative Literature as an academic discipline.[15] I have thus been positing a rather more problematic set of issues, which complicate the location of Pynchon's storylines within the well-known ur-narratives of U.S. Americanism: Pynchon's satirical defiance, his multifaceted, unsimplistic debunking of American exceptionalism through postnational satire.

"'If the U.S. was a person, . . . and it *sat down,* Ohio would instantly be plunged into darkness'" (*AD,* 66), one of the characters in *Against the Day,* Merle Rideout, becomes fond of saying. Once again, the sacred figure of the motherland, its body as well as its map, is eschatologically codified in satirical terms throughout *Against the Day* as Pynchon examines the (national) historical record at a different juncture: the turn of the nineteenth century. One of the central historical themes of the novel is the repressed history of labor resistance to capitalist expropriation in the United States at the height of its western expansion and robber baron liberalism with the aim to demarcate, in the most unequivocal manner, the partnership of local and transnational plutocracy, the "plutes" as they are referred to in the novel, with scientific and technological developments. Some of the central characters in *Against the Day* provide a different alternate American genealogy to that of Slothrop's Puritan forefathers: the oppositional actions of a working-class mining family, the Traverse, take center stage and they "foreshadow" their successors, the Traverses who had already appeared in *Vineland.* This family is characterized by an anti-nationalist trajectory of opposition to the inter-class nationalist consensus promoted by the economic and political elites, be they Rockefeller or Reagan. This explicitly anti-nationalist antagonism is summed up in the school essay on "What It Means to Be an American" written by Jess Traverse, Webb Traverse's grandchild and the grandfather of *Vineland*'s Frenesi Gates:

"It means do what they tell you and take what they give you and don't go on strike or their soldiers will shoot you down" (*AD*, 1076). The purported exceptionalism of the American experience is not by any means salvaged in this explicit literary exercise of historical continuum; instead the opposite happens and the history of America is cast as part of a larger history of human exploitation and conflict. For a Finno-Russian anarchist immigrant, Veikko Rautavaara, one of Webb Traverse's friends in *Against the Day,* Russia and the United States appear to be remarkably similar:

> He'd never seen much difference between the Tsar's regime and American capitalism. To struggle against one, he figured, was to struggle against the other. Sort of this world-wide outlook. "Was a little worse for us, maybe, coming to the U.S.A. after hearing so much about the "land of the free." Thinking he'd escaped something, only to find life out here just as mean and cold, same wealth without conscience, same poor people in misery, army and police free as wolves to commit cruelties on behalf of the bosses, bosses ready to do anything to protect what they had stolen. The main difference he could see was that the Russian aristocracy, after centuries of believing in nothing but its own entitlement, had grown weak, neurasthenic. "But American aristocracy is not even a century old, in peak of fighting condition, strong from efforts it took to acquire its wealth, more of a challenge. Good enemy." (*AD,* 83)

Later on in the novel the boss and villainous plutocrat Scarsdale Vibe sends two of his gunslingers to torture and execute Webb in a scene reminiscent of the "dirty wars" waged against leftist activists throughout the Americas during the Cold War years, but also of the deployment of the Colorado National Guard and other militia to put down a mining strike resulting in the Ludlow Massacre of 1914.[16] Before this central politically motivated assassination that will elicit a novel-long revenge plot on the part of Webb's children, the narrative had already exposed the violence and witlessness of capitalist thugs in a memorable scene: Ku Klux Klan members are shown in the raw as a vigilante bloodthirsty pack in the service of the business bosses. The satirical mode is key to decoding this scene: an eschatological depiction mobilizes references to "laundering deficiencies," stains and body humors, to highlight the sullied whiteness of the Klansmen's sheets and thus to accentuate their lack of (white) supremacy over humanity: "Seeing these sheet-sporting vigilantes out in the sunlight, their attire displaying all sorts of laundering deficiencies, including cigar burns, food spills, piss blotches, and shit streaks, Lew found, you'd say, a certain de-emphasis of the sinister, pointy hoods or not. 'Howdy, fellers!' he called out, friendly enough" (*AD*, 178). The "de-emphasis of the sinister" observed by Lew Basnight provides a farcical view of the Klansmen not as the "Patriots and Saints" portrayed by Thomas Dixon in his

Reconstruction Trilogy, but as sadistic foolish killers.[17] What Dixon—and with him Griffith in his adaptation of *The Clansman* (1905) in *The Birth of a Nation* (1915)—narrated as a foundational racialist form of white supremacist patriotism is depicted by Pynchon as sheer incompetence and the rule of a vigilante mob directed here to the repression of white workers: " 'What do we do? Shoot him? Hang him?' 'Nail his dick to a stump, and, and then, set him on fahr,' eagerly accompanied by a quantity of drool visibly soaking the speaker's hood. . . . 'Shh! Clovis, you hamhead, you ain't supposed to tell em your name' " (*AD,* 178). The racial consensus proclaimed by the earlier narratives of Griffith and Dixon is here challenged through the emphasis on class interests and class divisions, phrased elsewhere as "the terrible American divide, between hunter and prey" (*AD,* 186).

A surprisingly similar postnational satirical representation of the KKK can be found in Quentin Tarantino's recent *Django Unchained* (2013), when a bunch of grumbling Southern plantation bosses led by Big Daddy and their minions discuss the condition of the white "bags" they are wearing and the lack of visibility they offer for their imminent night raid.[18] The targets of these postnational satirical interventions are the racist foundational myths of American nationalism: the nation's alleged birth wrapped earlier in filmic and literary white sheets is here humanized and lampooned, historicized and portrayed in its more complex socioeconomic setting. As in *Against the Day,* the society born out of these repressive forces is not the official United States of white supremacy or vigilante "democracy," but the resistance of small and local multiethnic alliances and solidarities, Yash Traverse's "our own little Republic,"[19] a utopian project of secession recovered here as a plausible counternarrative to the U.S. violent history of (post)colonial barbarism, labor exploitation, and ethnic cleansing.

In his latest novel, *Bleeding Edge,* the older KKK's enforcement of "national values" has been replaced by the "patriotism police" (*Bleeding Edge,* 445), and the secretive "U.S. security apparatus" (117, 325), who might be in the know of the apparently predictable—scented, smelly—looming destruction of the Twin Towers by an amorphous military-industrial conglomerate. The intimation throughout the novel of an obscure conspiracy involving Gabriel Ice and his tentacular transnational companies appears to provide "Bush and his gang" with a *casus belli* for their endless War on Terror. "You really think Bush's people are behind this?" asks Maxine Tarnow, the overwhelmed fraud investigator who is, like Oedipa Maas, quite unable to put together a full picture of the enmeshed interests and frauds she is investigating. "You don't?" responds her friend, documentary expert Reg Despard. To which a laconic Maxine replies "I am just a fraud examiner. Bush, don't get me started . . ." (349). "Just a fraud examiner" emerges like a raw ironic joke on the character's self-perception. What type of examiner, what kind of reader would be needed then to delineate those larger conspiracies, those intricate connections intimated throughout the novel? One of Maxine's other friends, March

Kelleher, scribbles in her weblog an analysis of 9/11 following what she calls "her old-lefty tirade mode." She concludes in a similarly ironic negative that produces a palpable parodic effect on her nationalist penchant: ". . . it would take a mind hopelessly diseased with paranoia, indeed a screamingly anti-American nutcase, even to allow to cross her mind the possibility that that terrible day could have deliberately been engineered as a pretext to impose some endless Orwellian 'war' and the emergency decrees we will soon be living under. Nah, nah, perish that thought" (321–22). Perish the radically critical (postnational) thought; do not venture out of the national matrix. Where does Pynchon the satirist stand?

If Pynchon's fiction started by casting the history of Western culture as one of "death and repression," his most recent works expand to the whole of humanity that obsessive drive toward political and socio-economic repression, environmental destruction, and planetary annihilation. In *Inherent Vice* Pynchon critically reconstructs the historical layers of human occupation of the Western Hemisphere to reassert not its pre-European utopian state, but the "toxicity" brought over by different waves of humans to the landmass. In a slight departure from his earlier concentration on Northern/German/Western forms of brutality and subjugation, Pynchon presents a legend belonging to "hippie metaphysics,"[20] which imagines a pre-Columbian past in a more misanthropic vein, free from the utopian ur-narratives with which Europeans had imagined and mapped California and the Americas in the sixteenth and seventeenth centuries and beyond. According to the Lemuria story, the first occupants of California were not peaceful inhabitants of a Native American Eden but the survivors of Lemuria, a mythical continental mass in the Pacific Ocean said to have been flooded out of the surface of the earth just like Atlantis, due to their high levels of pollution: "both empires [Lemuria and Atlantis] were sunk into the sea because Earth couldn't accept the levels of toxicity they'd reached" (*IV,* 105). Following closely the Gaia Hypothesis or Gaia Theory proposed by British scientist James Lovelock,[21] Pynchon's characters Sortilège and her guru Vehi Fairfield are not merely animating the Earth in their account of the legend, but they are instead echoing the idea that the Earth is a tangible living organism and that "like any living creature, Earth has an immune system too, and sooner or later she's going to start rejecting agents of disease like the oil industry" (*IV,* 105). Pynchon's postnationalist ethics, born out of the Marcusian New Leftist opposition to technocracy, is here reinforced by the ecocritical denunciation of the materialist reification of nature and the land. The construction of the deserted, inanimate Promised Land as the rightful realm for the unfolding of the nation-state is confronted with a counter-narrative: the earth not as object, but as subject, planet Earth as a living organism and its corollary: modern man and its predatory industries as a viral infection. Neither geography nor history, neither past nor future appears to harbor any consolation for Pynchon, the consummate ecocritical satirist. Larry "Doc" Sportello, the stoned protagonist of *Inherent*

Vice, witnesses human history as a self-erasing maelstrom, a vortex: "Doc was left at his negligible altitude above the Pacific to find his way out of a vortex of corroded history, to evade somehow a future that seemed dark whichever way he turned" (*IV,* 110). From the lack of faith in Americanism, Pynchon has unremittingly moved forward into a denunciation of the belief in human or material progress, culminating in a Luddite postmodern environmentalist disavowal of the promises of technological modernity.[22]

Doc, like chef Dionisio in Fuentes's "El despojo," flees southward to escape the fog spreading over California in the early 1970s: "maybe he'd have to just keep driving, down past Long Beach, down through Orange County, and San Diego, and across a border where nobody could tell anymore in the fog who was Mexican, who was Anglo, who was anybody. Then again, he might run out of gas before that happened, and have to leave the caravan, and pull over on the shoulder, and wait. For whatever would happen" (*IV,* 369). Halted in transit, Doc never appears to reach his utopian destination on the other side of the border, in an idealized space where identity, Mexican, Anglo, appears to be superseded as a meaningful binary code. However, like the characters traveling southward in search of a Mexican salvation in Fuentes's short story or in Guillermo Arriaga's film *The Burning Plain* (2008),[23] who envision Mexico as a place to heal, Doc seeks in his planned trip across the border to do away with the indenture of identity and the binary operations of the hyper-racialized regime of the postcolonial United States. Of course, readers of Fuentes, and anyone familiar with Mexico's own long history of racism, xenophobia, (post)colonial *castas,* and discrimination might not harbor such high hopes about the other side's greenery—especially around the vast Chihuahua desert that straddles both sides of the U.S.-Mexico border. This is perhaps why Doc is left along the way rather than in a nonexistent safe haven, in transit, waiting "for whatever would happen."

In their satiric parodies of national histories both Fuentes and Pynchon avoid the nostalgic longing for a purer, morally higher past—the "image of pristine integrity" which Frank Palmeri and others have identified as the prime motivation of the satirist's work.[24] Their turn of the screw of the satirical genre compels readers in distinct and yet germane ways to place themselves above and beyond the national confines, both geographically and temporally, to appreciate history in a larger, postnational, and even at times post-human dimension. Their postnational satirical denunciations, their spatial disjunctions as well as their temporal ruptures, underwrite archival parodies, contemporary ironies, and future uncertainties as central aesthetic elements of a critical, alternate heuristic model and in so doing they intimate the contours of a plausible, more sustainable postnational ethics.

NOTES

Preface

1. Except for a few feet of Western International Street, no 3D street-view images were available on "Google Maps," http://maps.google.com.

2. Marc Lacey, "Smugglers of Drugs Burrow on Border," *New York Times,* October 3, 2010.

3. For Carlos Francisco Parra, at the beginning of the twentieth century "the absence of a physical barrier stimulated the close relationship between the two cities so that, like many other border towns of the period, they were in reality one bi-national community." Carlos Francisco Parra, "Valientes Nogalenses: The 1918 Battle Between the U.S. and Mexico That Transformed Ambos Nogales," *Journal of Arizona History* 51, no. 1 (2010): 2.

4. Scott Horsley, "Border Fence Firm Snared for Hiring Illegal Workers," http://www.npr.org/templates/story/story.php?storyId=6626823.

5. Sidney Weintraub, *Unequal Partners: The United States and Mexico* (Pittsburgh, Pa.: University of Pittsburgh Press, 2010), 116.

6. Wendy Brown, *Walled States, Waning Sovereignty* (New York; Cambridge, Mass.: Zone Books; MIT Press, 2010).

7. A pointed review of *The Cambridge Companion to Thomas Pynchon* notes how "the 'state of the art' in Pynchon studies is thus hard to untie from models of postmodernism that emerged during the process of his initial critical canonization" (143). It also points out the "straitjacket of precisely that theoretical moment" (144) which points up an important missing aspect of the *Companion:* "What's missing, however, is a sense of how Pynchon's relevance might endure once the identification between the contemporary and the canonically postmodern finally becomes untenable" (145). Ali Chetwynd, "The Cambridge Companion to Thomas Pynchon," *College Literature* 39, no. 4 (2012). It is precisely in this search for Pynchon's relevance beyond the "canonically postmodern" and within a postnational, post-Americanist canon that I intend to study Pynchon's works here.

8. The case of American literature and the creation of its curriculum has been amply studied; see, for instance, David R. Shumway, *Creating American Civilization: A Genealogy of American Literature as an Academic Discipline* (Minneapolis: University of Minnesota Press, 1994), 192–200.

9. For a definition of the polygenetic approach to literature and its associated cosmopolitanism "that will expose and defeat imperialism," see Cyrus R. K. Patell, "Comparative American Studies: Hybridity and Beyond," *American Literary History* 11, no. 1 (1999): 181–82. A good complementary model of postnational cultural history for the Mexico-U.S. border is provided by musicologists Ignacio

Corona and Alejandro Madrid, who have studied in detail the development of hybrid techno musical forms around the Nor-tec Collective in the city of Tijuana, where this group of musicians emerged in the 1990s. For Corona and Madrid, "[Nor-tec's] hybrid artistic identity places them in an ambivalent position regarding traditional discourses of national, regional, or family identity, class, and even gender. . . ." Ignacio Corona and Alejandro Madrid, eds., *Postnational Musical Identities: Cultural Production, Distribution, and Consumption in a Globalized Scenario* (Lanham, Md.: Lexington Books, 2008), 105.

10. Caroline Field Levander and Robert S. Levine, "Introduction: Essays Beyond the Nation," in *Hemispheric American Studies,* ed. Caroline Field Levander and Robert S. Levine (New Brunswick, N.J.: Rutgers University Press, 2008), 3.

11. The list of books and journals that have pioneered these kinds of approaches is long and increasingly rich and varied. These are just some titles that have been influential in the creation of this wider framework: Bell Gale Chevigny and Gari Laguardia, *Reinventing the Americas: Comparative Studies of Literature of the United States and Spanish America* (Cambridge: Cambridge University Press, 1986); Vera M. Kutzinski, *Against the American Grain: Myth and History in William Carlos Williams, Jay Wright, and Nicolás Guillén* (Baltimore: Johns Hopkins University Press, 1987); Gustavo Pérez Firmat, *Do the Americas Have a Common Literature?* (Durham, N.C.: Duke University Press, 1990); José David Saldívar, *The Dialectics of Our America: Genealogy, Cultural Critique, and Literary History* (Durham, N.C.: Duke University Press, 1991); Lois Parkinson Zamora, *Writing the Apocalypse: Historical Vision in Contemporary U.S. and Latin American Fiction* (Cambridge: Cambridge University Press, 1993); Amy Kaplan and Donald E. Pease, *Cultures of United States Imperialism* (Durham, N.C.: Duke University Press, 1993); Djelal Kadir, *The Other Writing: Postcolonial Essays in Latin America's Writing Culture* (West Lafayette, Ind.: Purdue University Press, 1993). Deborah N. Cohn, *History and Memory in the Two Souths: Recent Southern and Spanish American Fiction* (Nashville, Tenn.: Vanderbilt University Press, 1999); *The Latin American Literary Boom and U.S. Nationalism During the Cold War* (Nashville, Tenn.: Vanderbilt University Press, 2012); Alejandro Herrero-Olaizola, *Narrativas híbridas: Parodia y posmodernismo en la ficción contemporánea de las Américas* (Madrid: Editorial Verbum, 2000); John Carlos Rowe, *Post-Nationalist American Studies* (Berkeley: University of California Press, 2000); Anna Brickhouse, *Transamerican Literary Relations and Nineteenth-Century Public Sphere* (Cambridge: Cambridge University Press, 2004).

12. Jean Franco, "Narrador, autor, superestrella: La narrativa latinoamericana en la época de cultura de masas," *Revista Iberoamericana* 47, no. 114 (1981); Enrique Krauze, "The Guerrilla Dandy," *New Republic* 198, no. 26 (1988).

13. Dane S. Claussen, *Anti-Intellectualism in American Media: Magazines & Higher Education* (New York: P. Lang, 2004); Richard Hofstadter, *Anti-Intellectualism in American Life* (New York: Knopf, 1963).

14. Todd Gitlin singles out Thomas Pynchon as one of the ideological referents of the 1960s New Left and new members of Students for a Democratic Society: "When they discovered alienation, they looked to Thomas Pynchon more than to Karl Marx"; Todd Gitlin, *The Sixties: Years of Hope, Days of Rage* (New York: Bantam Books, 1993), 186.

15. Thomas Pynchon, *Against the Day* (New York: Penguin, 2006); Thomas Pynchon, *Inherent Vice* (New York: Penguin, 2009); Thomas Pynchon, *Bleeding Edge* (New York: Penguin, 2013). At the time of going to press, the first film adaptation of a Pynchon novel, *Inherent Vice,* directed by Paul Thomas Anderson, was in post-production and slated to appear sometime in 2014. "*Inherent Vice* (2014)," *Internet Movie Database,* accessed December 3, 2013, http://www.imdb.com/title/tt1791528/.

16. A great summary and well-established denunciation of this formalist tendency can be found in Michael Bérubé, *Marginal Forces/Cultural Centers: Tolson, Pynchon, and the Politics of the Canon* (Ithaca, N.Y.: Cornell University Press, 1992). See particularly chapter 5, pp. 266–315.

Introduction. Bordering Can(n)ons: Postnational Satire in the United States and Mexico

The chapter epigraph is from Barack H. Obama, "Remarks by the President in State of the Union Address," http://www.whitehouse.gov/the-press-office/2011/01/25/remarks-president-state-union-address.

1. Françoise Gaillard, "The Terror of Consensus," in *Terror and Consensus: Vicissitudes of French Thought,* ed. Jean-Joseph Goux and Philip R. Wood (Stanford, Calif.: Stanford University Press, 1998). Referring to contemporary France, Gaillard remarks that in modern democracies, "[to] deny conflicts also means eliminating from the consensual community all those who are not party to this consensus, in other words, all those to whom the provisions of the consensus do irremediable harm: the have-nots, the homeless, the unemployed, immigrants, and so on. Beware, too, the formation at the margins of the consensual society of pockets of minorities that can be neither integrated nor managed, whose only remaining mode of expression is despair, or in its more heated form, the explosion of violence not linked to any historical or political goal" (68).

2. For a very optimistic Donald E. Pease, Obama "aspired to change America through a radical transformation of three of the grand themes of American exceptionalism—the American dream, the perfectible Union, the land of promise—organizing the 'positionality' of the nation's citizens." Donald E. Pease, *The New American Exceptionalism* (Minneapolis: University of Minnesota Press, 2009), 209. Carlos Fuentes also shared in the optimism at the time and highlighted Obama's mixed racial descent, his *mestizaje,* as a welcome political innovation for the U.S. in his note "Obama: The First Mestizo Leader North of the Border," *New Perspectives Quarterly* 26.1 (2009): 34.

3. Terry Eagleton, *After Theory* (New York: Basic Books, 2003), 224.

4. Eric J. Hobsbawm, *Nations and Nationalism Since 1780: Programme, Myth, Reality,* 2nd ed. (Cambridge: Cambridge University Press, 1992), 9.

5. "Metonymy is about *referring:* a method of naming or identifying something by mentioning something else which is a component part or symbolically linked." Murray Knowles and Rosamund Moon, *Introducing Metaphor* (London: Routledge, 2006), 58.

6. Geoffrey Bennington, "Postal Politics and the Institution of the Nation," in *Nation and Narration,* ed. Homi Bhabha (London: Routledge, 1990), 132.

7. M. Montserrat Guibernau i Berdún, *The Identity of Nations* (Cambridge, Eng.: Polity, 2007), 25–30. Guibernau lists five "main strategies employed by the

state in its pursuit of a single national identity capable of uniting its citizens," of which number four is "the creation of common enemies," (25) a feature she considers "essential" (30).

8. Bennington, "Postal Politics and the Institution of the Nation," 132.

9. Eric J. Hobsbawm and Terence Ranger, *The Invention of Tradition* (Cambridge: Cambridge University Press, 1983); Ernest Gellner, *Nations and Nationalism* (London: Blackwell, 1983); Benedict Anderson, *Imagined Communities: Reflections on the Origin and Spread of Nationalism* (London: Verso, 1983).

10. A productive critique of liberalism as predicated on colonial expansion is Domenico Losurdo and Gregory Elliott, *Liberalism: A Counter-History* (London: Verso Books, 2011).

11. Gellner, *Nations and Nationalism,* 1.

12. Anderson, *Imagined Communities,* 191.

13. Etienne Balibar and Immanuel Wallerstein, *Race, Nation, Class: Ambiguous Identities,* trans. Chris Turner (London: Verso, 1991), 86.

14. This is a much debated issue, in particular in relation to postcolonial societies. See V. G. Kiernan, *Imperialism and Its Contradictions* (New York: Routledge, 1995), 121–43; Gellner, *Nations and Nationalism,* 111–12. See also Hobsbawm and Ranger, *The Invention of Tradition,* 1–14 (1); Arjun Appadurai, *Modernity at Large: Cultural Dimensions of Globalization* (Minneapolis: University of Minnesota Press, 1996).

15. Claudio Lomnitz-Adler, *Deep Mexico, Silent Mexico: An Anthropology of Nationalism* (Minneapolis: University of Minnesota Press, 2001), 126.

16. Frantz Fanon, *The Wretched of the Earth,* trans. Constance Farrington (New York: Grove, 1965), 148–205.

17. José Joaquín Fernández de Lizardi, *Obras. Novelas: El Periquillo Sarniento (Tomos I y II),* 9 vols., vol. 8 (México, D.F.: Universidad Nacional Autónoma de México, 1982).

18. Ignacio M. Altamirano, "Prólogo," in *El romancero nacional,* ed. Guillermo Prieto (México, D.F.: Oficina tip. de la secretaría de fomento, 1885), VIII.

19. Enrique Florescano, *Etnia, estado y nación: Ensayo sobre las identidades colectivas en México* (México, D.F.: Aguilar, 1997), 499.

20. Ibid., 502.

21. The standard corpus is still John Rutherford, *An Annotated Bibliography of the Novels of the Mexican Revolution of 1910–1917, in English and Spanish* (Troy, N.Y.: Whitston, 1972).

22. Ignacio Sánchez Prado has studied in great detail how this paradoxical situation came to be in the aftermath of the public literary debates of 1925 and 1932, after Francisco Monterde's "discovery" of *Los de abajo,* and how from these foundational moments "el campo literario en México adoptará para sí, de manera paradójica y simultánea, la responsabilidad de prescribir las características esenciales de 'lo mexicano,' a partir de la articulación de una literatura restringida siempre a la representación de dichas prescripciones, y el deber cívico de criticar al régimen cuando éste 'traiciona' el espíritu político de dichas prescripciones." Ignacio M. Sánchez Prado, *Naciones intelectuales: Las fundaciones de la modernidad literaria mexicana, 1917–1959* (West Lafayette, Ind.: Purdue University Press, 2009), 47.

23. Néstor García Canclini, *Culturas híbridas: Estrategias para entrar y salir de la modernidad* (Buenos Aires: Ediciones Paidós, 2001), 165–68.

24. Fredrick Turner suggested that the Mexican large-scale public murals of the 1920s–1940s are the "best artistic example of the nationalist movement." Frederick C. Turner, *The Dynamic of Mexican Nationalism* (Chapel Hill: University of North Carolina Press, 1968), 292.

25. Guillermo Bonfil Batalla, *México profundo: Una civilización negada* (México, D.F.: Grijalbo, 1990), 89–90. See also David Luis-Brown, *Waves of Decolonization: Discourses of Race and Hemispheric Citizenship in Cuba, Mexico, and the United States* (Durham, N.C.: Duke University Press, 2008).

26. Roger Bartra, *La jaula de la melancolía: Identidad y metamorfosis del mexicano* (México, D.F.: Grijalbo, 2000), 132.

27. Roger Bartra, *La sangre y la tinta: Ensayos sobre la condición postmexicana* (México, D.F.: Océano, 1999), 20.

28. Ronald Bush, *American Voice / American Voices: An Inaugural Lecture Delivered before the University of Oxford on 27th May 1999* (Oxford: Oxford University Press, 1999), 9. Perhaps the best study to date on the history and socio-political evolution of the U.S. national calendar of public festivities is Matthew Dennis, *Red, White, and Blue Letter Days: An American Calendar* (Ithaca, N.Y.: Cornell University Press, 2002).

29. For the editors of *Imagined Histories* "few [nations] have equalled America in promoting the claim of its special destiny" and its "allegedly exceptional history." See Anthony Molho and Gordon S. Wood, "Introduction," in *Imagined Histories: American Historians Interpret the Past,* ed. Anthony Molho and Gordon S. Wood (Princeton, N.J.: Princeton University Press, 1998), 4.

30. John Fousek, *To Lead the Free World: American Nationalism and the Cultural Roots of the Cold War* (London: University of California Press, 2000), 4.

31. Amy Kaplan, "The Tenacious Grasp of American Exceptionalism: A Response to Djelal Kadir," *Comparative American Studies* 2, no. 2 (2004): 155.

32. Timothy Brennan, "The National Longing for Form," in *Nation and Narration,* ed. Homi Bhabha (London: Routledge, 1990), 50. By way of contrast, Anderson associates the narration of national epics with an "ahistorical" formation: "the nation is outside history as it were." Benedict Anderson, *The Spectre of Comparisons: Nationalism, Southeast Asia, and the World* (London: Verso, 1998), 364. Fredric Jameson also maintained a fairly ethnocentric and stolid description of the relation between novel and epic, and the (Third World) novel as necessarily built around national allegory, in his widely commented article "Third-World Literature in the Era of Multinational Capitalism," *Social Text* 15 (1986): 65–88.

33. Alvin B. Kernan, *The Plot of Satire* (New Haven, Conn.: Yale University Press, 1965), 100.

34. Gary Saul Morson, *Narrative and Freedom: The Shadows of Time* (New Haven, Conn.: Yale University Press, 1994), 99–100.

35. Anderson, *Imagined Communities,* 24–25.

36. Homi K. Bhabha, *Nation and Narration* (London: Routledge, 1990), 311.

37. There is a dense bibliography dealing with canon formation and the cultural wars. Some particularly relevant contributions are Sarah E. L. Bowskill,

Gender, Nation and the Formation of the Twentieth-Century Mexican Literary Canon (London: Legenda, 2011); Joan Lipman Brown, *Confronting Our Canons: Spanish and Latin American Studies in the 21st Century* (Lewisburg, Pa.: Bucknell University Press, 2010); Lillian S. Robinson, *In the Canon's Mouth: Dispatches from the Culture Wars* (Bloomington: Indiana University Press, 1997); Henry Louis Gates Jr., *Loose Canons: Notes on the Culture Wars* (New York: Oxford University Press, 1993); Ignacio M. Sánchez Prado, *Naciones intelectuales: Las fundaciones de la modernidad literaria mexicana, 1917–1959* (West Lafayette, Ind.: Purdue University Press, 2009). A particularly articulate intervention in the intersection of hemispheric concerns and the U.S. literary canon is Michael Roy Hames-García, "Which America Is Ours?: Martí's 'Truth' and the Foundations of 'American Literature,'" *Modern Fiction Studies* 49, no. 1 (2003).

38. Van Gosse, *Rethinking the New Left: An Interpretative History* (New York: Palgrave Macmillan, 2005), 5. See also Stuart A. Kallen, *Sixties Counterculture, History Firsthand* (San Diego, Calif.: Greenhaven, 2001).

39. For a study of the 1960s countercultural movements within a larger international scope, see Arthur Marwick, *The Sixties: Cultural Revolution in Britain, France, Italy, and the United States, c. 1958–c. 1974* (London: Bloomsbury Reader, 2012). See also Eric Zolov, "Protest and Counterculture in the 1968 Student Movement in Mexico," in *Student Protest: The Sixties and After,* ed. Gerard J. De Groot (London: Longman, 1998).

40. Several other studies already offer a detailed discussion of the intellectual debates over postnationalism: its hypothetical co-optation by market globalization, and its emancipatory, liberating potential. Tom Nairn and Paul James, *Global Matrix: Nationalism, Globalism and State-Terrorism* (London: Pluto, 2005); Pheng Cheah and Bruce Robbins, *Cosmopolitics: Thinking and Feeling Beyond the Nation* (Minneapolis: University of Minnesota Press, 1998); Keith Breen and Shane O'Neill, *After the Nation? Critical Reflections on Nationalism and Postnationalism* (New York: Palgrave Macmillan, 2010). See also the opening chapters to Sascha Pohlmann, *Pynchon's Postnational Imagination* (Heidelberg, Ger.: Universitatsverlag Winter, 2010).

41. Anderson, *The Spectre of Comparisons,* 334.

42. Ibid. 334.

43. John Clement Ball, *Satire & the Postcolonial Novel: V. S. Naipaul, Chinua Achebe, Salman Rushdie* (New York: Routledge, 2003), 166.

44. Gary Saul Morson and Caryl Emerson, *Rethinking Bakhtin: Extensions and Challenges* (Evanston, Ill.: Northwestern University Press, 1989), 81.

45. Chalene Helmuth, *The Postmodern Fuentes* (Lewisburg, Pa.: Bucknell University Press, 1997), 42.

46. For Jean-François Lyotard, the unambiguous orientation of postmodernism is a suspicion of "all that has been received, if only yesterday." Jean-François Lyotard, *The Postmodern Condition: A Report on Knowledge,* trans. Geoffrey Bennington and Brian Massumi (Manchester: Manchester University Press, 1984), 27.

47. Frank Palmeri, *Satire in Narrative: Petronius, Swift, Gibbon, Melville, and Pynchon* (Austin: University of Texas Press, 1990), 1.

48. In his interview with Claudia Ferman, Fuentes claims that contemporary writers, including him, "are the poor epigones of Miguel de Cervantes via

Laurence Sterne." Claudia Ferman, "De exorcismos y profecías: Carlos Fuentes ente la modernidad y la posmodernidad," *Torre de Papel* 7, no. 3 (1997): 137.

49. Julia Kristeva, *La révolution du langage poétique; L'avant-garde à la fin du XIX siècle, Lautréamont et Mallarmé, tel quel* (Paris: Éditions du Seuil, 1974), 388–89.

50. Morson and Emerson, *Rethinking Bakhtin: Extensions and Challenges,* 63–86 (67). The object of parody need not be as specific as in traditional definitions, thus including ideas, or other cultural items, as Morson argues: "the class [of parody] I have described requires neither the parody nor its target to be a literary work; nor does it require the target to be a single work" (69). See also Margaret A. Rose, *Parody/Meta-Fiction: An Analysis of Parody as a Critical Mirror to the Writing and Reception of Fiction* (London: Croom Helm, 1979), 44.

51. Linda Hutcheon, *A Theory of Parody: The Teachings of Twentieth-Century Art Forms* (New York: Methuen, 1985).

52. Gérard Genette, *Palimpsests: Literature in the Second Degree,* trans. Channa Newman and Claude Doubinsky (Lincoln: University of Nebraska Press, 1997), 10.

53. Margaret A. Rose collects some of the most noted definitions of parody from Quintilian to Umberto Eco, and differentiates between ancient or classic, modern, late modern, and postmodern parody. Margaret A. Rose, *Parody: Ancient, Modern and Post-Modern* (Cambridge: Cambridge University Press, 1993), 5–99, and 280–83.

54. Linda Hutcheon, *Poetics of Postmodernism: History, Theory, Fiction* (New York: Routledge, 1988), 106.

55. Santiago Juan-Navarro, *Archival Reflections: Postmodern Fiction of the Americas (Self-Reflexivity, Historical Revisionism, Utopia)* (Lewisburg, Pa.; London: Bucknell University Press; Associated University Presses, 1999), 14.

56. Brian McHale, *Post Modernist Fiction* (London: Routledge, 1994); Herrero-Olaizola, *Narrativas híbridas;* Lois Parkinson Zamora, *The Usable Past: The Imagination of History in Recent Fiction of the Americas* (Cambridge: Cambridge University Press, 1997).

57. John Carlos Rowe, "Globalism and the New American Studies," in *Post-Nationalist American Studies,* ed. John Carlos Rowe (Berkeley: University of California Press, 2000), 28.

58. Nicola Miller, "The Historiography of Nationalism and National Identity in Latin America," *Nations and Nationalism* 12, no. 2 (2006): 203.

59. Ilan Stavans, *Spanglish: The Making of a New American Language* (New York: Rayo, 2004); John M. Lipski, *Varieties of Spanish in the United States* (Washington, D.C.: Georgetown University Press, 2008).

60. Jane H. Hill and Kenneth C. Hill, *Speaking Mexicano: Dynamics of Syncretic Language in Central Mexico* (Tucson: University of Arizona Press, 1986); Bárbara Cifuentes and Lucina García, *Letras sobre voces: Multilingüismo a través de la historia* (México, D.F.: CIESAS; INI, 1998).

61. A point noted by Carlos Fuentes: "el castellano es la lengua franca de la indianidad americana." Carlos Fuentes, *La gran novela latinoamericana* (México, D.F.: Alfaguara, 2011), 12.

62. Walter Lafeber, *The New Empire: An Interpretation of American Expansion, 1860–1898* (Ithaca, N.Y.: Cornell University Press, 1967), 4–5; Albert Katz

Weinberg, *Manifest Destiny: A Study of Nationalist Expansionism in American History* (Chicago: Quadrangle Books, 1963), 1–11; Richard Warner Van Alstyne, *The Rising American Empire* (Oxford: Blackwell, 1960), 1.

63. Lafeber, *The New Empire,* 4.

64. Bradford Perkins et al., eds., *The Cambridge History of American Foreign Relations,* 4 vols. (Cambridge: Cambridge University Press, 1993), 1:148.

65. Ibid., 168.

66. Shelley Streeby, *American Sensations: Class, Empire, and the Production of Popular Culture* (Berkeley: University of California Press, 2002), 10.

67. Juan González, *Harvest of Empire: A History of Latinos in America* (New York: Penguin, 2001). See also Noam Chomsky et al., *Latin America: From Colonization to Globalization* (Melbourne: Ocean, 1999).

68. Amy Kaplan, "Left Alone in America": The Absence of Empire in the Study of American Culture," in *Cultures of United States Imperialism,* ed. Amy Kaplan and Donald E. Pease (Durham, N.C.: Duke University Press, 1993), 14.

69. Ibid., 16.

70. One of the founding collections of this post-Americanist approach is Donald E. Pease, ed., *National Identities and Post-Americanist Narratives* (Durham, N.C.: Duke University Press, 1994). See also his *The New American Exceptionalism.*

71. Sacvan Bercovitch, *The American Jeremiad* (Madison: University of Wisconsin Press, 1978), 161; Sacvan Bercovitch, *The Rites of Assent* (New York: Routledge, 1992).

72. Bercovitch, *The Rites of Assent,* 53.

73. José E. Limón, *American Encounters: Greater Mexico, the United States, and the Erotics of Culture* (Boston: Beacon, 1998).

74. See Richard W. Slatta, *Comparing Cowboys and Frontiers* (Norman: University of Oklahoma Press, 1997); Robert N. Smead, *Vocabulario Vaquero = Cowboy Talk: A Dictionary of Spanish Terms from the American West* (Norman: University of Oklahoma Press, 2004).

75. Leonard L. Richards, *The California Gold Rush and the Coming of the Civil War* (New York: Alfred A. Knopf, 2007); Amy S. Greenberg, *A Wicked War: Polk, Clay, Lincoln, and the 1846 U.S. Invasion of Mexico* (New York: Alfred A. Knopf, 2012). González, *Harvest of Empire.*

76. Chicano scholars Héctor Calderón and José David Saldívar have extensively and persuasively argued in favor of a postcolonial rewriting of the literary and cultural history of the Western borderlands and annexed territories to reclaim and "affirm" Hispano-Mexican folklores and literary cultures. Héctor Calderón and José David Saldívar, *Criticism in the Borderlands: Studies in Chicano Literature, Culture, and Ideology, Post-Contemporary Interventions* (Durham, N.C.: Duke University Press, 1991). See also Saldívar's "Preface: Americanity Otherwise" in his *Trans-Americanity: Subaltern Modernities, Global Coloniality, and the Cultures of Greater Mexico* (Durham: Duke University Press, 2011), ix–xxviii.

77. John A. Ochoa, *The Uses of Failure in Mexican Literature and Identity* (Austin: University of Texas Press, 2004), 190.

78. Carlos Fuentes, *Nuevo tiempo mexicano* (México, D.F.: Aguilar, 1994), 89.

79. Carlos Fuentes, *A New Time for Mexico,* trans. Marina Gutman Castañeda and Carlos Fuentes (Los Angeles: University of California Press, 1997), 208.

80. Van Gosse's periodization of the New Left as an active political movement spans from the "early 1950s to roughly 1975." See Gosse, *Rethinking the New Left*, 5.

81. Lyotard, *The Postmodern Condition.*

82. David Harvey, *The Condition of Postmodernity: An Enquiry into the Origins of Cultural Change* (Oxford: Blackwell, 1989).

83. Ihab Habib Hassan, *The Postmodern Turn: Essays in Postmodern Theory and Culture* (Columbus: Ohio State University Press, 1987), 134–36.

Part One: Narrative Undergrounds in the Postnational City

1. John Rechy, *City of Night* (New York: Grove/Atlantic, 1984), 9.

2. Carlos Fuentes, *La región más transparente* (Madrid: Real Academia Española, 2008). English translation *Where the Air Is Clear, a Novel,* trans. Sam Hileman (New York: I. Obolensky, 1960). Quotations are followed by the abbreviation *RT* and page references to the Spanish original and the published English version, except in some cases where I offer my own translation.

3. Thomas Pynchon, *V.* (London: Vintage, 1995).

4. Anderson, *Imagined Communities.* See also Anderson, *The Spectre of Comparisons;* Balibar and Wallerstein, *Race, Nation, Class.*

5. Ezra Greenspan, *The Schlemiel Comes to America* (Metuchen, N.J.: Scarecrow, 1983).

6. Morris Dickstein, *Gates of Eden: American Culture in the Sixties* (Cambridge, Mass.: Harvard University Press, 1997), 97. See also Kharpertian: "the conventionally static character of the picaro serves Pynchon's satiric form, for Profane remains a 'yo-yo' and 'schlemihl' throughout." Theodore D. Kharpertian, *A Hand to Turn the Time: The Menippean Satires of Thomas Pynchon* (London: Fairleigh Dickinson University Press, 1990), 67.

7. Menachem Feuer and Andrew Schmitz, "Hup! Hup! We Must Tumble: Toward an Ethical Reading of the Schlemiel," *Modern Fiction Studies* 54, no. 1 (2008): 95.

8. Ochoa, *The Uses of Failure in Mexican Literature and Identity.*

9. Alan Knight, "The Rise and Fall of Cardenismo," in *Mexico Since Independence,* ed. Leslie Bethell (Cambridge: Cambridge University Press, 1991), 284. At the end of 2013, constitutional reforms promoted by a PRI-PAN coalition completely rolled back the provisions protecting mineral underground resources to allow for foreign investment, provoking a whole series of reactions regretting the loss of national sovereignty; see for instance Carlos Bonfil, "2014: olvidar la soberanía," *La Jornada,* December 29, 2013, http://www.jornada.unam.mx/2013/12/29/opinion/a09a1esp.

10. Enrique Krauze, *Mexico: Biography of Power: A History of Modern Mexico, 1810–1996* (New York: Harper-Collins, 1997), 417.

11. For a detailed account of Mexico's role in the Spanish Civil War, see T. G. Powell, *Mexico and the Spanish Civil War* (Albuquerque: University of New Mexico Press, 1981).

12. On the conflict between the Mexican revolution and the Catholic Church during the 1920s and 1930s, see Jean A. Meyer, *The Cristero Rebellion: The Mexican People Between Church and State, 1926–1929* (Cambridge: Cambridge

University Press, 1976); Alfonso Taracena, *José Vasconcelos* (México, D.F.: Editorial Porrúa, 1982).

13. Joshua Lund, *The Mestizo State: Reading Race in Modern Mexico* (Minneapolis: University of Minnesota Press, 2012), xviii.

14. A term used by Jean Franco, *The Modern Culture of Latin America: Society and the Artist* (New York: F.A. Praeger, 1967), 71–82. William Rowe and Vivian Schelling, *Memory and Modernity: Popular Culture in Latin America* (London: Verso, 1991), 160. Claire Fox discusses the ethnocentric limitations of the logics of *mestizaje* in the context of the formation of a pan-American art circuit during the postwar years: see Claire F. Fox, *Making Art Panamerican: Cultural Policy and the Cold War* (Minneapolis: University of Minnesota Press, 2013), 75–76.

15. This is Claire Fox's central critique of the muralist aesthetics of *mestizaje* in *Making Art Panamerican,* following the work of David Luis-Brown, *Waves of Decolonization,* 180.

16. Pynchon, *V.,* 62.

17. Marshall Berman, *All That Is Solid Melts into Air: The Experience of Modernity* (New York: Penguin Books, 1988), 15.

18. Seymour Menton, "La obertura nacional: Asturias, Gallegos, Mallea, Dos Passos, Yañez, Fuentes, Sarduy," *Revista Iberoamericana* 51 (1985): 151–166. For a recognition of Dos Passos's influence, see John King, "Carlos Fuentes: An Interview with John King," in *Modern Latin American Fiction: A Survey,* ed. John King (London: Faber, 1987).

19. John Dos Passos, *U.S.A.* (Harmondsworth, Eng.: Penguin Books, 2001), 7.

20. Mumford's uneasiness is predominantly concerned with the effects that the cultural hegemony of the central power has on the cultures that become incorporated into the national project. Practices such as education, information, and legislation are therefore perceived as contributing to the "deliberate effort" to hold together a national unity built from the urban centers of power, as Mumford reminds us in *The Culture of Cities:* "To the extent that such a unity does not grow out of spontaneous allegiances and natural affiliations it must constantly be held together by deliberate effort: indoctrination in the school, propaganda in the press, restrictive laws, extirpation of rival dialects and languages, either by mockery or mandate, suppression of the customs and privileges of minorities" (349). Lewis Mumford, *The Culture of Cities* (San Diego, Calif.: Harvest Books, 1970), 349.

21. Raymond Williams, *Marxism and Literature* (Oxford: Oxford University Press, 1985), 112–13.

22. Kernan, *The Plot of Satire,* 100.

23. "Shifting critical paradigms in American studies away from linear narratives of immigration, assimilation, and nationhood." José David Saldívar, *Border Matters: Remapping American Cultural Studies* (Berkeley: University of California Press, 1997), 1.

24. Brian Jarvis, *Postmodern Cartographies: The Geographical Imagination in Contemporary American Culture* (New York: St. Martin's, 1998), 58.

25. Carlos Fuentes, *Tiempo mexicano* (México, D.F.: Editorial J. Mortiz, 1971), 36–42.

26. Fredric Jameson, *A Singular Modernity: Essay on the Ontology of the Present* (New York: Verso Books, 2002), 35–41.

27. Brian May, "Back to the Future: History in/and the Postcolonial Novel," *Studies in the Novel* 29 (1997): 268.

28. John A. McClure, *Late Imperial Romance* (London: Verso, 1994), 6.

29. Bhabha, *Nation and Narration,* 311.

Chapter 1. Modernity Versus Its National Demons: *La región más transparente*

1. Mumford only credits nationalism with creating "the semblance of political unity between diverse regions and communities" (349) despite the fact that it is "a term inherently so vague and so contradictory that it must always be taken in a mystic sense, as meaning whatever the ruling classes hold it convenient to mean at the moment" (349). Mumford, *The Culture of Cities.*

2. Mircea Eliade, *The Sacred and the Profane: The Nature of Religion,* trans. Willard R. Trask (New York: Harper and Row, 1959), 42–47.

3. Germán Vázquez, *Origen de los mexicanos* (Madrid: Dastin, 2001), 55–57; Ignacio Bernal, *Tenochtitlán en una isla* (México, D.F.: Secretaría de Educación Pública, 1972), 117–19.

4. The most obvious instance of its literary use after the revolution is Martín Luis Guzmán, *El águila y la serpiente* (Madrid: Compañía ibero-americana de publicaciones, 1928).

5. Claudio Lomnitz-Adler, *Exits from the Labyrinth: Culture and Ideology in the Mexican National Space* (Berkeley: University of California Press, 1992), 255.

6. A point taken up by many of Eliade's critics, and which has been amply discussed in Bryan S. Rennie, *Reconstructing Eliade: Making Sense of Religion* (Albany: State University of New York Press, 1996).

7. Eliade, *The Sacred and the Profane.* Eliade's work, originally published in French in 1944, is one of the few sources credited by Octavio Paz in his 1950 book, *El laberinto de la soledad* (México, D.F.: Fondo de Cultura Económica, 1998), 253, n. 4.

8. Luis Vélez de Guevara, *El diablo cojuelo,* ed. Enrique Rodríguez Cepeda (Madrid: Cátedra, 1995). In his interview with Claude Dumas, Fuentes identifies the Spanish seventeenth-century picaresque novel as one of the direct intertexts of *Where the Air Is Clear.* Claude Dumas, "Théorie et pratique du nouveau roman Latino-Américain: *La región más transparente* (1958), une analyse de son auteur, le Mexicain Carlos Fuentes," in *Écrire le Mexique: Carlos Fuentes, La región más transparente*; *Paco Ignacio Taibo II, La vida misma, sombra de la sombra,* ed. Jean Franco and Yves Aguila (Paris: Ellipses, 1998).

9. Dumas, "Théorie et pratique," 18.

10. Bartra, *La jaula de la melancolía,* 32.

11. Bartra refers specifically to Fuentes's reading of Juan Rulfo's use of myth in *Pedro Páramo.* Ibid., 32–33.

12. Carlos Fuentes, *Los días enmascarados* (México, D.F.: Los Presentes, 1954).

13. Robin George Collingwood, *The Idea of History,* ed. Jan Van Der Dussen (Oxford: Oxford University Press, 1994), 321–34 (333).

14. In a contemporary interview, Carlos Fuentes noted that he was particularly interested in time play: "I was reading Dos Passos a lot, looking for a way to build dead time into a novel." Luis Harss and Barbara Dohmann, *Into the*

Mainstream: Conversations with Latin American Writers (New York: Harper, 1967), 294.

15. Fuentes, *Tiempo mexicano,* 27.

16. Maarten Van Delden, *Carlos Fuentes, Mexico, and Modernity* (Liverpool: Liverpool University Press, 1998), 19.

17. "Anáhuac," in *Encyclopædia Britannica* from *Encyclopædia Britannica Online.*

18. In the published English translation, the address to a second person is introduced earlier in the passage, accelerating and somehow defusing this gradation.

19. "Here we bide" (5) in the English translation.

20. Dumas, "Théorie et pratique," 20.

21. Honoré de Balzac, *History of the Thirteen,* trans. Herbert J. Hunt (Harmondsworth, Eng.: Penguin Books, 1974), 26–27.

22. Gilles Deleuze and Felix Guattari, *A Thousand Plateaus: Capitalism and Schizophrenia,* trans. Brian Massumi (London: Athlone, 1991), 340.

23. Guillermo Bonfil Batalla, *México Profundo: Reclaiming a Civilization,* trans. Philip Adams Dennis (Austin: University of Texas Press, 1996).

24. Lomnitz-Adler, *Exits from the Labyrinth,* 249.

25. Jean Franco, *Plotting Women: Gender and Representation in Mexico* (New York: Columbia University Press, 1989), 131.

26. A failure that Franco makes extensive to the Cuban Revolution, whose contradictory gender policies left in place age-old machismo and a patriarchal subjugation of homosexuals. Jean Franco, "South of Your Border," in *The 60s Without Apology,* ed. Sohnya Sayres (Minneapolis: University of Minnesota Press in cooperation with Social Text, 1984), 326.

27. Alma Guillermoprieto, *The Heart That Bleeds: Latin America Now* (New York: Knopf, 1994), 47.

28. Canclini, *Culturas híbridas.*

29. Yves Aguila, *Écrire le Mexique: Carlos Fuentes, La región más transparente* (Paris: Ed. Messene, 1998), 79–81.

30. For a discussion on the early reception of the novel, see Richard Reeve, "Octavio Paz and Hiperión in *La región más transparente:* Plagiarism, Caricature or . . . ?," *Chasqui* 3 (1974).

31. Aguila, *Ecrire le Mexique,* 81.

32. José Vasconcelos, *La raza cósmica* (México, D.F.: Editorial Porrúa, 2001). Vasconcelos's role in the building of the postrevolutionary "Mexican cultural nationalism" was studied in detail by Jean Franco. Franco, *The Modern Culture of Latin America,* 71–82. See also Ana María Alonso, "Conforming Disconformity: 'Mestizaje,' Hybridity, and the Aesthetics of Mexican Nationalism," *Cultural Anthropology* 19, no. 4 (2004); Carrie C. Chorba, *Mexico, from Mestizo to Multicultural: National Identity and Recent Representations of the Conquest* (Nashville, Tenn.: Vanderbilt University Press, 2007), 14–15.

33. Abelardo Villegas, *La filosofía de lo mexicano* (México, D.F.: Fondo de Cultura Económica, 1960), 127.

34. Frantz Fanon, *Black Skin, White Masks,* trans. Charles Lam Markmann (New York: Grove, 1991), 18.

35. Samuel Ramos, *El perfil del hombre y la cultura en México* (México, D.F.: P. Robredo, 1938); English translation *Profile of Man and Culture in Mexico,* trans. Peter G. Earle (Austin: University of Texas Press, 1962), 93.

36. Alfonso Reyes, "Notas sobre la inteligencia americana," in *Última tule* (México, D.F.: Imprenta Universitaria, 1942), 132–33; in *Obras Completas,* 21 vols. (México, D.F.: Fondo de Cultura Económica, 1955). 11:82. This image and Reyes's quote are invoked again by Fuentes in a more recent description of Mexico's psychological complex of being "displaced from 'modernity' "; see Carlos Fuentes, *En esto creo* (Barcelona: Editorial Seix Barral, 2002), 180.

37. This image of decay is unexplainably absent from the novel's irregular translation; contrast p. 79 of the Spanish edition with p. 48 of the English edition where it should appear.

38. Georg Hegel, *The Philosophy of History,* trans. J. Sibree (New York: Wiley, 1944).

39. Paz, *El laberinto de la soledad,* 233–34.

40. The origins of the phrase "La región más transparente del aire" go back to Alexander Von Humboldt, and it is echoed by Alfonso Reyes in the epigraph to his article "Visión de Anáhuac" (1917). Steven Boldy similarly notes the parodic tone in his thorough reading of this long tirade. In particular, he identifies a parody of two specific nationalistic texts: Pablo Neruda's "Alturas de Macchu Picchu" and Alfonso Reyes's "Visión de Anáhuac." Steven Boldy, *Memoria Mexicana* (México, D.F.: Taurus, 1998), 66–70.

41. Gérard de Nerval, "Les Doctrinaires," in *Poésies et souvenirs,* ed. Jean Richer (Paris: Gallimard, 1974), 75.

42. Trained under nationalist intellectuals who followed Ortega y Gasset's exiled disciple José Gaos's soul-searching philosophy: Leopoldo Zea, Emilio Uranga, Jorge Portilla, Luis Villoro, Fernando Salmerón, Joaquín Sánchez MacGregor, and Ricardo Guerra. Ver Guillermo Hurtado, *El Hiperión: Antología* (México, D.F.: Universidad Nacional Autónoma de México, 2006).

43. Leopoldo Zea, *Discurso desde la marginación y la barbarie* (Barcelona: Anthropos, Editorial del Hombre, 1988); Leopoldo Zea, *The Role of the Americas in History,* ed. Amy Oliver, trans. Sonja Karsen (Savage: Rowman and Littlefield, 1992).

44. A point powerfully argued by Aziza Bennani, *Monde mental et monde romanesque de Carlos Fuentes* (Rabat: Université Mohammed V, 1985), 367–68.

45. In Rubén Marin, ed., *Los narradores ante el público,* 2 vols. (México, D.F.: Editorial J. Mortiz, 1967). 1:141; Fuentes, *Tiempo mexicano,* 63.

46. Max Weber suggested that industrialization led to a feeling of growing disenchantment, in "Science as a Vocation" (1918–19). Weber writes: "The fate of our times is characterized by rationalization and intellectualization and, above all, by the 'disenchantment of the world.' " Max Weber, *From Max Weber: Essays in Sociology,* ed. H. H. Gerth and C. Wright Mills (New York: Oxford University Press, 1946), 155.

Chapter 2. Innocents Abroad and at Home: The Profane History of American Modernity in *V.*

The chapter epigraph is from Errol Morris, *The Fog of War: Eleven Lessons from the Life of Robert S. McNamara* (Culver City, Calif.: Columbia TriStar Home Entertainment, 2004).

1. Graham Greene, *The Quiet American* (New York: Viking, 1956); Eugene Burdick and William J. Lederer, *The Ugly American* (New York: Norton, 1999).

2. Young claims that "in the Cold War era, imperialism almost more than capitalism as such became the object of communism's ideological war with the west and the general system of global domination of the United States." Robert Young, *Postcolonialism: An Historical Introduction* (Oxford: Blackwell, 2001), 29.

3. David Wise and Thomas B. Ross, *The Invisible Government* (New York: Random House, 1964), 167–69. A few years later in 1972, the "quiet ugly American" published his own account: Edward Geary Lansdale, *In the Midst of Wars: An American's Mission to Southeast Asia* (New York: Fordham University Press, 1991). See also Cecil B. Currey, *Edward Lansdale, the Unquiet American* (Boston: Houghton Mifflin, 1988). For a more complete account, see Jonathan Nashel, *Edward Lansdale's Cold War* (Amherst: University of Massachusetts Press, 2005), 2–3.

4. Michael McClintock focuses on this point of Lansdale's counterinsurgent tactics: "Lansdale's plans for the warlords reflected his peculiarly simplistic vision of nation-building." Michael McClintock, *Instruments of Statecraft: U.S. Guerrilla Warfare, Counterinsurgency, and Counter-Terrorism, 1940–1990* (New York: Pantheon Books, 1992), 131.

5. Richard Slotkin, *Gunfighter Nation: The Myth of the Frontier in Twentieth-Century America* (Norman: University of Oklahoma Press, 1998), 445–46.

6. Löwy evokes the internationalist and humanist potential that communism inspired. See Michael Löwy, *Fatherland or Mother Earth?: Essays on the National Question* (London: Pluto Press with the International Institute for Research and Education, 1998), 53.

7. Richard Rodgers and Oscar Hammerstein, "Carefully Taught," in *South Pacific* (New York: Columbia, 1987); Amy Kaplan, *The Anarchy of Empire in the Making of U.S. Culture* (Cambridge, Mass.: Harvard University Press, 2002).

8. A feature that has attracted other scholars; see, for instance, McClure, *Late Imperial Romance;* Jeffrey Baker, "Amerikka über Alles: German Nationalism, American Imperialism, and the 60's Antiwar Movement in *Gravity's Rainbow,*" *Critique: Studies in Contemporary Fiction,* 40, no. 4 (1999): 323–41.

9. David Cowart, *Thomas Pynchon: The Art of Allusion* (Carbondale: Southern Illinois University Press, 1980), 2–4; Thomas Pynchon, *Slow Learner: Early Stories* (Boston: Little Brown, 1984), 4. For Pynchon's short stories, I will refer to the *Slow Learner* (*SL*) edition.

10. Ian Tyrrell, "American Exceptionalim in an Age of International History," *American Historical Review* 96, no. 4 (1991), 1031.

11. Dickstein, *Gates of Eden,* 121.

12. Ronald W. Cooley, "The Hothouse or the Street: Imperialism and Narrative in Pynchon's *V.,*" *Modern Fiction Studies* 39 (1993): 309. See also Stefan Mattessich, "Imperium, Misogyny, and Postmodern Parody in Thomas Pynchon's *V.,*" *ELH* 65 (1998).

13. By way of contrast, Francisco Collado offers a "postmodern" summary of the novel as a quest for an "impossible historical-contemporary knowledge," thus obfuscating its political readings. Francisco Collado, "History and Metafiction: *V.*'s Impossible Cognitive Quest," *Atlantis* 15, no. 1 (1993): 75.

14. Thomas Pynchon, "Letter to Thomas F. Hirsch," in *The Fictional Labyrinths of Thomas Pynchon,* ed. David Seed (Iowa City: University of Iowa Press, 1988), 242.

15. Mark Sanders perceptively points out that Pynchon's "challenge as a historian is to attempt to speak for Africans, while rejecting the idea of colonial guardianship." Mark Sanders, "The Politics of Literary Reinscription in Thomas Pynchon's *V.*," *Critique: Studies in Contemporary Fiction* 39, no. 1 (1997): 85.

16. Brian Jarvis has amply commented on the spatial aspects of Pynchon's *V.*, particularly the destruction of Valletta, 306–7, in Jarvis, *Postmodern Cartographies,* 51–79 (57).

17. Joseph Conrad's *Heart of Darkness* is frequently cited as an ur-text behind *V.* McClure, *Late Imperial Romance;* Luc Herman and John M. Krafft, "From the Ground Up: The Evolution of the South-West Africa Chapter in Pynchon's *V.*," *Contemporary Literature* 47, no. 2 (2006): 287.

18. Robert Holton, "In the Rathouse of History with Thomas Pynchon: Rereading *V.*," *Textual Practice* 2, no. 3 (1988): 337.

19. John Fousek, *To Lead the Free World: American Nationalism and the Cultural Roots of the Cold War* (Chapel Hill: University of North Carolina Press, 2000), 189.

20. Following Ihab Hassan, Judith Chambers defines the two questing characters as follows: "Stencil's character suggests the elitism and oppression that is the legacy of his father, and Profane's the apathetic rejection of any legacy . . . [and as] the fluctuation between immanence and indeterminacy . . . though neither is so lofty." Judith Chambers, *Thomas Pynchon* (New York: Twayne, 1992), 48.

21. Thomas Pynchon, "The Small Rain," in *Slow Learner,* 25–52. The story first appeared in *The Cornell Writer,* 6, no. 2 (1959): 14–32.

22. Pynchon himself recognizes these influences: "the Beats writers, the diction of Saul Bellow in *The Adventures of Augie March,* emerging voices like those of Herbert Gold and Philip Roth." Pynchon, *Slow Learner,* 7. A number of contemporary commentators observed this important move. Leslie Fiedler summarized it as follows: "At the moment that young Europeans everywhere (even, at last, in England) are becoming imaginary Americans, the American is becoming an imaginary Jew. . . . At the same moment, the Jew . . . may himself be in the process of becoming an imaginary Negro." Leslie A. Fiedler, *Waiting for the End: The American Literary Scene from Hemingway to Baldwin* (London: Jonathan Cape, 1965), 98.

23. Anders Stephanson, *Manifest Destiny: American Expansionism and the Empire of Right* (New York: Hill and Wang, 1996), 7.

24. Ruth Wisse offers a perceptive reading of the cultural and historical context: "when America as a whole began to experience itself as a 'loser' after World War II and ever more insistently in the 1950s, the schlemiel was lifted from its parochial setting into national prominence." Ruth R. Wisse, *The Schlemiel as Modern Hero* (Chicago: University of Chicago Press, 1971), 75.

25. J. Kerry Grant, *A Companion to V.* (Athens: University of Georgia Press, 2001), 8–9.

26. Peter Stallybrass and Allon White, *The Politics and Poetics of Transgression* (Ithaca, N.Y.: Cornell University Press, 1986), 143.

27. Another clear instance of this contrast between the closed domestic environment of the "Hothouse" and the military male outside are the two spheres in "Entropy."

28. Campbell demotes its parodic role, claiming that "'under the street' is the area of the fantastic, where events and reported events seem less credible."

Elizabeth Campbell, "Metaphor And *V.*: Metaphysics in the Mirror," *Pynchon Notes* 22–23 (1988): 60.

29. In one of the most interesting essays written in the 1990s on *V.*, Paul W. Celmer, Jr., performs a Bakhtinian reading of the novel's undermining of the conspiracy atmosphere of the Cold War and, in particular, of its carnivalization of the Communist Plot in order to promote a "healing laughter" in the face of apocalypse. Paul W. Celmer, Jr., "Pynchon's *V.* and the Rhetoric of the Cold War," *Pynchon Notes,* no. 32–33 (1993): 28.

30. Arnold Cassola, "Pynchon, *V.*, and the Malta Connection," in *Pynchon Malta and Wittgenstein,* ed. P. Bianchi, Arnold Cassola, and Peter Serracino Inglott (Malta: Malta University Publishers, 1994), 15.

31. Kharpertian, *A Hand to Turn the Time,* 75.

32. Thomas Pynchon, *Gravity's Rainbow* (London: Vintage, 1995), 713.

Part Two. Dissenting from the Nation: The New Left

1. Some critics even go as far as to point to *The Crying of Lot 49* as "the most emblematic text of the American sixties." Pierre Yves Petillon, "A Recognition of Her Errand into the Wilderness," in *New Essays on the Crying of Lot 49,* ed. Patrick O'Donnell, 127 (Cambridge: Cambridge University Press, 1991). Mexican writer Jorge Volpi has seen in *Cambio de piel* Fuentes's "most ambitious project"; Jorge Volpi, *La imaginación y el poder: Una historia intelectual de 1968* (México, D.F.: Ediciones Era, 1998), 61.

2. Carlos Fuentes, *La muerte de Artemio Cruz,* ed. José C. González Boixo (Madrid: Cátedra, 1995). English translation *The Death of Artemio Cruz,* trans. Sam Hileman (New York: Farrar, Straus and Giroux, 1964). Quotations will be followed by parenthetical page references to the Spanish original and the English version, except in those cases in which the translation itself becomes problematic, where I will offer my own.

3. Tom Nairn, *The Break-up of Britain: Crisis and Neonationalism* (London: NLB and Verso Editions, 1981), 329–63; Tom Nairn, *Faces of Nationalism: Janus Revisited* (London: Verso Books, 1998).

4. Carlos Fuentes, *Cambio de piel* (México, D.F.: Editorial J. Mortiz, 1967). English translation *A Change of Skin,* trans. Sam Hileman (New York: Farrar, Straus and Giroux, 1968). As elsewhere in the book, page numbers refer first to the Spanish original version followed by page numbers of the English translation.

5. Norman Mailer, *Advertisements for Myself* (Cambridge, Mass.: Harvard University Press, 1992), 187–90 (188).

6. Thomas Pynchon, *The Crying of Lot 49* (Philadelphia: Lippincott, 1966).

7. Direct American investment in Mexico increased from $922 million in 1959 to nearly $1.3 billion in 1964. Peter H. Smith, "Mexico Since 1946: Dynamics of an Authoritarian Regime," in *Mexico Since Independence,* ed. Leslie Bethell (Cambridge: Cambridge University Press, 1991), 354.

8. As set out in Kennedy's "Preliminary Formulations of the Alliance for Progress." Address by President Kennedy at a White House reception for Latin American diplomats and members of Congress, March 13, 1961. In it, apart from suggesting ten points that summarized the political program of the "Alliance," including $500 million to "combat illiteracy, improve the productivity and use of their land, wipe out disease, attack archaic tax and land-tenure structures, provide

educational opportunities, and offer a broad range of projects designed to make the benefits of increasing abundance available to all," Kennedy emphasized his interest in the Caribbean: "Therefore let us express our special friendship to the people of Cuba and the Dominican Republic—and the hope they will soon rejoin the society of free men, uniting with us in our common effort." However, no mention is made of Mexico's PRI as having been in power for over forty years by the early 1960s, an instance of the U.S. administration's connivance with its oligarchic practices. *Department of State Bulletin* 44, no. 1136, April 3, 1961, 471–74.

9. Greg Grandin, *Empire's Workshop: Latin America, the United States, and the Rise of the New Imperialism* (New York: Metropolitan Books, 2006).

10. Noam Chomsky, *American Power and the New Mandarins* (Harmondsworth, Eng.: Penguin, 1969), 202.

11. Nairn, *The Break-up of Britain,* 350.

12. Fredric Jameson, *Postmodernism: or, the Cultural Logic of Late Capitalism* (London: Verso, 1991), 68, a concept derived directly from the Frankfurt School, and in particular from Adorno's analysis of the ideological import contained in the new "culture industry" of the mass media. Theodor W. Adorno, *Culture Industry,* ed. J. M. Bernstein (London: Routledge, 2001).

13. The Cold War had inaugurated a new economic era in the capitalist bloc which was best defined not as the age of private property, but as "the age of corporate property," using C. Wright Mills's phrase. C. Wright Mills, *The Power Elite* (New York: Oxford University Press, 1956), 148.

14. Jameson, *Postmodernism,* 36. This expression was already present in his first version: "Postmodernism or the Cultural Logic of Late Capitalism," *New Left Review* 146 (1984), 78.

15. Jameson, *Postmodernism,* 38.

16. Adorno, *Culture Industry,* 98–106 (99).

17. Lewis Mumford, *The Pentagon of Power* (New York: Harcourt Brace Jovanovich, 1974), 166.

18. Herbert Marcuse, *One-Dimensional Man: Studies in the Ideology of Advanced Industrial Society,* ed. Douglas Kellner (London: Routledge, 1991), 33.

19. Theodore Roszak, *The Making of a Counter Culture: Reflections on the Technocratic Society and Its Youthful Opposition* (Berkeley: University of California Press, 1995), 5. Jeffrey Baker has looked at *Gravity's Rainbow* as rooted in the democratic ideals of the 1960s counterculture: Jeffrey S. Baker, "A Democratic Pynchon: Counterculture, Counterforce and Participatory Democracy," *Pynchon Notes* 32–33 (1993).

20. Wilhelm Reich, *The Mass Psychology of Fascism,* trans. Vincent R. Carfagno (New York: Farrar, Straus and Giroux, 1970).

21. Marcuse, *One-Dimensional Man,* 18.

22. Kennedy's obscure assassination was attributed to Lee Harvey Oswald, a member of the FPCC (Fair Play for Cuba Committee), but subsequent investigations have pointed to the possible participation of the CIA and the FBI. Peter Knight, *Conspiracy Culture: From Kennedy to "the X-Files"* (London: Routledge, 2001), 87–90. Van Gosse traces the significance of the Cuban cause before and after Castro's takeover, and anti-imperialism in general, as an agglutinating factor in the formation of the New Left. Van Gosse, *Where the Boys Are: Cuba, Cold War America and the Making of a New Left* (London: Verso, 1993).

23. Quoted in Marwick, *The Sixties,* 536.
24. Ibid.
25. Susan Lee Johnson, *Roaring Camp: The Social World of the California Gold Rush* (New York: W.W. Norton, 2000).
26. Adorno, *Culture Industry,* 163.
27. A totalizing definition of "the system" like the one offered by Charles Reich: "The System is a merger of governmental, corporate, and media power into a managerial entity more powerful by reason of technology, organization, and control of livelihood than any previously known form of rule. To describe the System in this way must inevitably sound alarmist. But before dismissing this picture, remember how powerless most people feel." Charles A. Reich, *Opposing the System* (New York: Crown, 1995), 17.
28. Gilles Deleuze and Felix Guattari, *Anti-Oedipus: Capitalism and Schizophrenia,* trans. R. Hurley (London: Athlone, 1983), 33.
29. Néstor García Canclini, *Hybrid Cultures: Strategies for Entering and Leaving Modernity,* trans. Christopher L. Chiappari and Silvia L. López (Minneapolis: University of Minnesota Press, 2005), 259.
30. Nairn, *The Break-up of Britain,* 344–52.

Chapter 3. *La muerte de Artemio Cruz* and the Agonic Mexican Nation

1. Carlos Fuentes, *La nueva novela hispanoamericana* (México, D.F.: Editorial J. Mortiz, 1969).
2. C. Wright Mills, *C. Wright Mills: Letters and Autobiographical Writings,* ed. Kathryn Mills, Pamela Mills, and Dan Wakefield (Berkeley: University of California Press, 2000), 323.
3. José Donoso attributes to Fuentes the birth of the so-called "boom" of the Spanish American novel, as he was "the first one to manage his works through literary agents, the first one to have friendships with important writers from Europe and the US." José Donoso and María Pilar Donoso, *Historia personal del "Boom"* (Barcelona: Seix Barral, 1983), 50.
4. See, for instance, the colloquium between Mills and a number of Mexican intellectuals, including Fuentes: C. Wright Mills, "Izquierda, subdesarrollo y guerra fría: Un coloquio sobre cuestiones fundamentales," *Cuadernos Americanos* 19 (1960).
5. Mills, *C. Wright Mills: Letters and Autobiographical Writings.* See also C. Wright Mills, *Listen, Yankee: The Revolution in Cuba* (New York: Ballantine Books, 1960), 180.
6. See George Vickers, *The Formation of the New Left: The Early Years* (Lexington, Mass.: Lexington Books, 1975), 86–87. Vickers points to the "emergence of anarchism and voluntarism as central features of the ideological development taking place within the organization" (87).
7. Marin, *Los narradores ante el público,* 1:154. He is referring here to Fyodor M. Dostoevsky, and to Lev Davidovich Landau, Soviet physicist and winner of the Nobel Prize in 1962.
8. Later in his career Fuentes has even compared and equated openly Cuba's "illogical imitation of 'really-existing socialism'" with the pernicious "illogical imitation of authoritarian capitalism in the rest of Latin America, which

translated into brutal military dictatorships in Chile, Argentina and Uruguay." Fuentes, *En esto creo,* 216.

9. Maarten Van Delden has studied in detail Carlos Fuentes's changing attitude in the period from 1959 to 1966, when he clearly completed his distancing act from Castro's administration. Delden, *Carlos Fuentes, Mexico, and Modernity,* 41–50. Of particular interest are Fuentes's articles throughout the 1960s in magazines such as *Política* and *Siempre!*

10. Fanon, *The Wretched of the Earth*, 166.

11. It is also significant to cite here one of Fuentes's opinions about post-Castro's Cuba in the wake of the fall of the Berlin Wall: "El acto más valiente de su vida sería heredar un país en plena transformación independiente." (The most courageous act of his life [Fidel's] would be to bequeath a country in full independent transformation.) *El País,* January 20, 1998. He also traces Castro's central role in the Cuban Revolution to the legacy of Hispano-Arabic "caudillismo." Fuentes, *En esto creo,* 232.

12. Rosario Castellanos, *Juicios sumarios: Ensayos* (Xalapa: Universidad Veracruzana, 1966), 125.

13. There have been some important critical contributions establishing Artemio as a national allegory, two of them by Lanin Gyurko, who compares Welles and Fuentes in this particular use of "characters who function not only as individuals but as national symbols." Lanin Gyurko, "*La muerte de Artemio Cruz* and *Citizen Kane,*" in *Carlos Fuentes: A Critical View,* ed. Robert Brody and Charles Rossman, 66 (Austin: University of Texas Press, 1982). For D'Lugo, Artemio is "the embodiment of Mexico and Mexicans." Carol Clark D'Lugo, *The Fragmented Novel in Mexico: The Politics of Form* (Austin: University of Texas Press, 1997), 111.

14. Characteristically, Aub points out parenthetically that these novels generally criticized "revolutionaries, not the Revolution itself." Max Aub, *Ensayos mexicanos* (México, D.F.: Universidad Nacional Autónoma de México, 1974), 33.

15. Referring to the 1857 liberal constitution reinstated throughout Mexican history, in this case by Porfirio Díaz, who used it to create a national consensus among the middle classes.

16. Justo Sierra, *Evolución política del pueblo mexicano,* ed. Edmundo O'Gorman (México, D.F.: Universidad Nacional Autónoma de México, 1948), 359.

17. Benedict Anderson, "El efecto tranquilizador del fratricidio: O de como las naciones imaginan sus genealogías," in *El nacionalismo en México,* ed. Cecilia Noriega Elío (Zamora: Colegio de Michoacán, 1992). Anderson applies there the concept of "reassuring fratricide" to the recent histories of Mexico and postwar Germany. See also Anderson, *Imagined Communities,* 199–203.

18. Aub also points out the fact that "even though it may sound like a contradiction in terms, it was after all the Revolution that made Mexico speak one language, Spanish" (Aub uses the expression "españolizar" in a purely linguistic sense). Aub, *Ensayos mexicanos,* 44.

19. All extracts from Paz's works are my own translation unless otherwise indicated. Paz, *El laberinto de la soledad.* 210.

20. Ibid., 217–19.

21. In her monograph on the novel, María Stoopen has advanced a reading of the text as the "possibility of making valid, in a fictional universe, the theoretical postulates offered by Paz." María Stoopen, *La muerte de Artemio Cruz: Una novela de denuncia y traición* (México D.F.: Universidad Nacional Autonóma de México, 1982), 11.

22. Leopoldo Zea, *Conciencia y posibilidad del mexicano* (México, D.F.: Porrúa, 1952), 23.

23. Octavio Paz, *Vuelta a El laberinto de la soledad* (México, D.F.: Fondo de Cultura Económica, 1998), 369.

24. Paz, *El laberinto de la soledad,* 90.

25. Time is a gendered metaphor and the temporal definitions of the imagined community or nation raises issues of gender and sexuality, as Andrew Parker has pointed out in his introduction. Andrew Parker, *Nationalisms & Sexualities* (New York: Routledge, 1992), 5.

26. Edna Aizenberg, "The Untruths of the Nation: Petals of Blood and Fuentes's *The Death of Artemio Cruz,*" *Research in African Literatures* 21, no. 4 (1990), 91. I agree, however, with Aizenberg's main contention, namely that "the novel now combats the very thing it once sought to constitute [the nation]" (86).

27. "Siempre los dos tiempos, en esta comunidad jánica, de rostro doble, tan lejana de lo que fue, y tan lejana de lo que quiere ser" (250). Note the English translation of *The Death of Artemio Cruz* excludes the reference to the two times represented by the god's double face. In addition, "comunidad" is mistakenly translated as "town."

28. Octavio Paz, "Postdata," in *El laberinto de la soledad,* 263–355 (323–24).

29. In the lines of Brushwood's evaluation: "it does seem that the life of Cruz can be understood as one way of looking at the attitudes of the nation and why they are as they are. If my assumption is correct, Fuentes sees Mexico as having deceived herself by accepting values that will not allow her to realize her potential." John Stubbs Brushwood, *Mexico in Its Novel; A Nation's Search for Identity* (Austin: University of Texas Press, 1966), 41. Sandra Messinger Cypess also reads Artemio Cruz as a *malinchista* character "in the way he sells out his ideals in order to reap material gain." Sandra Messinger Cypess, *La Malinche in Mexican Literature from History to Myth* (Austin: University of Texas Press, 1991), 153.

30. Artemio resembles in this respect the Latin American elite described by C. Wright Mills in his interview with several Mexican writers in 1960, when he accuses the ruling class of acting as an "inside imperialist power." Mills, "Izquierda," 62.

31. Wendy B. Faris, *Carlos Fuentes* (New York: Ungar, 1983), 47; and Jonathan Tittler, *Narrative Irony in the Contemporary Spanish-American Novel* (Ithaca, N.Y.: Cornell University Press, 1984). D'Lugo, *The Fragmented Novel,* 103–5.

32. In Sarah A. Radcliffe and Sallie Westwood, *Remaking the Nation: Place, Identity and Politics in Latin America* (London: Routledge, 1996), 11–12; John King, *Magical Reels: A History of Cinema in Latin America* (London: Verso, 1990), 53. See also Zuzana M. Pick, *Constructing the Image of the Mexican Revolution: Cinema and the Archive* (Austin: University of Texas Press, 2010), 152–59.

33. Seth Fein, "Myths of Cultural Imperialism and Nationalism in Golden Age Mexican Cinema," in *Fragments of a Golden Age: The Politics of Culture in Mexico since 1940,* ed. Anne Rubenstein, Gilbert M. Joseph, and Eric Zolov (Durham, N.C.: Duke University Press, 2001), 191.

34. See also *MAC,* 301–16.

35. Irvin D. Solomon wrongly misses this criticism of the novel by summarizing it as "based on the notion that females are lesser beings who need to be controlled and dominated" (74). Irvin D. Solomon, "A Feminist Perspective of the Latin-American Novel: Carlos Fuentes's *The Death of Artemio Cruz," Hispanófila,* no. 97 (1989).

36. Anderson, "El efecto tranquilizador del fratricidio," 99.

37. Fuentes finds in this Cainite tradition "the key to Mexico"; see "El México alucinado de Carlos Fuentes," in *Narradores de esta América,* ed. Emir Rodríguez Monegal, 2 vols. (Buenos Aires: Alfa Argentina, 1974), 2:259.

38. Due to this duplicity, Catalina Bernal is read by Messinger Cypess as an avatar of the Malinche herself; Cypess, *La Malinche in Mexican Literature from History to Myth,* 150.

39. Doris Sommer, *Foundational Fictions: The National Romances of Latin America* (Berkeley: University of California Press, 1991), 29.

40. Castellanos, *Juicios sumarios,* 125.

41. Carlos Fuentes, "El ángel exterminador: Nadie encontrará una respuesta dogmática," Suplemento de *Siempre!* (Junio 13, 1962): xix.

42. Linda Glanze, "La distorsión temporal y las técnicas cinematográficas En *La muerte de Artemio Cruz," Hispamérica* 14, no. 40 (1985): 116.

43. See his interview with Emmanuel Carballo. Emmanuel Carballo, "Carlos Fuentes," in *Protagonistas de la literatura mexicana* (México, D.F.: SEP, 1986). 548.

44. William Shakespeare, *The Norton Shakespeare,* ed. Stephen Greenblatt et al. (New York: Norton, 1997), 1755.

45. A detailed analysis of these first-person sequences can be found in Bienvenido de la Fuente, "*La muerte de Artemio Cruz:* Observaciones sobre la estructura y sentido de la narración en primera persona," *Explicación de Textos Literarios,* 6, no. 2 (1978): 143–51.

46. Steven Boldy, "Fathers and Sons in Fuentes's *La muerte de Artemio Cruz,*" *BHS* 61 (1984): 32.

47. Carballo, "Carlos Fuentes," 548. Translated by Faris, *Carlos Fuentes,* 61.

48. *Aura* in Carlos Fuentes, *Cuerpos y ofrendas* (Madrid: Alianza, 2001), 157.

49. Faris, *Carlos Fuentes,* 73. See also her interesting comparisons between *Aura* and *The Aspern Papers* by Henry James, and Hawthorne's "Rappacini's Daughter," 77.

50. Peter Brooks, *Reading for the Plot: Design and Intention in Narrative* (Cambridge, Mass.: Harvard University Press, 1992), 317.

51. A direct influence recognized by Pynchon in his introductory piece to Pynchon, *Slow Learner,* 13.

52. Thomas Pynchon, "Entropy," in *Slow Learner,* 98.

53. Hayden White, *The Content of the Form: Narrative Discourse and Historical Representation* (Baltimore: Johns Hopkins University Press, 1990), 208.

54. Boldy, "Fathers and Sons in Fuentes's *La muerte de Artemio Cruz,*" 36.

55. Wendy Faris sees in Ludivinia an echo of Faulkner's Miss Rosa in *Absalom, Absalom!;* see Faris, *Carlos Fuentes,* 52.

56. Lanin Gyurko, "Self, Double, and Mask in Fuentes's *La muerte de Artemio Cruz,*" *Texas Studies in Language and Literature* 16 (1974). Gyurko establishes a division between compensatory and antagonist doubles.

57. John H. Sinningen, "El desarrollo combinado y desigual y *La muerte de Artemio Cruz,*" *Cuadernos Hispanoamericanos* 396 (1983): 700.

58. Paz, *El laberinto de la soledad,* 233–34.

Chapter 4. *The Crying of Lot 49* and the Nationalist Colonization of the Unconscious

1. Kharpertian, *A Hand to Turn the Time,* 95.

2. Thomas Pynchon, "The World (This One), the Flesh (Mrs. Oedipa Maas), and the Testament of Pierce Inverarity," *Esquire Magazine,* December 1965.

3. For an interesting reading of the materiality of *The Crying of Lot 49* as a book, see T. R. Andersen, "Distorted Transmissions: Towards a Material Reading of Thomas Pynchon's *The Crying of Lot 49,*" *Orbis Litterarum* 68, no. 2 (2013). Andersen highlights how "in addition to being saturated by various media, the novel also frequently thematizes its own status as a medium" (115).

4. Raymond Williams, *Television: Technology and Cultural Form* (New York: Schocken Books, 1975).

5. These various layers of meaning have also been observed by Wendy Steiner, "Collage or Miracle: Historicism in a Deconstructed World," in *Reconstructing American Literary History,* ed. Sacvan Bercovitch (Cambridge, Mass.: Harvard University Press, 1986).

6. Ganter has also studied the relation between these two contemporary texts. "Pynchon's description of what lay behind the Watts riots suggests a new reading of one of his most enigmatic novels, *The Crying of Lot 49,* and in particular, a new reading of the novel's mysterious WASTE/Trystero conspiracy." G. Ganter, "Rioting, Textuality and *The Crying of Lot 49,*" *Found Object* 2 (1993): 67.

7. Thomas Pynchon, "A Journey into the Mind of Watts," *The New York Times Magazine,* June 12, 1966, 80. Between August 12 and December 10, 1965, a total of 606 news articles were written about Watts in the *LA Times, LA Sentinel, New York Times, New York Amsterdam News, Chicago Tribune,* and *Chicago Defender.* For a detailed analysis of this large sample see Ronald N. Jacobs, *Race, Media, and the Crisis of Civil Society: From Watts to Rodney King* (Cambridge: Cambridge University Press, 2000), 56–80.

8. This goes to show how hopeful Petillon's reading turns out to be since he described *Lot 49* as "a New Deal novel, concerned with gathering back into the American fold a 'third world' previously excluded"; see Petillon, "A Recognition of Her Errand into the Wilderness," 150.

9. J. A. Varsava, "Thomas Pynchon and Postmodern Liberalism," *Canadian Review of American Studies* 25, no. 3 (1995): 73.

10. Coincidentally, Arrabal in Spanish means "ghetto" or "poor urban periphery."

11. According to Fernando Arrabal, he visited Cornell in the late 1950s and met with Pynchon and others there. Private exchange with the author in 2004.

12. Fernando Arrabal, *El cementerio de automóviles: El arquitecto y el emperador de Asiria* (Madrid: Ediciones Cátedra, 1993), 144.

13. Pynchon, "A Journey into the Mind of Watts," 84.

14. Joe R. Feagin and Harlan Hahn, *Ghetto Revolts: The Politics of Violence in American Cities* (New York: Macmillan, 1973), 117.

15. Anderson points out the composition of this de facto apartheid in the American mid-1960s: "Over 40 percent of nonwhites were below the poverty line, and another study demonstrated that the average combined underemployed and unemployed rate for blacks was almost nine times that of whites. The contrast with white America was startling. A black Watts resident told a white from Los Angeles: 'You've got it made. Some nights on the roof of our rotten falling-down buildings we can actually see your lights shining in the distance. So near and yet so far. We want to reach out and grab it and punch it on the nose.' . . . 95 percent of suburban residents were white, and 80 percent of northern blacks lived in segregated ghettos." Terry H. Anderson, *The Sixties* (New York: Pearson Longman, 2007), 75.

16. Giorgio Agamben, *Homo Sacer: Sovereign Power and Bare Life,* trans. Daniel Heller-Roazen (Stanford, Calif.: Stanford University Press, 1998), 90.

17. Norman Mailer, "The White Negro," in Mailer, *Advertisements for Myself,* 340.

18. See Jack Barnes, *Malcolm X, Black Liberation & the Road to Workers' Power* (New York: Pathfinder, 2009), 99–106.

19. Pynchon, "A Journey into the Mind of Watts," 84.

20. A point extensively developed by some critics; among the earliest is Peter L. Abernethy, "Entropy in Pynchon's *The Crying of Lot 49,*" *Critique: Studies in Modern Fiction* 14, no. 2 (1972).

21. Frank Kermode, "Decoding the Trystero," in *Pynchon: A Collection of Critical Essays,* ed. Edward Mendelson (New Jersey: Prentice Hall, 1978), 164.

22. Ibid., 163.

23. Pynchon, "A Journey into the Mind of Watts," 84.

24. Peter Freese, *"America," Dream or Nightmare?: Reflections on a Composite Image* (Essen: Verlag Die Blaue Eule, 1990), 153.

25. Michael Harrington, *The Other America: Poverty in the United States* (New York: Macmillan, 1962), 159.

26. Kharpertian, *A Hand to Turn the Time,* 88.

27. John Krafft, "Thomas Pynchon," in Sayres, *The 60s Without Apology,* 283–86 (284).

28. Ralph Ellison, *Invisible Man* (New York: Modern Library, 1994), 7.

29. Gloria E. Anzaldúa, *Borderlands/La Frontera: The New Mestiza* (San Francisco: Aunt Lute Books, 1987), 84.

30. David Cowart, "Pynchon and the Sixties," *Critique: Studies in Contemporary Fiction* 41, no. 1 (1999): 9.

31. Jeffrey L. Decker has suggested that "a transcendent myth of national origins is endlessly deferred in Pynchon's dream text." Jeffrey L. Decker, "'The Enigma His Efforts Had Created': Thomas Pynchon and the Legacy of America," *Pynchon Notes* 28–29 (1991): 30.

32. McHale, *Postmodernist Fiction.* 9.

33. It is uncertain when this painting may have been exhibited in Mexico where Varo was exiled after the Spanish Civil War. There were a number of exhibits during the early 1960s in several private galleries; see Janet A. Kaplan, *Unexpected Journeys: The Art and Life of Remedios Varo* (New York: Abbeville, 2001), 266.

34. Adorno, *Culture Industry,* 171.

35. Sophocles, *The Oedipus Plays of Sophocles; Oedipus the King, Oedipus at Colonus, Antigone,* trans. Paul Roche (New York: Signet Classics, 2001), 23.

36. Jean Baudrillard, *Simulacra and Simulation,* trans. Sheila Faria Glaser (Ann Arbor: University of Michigan Press, 1994), 80.

37. Ganter, "Rioting, Textuality and *The Crying of Lot 49,*" 68.

38. Decker, "'The Enigma His Efforts Had Created,'" 39. In typical Americanist fashion, Cyrus Patell reads *Lot 49* in conversation with *Vineland* around the central debate between individualism and communitarism to hope once more for a nationalist, Americanist Pynchon who would be apparently hoping for "Vineland the Good"—an America that "will begin only when we find a way to develop a communitarism that will foster respect for individuality, autonomy, and self-expression, the ideals that the national narrative of individualism has always held up but has yet to uphold." Cyrus R. K. Patell, *Negative Liberties: Morrison, Pynchon, and the Problem of Liberal Ideology,* ed. Donald E. Pease (Durham, N.C.: Duke University Press, 2001), 173.

39. Fredric Jameson, *The Geopolitical Aesthetic: Cinema and Space in the World System* (Bloomington: Indiana University Press, 1995), 17.

40. Pastiche is the dominant mode of the postmodern era for Jameson, who also defines it as a blank parody; a "parody finds itself without a vocation . . . a neutral practice." Jameson, *Postmodernism,* 17.

41. Lois Tyson, "Existential Subjectivity on Trial: *The Crying of Lot 49* and the Politics of Despair," *Pynchon Notes* 28–29 (1991): 10.

42. Molly Hite, *Ideas of Order in the Novels of Thomas Pynchon* (Columbus: Ohio State University Press, 1983), 88. See also Prasanta Das, "Oedipa's Night Journey in Pynchon's *The Crying of Lot 49,*" *Notes on Contemporary Culture* 23, no. 2 (1993).

43. Tyson, "Existential Subjectivity on Trial," 13.

44. Deborah L. Madsen, *The Postmodernist Allegories of Thomas Pynchon* (New York: St. Martin's, 1991), 59.

45. The scene is a clear allusion to the students' protests at Berkeley in July 1964.

46. Dulles was a public apologist of fascism in the 1930s; see Lawrence S. Wittner, *Cold War America: From Hiroshima to Watergate* (New York: Praeger, 1974), 170. See also Albert Fried, *McCarthyism: The Great American Red Scare: A Documentary History* (New York: Oxford University Press, 1997), 4–5; Daniel Yergin, *Shattered Peace: The Origins of the Cold War and the National Security State* (Boston: Houghton Mifflin, 1977); John Prados, *Keepers of the Keys: A History of the National Security Council from Truman to Bush* (New York: Morrow, 1991).

47. For a similar critique, see Chris Hall, "'Behind the Hieroglyphic Streets': Pynchon's Oedipa Maas and the Dialectics of Reading," *Critique: Studies in Contemporary Fiction* 33, no. 1 (1991). "In *The Crying of Lot 49,* Pynchon is anxious to satirize the New Critics as the 'hidebound cops' of the text." However, and following my earlier reading of the sailor episode, I differ from Hall's Derridean view that "the constant pressure and presence of the differance finally allows Oedipa, through a simple pun, the changing significations of the letters 'dt,' an appreciation of the many worlds of experience known by an old sailor" (68).

48. "What Oedipa is doing is very much like reading a book." Kermode, "Decoding the Trystero," 163.

49. Pynchon also alludes to this mixture of subversion and consumerism in his introduction to Richard Fariña, *Been Down So Long It Looks Like Up to Me* (New York: Penguin Books, 1996).

50. *New York Times Book Review,* May 6, 1973, 36.

51. In Alexander Bloom and Wini Breines, eds., *"Takin' It to the Streets": A Sixties Reader* (New York: Oxford University Press, 1995), 13.

52. Gerard J. De Groot, "Student Protest: The Sixties and After," in *"Left, Left, Left!": The Vietnam Day Committee, 1965–66,* ed. Gerard J. De Groot (London: Longman, 1998), 89.

53. Betty Friedan, *The Feminine Mystique* (Harmondsworth, Eng.: Penguin Books, 1965), 264.

54. Sara M. Evans, *Personal Politics: The Roots of Women's Liberation in the Civil Rights Movement and the New Left* (New York: Knopf, 1979), 4.

55. Ibid.

56. Quoting Friedan, *The Feminine Mystique.* Gerd Hurm reads Oedipa as representative of housewives' victimization in patriarchal suburbs during the 1950s and 1960s. See Gerd Hurm, *Fragmented Urban Images: The American City in Modern Fiction from Stephen Crane to Thomas Pynchon* (Frankfurt am Main: Lang, 1991), 308. However, I disagree with him, as with other critics, in the suggestion that "Oedipa's concern . . . turns her into an involved citizen" (309).

57. Vance Packard, *The Hidden Persuaders* (New York: D. McKay, 1957), 12.

58. His name is also a play with the name of the proponent of LSD in the United States, the Harvard professor Timothy Leary, an echo also recognized by Petillon, "A Recognition of Her Errand into the Wilderness," 127.

59. Pynchon, "A Journey into the Mind of Watts," 84.

60. Earlier on in the decade "taking LSD was like being in a secret society. Hardly anything was being said about it publicly. As a matter of fact, LSD was: not an illegal drug, but people acted as if it were; it seemed illegal." Charles Perry and Bob Weir, *The Haight Ashbury* (New York: Wenner Books, 2005), 7.

61. Indeed, Pynchon proved to be more visionary here than some of his contemporaries, who would later on "endorse the notion that the CIA disseminated street acid en masse so as to deflate the political potency of the youth rebellion." See Martin A. Lee, Bruce Shlain, and Andrei Codrescu, *Acid Dreams: The Complete Social History of LSD: The CIA, the Sixties, and Beyond* (New York: Grove, 1986), 282.

62. Annette Kolodny and Daniel James Peters, "Pynchon's *The Crying of Lot 49:* The Novel as Subversive Experience," *Modern Fiction Studies* 19 (1973): 79.

Chapter 5. Epidermic Metamorphosis? Shedding the Nation in *Cambio de piel*

1. This is not to counter the well-established argument about the way in which images of death have been historically "nationalized" in Mexico in what Claudio Lomnitz has described as the "nationalization of a playful familiarity with and proximity to Death itself." Claudio Lomnitz-Adler, *Death and the Idea of Mexico* (New York: Zone; MIT Press, 2008), 36.

2. A number of critics have pointed to *A Change of Skin* as the "capital novel" that defines the beginning of a second period in Fuentes's works. See Carballo, "Carlos Fuentes," 574. Jorge Ruiz Basto enumerates six formal features that distinguish the novel from previous works by Fuentes. Jorge Ruiz Basto, *De la modernidad y otras creencias: En torno a Cambio de piel de Carlos Fuentes* (México, D.F.: Universidad Nacional Autónoma de México, 1992), 38–39.

3. David Gallagher, "Stifled Tiger," in *The New York Times Book Review,* February 4, 1968, 5–8. For the Spanish censor's report, see "Fuentes y la censura española," *Mundo Nuevo* 17 (1967): 90–91.

4. See his letter to the Spanish censor in "Fuentes y la censura española," 91.

5. Carlos Fuentes, "Letter to the Editor," *The New York Times,* March 3, 1968.

6. Ibid.

7. Marin, *Los narradores ante el público,* 1:147.

8. Harss and Dohmann, "Carlos Fuentes, or the New Heresy," in Harss and Dohmann, *Into the Mainstream,* 277–309.

9. Emir Rodríguez Monegal, "Entrevista con Emir Rodríguez Monegal," in *Homenaje a Carlos Fuentes: Variaciones interpretativas en torno a su obra,* ed. Helmy Fuad Giacoman (New York: Las Américas, 1971).

10. Harss and Dohmann, *Into the Mainstream,* 155.

11. Ibid., 152.

12. Honoré de Balzac, *Louis Lambert,* trans. Katherine Prescott Wormeley (Boston: Little, Brown, 1900), 10.

13. Ibid., 88.

14. Ibid., 97.

15. Michel Foucault, *Madness and Civilization: A History of Insanity in the Age of Reason,* trans. Richard Howard (London: Routledge, 1971), 107.

16. Julio Cortázar, *Rayuela,* ed. Andrés Amorós (Madrid: Ediciones Cátedra, 1984).

17. Carlos Fuentes, "*Rayuela:* La novela como caja de Pandora," *Mundo Nuevo* 9 (March 1967), 67–69.

18. Fyodor Dostoyevsky, *Notes from Underground,* trans. Michael R. Katz (New York: Norton, 2001), 3.

19. Klaus Meyer-Minnemann, "Narración homodiegética y 'segunda persona': *Cambio de piel* de Carlos Fuentes," *Acta Literaria* 9 (1984): 13–14.

20. Harss and Dohmann, *Into the Mainstream,* 308.

21. Ibid., 309.

22. Emir Rodríguez Monegal, "Entrevista con Emir Rodríguez Monegal," in *Homenaje a Carlos Fuentes,* ed. H. F. Giacoman (Madrid: Anaya, Colección Las Américas, 1971), 39.

23. Caryl Emerson has looked at the suggestion by Bakhtin that "in the realm of culture, outsideness is the most powerful lever of understanding." Caryl Emerson, "Keeping the Self Intact During the Culture Wars: A Centennial Essay for Mikhail Bakhtin," *New Literary History* 27, no. 1 (1996): 110.

24. Harss and Dohmann, *Into the Mainstream,* 309.

25. Ruiz Basto, *De la modernidad y otras creencias,* 66–73.

26. Monegal, "Entrevista," 7.

27. Margo Glantz has also discussed the feast as a process of "exorcismo" in the novel, Margo Glantz, *Repeticiones: Ensayos sobre literatura mexicana* (Xalapa: Universidad Veracruzana, 1979), 35–46 (41).

28. Susan Sontag, *Against Interpretation, and Other Essays* (New York: Anchor Books, 1990), 263–74 (263).

29. Ibid., 265.

30. A mixture that corresponds to Leslie Fiedler's 1960s definition of postmodernism. Fiedler, *Waiting for the End,* 174.

31. Jean Franco, "Modernización, resistencia y revolución: La producción literaria de los años sesenta," *Escritura: Teoría y Crítica Literarias* 3 (1977): 14.

32. Given Fuentes's customary creative concentration, it is not surprising that his definition of Cortázar's novel in his title to the *Mundo Nuevo* review, "*Rayuela:* La novela como caja de Pandora," should coincide with the title of the novel Javier is writing in *Cambio de piel.*

33. Glantz, *Repeticiones,* 42.

34. Steven Boldy, "*Cambio de piel:* Literature and Evil," *BHS* 66 (1989): 55.

35. Monegal, "Entrevista," 11.

36. Walter Benjamin, *Illuminations,* trans. Harry Zohn (London: Fontana, 1992), 249.

37. Fuentes, *Tiempo mexicano,* 13.

38. Marin, *Los narradores ante el público,* 1:140.

39. Ibid., 144.

40. Fanon, *The Wretched of the Earth,* 152–53.

41. Monegal, "Entrevista," 9.

42. Marin, *Los narradores ante el público,* 1:140. See also Carlos Fuentes, "De Quetzalcóatl a Pepsicóatl," in *Tiempo mexicano,* 17–42.

43. Marin, *Los narradores ante el público,* 1:140.

44. Fuentes, *Tiempo mexicano,* 26.

45. Sontag, *Against Interpretation,* 265.

46. Emir Rodríguez Monegal, "Entrevista con Emir Rodríguez Monegal," in *Homenaje a Carlos Fuentes,* ed. H. F. Giacoman (Madrid: Anaya, Colección Las Américas, 1971).

47. José Emilio Pacheco, *Morirás lejos* (México, D.F.: Editorial J. Mortiz, 1967).

Part Three: (Post)Colonial Enlightened Origins: Americanism Born

1. Carlos Fuentes, *La campaña* (México, D.F.: Fondo de Cultura Económica, 1990). English translation *The Campaign,* trans. Alfred J. Mac Adam (New York: Farrar, Straus and Giroux, 1991). Quotations are followed by parenthetical page references to the Spanish original and the English version, except in those cases in which the translation itself becomes problematic, where I offer my own.

2. Thomas Pynchon, *Mason & Dixon* (New York: Henry Holt, 1997). 678.

3. Henri Lefebvre, *The Production of Space* (Oxford: Blackwell, 1991), 28.

4. Carlos Fuentes, "El secreto de Diderot," in *Los novelistas como críticos,* ed. Norma Klahn and Wilfrido H. Corral (México, D.F.: Fondo de Cultura Económica, 1991), 105.

5. Zea, *Discurso desde la marginación y la barbarie.*

6. Elizabeth Jane Wall Hinds, "Sari, Sorry, and the Vortex of History: Calendar Reform, Anachronism, and Language Change in *Mason & Dixon*," *American Literary History* 12, no. 1–2 (2000): 198.

7. Theodor W. Adorno and Max Horkheimer, *Dialectic of Enlightenment*, trans. John Cumming (New York: Routledge, 1990), 92.

8. The novel has been described as a manifesto for Pynchon's Luddite agenda. David Cowart, "The Luddite Vision: *Mason & Dixon*," *American Literature: A Journal of Literary History* 71, no. 2 (1999).

9. Thomas Pynchon, "Is It O.K. to Be a Luddite?" *New York Times Book Review*, October 28, 1984.

10. Foucault, *Dits et écrits*, 4:565. Mauricio Passerin d'Entrèves points out the "deep affinity" between Foucault and the Frankfurt School's critique of instrumental reason, particularly in relation to Kant's essay. Mauricio Passerin d'Entrèves, "Critique and Enlightenment: Michel Foucault on 'Was Ist Aufklärung?'" in *The Enlightenment and Modernity*, ed. Norman Geras and Robert Wokler (New York: Saint Martin's, 2000), 189. Passerin claims for a reading of Foucault's article in tune with his more Nietzschean roots rather than as a child of the Enlightenment critiquing the "American "taming" of Foucault: "Foucault's critical ontology of ourselves, his ethos of transgression and aesthetic self-fashioning are indeed much closer to Nietzsche's vision of a transvaluation of values than to Kant's notion of maturity (Mündigkeit)" (200).

11. Immanuel Kant, "An Answer to the Question: 'What Is Enlightenment?'" in *Kant's Political Writings*, ed. H. Reiss (Cambridge: Cambridge University Press, 1970), 54.

12. A "Wahlspruch" or "device" as Foucault remarks in his "Qu'est ce que les Lumières?" Michel Foucault, *Dits et écrits: 1954–1988*, ed. Daniel Defert and François Ewald, 4 vols. (Paris: Éditions Gallimard, 1994), 4:565. For a complete study of the evolution of the motto from Horace through Gassendi and Shaftesbury to Kant, Franco Venturi, *Utopia and Reform in the Enlightenment* (Cambridge: Cambridge University Press, 1970), 6–9. Venturi asserts the predominant place of the German definition of Enlightenment: "From Kant to Cassirer and beyond, our understanding of the European Enlightenment has been dominated by the philosophical interpretation of the German Aufklärung" (1).

13. Fuentes, "El secreto de Diderot," 105.

14. Carlos Fuentes, *El espejo enterrado* (México, D.F.: Fondo de Cultura Económica, 1992), 307–8.

15. Anderson, *Imagined Communities*, 11.

16. Interestingly, Bercovitch shows the history of the American Revolution as staging a radical shift from the history of the "people," which becomes suppressed over time, to that of the "chosen people," in order to accommodate the recurrent theme of the Protestant "Errand" into the Revolution. Bercovitch, *The Rites of Assent*.

17. An instance of this classical interpretation about the relations between the British crown and the Anglo-American colonists is Peggy K. Liss, *Atlantic Empires: The Network of Trade and Revolution, 1713–1826* (Baltimore: Johns Hopkins University Press, 1983), 1–25. For an overview of the projects of reform promoted by the Iberian powers, see the second chapter, "'Rich in Intentions and Projects': Spain and Portugal," 48–74. In relation to the British colonies,

see Kevin P. Phillips, *The Cousins' Wars: Religion, Politics, and the Triumph of Anglo-America* (New York: Basic Books, 2000), 79–122.

18. "The reformers were in some senses more successful in Latin America, ultimately to their own undoing." Liss, *Atlantic Empires,* 74.

19. Bercovitch, *The Rites of Assent,* 147–67.

20. "'In the beginning' Locke had written—inadvertently earning his place as a prophet of the apocalypse—'all the world was America' and if in the end all the world should be America again, the mission of a chosen people would have been fulfilled. Virtue and commerce, liberty and culture, republic and history would have rendered their partnership perpetual by the only possible means—that of engaging all mankind perpetually in it; and in so doing would have attained that blend of millennium and utopia which was the outcome of the early modern secularization of biblical prophecy." J. G. A. Pocock, *The Machiavellian Moment: Florentine Political Thought and the Atlantic Republican Tradition* (Princeton, N.J.: Princeton University Press, 1975), 542.

21. "The preparatory steps [of the American Revolution] took place largely in England, among a group of radical Englishmen associated with non-Anglican (Nonconforming or Dissenting) Protestant denominations such as the Quakers to whom Paine's father belonged. These men transferred to secular political discourse their reliance on the individual conscience of uneducated man for which they had contended in religion." Staughton Lynd, *Intellectual Origins of American Radicalism* (Cambridge, Mass.: Harvard University Press, 1982), 19–20. For Bailyn: "a continuous flow of fresh information and ideas between Europe and the mainland colonies in America. Of these the most important were not conveyed principally by the writings of the great figures of the European Enlightenment but by the opposition publicists in British politics and the religious dissenters in constant touch with their numerous co-denominationalists in America." Bernard Bailyn, *The Ideological Origins of the American Revolution* (Cambridge, Mass.: Belknap Press of Harvard University Press, 1967), 190.

22. Frank Shuffleton, ed., *The American Enlightenment* (Rochester, N.Y.: University of Rochester Press, 1993), xi.

23. Arthur P. Whitaker, "Changing and Unchanging Interpretations of the Enlightenment in Spanish America," in *The Ibero-American Enlightenment,* ed. Alfred Owen Aldridge (Urbana: University of Illinois Press, 1971). See also Gabriel B. Paquette, *Enlightenment, Governance and Reform in Spain and Its Empire 1759-1808* (Basingstoke [England]: Palgrave Macmillan, 2008).

24. John Tate Lanning, "The Reception of the Enlightenment in Latin America," in *Latin America and the Enlightenment,* ed. Arthur Preston Whitaker (New York: Appleton-Century, 1942), 77–79. Lanning concludes his analysis by stating that "in reality, then, Americans did not so much receive the Enlightenment; they reproduced it from the sources upon which its exponents in Europe depended" (90). Pierre Chaunu also confirms that "la participation de l'Amerique aux "Lumières' du XVIIIe siècle n'est certes pas douteuse." Pierre Chaunu, *L'Amérique et les Amériques* (Paris: A. Colin, 1964), 192.

25. "The enthusiasm of Humboldt as he surveyed the intellectual status of America from Mexico and Havana to Caracas and Quito seems less strange to one who has looked at colonial writings than to writers who have looked only at nineteenth century propaganda." Roland D. Hussey, "Traces of French

Enlightenment in Colonial Hispanic America," in *Latin America and the Enlightenment,* ed. Arthur Preston Whitaker (New York: Appleton-Century, 1942), 49; Alexander von Humboldt, *Essai politique sur le royaume de la Nouvelle-Espagne,* 5 vols. (Paris: F. Schoell, 1811), 2:9–24; Gabriel B. Paquette, *Enlightened Reform in Southern Europe and Its Atlantic Colonies, c. 1750–1830* (Farnham, Eng.: Ashgate, 2009).

26. "Long before 1808 students at the University of Caracas heard openly of Bacon, Condillac, Brisson, Buffon, Descartes, Lamarck, Locke, and Newton." Similarly in Guatemala, Cuba, and Chile. Hussey, "Traces of French Enlightenment in Colonial Hispanic America," 39. "The Enlightenment clearly influenced many men in the eighteenth century, and the whole of the generation that came to maturity about 1808 and led the struggle for independence. A recent authority regards Rousseau's *Social Contract,* Quesnay's *General Maxims of Political Economy,* and Condillac's *Treatise on the Sensations* as the 'ideological sources of the revolution' in the Argentine" (ibid., 48).

27. For a discussion of the various definitions of the Hispanic versions of Enlightenment see Whitaker, "Changing and Unchanging Interpretations of the Enlightenment in Spanish America," 32–33. José Carlos Chiaramonte points to Bourbon reforms as a major influence in the birth of "new attitudes" toward science, trade, and society in the Río de la Plata. José Carlos Chiaramonte, *La ilustración en el Río de la Plata: Cultura eclesiástica y cultura laica durante el virreinato* (Buenos Aires: Puntosur Editores, 1989), 15.

28. Fuentes, *El espejo enterrado,* 255.

29. Ibid.

30. For a study of the book trade in eighteenth-century Spanish America, see Hussey, "Traces of French Enlightenment in Colonial Hispanic America," 28–30.

31. "De alguna forma el presente ensayo es una rama de la novela que me ha ocupado durante los pasados seis años." Carlos Fuentes, *Cervantes, o la crítica de la lectura* (Alcalá de Henares: Centro de Estudios Cervantinos, 1994), 36.

32. Whitaker criticizes the absence of Spanish American Enlightenment in Peter Gay's work as it "widens the gap that has always existed between the European core and the Hispanic periphery." Whitaker, "Changing and Unchanging Interpretations of the Enlightenment in Spanish America," 50. Whitaker perceives in this process the confirmation of a Eurocentric attitude toward displaced "Europeans."

33. Observing the transit of Venus over the face of the Sun from different points of the planet had been proposed as a method of finding the solar parallax by Halley in the seventeenth century. Harry Woolf, *The Transits of Venus: A Study of Eighteenth-Century Science* (Princeton, N.J.: Princeton University Press, 1959); Brooke Hindle, *The Pursuit of Science in Revolutionary America, 1735–1789* (Chapel Hill: University of North Carolina Press, 1956), particularly chapter 8 on the transit of Venus.

34. "The systematizing of nature, I am suggesting, is a European project of a new kind, a new form of what one might call planetary consciousness among Europeans." Mary Louise Pratt, *Imperial Eyes: Travel Writing and Transculturation* (London: Routledge, 1992), 29. This planetary consciousness is also associated by Pratt with the expansion of slave trade: "The systematization of nature coincides with the height of the slave trade, the plantation system, colonial

genocide in North America and South Africa, slave rebellions in the Andes, the Caribbean, North America, and elsewhere" (36).

35. Mignolo uses "local histories" as a qualified, critical synonym for the national. Walter D. Mignolo, *Local Histories/Global Designs: Coloniality, Subaltern Knowledges, and Border Thinking* (Princeton, N.J.: Princeton University Press, 2000), 317. See also Walter D. Mignolo, *The Darker Side of Western Modernity: Global Futures, Decolonial Options* (Durham & London: Duke University Press, 2011).

Chapter 6. Enlightened Nationalists: The Conquest Rides Again in *La campaña*

1. Arturo Uslar Pietri, *Las lanzas coloradas y cuentos selectos,* ed. Domingo Miliani (Caracas: Biblioteca Ayacucho, 1988), 130–31. English translation *The Red Lances,* trans. Harriet de Onís (New York: Knopf, 1963), 209.

2. Both Hussey and Lynch also mention Locke and Paine as authors that were widely read and accepted by the Spanish American colonists. Hussey, "Traces of French Enlightenment in Colonial Hispanic America," 48; R. A. Humphreys and John Lynch, *Latin American Revolutions, 1808–1826: Old and New World Origins* (Norman: University of Oklahoma Press, 1995), 33–34.

3. "The followers of Ignatius Loyola dominated the sphere of higher education in all but the royal and pontifical universities." John Tate Lanning, *Academic Culture in the Spanish Colonies* (London: Oxford University Press, 1940), 21. The expulsion of the Jesuits from all the Spanish territories in 1767 has sometimes been regarded as both the result of and the reason for Jesuit conspiracies against the Spanish monarchy. Although this conspiracy theory is seen as an exaggeration by some authors, see Whitaker, "Changing and Unchanging Interpretations of the Enlightenment in Spanish America," 34–35. In turn, their expulsion has also been associated with a Freemason conspiracy, which played against Spain's national interests, by conservative Catholic writers and Spanish liberal intellectuals alike: Magnus Mörner, *The Expulsion of the Jesuits from Latin America* (New York: Knopf, 1965). Crucially, the Jesuits influenced the formation of a Creole national conscience in the years leading to the period of independence; see Bernabé Navarro B, *Cultura mexicana moderna en el siglo XVIII* (México, D.F.: Universidad Nacional Autónoma de México, 1982). For a Marxist analysis of the economic aspects of the expulsion of the Jesuits, see Rodolfo Puiggrós, *De la colonia a la revolución* (Buenos Aires: Ediciones Leviatán, 1957), 256–67.

4. Even though in the last battle of the novel tragic and epic elements are closely interwoven: "nobody is any longer a man; each is but a lethal instrument capable of destroying, longing to destroy, bent solely on destruction . . . not men, but arms holding lances, red arms with red lances" (Arturo Uslar Pietri, *Las lanzas coloradas,* 218).

5. For Bennani, "la question de l'identité nationale constitue donc, en quelque sorte, la pièrre angulaire de la production littéraire de Carlos Fuentes." Bennani, *Monde mental et monde romanesque de Carlos Fuentes,* 370.

6. There are many studies dealing with the exchange between anthropology and political thought in the French Enlightenment; a thoroughly documented and very satisfactory survey is Michèle Duchet and Claude Blanckaert, *Anthropologie et histoire au siècle des lumières* (Paris: A. Michel, 1995).

7. Note here the careful use of the adjective "actual," rather than "moderno," to refer to Diderot as his contemporary.

8. Carlos Fuentes, *Valiente mundo nuevo: Épica, utopía y mito en la novela hispanoamericana* (México, D.F.: Fondo de Cultura Económica, 1990).

9. Chaunu, *L'Amérique et les Amériques,* 190; Tulio Halperín Donghi, *Politics Economics and Society in Argentina in the Revolutionary Period,* trans. Richard Southern (Cambridge: Cambridge University Press, 1975), 240.

10. Manuel Alvar, "Las castas coloniales en un cuadro de la Real Academia Española," *Boletín de la RAE* 78, no. 275 (1998); Magali M. Carrera, *Imagining Identity in New Spain: Race, Lineage, and the Colonial Body in Portraiture and Casta Paintings* (Austin: University of Texas Press, 2003); Ilona Katzew, *Casta Painting: Images of Race in Eighteenth-Century Mexico* (New Haven, Conn.: Yale University Press, 2004); Ilona Katzew and Susan Deans-Smith, *Race and Classification: The Case of Mexican America* (Stanford, Calif.: Stanford University Press, 2009).

11. These sixteen classical categories are "mestizo, castizo, español, mulato, morisco, albino, torna atrás, lobo, zambaigo, cambujo, albarazado, barcino, coyote, chamiso, coyote mestizo, ahí te estás." Though this classification is by no means definitive, as Mörner suggests: "este ejemplo de ningún modo agota la terminología" (89). For Mörner it is clear that there were only three clearly defined ethnic groups during the long colonial years: "había solamente tres grupos legal y socialmente definibles: 'españoles,' 'castas,' e 'indios'" and that despite the fact that "la distinción entre mestizos, por un lado, y negros, mulatos y zambos libres, por el otro, es demasiado importante como para ignorarla" (91). Magnus Mörner, *Estado, razas y cambio social en la Hispanoamérica colonial* (México, D.F.: Secretaría de Educación Pública, 1974).

12. Halperín Donghi, *Politics Economics and Society in Argentina in the Revolutionary Period,* 244.

13. For a comparison between different evolutions of the two movements, see Liss, *Atlantic Empires,* 235–36.

14. At this point, the translator used the less charged word "confusion." However, by keeping the original image, the text could have conveyed more convincingly Fuentes's point about the ideological saturation of the revolutionaries.

15. In a contemporary proposal, Fuentes advocated for an Ibero-American Federation of nations, alluding to a common postcolonial multicultural heritage: "Yet our contemporary crisis has made us realize that one thing stands on its own feet in the midst of our political and economic failures. And this is our cultural continuity, the multiracial and pluralistic culture we have created during the past 500 years." Carlos Fuentes, "Latin-America's Alternative: An Ibero-American Federation," *New Perspectives Quarterly* 8, no. 1 (1991): 16.

16. Whether the Spanish American Enlightenment and the subsequent movements for independence were more influenced by the French Enlightenment than by the English, or by their Spanish explicators, is not as clear to historians of the period as Fuentes presents it. Some authors appear openly opposed to the view of Spanish American revolutionaries as enlightened colonials who banished the reactionary metropolis. See Chaunu, who brands that viewpoint as "un stereotype"; Chaunu, *L'Amérique et les Amériques,* 193. Halperín rejects it as only appropriate for "popular histories"; Halperín Donghi, *Politics Economics*

and Society in Argentina in the Revolutionary Period, 119. A recent stupendous biography of Simón Bolívar has him reading Voltaire and Montesquieu in the mornings, even as he campaigned throughout the Venezuelan jungle; see Marie Arana, *Bolívar: American Liberator* (New York: Simon & Schuster, 2013), 253. Arana, however, acknowledges that Bolívar's conclusion that "Greater Colombia was governable only by a strong hand," was "far from the teachings of the Enlightenment," but had nevertheless become for Bolívar "the hard truth" (269) after his intense campaigns to secure independence and form a new nation-state.

17. Fuentes's approach to historiography is in tune with Dominick LaCapra's defense of an interpretative history, rejecting the over-contextualization of the neopositivistic schools; Dominick LaCapra, *History and Criticism* (Ithaca, N.Y.: Cornell University Press, 1985).

18. Pogolotti associates the parodic allegorical presentation of characters with a "vieja novela de ideas" though for her "ninguno de ellos resulta la mera encarnación de un concepto." Graziella Pogolotti, "*La campaña* de Carlos Fuentes: Una parábola de la utopía," *Literatura Mexicana* 5, no. 2 (1994): 447.

19. Julio A. Muzzio, *Diccionario histórico y biográfico de la República Argentina,* 2 vols. (Buenos Aires: J. Roldan, 1920), 1:95–96; Halperín Donghi, *Politics Economics and Society in Argentina in the Revolutionary Period,* 251–52, 318–22.

20. Muzzio, *Diccionario histórico y biográfico de la República Argentina,* 171–72; Halperín Donghi, *Politics Economics and Society in Argentina in the Revolutionary Period,* 366; Domingo Faustino Sarmiento, *Facundo: Civilización y barbarie,* ed. Susana Zanetti (Madrid: Alianza, 1988), 1:202–10.

21. Juan María Gutiérrez and Miguel Cané, *Juan Cruz Varela: Su vida, sus obras, su época* (Buenos Aires: Vaccaro, 1918).

22. "Por esta noble libertad se llama / El siglo en que vivimos / El siglo de las luces, aunque brama / Sañudo el Fanatismo, que quisiera / Muchos lustros al Tiempo en su carrera / Hacer retrogadar"; Juan Cruz Varela, *Poesías* (Buenos Aires: La Cultura Argentina, 1916), 150.

23. In Claudia Macías de Yoon, "Las falsas polifonías de un narrador monológico en *La campaña,* de Carlos Fuentes," *Texto Crítico* 4–5 (1997). The critic refers to the fact that Varela is "lost" on a number of occasions, when an "omniscient" narrator takes over the narrating voice. Macías de Yoon refers in particular to the following two passages as a proof of the inconsistency of the narration: "mientras él [Baltasar] actuaba esa noche en los dormitorios de la aristocracia, sus amigos, Dorrego y Varela, también proclamaron una junta" (Fuentes, *La campaña,* 27). And "La solitaria lejanía—¡cinco años ya!—sin ver a Dorrego y Varela y sentir que vivían juntos en la fraternidad loca" (ibid., 148). The examples provided by Macías are too ambiguous to sustain a whole theory about the lack of consistency of the narrator. It suggests rather a stylistic strategy to avoid the rather repetitious insistence on the narrator's identity ("I, Varela.").

24. Macías seems to miss Fuentes's point when she criticizes the novel's plurality because "aún faltaría el tiempo de hablar y actuar del indio, del negro, del mestizo, en donde ellos fueran seres con voz y presencia cultural." ("It would still need the time of speaking and acting of Indians, blacks and mestizos, where they would be human beings with a voice and a cultural presence.") Macías de Yoon, "Las falsas polifonías," 38.

25. Seymour Menton uses this motif to expand on the concept of the carnivalesque in the novel in the third of his six alternative readings of the novel, where he studies *La campaña* as "The Dialogic, Carnivalesque, Bakhtinian Novel" (174–77); Seymour Menton, *Latin America's New Historical Novel* (Austin: University of Texas Press, 1993), 163–85 (176).

26. There is a wide consensus among the many critics who have discussed *La campaña* about the parallel occurrence of more than one campaign in the novel, but there is little agreement as to the number of "campaigns" and their signification. Three opinion groups of critics can be distinguished depending on the number of plots in the novel identified. The two first groups identify only two main campaigns: Alonso, González Echevarría, and Menton emphasize the lover's plot as the alternative plot to the historical one. Even though it is true that the quest in search of his loved one parodies the quest for independence, this is not the decisive aspect that turns the narrative into the critique of the Enlightenment. A second line of opinion, Pogolotti's, underlines the relevance of the plot of self-discovery over the others. Finally, a last group emphasizes the concurrence of three campaigns, the novel as historical journey, the novel as bildungsroman, and the novel as a "gran metáfora antropológica sobre el destino del intelectual en Hispanoamérica" (Pogolotti, "*La campaña* de Carlos Fuentes," 89). Menton has described the novel as performing six types of novels.

27. For Maarten Van Delden, "Baltasar repeats don Quixote's discovery of the divorce between text and reality." Delden, *Carlos Fuentes, Mexico, and Modernity,* 192.

28. Alonso's emphasis. Carlos J. Alonso, *The Burden of Modernity: The Rhetoric of Cultural Discourse in Spanish America* (New York: Oxford University Press, 1998), 263.

29. According to him, the other campaign would be the military campaign. Menton, *Latin America's New Historical Novel,* 164.

30. José A. Rivas, "La historia y los papeles: *La campaña,*" *Antípodas* 8–9 (1996–97), 92. The intertextuality of *La campaña* has been widely studied in Menton, *Latin America's New Historical Novel,* 177–82; David Chávez, "Ideología y juego intertextual en *La campaña* de Carlos Fuentes," *Mester* 23, no. 2 (1994). Morson cites Don Quixote as the originating text of this subgenre, see Morson, "Parody, History, and Metaparody," in Gary Saul Morson and Caryl Emerson, *Rethinking Bakhtin: Extensions and Challenges* (Evanston, Ill.: Northwestern University Press, 1989), 75–6.

31. Gordon Brotherston suggests a reading of *Candide* as possessing a "latent Americanism," which has escaped critical attention. Gordon Brotherston, "*Candide* and Native America," in *The Enlightenment and Its Shadows,* ed. Peter Hulme and L. J. Jordanova (London: Routledge, 1990), 46.

32. The reader is told at the end of the novel that the child is the narrator's (*LC,* 258).

33. Macías de Yoon, "Las falsas polifonías," 45.

34. Roberto González Echevarría, *Alejo Carpentier: The Pilgrim at Home* (Austin: University of Texas Press, 1990), 232.

35. For an interpretation of the novel as a trip of initiation, see Menton, *Latin America's New Historical Novel,* 169–174; and Rivas, "La historia y los papeles," 93–94. For Menton, at the end of the trip the young revolutionary

has achieved maturity, without losing his enthusiasm (172). Rivas finds in this trip the character's war against himself, at the end of which Bustos has become skeptical, and bitter: in the critic's own words, "más sudamericano y más real" (Rivas, 94).

36. In his trip to Upper Peru, for instance, he "was made to feel that he was the representative of a new power as distant and despotic as Spain" (*LC*, 69).

37. These elites saw themselves as the regional intelligentsia destined to take over the rule of a new country, very much in the manner of the character Xavier Dorrego in *La campaña.* Such an assumption contradicts the views of the Spanish American colonies as necessarily "third worldly" already before their independence, which is Benedict Anderson's poor explanation of their inability to unite in a wide federation. See Anderson, *Imagined Communities,* 50–53. For a more recent discussion of the diverse and complex drive toward nation building in the nineteenth century in both Spain and Latin America see Miguel A. Centeno and Agustín Ferraro, *State and Nation Making in Latin America and Spain: Republics of the Possible* (Cambridge: Cambridge University Press, 2013).

38. Maarten Van Delden has succinctly described *La campaña* as "on one level a satire of the attempt to apply Enlightenment ideals to the specific conditions of Spanish America in the early nineteenth century. It illustrates the thesis that many of Spanish America's ills are attributable to the profound disjunction between, on the one hand, the ideas of rhetoric, the laws and books of a small educated elite, and on the other hand the practices and actions, the beliefs and customs of the vast majority of the continent's people." Delden, *Carlos Fuentes, Mexico, and Modernity,* 187.

39. Fuentes, *Tiempo mexicano.* 125.

40. See Valiente Mundo Nuevo, *Épica, utopía y mito en la novela hispanoamericana,* 14–18, for a detailed analysis of the effects of these two separate nations.

41. There is also a constant reference to French republican forms. See Sarmiento, *Facundo,* 268, for an example of fluvial work in the United States as "civilizing." For a critique of Sarmiento by Fuentes, see Fuentes, *Valiente mundo nuevo,* 18.

42. Macías de Yoon fails to understand that Fuentes is trying to find in Bakhtinian dialogism a provisional solution to the debate civilization/barbarism. She affirms that Fuentes is "más cerca todavía del conflicto 'civilización o barbarie' . . . que de la problematización del discurso monológico bajo los términos de Bajtín." ("Still closer to the conflict 'civilization and barbarity' . . . than to the problematization of the monologic discourse under Bakhtin's terms"). Macías de Yoon, "Las falsas polifonías," 37.

43. As one of the characters reminds us in *La campaña,* concepts such as "popular sovereignty" were already available to Spanish intellectuals.

44. "Estaba convencido de que había llegado al pasado más remoto, al origen de todas las cosas, y que este origen mágico, de brujería y engaño, no era el de una perfecta asimilación del hombre con la naturaleza, sino, nuevamente, un divorcio intolerable, una separación que lo hería en lo más seguro de sus convicciones ilustradas" (*LC,* 97).

45. On the El Dorado cavern as a form of inverse Platonism, see Estela Saint-Andre, "Acerca de la escritura y la lectura en *La campaña* de Carlos Fuentes," *Revista de Literaturas Modernas* 27 (1994): 134.

Chapter 7. Surveying American Exceptionalism in *Mason & Dixon*

The first chapter epigraph is from Washington Irving, "Traits of Indian Character," in *The Sketch Book of Geoffrey Crayon* (London: John Murray, 1820), 235–36.

The second chapter epigraph is from "Verses on the Prospect of Planting Arts and Learning in America" (appeared in a private letter in 1726, first published in 1752). George Berkeley, "Verses on the Prospect of Planting Arts and Learning in America," in *The Works of George Berkeley, Bishop of Cloyne,* ed. A. A. Luce and T. E. Jesson (London: Nelson, 1967). Another rendering for the last verse reads: "The world's great effort is the last," 370.

1. Irving, "Traits of Indian Character," 235. The idea that Native Americans were condemned to either extermination or absorption is thoroughly studied in D'Arcy McNickle, *Native American Tribalism: Indian Survivals and Renewals* (New York: published for the Institute of Race Relations by Oxford University Press, 1973).

2. These two terms are often used to describe some of the ideological debates associated with Pynchon's fiction. They are taken from *Gravity's Rainbow,* 555, where Lt. Tyrone, Slothrop's first American ancestor, William Slothrop, is presented as a dissenter of Puritan theology—itself a dissenting creed. Steven Weisenburger has succinctly illustrated the biographical subtext of this reference to Pynchon's Puritan ancestor, William Pynchon. Steven C. Weisenburger, *A Gravity's Rainbow Companion: Sources and Contexts for Pynchon's Novel* (Athens: University of Georgia Press, 1990), 237–38.

3. Bercovitch, *The Rites of Assent.* See particularly "The Ritual of Consensus," 29–67, and "The Typology of Mission, from Edwards to Independence," 147–67 (158). In an earlier version of that essay Bercovitch claims that "America was not a territorial definition (except in the vague sense of 'New World'), but the symbol of an ideological consensus." Bercovitch, *The American Jeremiad,* 161. "American, after all, was a consensual term. Like biblical exegesis and the Puritan rhetoric of ambiguity, it encouraged multiplicity of meaning while precluding contradiction in fact" (170).

4. Bercovitch, *The Rites of Assent,* 53.

5. Ibid., 185.

6. In his chapter on *Mason & Dixon,* David Seed also concludes that "the novel demonstrates a postcolonial alertness to mapping as a culturally inflected exercise, an exercise in territorial appropriation where the first casualties to be displaced are the native Americans." David Seed, "Mapping the Course of Empire in the New World," in *Pynchon and Mason & Dixon,* ed. Brooke Horvath and Irving Malin (Newark: University of Delaware Press, 2000), 99.

7. Pynchon, *Mason & Dixon,* 678.

8. William Logan, "Pynchon in the Poetic," *Southern Review* 83, no. 4 (1998).

9. Bérubé, *Marginal Forces/Cultural Centers,* 310. Bérubé is using here an expression coined by Nina Baym, "Melodramas of Beset Manhood: New Theories of American Fiction Exclude Women Authors," in *The New Feminist Criticism: Essays on Women, Literature and Theory,* ed. Elaine Showalter (New York: Pantheon Books, 1985).

10. Bercovitch, *The American Jeremiad.* In the note to 204, Bercovitch explicitly mentions Pynchon as one of the modern practitioners of the American anti-jeremiad.

11. Bérubé, *Marginal Forces/Cultural Centers,* 309.

12. In Pynchon's case, this is true even from a biographical viewpoint; see comments on his Puritan ancestors by Weisenburger and Tanner.

13. Pease, *The New American Exceptionalism,* 141.

14. "Could we ever narrativize without moralizing?" asks Hayden White in White, *The Content of the Form,* 25.

15. Douglas Keesey, "*Mason & Dixon* on the Line: A Reception Study," *Pynchon Notes* 36–39 (1995–96 [1998]), 171. Linda Hutcheon's defense of parody in historiographic metafiction as a way of articulating a postmodern political critique clearly resonates in this assertion. In reference to Pynchon, Hutcheon affirms: "Pynchon's intertextually overdetermined, discursively overloaded fictions both parody and enact the totalizing tendency of all discourses to create systems and structures" Hutcheon, *Poetics of Postmodernism,* 133.

16. White, *The Content of the Form,* 25.

17. Jarvis, *Postmodern Cartographies,* 53.

18. Not unlike those described by Anderson, *Imagined Communities,* 55.

19. "We can now be certain that Charles Mason, the astronomer, was born at Wherr in the parish of Bisley in Gloucestershire in the early part of 1728, for he was baptized at Sapperton Church on 1 May 1728." In H. W. Robinson, "A Note on Charles Mason's Ancestry and His Family," *Proceedings of the American Philosophical Society* 93, no. 2 (1949): 135.

20. For a short account of Jeremiah Dixon's life, see H. W. Robinson, "Jeremiah Dixon (1733–1779)—A Biographical Note." In *Proceedings of the American Philosophical Society* 94, no. 3 (1950). "Jeremiah Dixon was born at Bishop Auckland on 27 July 1733" (272). See also H. P. Hollis, "Jeremiah Dixon and his Brother," *Journal of the British Astronomy Association,* 44, no. 8 (1934): 294–99.

21. Some available sources are Thomas D. Cope, "Collecting Source Material About Charles Mason and Jeremiah Dixon," *Proceedings of the American Philosophical Society,* 92, no. 2 (1948): 111–14 and, by the same author, "First Scientific Expedition of Mason and Dixon," *Pennsylvania History* 12, no. 1 (1945), 24–33; R. H. Heindel, "An Early Episode in the Career of Mason and Dixon," *Pennsylvania History,* 6, no. 1 (1939): 20–24; C. R. Weld, *History of the Royal Society* (London, 1848), vol. 2, 11–17.

22. For the dates and place of Charles Mason's burial, see Thomas D. Cope, "Collecting Source Material About Charles Mason and Jeremiah Dixon," *Proceedings of the American Philosophical Society* 92, no. 2 (1948): 114. Cope also notes about Mason: "He was laid to rest on October 26, 1786, in Christ Church Burying Ground at Fifth and Arch Streets, Philadelphia. The grave is not marked and its exact location is unknown. Benjamin Franklin and his wife Deborah rest nearby." Thomas D. Cope, "A Mountain in Perthshire," *Pennsylvania History* 21, no. 7 (1954): 231.

23. Charles Mason's *Journal* was found at Halifax, Nova Scotia, in 1860. See the "Preface" to Charles Mason and Jeremiah Dixon, *The Journal of Charles Mason and Jeremiah Dixon,* ed. A. Hughett Mason (Philadelphia: American Philosophical Society, 1969), iv.

24. Foucault, *Madness and Civilization.*

25. H. W. Robinson, "Jeremiah Dixon (1733–1779): A Biographical Note," *Proceedings of the American Philosophical Society* 94, no. 3 (1950): 272.

26. It is still unclear who did Berkeley himself refer to when he talked about this offspring; was it the creoles or the Indians?

27. Jarvis, *Postmodern Cartographies,* 58.

28. The ideological defense of unconquered territories is carried out through this opposition of "subjunctive" versus "indicative," rather than through that "sharp line between past and present" noticed by Hinds, "Sari, Sorry, and the Vortex of History," 206. A detailed explanation of the uses of the subjunctive in the novel is Brian McHale, "*Mason & Dixon* in the Zone, or a Brief Poetics of Pynchon-Space," in *Pynchon and Mason & Dixon,* ed. Brooke Hovarth and Irving Malin (Newark: University of Delaware Press, 2000).

29. The *Journal* is written in the first person by Charles Mason: "Thus ends my restless progress in America" (211).

30. Mason and Dixon, *The Journal of Charles Mason and Jeremiah Dixon,* 66. I have italicized the section of Charles Mason's entry quoted by Cherrycoke in the novel.

31. Another aspect of Pynchon's accurate historical research: "Dixon wore military uniform from 1760 until his death consisting of a long red coat and a cocked hat"; in Robinson, "Jeremiah Dixon (1733–1779): A Biographical Note," 273.

32. "Whether Dixon accompanied him is not clear." Thomas D. Cope, "The Stargazers' Stone," *Pennsylvania History* 6, no. 4 (1939): 206.

33. The epigraph for this section is from Genevieve Blatt's preface to Hubertis M. Cummings, *The Mason and Dixon Line: Story for a Bicentenary* (Harrisburg, Pa.: Commonwealth of Pennsylvania, 1962), iv.

34. Despite efforts to directly contact this author, I have been unable to this date to trace her present address.

35. Barbara Susan Lefever, *The Stargazers, Story of Mason and Dixon: An Historical Biographical Novel by Barbara Susan Lefever* (York, Pa.: the author, 1986), 326.

36. The other published material by the surveyors can be found in *Philosophical Transactions of the Royal Society of London* 52 (1761–62), Article LX, "Observations made at the Cape of Good Hope" (read April 22, 1762), 378–94; Article LXI, "Latitude of the Observatory at the Cape of Good Hope" (read June 17, 1762), 395; Vol. 58: 1768; Article XLII, "Observations for determining the Length of a Degree of Latitude, in the Provinces of Maryland and Pennsylvania, in North America" (read November 24, 1768), 274–328; Article XLII, "Astronomical Observations, made in the Forks of the River Brandiwine [*sic*] in Pennsylvania, for determining the going of a Clock sent thither by the Royal Society, in order to find the Difference of Gravity between the Royal Observatory at Greenwich, and the Place where the Clock was set up in Pennsylvania: To which are added, an Observation of the End of an Eclipse of the Moon, and some Immersions of Jupiter's First Satellite observed at the Same Place in Pennsylvania" (read December 15, 1768), 329–35.

37. John H. B. Latrobe, *The History of Mason and Dixon's Line Contained in an Address* ([Philadelphia]: Press of the Historical Society of Pennsylvania, 1855).

38. Unmentioned albeit clearly suggested, the train is an obvious reference given Latrobe's personal investments in the Virginia/Ohio train company. See

John E. Semmes, *John H. B. Latrobe and His Times, 1803–1891* (Baltimore: Norman, Remington, 1917).

39. "The slavery question of the United States is a question of interest; and its solution will be found in the increasing white population of the country, the consequent reduction of wages, and the great ultimate result—the production, by free labor, of the chief staples of the country cheaper than they can be produced by slave-labor." Latrobe, *The History of Mason and Dixon's Line Contained in an Address,* 6.

40. Latrobe here slips one of his many historical inaccuracies because both Mason and Dixon lived to see the first episodes of the American Revolution. Charles Mason himself died in Philadelphia in 1786.

41. David Bidney interestingly suggests the historical continuities between the two: "It is of interest in this connection [contemporary reassessment of attitudes toward Indians] to reflect that the typical rationalization employed by nineteenth-century Americans to validate their claim to expansion on the North American continent and to exclude the Indians from participating in their civilization, was duplicated in the twentieth century by the claims of land-hungry nations of Europe, Germany and Italy, before the Second World War. In their quest for *Lebensraum* similar claims were made as to the rights of powerful civilized peoples at the expense of the so-called less civilized, weaker peoples." David Bidney, "The Idea of the Savage in North American Ethnohistory," in *The American Enlightenment,* ed. Frank Shuffelton (Rochester, N.Y.: University of Rochester Press, 1993), 102.

42. "A story is told that one day, whilst in America, Dixon came across a slave driver mercilessly beating a poor black woman. Going up to him he said: 'Thou must not do that!' He received the curt answer: 'You be d. . .d! Mind your own business.' Dixon's reply was: 'If thou doesn't desist I'll thrash thee!' Then righteous wrath overcame his Quaker principles. He was a tall and powerful man, and an imposing figure, so without more ado he seized the slave-driver's whip and with it gave him the sound thrashing that he richly deserved. Dixon kept the whip as a trophy and took it back with him to Cockfield, where it was long regarded as a family treasure." In H. W. Robinson, "Jeremiah Dixon," 273.

Conclusion. Beyond the Nation

1. Sommer, *Foundational Fictions,* 27. Throughout his book *Mexican Masculinities* Robert McKee Irwin argues that Mexican literary history does not adhere fully to Sommer's assumption: "While gender, particularly masculinity, was uniformly a key term in this discourse, notions of nation were not constructed only through allegories of male-female bonding." Robert McKee Irwin, *Mexican Masculinities* (Minneapolis: University of Minnesota Press, 2003), 4.

2. Kwame Anthony Appiah, "Is the Post- in Postmodernism the Post- in Postcolonial?" *Critical Inquiry* 17, no. 2 (1991), 353.

3. "No quiso mirar hacia abajo porque temía descubrir algo horrible que quizás sólo desde el cielo podía verse; ya no había país, ya no había México, el país era una ficción o, más bien, un sueño mantenido por un puñado de locos que alguna vez creyeron en la existencia de México." Carlos Fuentes, *La frontera de cristal: Una novela en nueve cuentos* (Madrid: Alfaguara, 1995), 204.

4. Fuentes, *En esto creo.*

5. Jürgen Habermas, *The Postnational Constellation: Political Essays,* trans. Max Pensky (Cambridge, Eng.: Polity, 2007), 56–57.

6. See Paul James, "Dark Nationalism or Transparent Postnationalism?" in *Global Matrix: Nationalism, Globalism and State-Terrorism,* ed. Tom Nairn and Paul James (London: Pluto, 2005).

7. Julia Kristeva, *Nations Without Nationalism* (New York: Columbia University Press, 1993), 16.

8. James, "Dark Nationalism or Transparent Postnationalism?" 117.

9. Christopher Domínguez Michael, *Diccionario crítico de la literatura mexicana,* 1955–2005 (México, D.F.: Fondo de Cultura Económica, 2007), 137.

10. This discussion was part of the obituary I published in the wake of Fuentes's death in 2012. Pedro García-Caro, "The Death of Carlos Fuentes: An Impossible Silencing Act. In Memoriam (1928–2012)," *A Contracorriente* 9, no. 3 (2012).

11. At the center of this novel, as in other earlier works by Fuentes, is the ethical choice between the loyalty to the genetic family or to the family of interests, and thus a restaging of the issue of inheritance and democracy resonant of his earlier works. This interpretation counters the drift away from this preoccupation with inheritance and family noted by Boldy. Steven Boldy, "De la afrenta al melodrama: La familia, la violencia y el crimen en las últimas obras de Carlos Fuentes," *Mexican Studies/Estudios Mexicanos* 28, no. 2 (2012): 262.

12. See Deborah N. Cohn, *The Latin American Literary Boom and U.S. Nationalism During the Cold War* (Nashville: Vanderbilt University Press, 2012).

13. Thomas H. Schaub, "*The Crying of Lot 49* and Other California Novels," in *The Cambridge Companion to Thomas Pynchon,* ed. Inger Dalsgaard, Luc H. Herman, and Brian McHale (Cambridge: Cambridge University Press, 2012), 40.

14. David Cowart, *Thomas Pynchon & the Dark Passages of History* (Athens: University of Georgia Press, 2011), 127.

15. Linda Hutcheon, "Comparative Literature: Congenitally Contrarian," in *Comparative Literature in an Age of Globalization,* ed. Haun Saussy (Baltimore, Md.: Johns Hopkins University Press, 2006), 225.

16. For a thorough study of class warfare in the settling of the West and the Ludlow Massacre, see Scott Martelle, *Blood Passion: The Ludlow Massacre and Class War in the American West* (New Brunswick, N.J.: Rutgers University Press, 2007).

17. Thomas Dixon, *The Reconstruction Trilogy: The Leopard's Spots; The Clansman; The Traitor,* ed. Sam Dickson (Newport Beach, Calif.: Noontide, 1994). I am referring to the scene in Dixon's novel *The Clansman* when the war hero (in both Mexico and the Civil War), Ben Cameron, addresses his fellow Klan members: "We are going to make a daring experiment of the utmost importance . . . There are laws of our race, old before this Republic was born in the souls of white freemen. The fiat of fools has repealed on papers these laws. Your fathers who created this Nation were first Conspirators, then Revolutionists, now Patriots and Saints. I need tonight ten volunteers to lead the coming clansmen over this county and disarm every Negro in it" (401). *The Birth of a Nation* was a direct adaptation of Dixon's novel: D. W. Griffith, *The Birth of a Nation* (Southgate, Mich.: Triad Productions, 2009).

18. Quentin Tarantino, *Django Unchained* (Beverly Hills, Calif.: Anchor Bay Entertainment, 2013).

19. Pynchon, *Against the Day.*

20. Pynchon, *Inherent Vice,* 101.

21. James Lovelock, *Gaia, a New Look at Life on Earth* (Oxford: Oxford University Press, 1979). Even more interestingly for this connection, see his later *The Revenge of Gaia: Earth's Climate Crisis and the Fate of Humanity* (New York: Basic Books, 2006).

22. One of the earliest definitions of postmodernism in this environmental framework is perhaps Hassan's: "What concerns us now is the Denaturalization of the Planet and the End of Man. We are, I believe, inhabitants of another Time and another Space, and we no longer know what response is adequate to our reality. In a sense we have all learned to become minimalists—of that time and space we can call our own—although the globe may have become our village." Hassan, *The Postmodern Turn,* 39.

23. Guillermo Arriaga Jordán, *The Burning Plain* ([Los Angeles]: Magnolia Home Entertainment, 2010).

24. Palmeri, *Satire in Narrative.* Particularly interesting as a classification of theories of satire that allude to this Edenic past is Ball, *Satire & the Postcolonial Novel,* 9–40.

BIBLIOGRAPHY

Abernethy, Peter L. "Entropy in Pynchon's *The Crying of Lot 49.*" *Critique: Studies in Modern Fiction* 14, no. 2 (1972): 18–33.

Adorno, Theodor W. *Culture Industry.* Edited by J. M. Bernstein. London: Routledge, 2001.

Adorno, Theodor W., and Max Horkheimer. *Dialectic of Enlightenment.* Translated by John Cumming. New York: Routledge, 1990.

Agamben, Giorgio. *Homo Sacer: Sovereign Power and Bare Life.* Translated by Daniel Heller-Roazen. Stanford, Calif.: Stanford University Press, 1998.

Aguila, Yves. *Écrire le Mexique: Carlos Fuentes, La región más transparente.* Paris: Ed. Messene, 1998.

Aizenberg, Edna. "The Untruths of the Nation: Petals of Blood and Fuentes's *The Death of Artemio Cruz. Research in African Literatures* 21, no. 4 (1990): 85–103.

Aleksandrov, Grigoriĭ Vasil'evich, and Sergei Eisenstein. 1985. *¡Que viva México!.* New York: IFEX Films.

Alonso, Ana María. "Conforming Disconformity: "'Mestizaje,' Hybridity, and the Aesthetics of Mexican Nationalism." *Cultural Anthropology* 19, no. 4 (2004): 459–90.

Alonso, Carlos J. *The Burden of Modernity: The Rhetoric of Cultural Discourse in Spanish America.* New York: Oxford University Press, 1998.

Altamirano, Ignacio M. "Prólogo." In *El romancero nacional,* edited by Guillermo Prieto. México, D.F.: Oficina tip. de la secretaría de fomento, 1885.

Alvar, Manuel. "Las castas coloniales en un cuadro de la Real Academia Española." *Boletín de la RAE* 78, no. 275 (1998): 307–38.

Andersen, T. R. "Distorted Transmissions: Towards a Material Reading of Thomas Pynchon's *The Crying of Lot 49.*" *Orbis Litterarum* 68, no. 2 (2013): 110–42.

Anderson, Benedict. "El efecto tranquilizador del fratricidio: O de como las naciones imaginan sus genealogías." In *El nacionalismo en México,* edited by Cecilia Noriega Elío. Zamora: Colegio de Michoacán, 1992.

———. *Imagined Communities: Reflections on the Origin and Spread of Nationalism.* London: Verso Books, 1983, 1991.

———. *The Spectre of Comparisons: Nationalism, Southeast Asia, and the World.* London: Verso, 1998.

Anderson, Terry H. *The Sixties.* New York: Pearson Longman, 2007.

Anzaldúa, Gloria E. *Borderlands/La Frontera: The New Mestiza.* San Francisco: Aunt Lute Books, 1987.

Appadurai, Arjun. *Modernity at Large: Cultural Dimensions of Globalization.* Minneapolis: University of Minnesota Press, 1996.

Appiah, Kwame Anthony. "Is the Post- in Postmodernism the Post- in Postcolonial?" *Critical Inquiry* 17, no. 2 (1991): 336–57.

Arana, Marie. *Bolívar: American Liberator.* New York: Simon & Schuster, 2013.

Arrabal, Fernando. *El cementerio de automóviles: El arquitecto y el emperador de Asiria.* Madrid: Ediciones Cátedra, 1993.

Arriaga Jordán, Guillermo. *The Burning Plain.* [Los Angeles]: Magnolia Home Entertainment, 2010.

Aub, Max. *Ensayos mexicanos.* México, D.F.: Universidad Nacional Autónoma de México, 1974.

Bailyn, Bernard. *The Ideological Origins of the American Revolution.* Cambridge, Mass.: Belknap Press of Harvard University Press, 1967.

Baker, Jeffrey S. "A Democratic Pynchon: Counterculture, Counterforce and Participatory Democracy." *Pynchon Notes* 32–33 (1993): 99–131.

Bakhtin, M. M. "Epic and Novel: Toward a Methodology for the Study of the Novel." Translated by Caryl Emerson and Michael Holquist. In *The Dialogic Imagination: Four Essays,* edited by Michael Holquist, 3–40. Austin: University of Texas Press, 1981.

Balibar, Etienne, and Immanuel Wallerstein. *Race, Nation, Class: Ambiguous Identities.* Translated by Chris Turner. London: Verso, 1991.

Ball, John Clement. *Satire & the Postcolonial Novel: V. S. Naipaul, Chinua Achebe, Salman Rushdie.* New York: Routledge, 2003.

Balzac, Honoré de. *History of the Thirteen.* Translated by Herbert J. Hunt. Harmondsworth, Eng.: Penguin Books, 1974.

Barnes, Jack. *Malcolm X, Black Liberation & the Road to Workers Power.* New York: Pathfinder, 2009.

Bartra, Roger. *La jaula de la melancolía: Identidad y metamorfosis del mexicano.* México, D.F.: Grijalbo, 2000.

———. *La sangre y la tinta: Ensayos sobre la condición postmexicana.* México, D.F.: Océano, 1999.

Baudrillard, Jean. *Simulacra and Simulation.* Translated by Sheila Faria Glaser. Ann Arbor: University of Michigan Press, 1994.

Baym, Nina. "Melodramas of Beset Manhood: New Theories of American Fiction Exclude Women Authors." In *The New Feminist Criticism: Essays on Women, Literature and Theory,* edited by Elaine Showalter, 63–80. New York: Pantheon Books, 1985.

Bell-Villada, Gene H. *García Márquez: el hombre y su obra.* Barcelona and Miami: Ediciones B, 2012.

Benjamin, Walter. *Illuminations.* Translated by Harry Zohn. London: Fontana, 1992.

Bennani, Aziza. *Monde mental et monde romanesque de Carlos Fuentes.* Rabat: Université Mohammed V, 1985.

Bennington, Geoffrey. "Postal Politics and the Institution of the Nation." In *Nation and Narration,* edited by Homi Bhabha, 121–37. London: Routledge, 1990.

Bercovitch, Sacvan. *The American Jeremiad.* Madison: University of Wisconsin Press, 1978.

———. *The Rites of Assent.* New York: Routledge, 1992.

Berkeley, George. "Verses on the Prospect of Planting Arts and Learning in America." In *The Works of George Berkeley, Bishop of Cloyne,* edited by A. A. Luce and T. E. Jesson, 370–73. London: Nelson, 1967.

Berman, Marshall. *All That Is Solid Melts into Air: The Experience of Modernity.* New York: Penguin Books, 1988.

Bernal, Ignacio. *Tenochtitlán en una isla.* México, D.F.: Secretaría de Educación Pública, 1972.

Bérubé, Michael. *Marginal Forces/Cultural Centers: Tolson, Pynchon, and the Politics of the Canon.* Ithaca, N.Y.: Cornell University Press, 1992.

Bhabha, Homi K. *Nation and Narration.* London: Routledge, 1990.

Bidney, David. "The Idea of the Savage in North American Ethnohistory." In *The American Enlightenment,* edited by Frank Shuffelton, 97–102. Rochester, N.Y.: University of Rochester Press, 1993.

Bloom, Alexander, and Wini Breines, eds. *"Takin' It to the Streets": A Sixties Reader.* New York: Oxford University Press, 1995.

Boldy, Steven. "*Cambio de piel:* Literature and Evil." *BHS* 66 (1989): 55–72.

———. "De la afrenta al melodrama: La familia, la violencia y el crimen en las últimas obras de Carlos Fuentes." *Mexican Studies/Estudios Mexicanos* 28, no. 2 (2012): 243–63.

———. "Fathers and Sons in Fuentes's *La muerte de Artemio Cruz.*" *BHS* 61 (1984): 31–40.

———. *Memoria mexicana.* México, D.F.: Taurus, 1998.

Bonfil, Carlos. "2014: olvidar la soberanía." *La Jornada,* December 29, 2013. Accessed December 30, 2013, http://www.jornada.unam.mx/2013/12/29/opinion/a09a1esp.

Bonfil Batalla, Guillermo. *México Profundo: Reclaiming a Civilization.* Translated by Philip Adams Dennis. Austin: University of Texas Press, 1996.

———. *México profundo: Una civilización negada.* México, D.F.: Grijalbo, 1990.

Bowskill, Sarah E. L. *Gender, Nation and the Formation of the Twentieth-Century Mexican Literary Canon.* London: Legenda, 2011.

Breen, Keith, and Shane O'Neill. *After the Nation? Critical Reflections on Nationalism and Postnationalism.* New York: Palgrave Macmillan, 2010.

Brennan, Timothy. "The National Longing for Form." In *Nation and Narration,* edited by Homi Bhabha, 44–70. London: Routledge, 1990.

Brickhouse, Anna. *Transamerican Literary Relations and Nineteenth-Century Public Sphere.* Cambridge: Cambridge University Press, 2004.

Brooks, Peter. *Reading for the Plot: Design and Intention in Narrative.* Cambridge, Mass.: Harvard University Press, 1992.

Brotherston, Gordon. "*Candide* and Native America." In *The Enlightenment and Its Shadows,* edited by Peter Hulme and L. J. Jordanova, 35–46. London: Routledge, 1990.

Brown, Joan Lipman. *Confronting Our Canons: Spanish and Latin American Studies in the 21st Century.* Lewisburg, Pa.: Bucknell University Press, 2010.

Brown, Wendy. *Walled States, Waning Sovereignty.* New York; Cambridge, Mass.: Zone Books; MIT Press, 2010.

Brushwood, John Stubbs. *Mexico in Its Novel; A Nation's Search for Identity.* Austin: University of Texas Press, 1966.

Burdick, Eugene, and William J. Lederer. *The Ugly American.* New York: Norton, 1999.

Calderón, Héctor, and José David Saldívar. *Criticism in the Borderlands: Studies in Chicano Literature, Culture, and Ideology, Post-Contemporary Interventions.* Durham, N.C.: Duke University Press, 1991.

Campbell, Elizabeth. "Metaphor and *V.*: Metaphysics in the Mirror." *Pynchon Notes* 22–23 (1988): 57–69.

Canclini, Néstor García. *Culturas híbridas: Estrategias para entrar y salir de la modernidad.* Buenos Aires: Ediciones Paidós, 2001.

Carballo, Emmanuel. "Carlos Fuentes." In *Protagonistas de la literatura mexicana,* 534–76. México, D.F.: SEP, 1986.

Carrera, Magali M. *Imagining Identity in New Spain: Race, Lineage, and the Colonial Body in Portraiture and Casta Paintings.* Austin: University of Texas Press, 2003.

Cassola, Arnold. "Pynchon, *V.*, and the Malta Connection." In *Pynchon Malta and Wittgenstein,* edited by P. Bianchi, Arnold Cassola, and Peter Serracino Inglott, 15–38. Malta: Malta University Publishers, 1994.

Castellanos, Rosario. *Juicios sumarios: Ensayos.* Xalapa: Universidad Veracruzana, 1966.

Centeno, Miguel A. and Agustín Ferraro. *State and Nation Making in Latin America and Spain: Republics of the Possible.* Cambridge: Cambridge University Press, 2013.

Celmer Jr., Paul W. "Pynchon's *V.* and the Rhetoric of the Cold War." *Pynchon Notes,* no. 32–33 (1993): 5–32.

Chambers, Judith. *Thomas Pynchon.* New York: Twayne, 1992.

Chaunu, Pierre. *L'Amérique et les Amériques.* Paris: A. Colin, 1964.

Chávez, David. "Ideología y juego intertextual en *La campaña* de Carlos Fuentes." *Mester* 23, no. 2 (1994): 31–43.

Cheah, Pheng, and Bruce Robbins. *Cosmopolitics: Thinking and Feeling Beyond the Nation.* Minneapolis: University of Minnesota Press, 1998.

Chetwynd, Ali. "The Cambridge Companion to Thomas Pynchon." *College Literature* 39, no. 4 (2012): 142–45.

Chevigny, Bell Gale, and Gari Laguardia. *Reinventing the Americas: Comparative Studies of Literature of the United States and Spanish America.* Cambridge: Cambridge University Press, 1986.

Chiaramonte, José Carlos. *La ilustración en el Río de la Plata: Cultura eclesiástica y cultura laica durante el Virreinato.* Buenos Aires: Puntosur Editores, 1989.

Chomsky, Noam. *American Power and the New Mandarins.* Harmondsworth, Eng.: Penguin, 1969.

Chomsky, Noam, Heinz Dieterich, Denise Glasbeek, and Julian Sempill. *Latin America: From Colonization to Globalization.* Melbourne: Ocean, 1999.

Chorba, Carrie C. *Mexico, from Mestizo to Multicultural: National Identity and Recent Representations of the Conquest.* Nashville, Tenn.: Vanderbilt University Press, 2007.

Cifuentes, Bárbara, and Lucina García. *Letras sobre voces: Multilingüismo a través de la historia.* México, D.F.: CIESAS; INI, 1998.

Claussen, Dane S. *Anti-Intellectualism in American Media: Magazines & Higher Education.* New York: P. Lang, 2004.

Cohn, Deborah N. *History and Memory in the Two Souths: Recent Southern and Spanish American Fiction.* Nashville, Tenn.: Vanderbilt University Press, 1999.

———. *The Latin American Literary Boom and U.S. Nationalism During the Cold War.* Nashville, Tenn.: Vanderbilt University Press, 2012.

Collado, Francisco. "History and Metafiction: *V.*'s Impossible Cognitive Quest." *Atlantis* 15, no. 1 (1993): 61–77.

Collingwood, Robin George. *The Idea of History.* Edited by Jan Van Der Dussen. Oxford: Oxford University Press, 1994.

Cooley, Ronald W. "The Hothouse or the Street: Imperialism and Narrative in Pynchon's *V.*" *Modern Fiction Studies* 39 (1993): 307–25.

Cope, Thomas D. "Collecting Source Material About Charles Mason and Jeremiah Dixon." *Proceedings of the American Philosophical Society* 92, no. 2 (1948): 111–14.

———. "A Mountain in Perthshire." *Pennsylvania History* 21, no. 7 (1954): 228–38.

———. "The Stargazers' Stone." *Pennsylvania History* 6, no. 4 (1939): 205–20.

Corona, Ignacio, and Alejandro Madrid, eds. *Postnational Musical Identities: Cultural Production, Distribution, and Consumption in a Globalized Scenario.* Lanham, Md.: Lexington Books, 2008.

Cortázar, Julio. *Rayuela.* Edited by Andrés Amorós. Madrid: Ediciones Cátedra, 1984.

Cowart, David. "The Luddite Vision: *Mason & Dixon.*" *American Literature: A Journal of Literary History* 71, no. 2 (1999): 341–63.

———. "Pynchon and the Sixties." *Critique: Studies in Contemporary Fiction* 41, no. 1 (1999): 3–13.

———. *Thomas Pynchon & the Dark Passages of History.* Athens: University of Georgia Press, 2011.

———. *Thomas Pynchon: The Art of Allusion.* Carbondale: Southern Illinois University Press, 1980.

Cummings, Hubertis M. *The Mason and Dixon Line: Story for a Bicentenary.* Harrisburg: Commonwealth of Pennsylvania, 1962.

Currey, Cecil B. *Edward Lansdale, the Unquiet American.* Boston: Houghton Mifflin, 1988.

Cypess, Sandra Messinger. *La Malinche in Mexican Literature from History to Myth.* Austin: University of Texas Press, 1991.

Das, Prasanta. "Oedipa's Night Journey in Pynchon's *The Crying of Lot 49.*" *Notes on Contemporary Culture* 23, no. 2 (1993): 4–5.

De Groot, Gerard J. "Student Protest: The Sixties and After." In *"Left, Left, Left!": The Vietnam Day Committee, 1965–66,* edited by Gerard J. De Groot. London: Longman, 1998.

de Nerval, Gérard. "Les Doctrinaires." In *Poésies et souvenirs,* edited by Jean Richer, 73–75. Paris: Gallimard, 1974.

Decker, Jeffrey L. "'The Enigma His Efforts Had Created': Thomas Pynchon and the Legacy of America." *Pynchon Notes* 28–29 (1991): 27–42.

Delden, Maarten Van. *Carlos Fuentes, Mexico, and Modernity.* Liverpool: Liverpool University Press, 1998.

Deleuze, Gilles, and Felix Guattari. *Anti-Oedipus: Capitalism and Schizophrenia.* Translated by R. Hurley. London: Athlone, 1983.

———. *A Thousand Plateaus: Capitalism and Schizophrenia.* Translated by Brian Massumi. London: Athlone, 1991.

Dennis, Matthew. *Red, White, and Blue Letter Days: An American Calendar.* Ithaca, N.Y.: Cornell University Press, 2002.

Dickstein, Morris. *Gates of Eden: American Culture in the Sixties.* Cambridge, Mass.: Harvard University Press, 1997.

Dixon, Thomas, Jr. *The Reconstruction Trilogy: The Leopard's Spots; The Clansman; The Traitor.* Edited by Sam Dickson. Newport Beach, Calif.: Noontide, 1994.

D'Lugo, Carol Clark. *The Fragmented Novel in Mexico: The Politics of Form.* Austin: University of Texas Press, 1997.

Domínguez Michael, Christopher. *Diccionario crítico de la literatura mexicana, 1955–2005.* México, D.F.: Fondo de Cultura Económica, 2007.

Donoso, José, and María Pilar Donoso. *Historia personal del "Boom."* Barcelona: Seix Barral, 1983.

Dos Passos, John. *U.S.A.* Harmondsworth, Eng.: Penguin Books, 2001.

Dostoyevsky, Fyodor. *Notes from Underground.* Translated by Michael R. Katz. New York: Norton, 2001.

Duchet, Michèle, and Claude Blanckaert. *Anthropologie et histoire au siècle des lumières.* Paris: A. Michel, 1995.

Dumas, Claude. "Théorie et pratique du nouveau roman Latino-Américain: *La región más transparente* (1958), Une analyse de son auteur, le Mexicain Carlos Fuentes." In *Écrire le Mexique: Carlos Fuentes, La región más transparente;* Paco Ignacio Taibo Ii, La vida misma, Sombra de la sombra, edited by Jean Franco and Yves Aguila, 14–28. Paris: Ellipses, 1998.

Eagleton, Terry. *After Theory.* New York: Basic Books, 2003.

Eliade, Mircea. *The Sacred and the Profane: The Nature of Religion.* Translated by Willard R. Trask. New York: Harper and Row, 1959.

Ellison, Ralph. *Invisible Man.* New York: Modern Library, 1994.

Emerson, Caryl. "Keeping the Self Intact During the Culture Wars: A Centennial Essay for Mikhail Bakhtin." *New Literary History* 27, no. 1 (1996): 107–26.

Evans, Sara M. *Personal Politics: The Roots of Women's Liberation in the Civil Rights Movement and the New Left.* New York: Knopf, 1979.

Fanon, Frantz. *Black Skin, White Masks.* Translated by Charles Lam Markmann. New York: Grove, 1991.

———. *The Wretched of the Earth.* Translated by Constance Farrington. New York: Grove, 1965.

Fariña, Richard. *Been Down So Long It Looks Like Up to Me.* New York: Penguin Books, 1996.

Faris, Wendy B. *Carlos Fuentes.* New York: Ungar, 1983.

Feagin, Joe R., and Harlan Hahn. *Ghetto Revolts: The Politics of Violence in American Cities.* New York: Macmillan, 1973.

Fein, Seith. "Myths of Cultural Imperialism and Nationalism in Golden Age Mexican Cinema." In *Fragments of a Golden Age: The Politics of Culture in Mexico since 1940,* edited by Anne Rubenstein, Gilbert Joseph, and Eric Zolov, 159–98. Durham, N.C.: Duke University Press, 2001.

Ferman, Claudia. "De exorcismos y profecías: Carlos Fuentes ente la modernidad y la posmodernidad." *Torre De Papel* 7, no. 3 (1997): 126–47.

Fernández de Lizardi, José Joaquín. *Obras. Novelas: El Periquillo Sarniento (tomos I y II)*. 9 vols. Vol. 8. México, D.F.: Universidad Nacional Autónoma de México, 1982.

Feuer, Menachem, and Andrew Schmitz. "Hup! Hup! We Must Tumble: Toward an Ethical Reading of the Schlemiel." *Modern Fiction Studies* 54, no. 1 (2008): 91–114.

Fiedler, Leslie A. *Waiting for the End: The American Literary Scene from Hemingway to Baldwin.* London: Jonathan Cape, 1965.

Florescano, Enrique. *Etnia, estado y nación: Ensayo sobre las identidades colectivas en México*. México, D.F.: Aguilar, 1997.

Foucault, Michel. *Dits et écrits: 1954–1988*. Edited by Daniel Defert and François Ewald. 4 vols. Vol. 4. Paris: Editions Gallimard, 1994.

———. *Madness and Civilization: A History of Insanity in the Age of Reason.* Translated by Richard Howard. London: Routledge, 1971.

———. *The Order of Things: An Archaeology of the Human Sciences*. London: Routledge, 1970.

Fousek, John. *To Lead the Free World: American Nationalism and the Cultural Roots of the Cold War.* Chapel Hill: University of North Carolina Press, 2000.

Fox, Claire F. *Making Art Panamerican: Cultural Policy and the Cold War.* 2013.

Franco, Jean. *The Modern Culture of Latin America: Society and the Artist.* New York: F. A. Praeger, 1967.

———. "Modernización, resistencia y revolución. La producción literaria de los años sesenta." *Escritura: Teoría y Crítica Literarias* 3 (1977): 3–19.

———. "Narrador, autor, superestrella: La narrativa latinoamericana en la época de cultura de masas." *Revista Iberoamericana* 47, no. 114 (1981): 129–48.

———. *Plotting Women: Gender and Representation in Mexico*. New York: Columbia University Press, 1989.

Freese, Peter. *"America," Dream or Nightmare?: Reflections on a Composite Image*. Essen: Verlag Die Blaue Eule, 1990.

Fried, Albert. *McCarthyism: The Great American Red Scare: A Documentary History.* New York: Oxford University Press, 1997.

Friedan, Betty. *The Feminine Mystique.* Harmondsworth, Eng.: Penguin Books, 1965.

Fuentes, Carlos. *Cambio de piel.* México, D.F.: Editorial J. Mortiz, 1967.

———. *The Campaign.* Translated by Alfred J. Mac Adam. New York: Farrar, Straus and Giroux, 1991.

———. *Cervantes, o la crítica de la lectura.* Alcalá de Henares: Centro de Estudios Cervantinos, 1994.

———. *A Change of Skin.* Translated by Sam Hileman. New York: Farrar, Straus and Giroux, 1968.

———. *Cuerpos y ofrendas.* Madrid: Alianza, 2001.

———. *The Death of Artemio Cruz.* Translated by Sam Hileman. New York: Farrar, Straus and Giroux, 1964.

———. "El ángel exterminador: Nadie encontrará una respuesta dogmática." *Siempre!*, 1962, 19.

———. *El espejo enterrado.* México, D.F.: Fondo de Cultura Económica, 1992.

———. "El secreto de Diderot." In *Los novelistas como críticos*, edited by Norma Klahn and Wilfrido H. Corral. México, D.F.: Fondo de Cultura Económica, 1991.

———. *En esto creo*. Barcelona: Editorial Seix Barral, 2002.

———. *La campaña*. México, D.F.: Fondo de Cultura Económica, 1990.

———. *La frontera de cristal: Una novela en nueve cuentos*. Madrid: Alfaguara, 1995.

———. *La gran novela latinoamericana*. México, D.F.: Alfaguara, 2011.

———. *La muerte de Artemio Cruz*. Edited by José C. González Boixo. Madrid: Cátedra, 1995.

———. *La nueva novela hispanoamericana*. México, D.F.: Editorial J. Mortiz, 1969.

———. *La región más transparente*. Madrid: Real Academia Española, 2008.

———. "Latin-America's Alternative: An Ibero-American Federation." *New Perspectives Quarterly* 8, no. 1 (1991): 15–17.

———. *Los días enmascarados*. México, D.F.: Los Presentes, 1954.

———. *A New Time for Mexico*. Translated by Marina Gutman Castañeda and Carlos Fuentes. Los Angeles: University of California Press, 1997.

———. *Nuevo tiempo mexicano*. México, D.F.: Aguilar, 1994.

———. "Obama: The First Mestizo Leader North of the Border." *New Perspectives Quarterly* 26.1 (2009): 34.

———. "*Rayuela:* La novela como caja de Pandora." *Mundo Nuevo*, 1967, 69.

———. *Tiempo mexicano*. México, D.F.: Editorial J. Mortiz, 1971.

———. *Valiente mundo nuevo: Épica, utopía y mito en la novela hispanoamericana*. México, D.F.: Fondo de Cultura Económica, 1990.

———. *Where the Air Is Clear, a Novel*. Translated by Sam Hileman. New York: I. Obolensky, 1960.

Gaillard, Françoise. "The Terror of Consensus." Translated by Jennifer Curtis Gage. In *Terror and Consensus: Vicissitudes of French Thought*, edited by Jean-Joseph Goux and Philip R. Wood, 65–74. Stanford, Calif.: Stanford University Press, 1998.

Ganter, G. "Rioting, Textuality, and *The Crying of Lot 49*." *Found Object* 2 (1993): 67–81.

García Canclini, Néstor. *Hybrid Cultures: Strategies for Entering and Leaving Modernity* [a translation of *Culturas híbridas: Estrategias para entrar y salir de la modernidad*]. Translated by Christopher L. Chiappari and Silvia L. López. Minneapolis: University of Minnesota Press, 2005.

García-Caro, Pedro. "The Death of Carlos Fuentes: An Impossible Silencing Act. In Memoriam (1928–2012)." *A Contracorriente* 9, no. 3 (2012): i–x.

Gates, Henry Louis, Jr. *Loose Canons: Notes on the Culture Wars*. New York: Oxford University Press, 1993.

Gellner, Ernest. *Nations and Nationalism*. London: Blackwell, 1983.

Genette, Gérard. *Palimpsests: Literature in the Second Degree*. Translated by Channa Newman and Claude Doubinsky. Lincoln: University of Nebraska Press, 1997.

Gitlin, Todd. *The Sixties: Years of Hope, Days of Rage*. New York: Bantam Books, 1993.

Glantz, Margo. *Repeticiones: Ensayos sobre literatura mexicana.* Xalapa: Universidad Veracruzana, 1979.

Glanze, Linda. "La distorsión temporal y las técnicas cinematográficas en *La muerte de Artemio Cruz.*" *Hispamérica* 14, no. 40 (1985): 115–20.

González, Juan. *Harvest of Empire: A History of Latinos in America.* New York: Penguin, 2001.

González Echevarría, Roberto. *Alejo Carpentier: The Pilgrim at Home.* Ithaca, N.Y.: Cornell University Press, 1977.

———. *Myth and Archive: a Theory of Latin American Narrative.* Cambridge: Cambridge University Press, 1990.

———. *Mito y archivo: Una teoría de la narrativa latinoamericana.* México, D.F.: Fondo de Cultura Económica, 2011.

Google Maps. http://maps.google.com.

Gosse, Van. *Rethinking the New Left: An Interpretative History.* New York: Palgrave Macmillan, 2005.

———. *Where the Boys Are: Cuba, Cold War America and the Making of a New Left.* London: Verso, 1993.

Grandin, Greg. *Empire's Workshop: Latin America, the United States, and the Rise of the New Imperialism.* New York: Metropolitan Books, 2006.

Grant, J. Kerry. *A Companion to V.* Athens: University of Georgia Press, 2001.

Greenberg, Amy S. *A Wicked War: Polk, Clay, Lincoln, and the 1846 U.S. Invasion of Mexico.* New York: Alfred A. Knopf, 2012.

Greene, Graham. *The Quiet American.* New York: Viking, 1956.

Greenspan, Ezra. *The Schlemiel Comes to America.* Metuchen, N.J.: Scarecrow, 1983.

Griffith, D. W. *The Birth of a Nation.* Southgate, Mich.: Triad Productions, 2009.

Guibernau i Berdún, M. Montserrat. *The Identity of Nations.* Cambridge, Eng.: Polity, 2007.

Guillermoprieto, Alma. *The Heart That Bleeds: Latin America Now.* New York: Knopf, 1994.

Gutiérrez, Juan María, and Miguel Cané. *Juan Cruz Varela: Su vida, sus obras, su época.* Buenos Aires: Vaccaro, 1918.

Guzmán, Martín Luis. *El águila y la serpiente.* Madrid: Compañía iberoamericana de publicaciones, 1928.

Gyurko, Lanin. "*La muerte de Artemio Cruz* and *Citizen Kane.*" In *Carlos Fuentes: A Critical View,* edited by Robert Brody and Charles Rossman, 64–94. Austin: University of Texas Press, 1982.

———. "Self, Double, and Mask in Fuentes's *La Muerte De Artemio Cruz.*" *Texas Studies in Language and Literature* 16 (1974): 363–84.

Habermas, Jürgen. *The Postnational Constellation: Political Essays.* Translated by Max Pensky. Cambridge, Eng.: Polity, 2007.

Hall, Chris. "'Behind the Hieroglyphic Streets': Pynchon's Oedipa Maas and the Dialectics of Reading." *Critique: Studies in Contemporary Fiction* 33, no. 1 (1991): 63–77.

Halperín Donghi, Tulio. *Politics Economics and Society in Argentina in the Revolutionary Period.* Translated by Richard Southern. Cambridge: Cambridge University Press, 1975.

Hames-García, Michael Roy. "Which America Is Ours?: Martí's 'Truth' and the Foundations of 'American Literature.'" *Modern Fiction Studies* 49, no. 1 (2003): 19–53.

Harrington, Michael. *The Other America: Poverty in the United States.* New York: Macmillan, 1962.

Harss, Luis, and Barbara Dohmann. *Into the Mainstream: Conversations with Latin American Writers.* New York: Harper, 1967.

Harvey, David. *The Condition of Postmodernity: An Enquiry into the Origins of Cultural Change.* Oxford: Blackwell, 1989.

Hassan, Ihab Habib. *The Postmodern Turn: Essays in Postmodern Theory and Culture.* Columbus: Ohio State University Press, 1987.

Hegel, Georg. *The Philosophy of History.* Translated by J. Sibree. New York: Wiley, 1944.

Helmuth, Chalene. *The Postmodern Fuentes.* Lewisburg, Pa: Bucknell University Press, 1997.

Herman, Luc, and John M. Krafft. "From the Ground Up: The Evolution of the South-West Africa Chapter in Pynchon's *V.*" *Contemporary Literature* 47, no. 2 (2006): 261–88.

Herrero-Olaizola, Alejandro. *Narrativas híbridas: Parodia y posmodernismo en la ficción contemporánea de las Américas.* Madrid: Editorial Verbum, 2000.

Hill, Jane H., and Kenneth C. Hill. *Speaking Mexicano: Dynamics of Syncretic Language in Central Mexico.* Tucson: University of Arizona Press, 1986.

Hindle, Brooke. *The Pursuit of Science in Revolutionary America, 1735–1789.* Chapel Hill: University of North Carolina Press, 1956.

Hinds, Elizabeth J. W. "Sari, Sorry, and the Vortex of History: Calendar Reform, Anachronism, and Language Change in *Mason & Dixon.*" *American Literary History* 12, no. 1–2 (2000): 187–215.

Hite, Molly. *Ideas of Order in the Novels of Thomas Pynchon.* Columbus: Ohio State University Press, 1983.

Hobsbawm, Eric J. *Nations and Nationalism Since 1780: Programme, Myth, Reality.* 2nd ed. Cambridge: Cambridge University Press, 1992.

Hobsbawm, Eric J., and Terence Ranger. *The Invention of Tradition.* Cambridge: Cambridge University Press, 1983.

Hofstadter, Richard. *Anti-Intellectualism in American Life.* New York: Knopf, 1963.

Holton, Robert. "In the Rathouse of History with Thomas Pynchon: Rereading *V.*" *Textual Practice* 2, no. 3 (1988): 324–44.

Horsley, Scott. "Border Fence Firm Snared for Hiring Illegal Workers." http://www.npr.org/templates/story/story.php?storyId=6626823.

Humboldt, Alexander von. *Essai politique sur le royaume de la Nouvelle-Espagne.* 5 vols. Vol. 2. Paris: F. Schoell, 1811.

Humphreys, R. A., and John Lynch. *Latin American Revolutions, 1808–1826: Old and New World Origins.* Norman: University of Oklahoma Press, 1995.

Hurm, Gerd. *Fragmented Urban Images: The American City in Modern Fiction from Stephen Crane to Thomas Pynchon.* Frankfurt am Main: Lang, 1991.

Hurtado, Guillermo. *El Hiperión: Antología.* México, D.F.: Universidad Nacional Autónoma de México, 2006.

Hussey, Roland D. "Traces of French Enlightenment in Colonial Hispanic America." In *Latin America and the Enlightenment,* edited by Arthur Preston Whitaker, 23–51 New York: Appleton-Century, 1942.

Hutcheon, Linda. "Comparative Literature: Congenitally Contrarian." In *Comparative Literature in an Age of Globalization,* edited by Haun Saussy, 224–29. Baltimore, Md.: Johns Hopkins University Press, 2006.

———. *Poetics of Postmodernism: History, Theory, Fiction.* New York: Routledge, 1988.

———. *A Theory of Parody: The Teachings of Twentieth-Century Art Forms.* New York: Methuen, 1985.

"*Inherent Vice* (2014)," *Internet Movie Database.* Accessed December 3, 2013. http://www.imdb.com/title/tt1791528/.

Irving, Washington. "Traits of Indian Character." In *The Sketch Book of Geoffrey Crayon,* 211–36. London: John Murray, 1820.

Irwin, Robert McKee. *Mexican Masculinities.* Minneapolis: University of Minnesota Press, 2003.

Jacobs, Ronald N. *Race, Media, and the Crisis of Civil Society: From Watts to Rodney King.* Cambridge: Cambridge University Press, 2000.

James, Paul. "Dark Nationalism or Transparent Postnationalism?" In *Global Matrix: Nationalism, Globalism and State-Terrorism,* edited by Tom Nairn and Paul James, 104–21. London: Pluto, 2005.

Jameson, Fredric. *The Geopolitical Aesthetic: Cinema and Space in the World System.* Bloomington: Indiana University Press, 1995.

———. "Postmodernism or the Cultural Logic of Late Capitalism." *New Left Review* 146 (1984): 59–92.

———. *Postmodernism: or, the Cultural Logic of Late Capitalism.* London: Verso, 1991.

———. *A Singular Modernity: Essay on the Ontology of the Present.* New York: Verso Books, 2002.

———. "Third-World Literature in the Era of Multinational Capitalism." *Social Text* 15 (1986): 65–88.

Jarvis, Brian. *Postmodern Cartographies: The Geographical Imagination in Contemporary American Culture.* New York: St. Martin's, 1998.

Johnson, Susan Lee. *Roaring Camp: The Social World of the California Gold Rush.* New York: W.W. Norton, 2000.

Juan-Navarro, Santiago. *Archival Reflections: Postmodern Fiction of the Americas (Self-Reflexivity, Historical Revisionism, Utopia).* Lewisburg, Pa.; London: Bucknell University Press; Associated University Presses, 1999.

Kadir, Djelal. *The Other Writing: Postcolonial Essays in Latin America's Writing Culture.* West Lafayette, Ind.: Purdue University Press, 1993.

Kallen, Stuart A. *Sixties Counterculture, History Firsthand.* San Diego, Calif.: Greenhaven, 2001.

Kant, Immanuel. "An Answer to the Question: 'What Is Enlightenment?' " In *Kant's Political Writings,* edited by H. Reiss, 54–60. Cambridge: Cambridge University Press, 1970.

Kaplan, Amy. *The Anarchy of Empire in the Making of U.S. Culture.* Cambridge, Mass.: Harvard University Press, 2002.

———. "'Left Alone in America': The Absence of Empire in the Study of American Culture." In *Cultures of United States Imperialism,* edited by Amy Kaplan and Donald E. Pease, 3–21. Durham, N.C.: Duke University Press, 1993.

———. "The Tenacious Grasp of American Exceptionalism: A Response to Djelal Kadir." *Comparative American Studies* 2, no. 2 (2004): 153–59.

Kaplan, Amy, and Donald E. Pease. *Cultures of United States Imperialism.* Durham, N.C.: Duke University Press, 1993.

Kaplan, Janet A. *Unexpected Journeys: The Art and Life Of Remedios Varo.* New York: Abbeville, 2001.

Katzew, Ilona. *Casta Painting: Images of Race in Eighteenth-Century Mexico.* New Haven, Conn.: Yale University Press, 2004.

Katzew, Ilona, and Susan Deans-Smith. *Race and Classification: The Case of Mexican America.* Stanford, Calif.: Stanford University Press, 2009.

Keesey, Douglas. "*Mason & Dixon* on the Line: A Reception Study." *Pynchon Notes* 36–39 (1995–96 [1998]): 165–78.

Kermode, Frank. "Decoding the Trystero." In *Pynchon: A Collection of Critical Essays,* edited by Edward Mendelson, 162–66. New Jersey: Prentice Hall, 1978.

Kernan, Alvin B. *The Plot of Satire.* New Haven, Conn.: Yale University Press, 1965.

Kharpertian, Theodore D. *A Hand to Turn the Time: The Menippean Satires of Thomas Pynchon.* London: Fairleigh Dickinson University Press, 1990.

Kiernan, V. G. *Imperialism and Its Contradictions.* New York: Routledge, 1995.

King, John. "Carlos Fuentes: An Interview with John King." In *Modern Latin American Fiction: A Survey,* edited by John King, 136–54. London: Faber, 1987.

———. *Magical Reels: A History of Cinema in Latin America.* London: Verso, 1990.

Knight, Alan. "The Rise and Fall of Cardenismo." In *Mexico Since Independence,* edited by Leslie Bethell, 241–320. Cambridge: Cambridge University Press, 1991.

Knight, Peter. *Conspiracy Culture: From Kennedy to "the X-Files."* London: Routledge, 2001.

Knowles, Murray, and Rosamund Moon. *Introducing Metaphor.* London: Routledge, 2006.

Kolodny, Annette, and Daniel James Peters. "Pynchon's *The Crying of Lot 49:* The Novel as Subversive Experience." *Modern Fiction Studies* 19 (1973): 79–87.

Krauze, Enrique. "The Guerrilla Dandy." *New Republic* 198, no. 26 (1988): 28–31.

———. *Mexico: Biography of Power: A History of Modern Mexico, 1810–1996.* New York: Harper-Collins, 1997.

Kristeva, Julia. *La révolution du langage poétique; L'avant-garde à la fin du XIX siècle, Lautréamont et Mallarmé, tel quel.* Paris: Éditions du Seuil, 1974.

———. *Nations Without Nationalism.* New York: Columbia University Press, 1993.

Kutzinski, Vera M. *Against the American Grain: Myth and History in William Carlos Williams, Jay Wright, and Nicolás Guillén.* Baltimore: Johns Hopkins University Press, 1987.

LaCapra, Dominick. *History and Criticism.* Ithaca, N.Y.: Cornell University Press, 1985.

Lacey, Marc. "Smugglers of Drugs Burrow on Border." *The New York Times,* October 3, 2010, 16.

Lafeber, Walter. *The New Empire: An Interpretation of American Expansion, 1860–1898.* Ithaca, N.Y.: Cornell University Press, 1967.

Lanning, John Tate. *Academic Culture in the Spanish Colonies.* London: Oxford University Press, 1940.

———. "The Reception of the Enlightenment in Latin America." In *Latin America and the Enlightenment,* edited by Arthur Preston Whitaker, 71–90. New York: Appleton-Century, 1942.

Lansdale, Edward Geary. *In the Midst of Wars: An American's Mission to Southeast Asia.* New York: Fordham University Press, 1991.

Latrobe, John H. B. *The History of Mason and Dixon's Line Contained in an Address.* [Philadelphia]: Press of the Historical Society of Pennsylvania, 1855.

Lee, Martin A., Bruce Shlain, and Andrei Codrescu. *Acid Dreams: The Complete Social History of LSD: The CIA, the Sixties, and Beyond.* New York: Grove, 1986.

Lefebvre, Henri. *The Production of Space* [a translation of *La production de l'espace*]. Oxford: Blackwell, 1991.

Lefever, Barbara Susan. *The Stargazers, Story of Mason and Dixon: An Historical Biographical Novel by Barbara Susan Lefever.* York, Pa.: the author, 1986.

Levander, Caroline Field, and Robert S. Levine. "Introduction: Essays Beyond the Nation." In *Hemispheric American Studies,* edited by Caroline Field Levander and Robert S. Levine, 1–17. New Brunswick, N.J.: Rutgers University Press, 2008.

Limón, José E. *American Encounters: Greater Mexico, the United States, and the Erotics of Culture.* Boston: Beacon, 1998.

Lipski, John M. *Varieties of Spanish in the United States.* Washington, D.C.: Georgetown University Press, 2008.

Liss, Peggy K. *Atlantic Empires: The Network of Trade and Revolution, 1713–1826.* Baltimore: Johns Hopkins University Press, 1983.

Logan, William. "Pynchon in the Poetic." *Southern Review* 83, no. 4 (1998): 424–37.

Lomnitz-Adler, Claudio. *Death and the Idea of Mexico.* New York; London: Zone; MIT, 2008.

———. *Deep Mexico, Silent Mexico: An Anthropology of Nationalism.* Minneapolis: University of Minnesota Press, 2001.

———. *Exits from the Labyrinth: Culture and Ideology in the Mexican National Space.* Berkeley: University of California Press, 1992.

Losurdo, Domenico, and Gregory Elliott. *Liberalism: A Counter-History.* London: Verso Books, 2011.

Lovelock, James. *Gaia, a New Look at Life on Earth.* Oxford: Oxford University Press, 1979.

———. *The Revenge of Gaia: Earth's Climate Crisis and the Fate of Humanity.* New York: Basic Books, 2006.

Löwy, Michael. *Fatherland or Mother Earth?: Essays on the National Question.* London: Pluto Press with the International Institute for Research and Education, 1998.

Luis-Brown, David. *Waves of Decolonization: Discourses of Race and Hemispheric Citizenship in Cuba, Mexico, and the United States.* Durham, N.C.: Duke University Press, 2008.

Lund, Joshua. *The Mestizo State: Reading Race in Modern Mexico.* Minneapolis: University of Minnesota Press, 2012.

Lynd, Staughton. *Intellectual Origins of American Radicalism.* Cambridge, Mass.: Harvard University Press, 1982.

Lyotard, Jean-François. *The Postmodern Condition: A Report on Knowledge.* Translated by Geoffrey Bennington and Brian Massumi. Manchester: Manchester University Press, 1984.

Macías de Yoon, Claudia. "Las falsas polifonías de un narrador monológico en *La campaña,* de Carlos Fuentes." *Texto Crítico* 4–5 (1997): 33–47.

Madsen, Deborah L. *The Postmodernist Allegories of Thomas Pynchon.* New York: St. Martin's, 1991.

Mailer, Norman. *Advertisements for Myself.* Cambridge, Mass.: Harvard University Press, 1992.

Marcuse, Herbert. *One-Dimensional Man: Studies in the Ideology of Advanced Industrial Society.* Edited by Douglas Kellner London: Routledge, 1991.

Marin, Rubén, ed. *Los narradores ante el público.* 2 vols. Vol. 1. México, D.F.: Editorial J. Mortiz, 1967.

Martelle, Scott. *Blood Passion: The Ludlow Massacre and Class War in the American West.* New Brunswick, N.J.: Rutgers University Press, 2007.

Marwick, Arthur. *The Sixties: Cultural Revolution in Britain, France, Italy, and the United States, c. 1958–c. 1974.* London: Bloomsbury Reader, 2012.

Mason, Charles, and Jeremiah Dixon. *The Journal of Charles Mason and Jeremiah Dixon.* Edited by A. Hughett Mason. Philadelphia: American Philosophical Society, 1969.

Mattessich, Stefan. "Imperium, Misogyny, and Postmodern Parody in Thomas Pynchon's *V.*" *ELH* 65 (1998): 503–21.

May, Brian. "Back to the Future: History in/and the Postcolonial Novel." *Studies in the Novel* 29 (1997): 267–73.

McClintock, Michael. *Instruments of Statecraft: U.S. Guerrilla Warfare, Counterinsurgency, and Counter-Terrorism, 1940–1990.* New York: Pantheon Books, 1992.

McClure, John A. *Late Imperial Romance.* London: Verso, 1994.

McHale, Brian. "Mason & Dixon in the Zone, or a Brief Poetics of Pynchon-Space." In *Pynchon and Mason & Dixon,* edited by Brooke Hovarth and Irving Malin, 43–62. Newark: University of Delaware Press, 2000.

———. *Postmodernist Fiction.* London: Routledge, 1994.

McNickle, D'Arcy. *Native American Tribalism: Indian Survivals and Renewals.* New York: published for the Institute of Race Relations by Oxford University Press, 1973.

Menton, Seymour. *Latin America's New Historical Novel.* Austin: University of Texas Press, 1993.

Meyer, Jean A. *The Cristero Rebellion: The Mexican People Between Church and State, 1926–1929.* Cambridge: Cambridge University Press, 1976.

Meyer-Minnemann, Klaus. "Narración homodiegética y "Segunda Persona": *Cambio de piel* de Carlos Fuentes." *Acta Literaria* 9 (1984): 5–27.

Mignolo, Walter D. *Local Histories/Global Designs: Coloniality, Subaltern Knowledges, and Border Thinking.* Princeton, N.J.: Princeton University Press, 2000.

———. *The Darker Side of Western Modernity: Global Futures, Decolonial Options.* Durham, N.C.; London: Duke University Press, 2011.

Miller, Nicola. "The Historiography of Nationalism and National Identity in Latin America." *Nations and Nationalism* 12, no. 2 (2006): 201–21.

Mills, C. Wright. *C. Wright Mills: Letters and Autobiographical Writings.* Edited by Kathryn Mills, Pamela Mills, and Dan Wakefield Berkeley; London: University of California Press, 2000.

———. "Izquierda, subdesarrollo y guerra fría: Un coloquio sobre cuestiones fundamentales." *Cuadernos Americanos* 19 (1960): 53–69.

———. *Listen, Yankee: The Revolution in Cuba.* New York: Ballantine Books, 1960.

———. *The Power Elite.* New York: Oxford University Press, 1956.

Molho, Anthony, and Gordon S. Wood. "Introduction." In *Imagined Histories: American Historians Interpret the Past,* edited by Anthony Molho and Gordon S. Wood, 3–20. Princeton, N.J.: Princeton University Press, 1998.

Mörner, Magnus. *Estado, razas y cambio social en la Hispanoamérica colonial.* México, D.F.: Secretaría de Educación Pública, 1974.

———. *The Expulsion of the Jesuits from Latin America.* New York: Knopf, 1965.

Morris, Errol. *The Fog of War: Eleven Lessons from the Life of Robert S. McNamara.* Culver City, Calif.: Columbia TriStar Home Entertainment, 2004.

Morson, Gary Saul. *Narrative and Freedom: The Shadows of Time.* New Haven, Conn.: Yale University Press, 1994.

Morson, Gary Saul, and Caryl Emerson. *Rethinking Bakhtin: Extensions and Challenges.* Evanston, Ill.: Northwestern University Press, 1989.

Mumford, Lewis. *The Culture of Cities.* San Diego, Calif.: Harvest Books, 1970.

———. *The Pentagon of Power.* New York: Harcourt Brace Jovanovich, 1974.

Muzzio, Julio A. *Diccionario histórico y biográfico de la república Argentina.* 2 vols. Buenos Aires: J. Roldan, 1920.

Nairn, Tom. *The Break-up of Britain: Crisis and Neonationalism.* London: NLB and Verso Editions, 1981.

———. *Faces of Nationalism: Janus Revisited.* London: Verso Books, 1998.

Nairn, Tom, and Paul James. *Global Matrix: Nationalism, Globalism and State-Terrorism.* London: Pluto, 2005.

Nashel, Jonathan. *Edward Lansdale's Cold War.* Amherst: University of Massachusetts Press, 2005.

Navarro B., Bernabé. *Cultura mexicana moderna en el siglo XVIII.* México, D.F.: Universidad Nacional Autónoma de México, 1982.

Obama, Barack H. "Remarks by the President in State of the Union Address." http://www.whitehouse.gov/the-press-office/2011/01/25/remarks-president-state-union-address.

Ochoa, John A. *The Uses of Failure in Mexican Literature and Identity.* Austin: University of Texas Press, 2004.

Pacheco, José Emilio. *Morirás lejos.* México, D.F.: Editorial J. Mortiz, 1967.

Packard, Vance. *The Hidden Persuaders.* New York: D. McKay, 1957.

Palmeri, Frank. *Satire in Narrative: Petronius, Swift, Gibbon, Melville, and Pynchon.* Austin: University of Texas Press, 1990.

Paquette, Gabriel B. *Enlightened Reform in Southern Europe and Its Atlantic Colonies, c. 1750–1830.* Farnham, Eng.: Ashgate, 2009.

———. *Enlightenment, Governance and Reform in Spain and Its Empire 1759–1808.* Basingstoke, Eng.: Palgrave Macmillan, 2008.

Parker, Andrew. *Nationalisms & Sexualities.* New York: Routledge, 1992.

Parkinson Zamora, Lois. *The Usable Past: The Imagination of History in Recent Fiction of the Americas.* Cambridge: Cambridge University Press, 1997.

Parra, Carlos Francisco. "Valientes Nogalenses: The 1918 Battle Between the U.S. and Mexico That Transformed Ambos Nogales." *Journal of Arizona History* 51, no. 1 (2010): 1–32.

Passerin d'Entrèves, Mauricio. "Critique and Enlightenment: Michel Foucault on 'Was Ist Aufklärung?'" In *The Enlightenment and Modernity,* edited by Norman Geras and Robert Wokler, 184–203. New York: Saint Martin's, 2000.

Patell, Cyrus R. K. "Comparative American Studies: Hybridity and Beyond." *American Literary History* 11, no. 1 (1999): 166–86.

———. *Negative Liberties: Morrison, Pynchon, and the Problem of Liberal Ideology.* Edited by Donald E. Pease. Durham, N.C.: Duke University Press, 2001.

Paz, Octavio. *El laberinto de la soledad.* México, D.F.: Fondo de Cultura Económica, 1998.

———. *Vuelta a El laberinto de la soledad.* México, D.F.: Fondo de Cultura Económica, 1998.

Pease, Donald E., ed. *National Identities and Post-Americanist Narratives.* Durham, N.C.: Duke University Press, 1994.

———. *The New American Exceptionalism.* Minneapolis: University of Minnesota Press, 2009.

Pérez Firmat, Gustavo. *Do the Americas Have a Common Literature?* Durham, N.C.: Duke University Press, 1990.

Perkins, Bradford, Walter LaFeber, Akira Iriye, and Warren I. Cohen, eds. *The Cambridge History of American Foreign Relations.* 4 vols. Vol. 1. Cambridge: Cambridge University Press, 1993.

Perry, Charles, and Bob Weir. *The Haight Ashbury.* New York: Wenner Books, 2005.

Petillon, Pierre Yves. "A Recognition of Her Errand into the Wilderness." In *New Essays on The Crying of Lot 49,* edited by Patrick O'Donnell, 127–70. Cambridge: Cambridge University Press, 1991.

Phillips, Kevin P. *The Cousins' Wars: Religion, Politics, and the Triumph of Anglo-America.* New York: Basic Books, 2000.

Pick, Zuzana M. *Constructing the Image of the Mexican Revolution: Cinema and the Archive.* Austin: University of Texas Press, 2010.

Pocock, J. G. A. *The Machiavellian Moment: Florentine Political Thought and the Atlantic Republican Tradition.* Princeton, N.J.: Princeton University Press, 1975.

Pogolotti, Graziella. "*La campaña* de Carlos Fuentes: Una parábola de la utopía." *Literatura Mexicana* 5, no. 2 (1994): 443–53.

Pohlmann, Sascha. *Pynchon's Postnational Imagination.* Heidelberg, Ger.: Universitatsverlag Winter, 2010.

Powell, T. G. *Mexico and the Spanish Civil War.* Albuquerque: University of New Mexico Press, 1981.

Prados, John. *Keepers of the Keys: A History of the National Security Council from Truman to Bush.* New York: Morrow, 1991.

Pratt, Mary Louise. *Imperial Eyes: Travel Writing and Transculturation.* London: Routledge, 1992.

Puiggrós, Rodolfo. *De la colonia a la revolución.* Buenos Aires: Ediciones Leviatán, 1957.

Pynchon, Thomas. *Against the Day.* New York: Penguin, 2006.

———. *The Crying of Lot 49.* 1st ed. Philadelphia: Lippincott, 1966.

———. *Gravity's Rainbow.* London: Vintage, 1995.

———. *Inherent Vice.* New York: Penguin, 2009.

———. *Bleeding Edge.* New York: Penguin, 2013.

———. "Is It O.K. to Be a Luddite?" *New York Times Book Review,* October 28, 1984, 40–41.

———. "A Journey into the Mind of Watts." *New York Times Magazine,* June 12, 1966, 34–35, 78, 80–82, 84.

———. "Letter to Thomas F. Hirsch." In *The Fictional Labyrinths of Thomas Pynchon,* edited by David Seed, 240–43. Iowa City: University of Iowa Press, 1988.

———. *Mason & Dixon.* New York: Henry Holt, 1997.

———. *Slow Learner: Early Stories.* Boston: Little Brown, 1984.

———. *V.* London: Vintage, 1995.

———. "The World (This One), the Flesh (Mrs. Oedipa Maas), and the Testament of Pierce Inverarity." *Esquire Magazine,* December 1965, 170–73, 296–303.

Radcliffe, Sarah A., and Sallie Westwood. *Remaking the Nation: Place, Identity and Politics in Latin America.* London: Routledge, 1996.

Ramos, Samuel. *El perfil del hombre y la cultura en México.* México, D.F.: P. Robredo, 1938.

———. *Profile of Man and Culture in Mexico.* Translated by Peter G. Earle. Austin: University of Texas Press, 1962.

Rechy, John. *City of Night.* New York: Grove/Atlantic, 1984.

Reeve, Richard. "Octavio Paz and Hiperión in *La región más transparente:* Plagiarism, Caricature or . . .?" *Chasqui* 3 (1974): 13–25.

Reich, Charles A. *Opposing the System.* New York: Crown, 1995.

Reich, Wilhelm. *The Mass Psychology of Fascism.* Translated by Vincent R. Carfagno. New York: Farrar, Straus and Giroux, 1970.

Rennie, Bryan S. *Reconstructing Eliade: Making Sense of Religion.* Albany: State University of New York Press, 1996.

Reyes, Alfonso. "Notas sobre la inteligencia americana." In *Última Tule,* 131–45. México, D.F.: Imprenta Universitaria, 1942.

———. *Obras Completas.* 21 vols. Vol. 11. México, D.F.: Fondo de Cultura Económica, 1955.

Richards, Leonard L. *The California Gold Rush and the Coming of the Civil War.* New York: Alfred A. Knopf, 2007.

Rivas, José A. "La historia y los papeles: *La campaña.*" *Antípodas* 8–9 (1996–97): 88–96.

Robinson, H. W. "Jeremiah Dixon (1733–1779): A Biographical Note." *Proceedings of the American Philosophical Society* 94, no. 3 (1950): 272–74.

———. "A Note on Charles Mason's Ancestry and His Family." *Proceedings of the American Philosophical Society* 93, no. 2 (1949): 134–36.

Robinson, Lillian S. *In the Canon's Mouth: Dispatches from the Culture Wars.* Bloomington: Indiana University Press, 1997.

Rodgers, Richard, and Oscar Hammerstein. *South Pacific.* New York: Columbia, 1987.

Rodríguez Monegal, Emir. "Entrevista con Emir Rodríguez Monegal." In *Homenaje a Carlos Fuentes: Variaciones interpretativas en torno a su obra,* edited by Helmy Fuad Giacoman. New York: Las Américas, 1971.

———, ed. *Narradores de esta América.* 2 vols. Vol. 2. Buenos Aires: Alfa Argentina, 1974.

Rose, Margaret A. *Parody/Meta-Fiction: An Analysis of Parody as a Critical Mirror to the Writing and Reception of Fiction.* London: Croom Helm, 1979.

———. *Parody: Ancient, Modern and Post-Modern.* Cambridge: Cambridge University Press, 1993.

Roszak, Theodore. *The Making of a Counter Culture: Reflections on the Technocratic Society and Its Youthful Opposition.* Berkeley: University of California Press, 1995.

Rowe, John Carlos. "Globalism and the New American Studies." In *Post-Nationalist American Studies,* edited by John Carlos Rowe, 23–37. Berkeley: University of California Press, 2000.

———. *Post-Nationalist American Studies.* Berkeley: University of California Press, 2000.

Rowe, William, and Vivian Schelling. *Memory and Modernity: Popular Culture in Latin America.* London: Verso, 1991.

Ruiz Basto, Jorge. *De la modernidad y otras creencias: En torno a Cambio de piel de Carlos Fuentes.* México, D.F.: Universidad Nacional Autónoma de México, 1992.

Rutherford, John. *An Annotated Bibliography of the Novels of the Mexican Revolution of 1910–1917. In English and Spanish.* Troy, N.Y.: Whitston, 1972.

Saint-Andre, Estela. "Acerca de la escritura y la lectura en *La campaña* de Carlos Fuentes." *Revista de Literaturas Modernas* 27 (1994): 129–43.

Saldívar, José David. *Border Matters: Remapping American Cultural Studies.* Berkeley: University of California Press, 1997.

———. *The Dialectics of Our America: Genealogy, Cultural Critique, and Literary History.* Edited by Stanley Fish and Fredric Jameson. Durham, N.C.: Duke University Press, 1991.

———. *Trans-Americanity: Subaltern Modernities, Global Coloniality, and the Cultures of Greater Mexico.* Durham: Duke University Press, 2011.

Sánchez Prado, Ignacio M. *Naciones intelectuales: Las fundaciones de la modernidad literaria mexicana, 1917–1959.* West Lafayette, Ind.: Purdue University Press, 2009.

Sanders, Mark. "The Politics of Literary Reinscription in Thomas Pynchon's *V.*" *Critique: Studies in Contemporary Fiction* 39, no. 1 (1997): 81–97.

Sarmiento, Domingo Faustino. *Facundo: Civilización y barbarie.* Edited by Susana Zanetti. Madrid: Alianza, 1988.

Sayres, Sohnya, ed. *The 60s Without Apology.* Minneapolis: University of Minnesota Press in cooperation with Social Text, 1984.

Schaub, Thomas H. "*The Crying of Lot 49* and Other California Novels." In *The Cambridge Companion to Thomas Pynchon,* edited by Inger Dalsgaard, Luc H. Herman, and Brian McHale. Cambridge: Cambridge University Press, 2012.

Seed, David. "Mapping the Course of Empire in the New World." In *Pynchon and Mason & Dixon,* edited by Brooke Horvath and Irving Malin, 84–99. Newark: University of Delaware Press, 2000.

Semmes, John E. *John H. B. Latrobe and His Times, 1803–1891.* Baltimore: Norman, Remington, 1917.

Shuffelton, Frank, ed. *The American Enlightenment.* Rochester, N.Y.: University of Rochester Press, 1993.

Shumway, David R. *Creating American Civilization: A Genealogy of American Literature as an Academic Discipline.* Minneapolis: University of Minnesota Press, 1994.

Sierra, Justo. *Evolución política del pueblo mexicano.* Edited by Edmundo O'Gorman. México, D.F.: Universidad Nacional Autónoma de México, 1948.

Sinningen, John H. "El desarrollo combinado y desigual y *La muerte de Artemio Cruz.*" *Cuadernos Hispanoamericanos* 396 (1983): 697–707.

Slatta, Richard W. *Comparing Cowboys and Frontiers.* Norman: University of Oklahoma Press, 1997.

Slotkin, Richard. *Gunfighter Nation: The Myth of the Frontier in Twentieth-Century America.* Norman: University of Oklahoma Press, 1998.

Smead, Robert N. *Vocabulario Vaquero = Cowboy Talk: A Dictionary of Spanish Terms from the American West.* Norman: University of Oklahoma Press, 2004.

Smith, Peter H. "Mexico Since 1946: Dynamics of an Authoritarian Regime." In *Mexico Since Independence,* edited by Leslie Bethell, 321–96. Cambridge: Cambridge University Press, 1991.

Solomon, Irvin D. "A Feminist Perspective of the Latin-American Novel: Carlos Fuentes's *The Death of Artemio Cruz.*" *Hispanófila,* no. 97 (1989): 69–75.

Sommer, Doris. *Foundational Fictions: The National Romances of Latin America.* Berkeley: University of California Press, 1991.

Sontag, Susan. *Against Interpretation and Other Essays.* New York: Anchor Books, 1990.

Sophocles. *The Oedipus Plays of Sophocles; Oedipus the King, Oedipus at Colonus, Antigone.* Translated by Paul Roche. New York: Signet Classics, 2001.

Stallybrass, Peter, and Allon White. *The Politics and Poetics of Transgression.* Ithaca, N.Y.: Cornell University Press, 1986.

Stavans, Ilan. *Spanglish: The Making of a New American Language.* New York: Rayo, 2004.

Steiner, Wendy. "Collage or Miracle: Historicism in a Deconstructed World." In *Reconstructing American Literary History,* edited by Sacvan Bercovitch, 323–51. Cambridge, Mass.: Harvard University Press, 1986.

Stephanson, Anders. *Manifest Destiny: American Expansionism and the Empire of Right.* New York: Hill and Wang, 1996.

Stoopen, María. *La muerte de Artemio Cruz: Una novela de denuncia y traición.* México, D.F.: Universidad Nacional Autonóma de México, 1982.

Streeby, Shelley. *American Sensations: Class, Empire, and the Production of Popular Culture.* Berkeley: University of California Press, 2002.

Taracena, Alfonso. *José Vasconcelos*. México, D.F.: Editorial Porrúa, 1982.
Tarantino, Quentin. *Django Unchained*. Beverly Hills, Calif.: Anchor Bay Entertainment, 2013.
Tittler, Jonathan. *Narrative Irony in the Contemporary Spanish-American Novel*. Ithaca, N.Y.: Cornell University Press, 1984.
Turner, Frederick C. *The Dynamic of Mexican Nationalism*. Chapel Hill: University of North Carolina Press, 1968.
Tyrrell, Ian. "American Exceptionalim in an Age of International History." *American Historical Review* 96, no. 4 (1991): 1031–55.
Tyson, Lois. "Existential Subjectivity on Trial: *The Crying of Lot 49* and the Politics of Despair." *Pynchon Notes* 28–29 (1991): 5–25.
Uslar Pietri, Arturo. *Las lanzas coloradas y cuentos selectos*. Edited by Domingo Miliani. Caracas: Biblioteca Ayacucho, 1988.
———. *The Red Lances*. Translated by Harriet de Onís. New York: Knopf, 1963.
Van Alstyne, Richard Warner. *The Rising American Empire*. Oxford: Blackwell, 1960.
Varela, Juan Cruz. *Poesías*. Buenos Aires: La Cultura Argentina, 1916.
Varsava, J. A. "Thomas Pynchon and Postmodern Liberalism." *Canadian Review of American Studies* 25, no. 3 (1995): 63–100.
Vasconcelos, José. *La raza cósmica*. México, D.F.: Editorial Porrúa, 2001.
Vázquez, Germán. *Origen de los mexicanos*. Madrid: Dastin, 2001.
Vélez de Guevara, Luis. *El diablo cojuelo*. Edited by Enrique Rodríguez Cepeda. Madrid: Cátedra, 1995.
Venturi, Franco. *Utopia and Reform in the Enlightenment*. Cambridge: Cambridge University Press, 1970.
Vickers, George. *The Formation of the New Left: The Early Years*. Lexington, Mass.: Lexington Books, 1975.
Villegas, Abelardo. *La filosofía de lo mexicano*. México, D.F.: Fondo de Cultura Económica, 1960.
Volpi, Jorge. *La imaginación y el poder: Una historia intelectual de 1968*. México, D.F.: Ediciones Era, 1998.
Weber, Max. *From Max Weber: Essays in Sociology*. Edited by H. H. Gerth and C. Wright Mills. New York: Oxford University Press, 1946.
Weinberg, Albert Katz. *Manifest Destiny: A Study of Nationalist Expansionism in American History*. Chicago: Quadrangle Books, 1963.
Weintraub, Sidney. *Unequal Partners: The United States and Mexico*. Pittsburgh: University of Pittsburgh Press, 2010.
Weisenburger, Steven C. *A Gravity's Rainbow Companion: Sources and Contexts for Pynchon's Novel*. Athens: University of Georgia Press, 1990.
Whitaker, Arthur P. "Changing and Unchanging Interpretations of the Enlightenment in Spanish America." In *The Ibero-American Enlightenment*, edited by Alfred Owen Aldridge, 21–57. Urbana: University of Illinois Press, 1971.
White, Hayden. *The Content of the Form: Narrative Discourse and Historical Representation*. Baltimore: Johns Hopkins University Press, 1990.
Williams, Raymond. *Marxism and Literature*. Oxford: Oxford University Press, 1985.
———. *Television: Technology and Cultural Form*. New York: Schocken Books, 1975.

Wise, David, and Thomas B. Ross. *The Invisible Government.* New York: Random House, 1964.

Wisse, Ruth R. *The Schlemiel as Modern Hero.* Chicago: University of Chicago Press, 1971.

Wittner, Lawrence S. *Cold War America: From Hiroshima to Watergate.* New York: Praeger, 1974.

Woolf, Harry. *The Transits of Venus: A Study of Eighteenth-Century Science.* Princeton, N.J.: Princeton University Press, 1959.

Yergin, Daniel. *Shattered Peace: The Origins of the Cold War and the National Security State.* Boston: Houghton Mifflin, 1977.

Young, Robert. *Postcolonialism: An Historical Introduction.* Oxford: Blackwell, 2001.

Zamora, Lois Parkinson. *Writing the Apocalypse: Historical Vision in Contemporary U.S. and Latin American Fiction.* Cambridge: Cambridge University Press, 1993.

Zamora, Lois Parkinson, and Wendy Faris, eds. *Magical Realism: Theory, History, Community.* Durham, N.C.: Duke University Press, 1995.

Zea, Leopoldo. *Conciencia y posibilidad del mexicano.* México, D.F.: Porrúa, 1952.

———. *Discurso desde la marginación y la barbarie.* Barcelona: Anthropos, Editorial del Hombre, 1988.

———. *The Role of the Americas in History.* Translated by Sonja Karsen. Edited by Amy Oliver. Savage: Rowman and Littlefield, 1992.

Zolov, Eric. "Protest and Counterculture in the 1968 Student Movement in Mexico." In *Student Protest: The Sixties and After,* edited by Gerard J. De Groot. London: Longman, 1998.

INDEX